Yamaha YZF-R6
Service and Repair Manual

by Tim Griffiths

Models covered

(5544-288-7AT1)

YZF-R6. 599cc. 2006 to 2013

© J H Haynes & Co Ltd 2020

A book in the Haynes Service and Repair Manual Series

ISBN: **978 1 78521 494 3**

British Library Cataloguing in Publication Data
A catalogue record for this book is available from the British Library.

Library of Congress Catalog Card Number 2012938334

J H Haynes & Co Ltd
Sparkford, Yeovil, Somerset BA22 7JJ, England

Haynes North America, Inc
859 Lawrence Drive, Newbury Park, California 91320, USA

Contents

LIVING WITH YOUR YAMAHA YZF-R6

Introduction

Pre-ride checks

MAINTENANCE

Routine maintenance and servicing

Contents

REPAIRS AND OVERHAUL

Engine, transmission and associated systems

Chassis components

Electrical system

Wiring diagrams

REFERENCE

Index

Yamaha
Musical instruments to motorcycles

The FS1E -
first bike of many sixteen year olds in the UK

The Yamaha Motor Company

The Yamaha name can be traced back to 1889, when Torakusu Yamaha founded the Yamaha Organ Manufacturing Company. Such was the success of the company, that in 1897 it became Nippon Gakki Limited and manufactured a wide range of reed organs and pianos.

During World War II, Nippon Gakki's manufacturing base was utilised by the Japanese authorities to produce propellers and fuel tanks for their aviation industry. The end of the war brought about a huge public demand for low cost transport and many firms decided to utilise their obsolete aircraft tooling for the production of motorcycles. Nippon Gakki's first motorcycle went on sale in February 1955 and was named the 125 YA-1 Red Dragonfly. This machine was a copy of the German DKW RT125 motorcycle, featuring a single cylinder two-stroke engine with a four-speed gearbox. Due to the outstanding success of this model the motorcycle operation was separated from Nippon Gakki in July 1955 and the Yamaha Motor Company was formed.

The YA-1 also received acclaim by winning two of Japan's biggest road races, the Mount Fuji Climbing race and the Asama Volcano race. The high level of public demand for the YA-1 led to the development of a whole series of two-stroke singles and twins.

Having made a large impact on their home market, Yamahas were exported to the USA in 1958 and to the UK in 1962. In the UK the signing of an Anglo-Japanese trade agreement during 1962 enabled the sale of Japanese lightweight motorcycles and scooters in Britain. At that time, competition between the many motorcycle producers in Japan had reduced numbers significantly and by the end of the sixties, only the big-four which are familiar with today remained.

Yamaha Europe was founded in 1968 and based in Holland. Although originally set up to market marine products, the Dutch base is now the official European Headquarters and distribution centre. Yamaha motorcycles are built at factories in Holland, Denmark, Norway, Italy, France, Spain and Portugal. Yamahas are imported into the UK by Yamaha Motor UK Ltd, formerly Mitsui Machinery Sales (UK) Ltd. Mitsui and Co. were originally a trading house, handling the shipping, distribution and marketing of Japanese products into western countries. Ultimately Mitsui Machinery Sales was formed to handle Yamaha motorcycles and outboard motors.

Based on the technology derived from its motorcycle operation, Yamaha have produced many other products, such as automobile and lightweight aircraft engines, marine engines and boats, generators, pumps, ATVs, snowmobiles, golf cars, industrial robots, lawnmowers, swimming pools and archery equipment.

Two-strokes first

Part of Yamaha's success was a whole string of innovations in the two-stroke world. Autolube engine lubrication, torque induction, multi-ported engines, reed valves and power valves kept their two-strokes at the forefront of technology. Many advances were achieved with the use of racing as a development laboratory. They went to the USA in the late 1950s with an air-cooled 250cc twin but didn't hit the GPs until the early 1960s when Fumio Ito scored a hat-trick of sixth places in the Isle of Man TT, the Dutch TT and the Belgian GP. This experiment gave rise to the idea of the over-the-counter racer, an idea that became reality in the TD1, the first in an unmatched series of two-stroke racers that were the standard issue for privateers at national and international level for years and helped Yamaha develop their road engines. While privateers raced the twins, Yamaha built the outrageously complicated vee-four 250 for Phil Read and followed it with a vee-four 125 that Bill Ivy lapped the Isle of Man on at over 100mph! When the FIM regulations were changed to limit the smaller GP classes to two cylinders, these exotic bikes died but set the scene for an unparalleled dynasty of mass-produced racers based on the same technology as the road bikes.

In the 1960s and 70s the two-stroke engined YAS3 125, YDS1 to YDS7 250 and YR5 350 formed the core of Yamaha's range. By the mid-70s they had been superseded by the RD (Race-Developed) 125, 250, and 350 range of two-stroke twins, featuring improved 7-port engines with reed valve induction. Braking was improved by the use of an hydraulic brake on the front wheel of DX models, instead of the drum arrangement used previously, and cast alloy wheels were available as an option on later RD models. The RD350 was replaced by the RD400 in 1976.

Running parallel with the RD twins was a range of single-cylinder two-strokes. Used in a variety of chassis types, the engine was used in the popular 50 cc FS1-E moped, the V50 to 90 step-thrus, RS100 and 125, YB100 and the DT trail range.

The TD racers got water-cooling in 1973 to become the TZs, the most successful and numerous over-the-counter racers ever built. That same year, Jarno Saarinen became the first rider to win a 500cc GP on a four-cylinder two-stroke on the new in-line four which was effectively a pair of TZs side-by-side. TZs won everywhere – including the Daytona 200 and 500 races when overbored to 351cc. A 700cc TZ also appeared, one year later taken out to 750cc. Steve Baker won the first Formula 750 world title – one of the precursors of Superbike – on one in 1977. The following year Kenny Roberts won Yamaha's first world 500 title and would be succeeded by Wayne Rainey and Eddie Lawson before Mick Doohan and the NSR500 took over.

The air-cooled single and twin cylinder RD road bikes were eventually replaced by the LC series in 1980, featuring liquid-cooled engines, radical new styling, spiral pattern cast wheels and cantilever rear suspension (Yamaha's Monoshock). Of all the LC models, the RD350LC, or RD350R as it was later known, has made the most impact in the market. Later models had YPVS (Yamaha Power Valve System) engines, another first for Yamaha – this was essentially a valve located in the exhaust ports which was electronically operated to alter port timing to achieve maximum power output. The RD500LC was the largest two-stroke made by Yamaha and differed from the other LCs by the use of its vee-four cylinder engine.

With the exception of the RD350R, now manufactured in Brazil, the LC range has been discontinued. Two-stroke engined models have given way to environmental pressure, and thus with a few exceptions, such as the TZR125 and TZR250, are used only in scooters and small capacity bikes.

The Four-strokes

Yamaha concentrated solely on two-stroke models until 1970 when the XS1 was produced, their first four-stroke motorcycle. It was perhaps Yamaha's success with two-strokes that postponed an earlier

The distinctive paintwork and trim of the RD models

move into the four-stroke motorcycle market, although their work with Toyota during the 1960s had given them a sound base in four-stroke technology.

The XS1 had a 650 cc twin-cylinder SOHC engine and was later to become known as the XS650, appearing also in the popular SE custom form. Yamaha introduced a three cylinder 750 cc engine in 1976, fitted in a sport-tourer frame and called the XS750, TX750 in the USA . The XS750 established itself well in the sport tourer class and remained in production with very few changes until uprated to 850 cc in 1980.

Other four-strokes followed in 1976, with the introduction of the XS250/360/400 series twins. The XS range was strengthened in 1978 by the four-cylinder XS1100.

The 1980s saw a new family of four-strokes, the XJ550, 650, 750 and 900 Fours. Improvements over the XS range amounted to a slimmer DOHC engine unit due to the relocation of the alternator behind the cylinders, electronic ignition and uprated braking and suspension systems. Models were available mainly in standard trim, although custom-styled Maxims were produced especially for the US market. The XJ650T was the first model from Yamaha to have a turbo-charged engine. Although these early XJ models have now been discontinued, their roots live on in the XJ600S and XJ900S Diversion (Seca II) models.

The FZR prefix encompasses the pure

The XS650 led the way for Yamaha's four-stroke range

sports Yamaha models. With the exception of the 16-valve FZR400 and FZR600 models, the FZ/FZR750 and FZR1000 used 20-valve engines, two exhaust valves and three inlet valves per cylinder. This concept was called Genesis and gave improved gas flow to the combustion chambers. Other features of the new engine were the use of down-draught carburetors and the engine's inclined angle in the frame, plus the change to liquid-cooling.

Yamaha's XS750 was produced from 1976 to 1982 and then uprated to 850 cc

Lightweight Deltabox design aluminium frames and uprated suspension improved the bikes's handling. The Genesis engine lives on in the YZF750 and 1000 models.

The Genesis concept was the basis of Yamaha's foray into four-stroke racing, first with a bike known simply as 'The Genesis', an FZ750 motor in a TT Formula 1 bike with which the factory attempted to steal the Honda RVF750's thunder at important events like the Suzuka 8 Hours and the Bol d'Or although they never fielded it for a whole World Championship season. That had to wait for the advent of the World Superbike Championship, although there was no full works team until 1995, instead it was left to individual importers to support teams. It was the Australian Dealer Team Yamaha which scored the factory's first World Superbike win in the series debut year of 1988. The rider? Mick Doohan. Slightly, embarrassingly, it was the steel framed FZ750 rather than the FZR homologation special that won races. The OW01 was a race winner, mainly in the hands of Fabrizio Pirovano, the factory's most successful Superbike racer with ten victories, but national success in the UK, Japan, and in the Daytona 200 has not been translated into World Championships for any of Yamaha's 750s.

The vee-twin engine has been the mainstay of the XV Virago range. Since 1981 XVs have been produced in 535, 700, 750, 920, 1000 and 1100 engine sizes, all using the same basic air-cooled sohc vee-twin engine. Other uses of vee engines have been in the XZ550 of the early 1980s, the XVZ12 Venture and the mighty VMX-12 V-Max.

Yamaha has always been a sporting-orientated company whose motto could be 'Racing Improves the Breed', so it's no surprise that

A new family of four-strokes was released in 1980 with the introduction of the XJ range

the latest generation of lightweight sportsters are at the cutting edge of performance on and off the track. The R6 won more races than any other machine in the inaugural year of the World Supersports Championship, the R7 won a race in its debut year in World Superbike in the hands of the mercurial Noriyuki Haga, and the mighty 1000cc R1 ended Honda's domination of the Isle of Man F1 TT when David Jefferies won three races in a week in 1999.

The Cutting Edge

Despite the buying public apparently falling out of love with big, litre-plus supersports bikes, the middleweight 600cc sector remains relatively healthy. And it's not just in the showrooms that the class is competitive; the World Supersports Championship for lightly tuned and modified 600s remains the most cut-throat class on the world's tracks. Since the financial meltdown started in 2008, the World Supersport Championship has been won twice by Honda with the CBR600, twice by Yamaha with the R6 and once by Kawasaki.

If a manufacturer wants to stay on the pace in this sort of racing class then it needs to keep throwing technical developments at the road bike that is homologated for the racing class. In Yamaha's case, that means the R6. Like all of its competition, the R6 started life as a simple across-the-frame four but with all the design emphasis on race-track readiness rather than ease of use on the road. The first R6 appeared in 1999 and won the World Supersport Championship the following year in the hands of the German Jorg Teuchert. The first major update came in 2003 when the R6's carburettors were replaced with fuel-injection.

Anyone who has followed MotoGP racing in the past few years knows that the factories have put major effort into the development of electronic engine control systems, and the third-generation R6, launched in 2006, reaped the benefits. The motor went ultra-short stroke, from 65.5 x 44.5 to 67 x 42.5 mm, and the throttles became fully fly-by wire thanks to Yamaha's YCC-T (Yamaha Chip-Controlled Throttle). In other words, the twistgrip was no longer directly connected to the throttle

The 2006 YZF-R6

The 2012 YZF-R6 in WGP 50th Anniversary livery

accurate, they are two-piece intake trumpets and at high revs and high throttle openings the longer, rear part is lifted away leaving a short intake trumpet sticking into the airbox. The ECU controls the action which is carried out by an electric servomotor and happens very quickly.

All these high-technology electronics have the same aim; spreading the power over a useful range but Yamaha's own publicity showed where the emphasis really was. It talked about the rush of power above 10,000rpm and maximum power at a heady 14,500rpm! The first of the short-stroke R6s had the red line marked at 17,500rpm, the highest of any production four-stroke motorcycle, although there was some dispute about the tachometer reading high. Whatever the exact number, it is certain that a production engine revved to over 16,000rpm.

The electronics and the short-stroke motor had the desired effect. Two British Yamaha R6 riders, Cal Crutchlow and Chaz Davies, won the world Supersport Championship in 2009 and 2011, respectively. It shows the level of technology of the third-generation R6 that two years after Crutchlow's winning season, Davies was given the self-same bike to run with his private team and was able to retake the title for Yamaha. All three generations of the R6, the first carbureted version, the early fuel-injected one, and the fully electronic latest iteration, have had the same objective; to win races. To that end, the bike has always been at the cutting edge of sports bike technology and given the market's lack of interest in large-capacity super-sportsters, it is the R6 and other middleweight four- (and three-) cylinder machines which will be the first to bring Grand Prix technology to the road.

butterflies. The twistgrip's position was just one of many inputs delivered to an ECU with around five times the processing capacity of the previous system, along with crank position, revs, intake pressure, temperature, and more. The ECU then decides how far to open the throttle valves, which it does with the help of an electric stepping motor.

This technology had been developed over the previous few years in MotoGP; the

2006 Yamaha R6 was the first street bike to be fully fly-by-wire. Its other MotoGP developed components were a slipper clutch and secondary fuel injectors. Incidently, a old piece of 1980s hi-tech also made its first appearance on a 600, the EXUP exhaust-valve system. Two years later another bit of race-track electronics arrived, YCC-I (Yamaha Chip-Controlled Intake) which is essentially variable-length intake tracts. To be strictly

Acknowledgements

Our thanks are due to Total Triumph of Taunton for supplying the 2010 R6 and Sander Hammelburg of Yeovil for supplying the 2006 R6 featured in the illustrations throughout this manual. We would also like to thank NGK Spark Plugs (UK) Ltd for supplying the colour spark plug condition photographs, the Avon Rubber Company for supplying information on tyre fitting and Draper Tools Ltd for some of the workshop tools shown.

Thanks are also due to Yamaha Motor (UK) Ltd who supplied model photographs, and to Julian Ryder who wrote the introduction 'Musical Instruments to Motorcycles'.

About this Manual

The aim of this manual is to help you get the best value from your motorcycle. It can do so in several ways. It can help you decide what

work must be done, even if you choose to have it done by a dealer; it provides information and procedures for routine maintenance and servicing; and it offers diagnostic and repair procedures to follow when trouble occurs.

We hope you use the manual to tackle the work yourself. For many simpler jobs, doing it yourself may be quicker than arranging an appointment to get the motorcycle into a dealer and making the trips to leave it and pick it up. More importantly, a lot of money can be saved by avoiding the expense the shop must pass on to you to cover its labour and overhead costs. An added benefit is the sense of satisfaction and accomplishment that you feel after doing the job yourself.

References to the left or right side of the motorcycle assume you are sitting on the seat, facing forward.

We take great pride in the accuracy of information given in this manual, but motorcycle manufacturers make alterations and design changes during the production run of a particular motorcycle of which they do not inform us. No liability can be accepted by the authors or publishers for loss, damage or injury caused by any errors in, or omissions from, the information given.

Frame and engine numbers

The frame serial number is stamped into the right-hand side of the steering head and is repeated on the VIN label just to the rear. The engine number is stamped into the right-hand rear of the crankcase. Further identification is provided by the model type code label stuck to the frame under the passenger's seat. These numbers should be recorded and kept in a safe place so they are available when purchasing parts or can be given to the police in the event of a theft.

The frame serial number, engine serial number, and model code should also be kept in a handy place (such as with your driver's licence) so that they are always available when ordering parts for your machine.

The procedures in this manual identify models by their production year (see below). Models can also be identified by their model type code and in certain markets also by the production year letter.

Prod. yr	Type code	Prod. yr letter
2006	2C0	V
2007	2C0	W
2008	13S	X
2009	13S	Y
2010	13S	Z
2011	13S	A
2012	13S	B
2013	13S	C

The model code label (arrowed) can be found under the passenger's seat

The frame number (A) is stamped into the right-hand side of the steering head and repeated on the VIN label (B)

Buying spare parts

Once you have found all the identification numbers, record them for reference when buying parts. Since the manufacturers change specifications, parts and vendors (companies that manufacture various components on the machine), providing the ID numbers is the only way to be reasonably sure that you are buying the correct parts.

Whenever possible, take the worn part to the dealer so direct comparison with the new component can be made. Along the trail from the manufacturer to the parts shelf, there are numerous places that the part can end up with the wrong number or be listed incorrectly.

The two places to purchase new parts for your motorcycle – the accessory store and the franchised dealer – differ in the type of parts they carry. While dealers can obtain virtually every part for your motorcycle, the accessory dealer is usually limited to normal high wear items such as shock absorbers, tune-up parts, various engine gaskets, cables, chains, brake parts, etc. Rarely will an accessory outlet have major suspension components, cylinders, transmission gears, or cases.

Used parts can be obtained for roughly half the price of new ones, but you can't always be sure of what you're getting. Once again, take your worn part to the breaker's yard for direct comparison.

Whether buying new, used or rebuilt parts, the best course is to deal directly with someone who specialises in parts for your particular make.

The engine number is stamped into the right-hand rear of the crankcase . . .

. . . and is viewed from the right-hand rear of the engine (arrowed)

Professional mechanics are trained in safe working procedures. However enthusiastic you may be about getting on with the job at hand, take the time to ensure that your safety is not put at risk. A moment's lack of attention can result in an accident, as can failure to observe simple precautions.

There will always be new ways of having accidents, and the following is not a comprehensive list of all dangers; it is intended rather to make you aware of the risks and to encourage a safe approach to all work you carry out on your bike.

Asbestos

● Certain friction, insulating, sealing and other products - such as brake pads, clutch linings, gaskets, etc. - contain asbestos. Extreme care must be taken to avoid inhalation of dust from such products since it is hazardous to health. If in doubt, assume that they do contain asbestos.

Fire

● Remember at all times that petrol is highly flammable. Never smoke or have any kind of naked flame around, when working on the vehicle. But the risk does not end there - a spark caused by an electrical short-circuit, by two metal surfaces contacting each other, by careless use of tools, or even by static electricity built up in your body under certain conditions, can ignite petrol vapour, which in a confined space is highly explosive. Never use petrol as a cleaning solvent. Use an approved safety solvent.

● Always disconnect the battery earth terminal before working on any part of the fuel or electrical system, and never risk spilling fuel on to a hot engine or exhaust.
● It is recommended that a fire extinguisher of a type suitable for fuel and electrical fires is kept handy in the garage or workplace at all times. Never try to extinguish a fuel or electrical fire with water.

Fumes

● Certain fumes are highly toxic and can quickly cause unconsciousness and even death if inhaled to any extent. Petrol vapour comes into this category, as do the vapours from certain solvents such as trichloro-ethylene. Any draining or pouring of such volatile fluids should be done in a well ventilated area.
● When using cleaning fluids and solvents, read the instructions carefully. Never use materials from unmarked containers - they may give off poisonous vapours.
● Never run the engine of a motor vehicle in an enclosed space such as a garage. Exhaust fumes contain carbon monoxide which is extremely poisonous; if you need to run the engine, always do so in the open air or at least have the rear of the vehicle outside the workplace.

The battery

● Never cause a spark, or allow a naked light near the vehicle's battery. It will normally be giving off a certain amount of hydrogen gas, which is highly explosive.

● Always disconnect the battery ground (earth) terminal before working on the fuel or electrical systems (except where noted).
● If possible, loosen the filler plugs or cover when charging the battery from an external source. Do not charge at an excessive rate or the battery may burst.
● Take care when topping up, cleaning or carrying the battery. The acid electrolyte, evenwhen diluted, is very corrosive and should not be allowed to contact the eyes or skin. Always wear rubber gloves and goggles or a face shield. If you ever need to prepare electrolyte yourself, always add the acid slowly to the water; never add the water to the acid.

Electricity

● When using an electric power tool, inspection light etc., always ensure that the appliance is correctly connected to its plug and that, where necessary, it is properly grounded (earthed). Do not use such appliances in damp conditions and, again, beware of creating a spark or applying excessive heat in the vicinity of fuel or fuel vapour. Also ensure that the appliances meet national safety standards.
● A severe electric shock can result from touching certain parts of the electrical system, such as the spark plug wires (HT leads), when the engine is running or being cranked, particularly if components are damp or the insulation is defective. Where an electronic ignition system is used, the secondary (HT) voltage is much higher and could prove fatal.

Remember...

✗ **Don't** start the engine without first ascertaining that the transmission is in neutral.
✗ **Don't** suddenly remove the pressure cap from a hot cooling system - cover it with a cloth and release the pressure gradually first, or you may get scalded by escaping coolant.
✗ **Don't** attempt to drain oil until you are sure it has cooled sufficiently to avoid scalding you.
✗ **Don't** grasp any part of the engine or exhaust system without first ascertaining that it is cool enough not to burn you.
✗ **Don't** allow brake fluid or antifreeze to contact the machine's paintwork or plastic components.
✗ **Don't** siphon toxic liquids such as fuel, hydraulic fluid or antifreeze by mouth, or allow them to remain on your skin.
✗ **Don't** inhale dust - it may be injurious to health (see Asbestos heading).
✗ **Don't** allow any spilled oil or grease to remain on the floor - wipe it up right away, before someone slips on it.
✗ **Don't** use ill-fitting spanners or other tools which may slip and cause injury.
✗ **Don't** lift a heavy component which may be beyond your capability - get assistance.

✗ **Don't** rush to finish a job or take unverified short cuts.
✗ **Don't** allow children or animals in or around an unattended vehicle.
✗ **Don't** inflate a tyre above the recommended pressure. Apart from overstressing the carcass, in extreme cases the tyre may blow off forcibly.
✔ **Do** ensure that the machine is supported securely at all times. This is especially important when the machine is blocked up to aid wheel or fork removal.
✔ **Do** take care when attempting to loosen a stubborn nut or bolt. It is generally better to pull on a spanner, rather than push, so that if you slip, you fall away from the machine rather than onto it.
✔ **Do** wear eye protection when using power tools such as drill, sander, bench grinder etc.
✔ **Do** use a barrier cream on your hands prior to undertaking dirty jobs - it will protect your skin from infection as well as making the dirt easier to remove afterwards; but make sure your hands aren't left slippery. Note that long-term contact with used engine oil can be a health hazard.
✔ **Do** keep loose clothing (cuffs, ties etc. and long hair) well out of the way of moving mechanical parts.

✔ **Do** remove rings, wristwatch etc., before working on the vehicle - especially the electrical system.
✔ **Do** keep your work area tidy - it is only too easy to fall over articles left lying around.
✔ **Do** exercise caution when compressing springs for removal or installation. Ensure that the tension is applied and released in a controlled manner, using suitable tools which preclude the possibility of the spring escaping violently.
✔ **Do** ensure that any lifting tackle used has a safe working load rating adequate for the job.
✔ **Do** get someone to check periodically that all is well, when working alone on the vehicle.
✔ **Do** carry out work in a logical sequence and check that everything is correctly assembled and tightened afterwards.
✔ **Do** remember that your vehicle's safety affects that of yourself and others. If in doubt on any point, get professional advice.
● If in spite of following these precautions, you are unfortunate enough to injure yourself, seek medical attention as soon as possible.

Coolant level

> ⚠️ **Warning: DO NOT remove the radiator pressure cap to add coolant. Topping up is done via the coolant reservoir tank filler. DO NOT leave open containers of coolant about, as it is poisonous.**

Before you start:

✔ Make sure you have a supply of coolant available – a mixture of 50% distilled water and 50% corrosion inhibited ethylene glycol anti-freeze is needed – alternatively you can purchase ready-mixed coolant. **Note:** *Yamaha specify that soft tap water can be used if necessary, but NOT hard water. If in doubt, boil the water first or use only distilled water.*
✔ Always check the coolant level when the engine is cold.
✔ Support the motorcycle in an upright position, using an auxiliary stand if required. Make sure it is on level ground.

Bike care:

● Use only the specified coolant mixture. It is important that anti-freeze is used in the system all year round, and not just in the winter. Do not top the system up using only water, as the system will become too diluted.
● Do not overfill the reservoir. If the coolant is significantly above the FULL level line at any time, the surplus should be siphoned or drained off to prevent the possibility of it being expelled out of the overflow hose.
● If the coolant level falls steadily, check the system for leaks (see Chapter 1). If no leaks are found and the level continues to fall, it is recommended that the machine be taken to a Yamaha dealer for a pressure test.

1 The reservoir is mounted on the right-hand side of the motorcycle, behind the fairing side panel. The coolant FULL and LOW level lines (arrowed) are marked on the reservoir and can be checked from under the front of the fairing.

2 If the coolant level is not between the FULL and LOW level lines, remove the cockpit trim panel to access the filler cap.

3 Remove the reservoir filler cap and draw the hose out, catching any drops of coolant with a rag.

4 Top the coolant level up with the recommended coolant mixture using a suitable funnel, and a piece of extension tubing if necessary. Fit the filler cap and refit the cockpit trim panel.

Suspension, steering and drive chain

Suspension and steering:

● Check that the front and rear suspension operates smoothly without binding.
● Check that the suspension is adjusted as required. Make sure each front fork is set equally.
● Check that the steering moves smoothly from lock-to-lock.

Final drive:

● Check that the drive chain slack isn't excessive, and adjust it if necessary (see Chapter 1).
● If the chain looks dry, lubricate it (see Chapter 1).

Engine oil level

Before you start:
✔ Support the motorcycle in an upright position, using an auxiliary stand if required. Make sure it is on level ground.
✔ Start the engine and let it idle for several minutes to allow it to reach normal operating temperature.
Caution: Do not run the engine in an enclosed space such as a garage or workshop.
✔ Leave the motorcycle undisturbed for a few minutes to allow the oil level to stabilise.

The correct oil:
● Modern, high-revving engines place great demands on their oil. It is very important that the correct oil for your bike is used.
● Always top up with a good quality oil of the specified type and viscosity and do not overfill the engine.

Oil type	API grade SG or higher motorcycle engine oil to JASO MA standard
Oil viscosity	SAE 10W/40, 10W/50, 15W/40, 20W/40 or 20W50 according to climate

Caution: Do not use chemical additives or oils with a grade of CD or higher, or use oils labelled 'ENERGY CONSERVING II'. Such additives or oils could cause clutch slip.

Bike care:
● If you have to add oil frequently, you should check whether you have any oil leaks. If there is no sign of oil leakage from the joints and gaskets the engine could be burning oil (see *Fault Finding*).

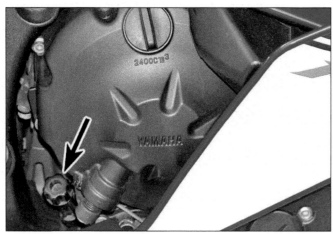

1 The dipstick (arrowed) is located on the right-hand side of the engine

2 The oil level should be checked with a warm engine, so if necessary allow the engine to run for a few minutes then switch it off and allow the oil level to settle before unscrewing the dipstick and wiping it clean with a rag.

3 With the machine upright, place the dipstick back in its hole but **DO NOT** screw it in. Remove the dipstick and inspect the oil level. The level should lie in the hatched area (arrowed).

4 If the level is below, or on the lower edge of the hatched area remove the filler cap

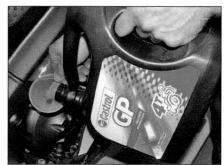

5 Top up the engine with the recommended grade and type of oil to bring the level almost up to the top of the hatched area on the dipstick. Do not overfill. On completion, fit the filler cap, making sure the O-ring is in its groove and in good condition.

Tyres

Tyre tread depth:

● At the time of writing UK law requires that tread depth must be at least 1 mm over the entire tread breadth all the way around the tyre, with no bald patches. Many riders, however, consider 2 mm tread depth minimum to be a safer limit. Yamaha recommend a minimum of 1.6 mm.

● Many tyres now incorporate wear indicators in the tread. Identify the triangular pointer, manufacturer's mark or TWI mark on the tyre sidewall to locate the indicator bar and replace the tyre with a new one if the tread has worn down to the bar.

The correct pressures:

● The tyres must be checked when **cold**, not immediately after riding. Note that low tyre pressures will cause unsafe handling, and may cause the tyre to slip on the rim or come off. High tyre pressures will cause abnormal tread wear and unsafe handling.

● Use an accurate pressure gauge. Spend as much as you can justify on a quality gauge.

● Correct air pressure will increase tyre life and provide maximum stability, handling capability and ride comfort.

Tyre care:

● Check the tyres carefully for cuts, tears, embedded nails or other sharp objects and excessive wear. Operation of the motorcycle with excessively worn tyres is extremely hazardous, as traction and handling are directly affected.

● Check the condition of the tyre valve and ensure the dust cap is in place.

● Pick out any stones or nails which may have become embedded in the tyre tread. If left, they could eventually penetrate through the casing and cause a puncture.

● If tyre damage is apparent, or unexplained loss of pressure is experienced, seek the advice of a tyre fitting specialist without delay.

Load	Front	Rear
2006 and 2007 models		
0-198lbs (0-90kg)	36 psi (2.5 Bar)	36 psi (2.5 Bar)
198-425lbs (90-193kg)	36 psi (2.5 Bar)	42 psi (2.9 Bar)
High Speed riding	36 psi (2.5 Bar)	36 psi (2.5 Bar)
2008-on models		
0-198lbs (0-90kg)	36 psi (2.5 Bar)	42 psi (2.9 Bar)
198-410lbs (90-186kg)	36 psi (2.5 Bar)	42 psi (2.9 Bar)
High Speed riding	36 psi (2.5 Bar)	42 psi (2.9 Bar)

1 Remove the cap from the valve – if there isn't one there buy a new one.

2 Check the tyre pressures when the tyres are **cold** and keep them properly inflated. Fit the cap on completion.

3 Measure tread depth at the centre of the tyre using a tread depth gauge.

4 Tyre tread wear indicator bar (A) and its location marking (B) – usually either an arrow, a triangle, the manufacturer's logo, or the letters TWI on the sidewall.

Brake fluid levels

> ⚠️ *Warning: Brake hydraulic fluid can harm your eyes and damage painted surfaces, so use extreme caution when handling and pouring it and cover surrounding surfaces with rag. Do not use fluid that has been standing open for some time, as it absorbs moisture from the air which can cause a dangerous loss of braking effectiveness.*

Before you start:

✔ The front brake fluid reservoir is on the right-hand handlebar. The rear brake fluid reservoir is located below the rider's seat on the right-hand side.

✔ When checking the fluid level in the front reservoir, either place the motorcycle on its sidestand and turn the handlebars to full right lock, or support it upright on an auxiliary stand with the handlebars straight, so the reservoir is level.

✔ When checking the fluid in the rear reservoir support the motorcycle upright, if available using an auxiliary stand.

✔ If topping up is necessary make sure you have the correct hydraulic fluid. DOT 4 is recommended.

✔ Wrap a rag around the reservoir being worked on to ensure that any spillage does not come into contact with painted surfaces.

Bike care:

● The fluid in the front and rear brake master cylinder reservoirs will drop as the brake pads wear down. If the fluid level is low check the brake pads for wear (see Chapter 1), and replace them with new ones if necessary (see Chapter 6).

● If either fluid reservoir requires repeated topping-up there could be a leak somewhere in the system, which must be investigated immediately.

● Check for signs of fluid leakage from the hydraulic hoses and brake system components – if found, rectify immediately (see Chapter 6).

● Check the operation of both brakes before taking the machine on the road; if there is evidence of air in the system (spongy feel to lever or pedal), it must be bled (see Chapter 6).

FRONT BRAKE

1 The front brake fluid level is visible through the reservoir body – it must be between the UPPER and LOWER level lines (arrowed).

2 If the level is below the LOWER level line, undo the reservoir cap clamp screw and remove the clamp . . .

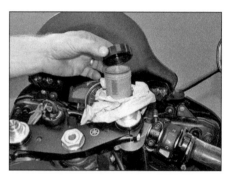

3 . . . then unscrew the cap and remove the diaphragm plate and the diaphragm.

4 Top up with new, clean DOT 4 hydraulic fluid, until the level is between the level lines. Take care to avoid spills (see **Warning** above) and do not overfill.

5 Wipe any moisture out of the diaphragm using a clean lint-free cloth.

6 Ensure that the diaphragm is correctly seated before installing the plate and cap. Secure the cap with its clamp.

REAR BRAKE

1 The rear brake fluid level is visible through the reservoir body – it must be between the UPPER and LOWER level lines (arrowed).

2 If the level is below the LOWER level line, slacken the reservoir mounting screw enough to tilt the reservoir so the cap clears the bracket.

3 Hold the reservoir, then unscrew the cap and remove the plate and the diaphragm.

4 Top up with new, clean DOT 4 hydraulic fluid, until the level is between the level lines. Take care to avoid spills (see **Warning** on page 0•14) and do not overfill.

5 Wipe any moisture out of the diaphragm using a clean lint-free cloth.

6 Ensure that the diaphragm is correctly seated before installing the plate and cap. Tighten the reservoir mounting screw.

Legal and safety

Lighting and signalling:
● Check that the headlight, tail light, brake light, licence plate light, instrument lights and turn signals all work correctly.
● Check that the horn sounds when the button is pushed.
● A working speedometer graduated in mph is a statutory requirement in the UK.

Safety:
● Check that the throttle grip rotates smoothly and snaps shut when released, in all steering positions. Also check for the correct amount of freeplay (see Chapter 1).
● Check that the steering moves freely from lock-to-lock.
● Check that the brake lever and pedal, clutch lever and gearchange lever operate smoothly. Lubricate them at the specified intervals or when necessary (see Chapter 1).
● Check that the engine shuts off when the kill switch is operated. Check the starter safety circuit (see Chapter 1).
● Check that the sidestand return spring holds the stand up securely when it is retracted.

Fuel:
● If the low fuel level warning light stays on check that you have enough fuel to get you to a fuel station. If you notice signs of fuel leakage – rectify the cause immediately.
● Ensure you use the correct grade fuel – premium unleaded petrol/gasoline (95 RON or higher).

2006

The 2006 R6 was completely revised from the previous year's model. The chain driven double overhead cam four cylinder engine having a different bore and stroke of 67 x 42.5 mm, a lighter crankshaft and pistons, larger intake and exhaust tracts, revised transmission layout, and a 'slipper' clutch. Other differences included the valves and their included angles, the alternator and the use of magnesium for some of the engine covers. The newly introduced digital fuel injection system with its secondary injectors and the Yamaha Chip-Controlled Throttle system (YCC-T) were all controlled by a powerful new ECU. The titanium exhaust silencer featured three catalytic convertor elements, an oxygen sensor, and the first appearance of Yamaha's EXUP system on a 600 supersport motorcycle. The 'Deltabox' frame was an all-new design, following Moto GP practice and keeping the steering head, swinging arm pivot and rear wheel axle in as close to a straight line as possible, it also formed part of the induction system and featured a longer swinging arm than the previous generation R6. The suspension featured new 41 mm upside-down oil damped forks with adjustable bump and rebound damping, and a rear shock absorber with the same features operated by a revised suspension linkage. Braking at the front was by 310mm floating discs, radially mounted four opposed piston Sumitomo calipers, and a Brembo radial master cylinder. Rear braking was by a 220mm disc and Sumitomo caliper. The all new bodywork included a cover for the pillion seat as standard.

2007

There were no significant changes for 2007.

2008

Modifications were made to the pistons, cam chain tensioner, valve springs, con-rod bearings and the main bearings. The YCC-I variable length intake tract system was introduced along with a new ECU and revised air filter housing. The exhaust connecting pipe between cylinders two and three was made 30% larger in diameter and there were revisions to the silencer. The fuel delivery pipe was changed from a two-piece design to a one-piece design. Minor changes to the upper radiator mountings and front forks specifications and design were also made. The frame had changes made in the area of the steering head and a new magnesium alloy rear sub-frame with the result that while it was substantially new it remained very similar in appearance. Front brake disc thickness was increased from 4.5mm to 5mm. The bodywork was redesigned with a slightly smaller fuel tank, LED front sidelight, and revised riding position although the same front mudguard was retained. The rear suspension featured internal design and material changes to the swingingarm along with a lighter suspension linkage.

2009 onwards

No changes since 2008. In 2012 Yamaha released a 50th Anniversary WGP version of the R6, with speedblock tank decals reminiscent of the 70s. This livery was applied to several other models in Yamaha's 2012 line up and commemorates 50 years of Grand Prix racing.

Dimensions and weights

Overall length	2040 mm
Overall width	
2006 and 2007 models	700 mm
2008-on models	705 mm
Overall height	1100 mm
Wheelbase	1380 mm
Seat height	850 mm
Ground clearance	130 mm
Wet weight (with all fluids and full fuel tank)	
2006 and 2007 models	182 kg
2008-on models	185 kg
Maximum load (rider, passenger, luggage, accessories)	
2006 and 2007 models	193 kg
2008-on models	186 kg

Engine

Type	Four-stroke 16V in-line four
Capacity	599 cc
Bore	67.0 mm
Stroke	42.5 mm
Compression ratio	
2006 and 2007 models	12.8 to 1
2008-on models	13.1 to 1
Cooling system	Liquid cooled
Clutch	Wet multi-plate
Transmission	Six-speed constant mesh
Final drive	Chain and sprockets
Camshafts	DOHC, chain-driven
Throttle bodies	Mikuni 41EIDW/1
Ignition system	Digital electronic CDI

Chassis

Frame type	Twin spar aluminium Deltabox
Rake	24°
Trail	97 mm
Fuel tank capacity (including reserve)	
2006 and 2007 models	17.5 litres (3.85 Imp gal, 4.62 US gal)
2008-on models	17.3 litres (3.81 Imp gal, 4.57 US gal)
Reserve capacity all models (with fuel light on)	3.5 litres (0.77 Imp gal, 0.92 US gal)
Front suspension	
Type	41 mm oil-damped USD telescopic forks
Travel	
2006 and 2007 models	120 mm
2008-on models	115 mm
Adjustment	Pre-load, compression and rebound damping
Rear suspension	
Type	Single shock absorber, rising rate linkage, box-section aluminium swingarm
Travel	60 mm
Adjustment	Pre-load, compression and rebound damping
Wheels	17 inch 5-spoke cast alloys
Tyres	
Front	120/70 ZR17 Tubeless radial
Rear	180/55 ZR17 Tubeless radial
Front brake	Twin 320 mm discs with Sumitomo 4-piston opposed calipers, radially mounted, radial master cylinder
Rear brake	Single 220 mm disc with Sumitomo single piston sliding caliper

Chapter 1
Routine maintenance and Servicing

Contents

Degrees of difficulty

Easy, suitable for novice with little experience	**Fairly easy,** suitable for beginner with some experience	**Fairly difficult,** suitable for competent DIY mechanic	**Difficult,** suitable for experienced DIY mechanic	**Very difficult,** suitable for expert DIY or professional 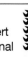

Engine

Spark plugs
    Type . . . . NGK CR10EK
    Electrode gap . . . . 0.6 to 0.7 mm
Engine idle speed . . . . 1250 to 1350 rpm
Cylinder identification . . . . numbered 1 to 4 from left to right
Throttle body synchronisation – intake vacuum at idle . . . . 150 mmHg
Throttle body synchronisation – max. difference between bodies . . . . . 10 mmHg
Valve clearances (COLD engine)
    Intake valves . . . . 0.12 to 0.19 mm
    Exhaust valves . . . . 0.16 to 0.23 mm
EXUP cable freeplay (see text) . . . . 1.0 to 2.0 mm

Cycle parts

Drive chain slack (see text):
    2006 and 2007 models . . . . 35 to 45 mm
    2008-on models . . . . 30 to 45 mm
Drive chain stretch limit (see text) . . . . 239.3 mm
Drive chain type . . . . 525V8, 114 links
Brake pad friction material wear limit
    Front calipers . . . . 0.5 mm
    Rear caliper . . . . 1.0 mm
Throttle cable freeplay . . . . 3 to 5 mm at twistgrip flange
Clutch cable freeplay . . . . 10 to 15 mm at lever ball end
Tyre pressures (cold) . . . . see *Pre-ride checks*
Steering head bearing tension . . . . 200 to 500g

Lubricants and fluids

Fuel . . . . Premium unleaded, minimum 95 RON (Research Octane Number)
Engine oil type . . . . SAE 10W/40, 10W/50, 15W/40, 20W/40 or 20W50 motorcycle engine oil to JASO MA standard or equivalent API grade SG or higher but NOT if it has a "CD" or "Energy Absorbing II" suffix

Engine oil capacity
    Oil change . . . . 2.4 litres
    Oil and filter change . . . . 2.6 litres
    Following engine overhaul – dry engine, new filter . . . . 3.4 litres
Coolant type . . . . 50% distilled water, 50% ethylene glycol anti-freeze with corrosion inhibitors for aluminium engines. **Note:** *Yamaha specify distilled water, but state that SOFT tap water may be used*

Coolant capacity
    Radiator . . . . 2.30 litres
    Reservoir . . . . 0.25 litre
Brake fluid . . . . DOT 4
Drive chain . . . . Engine oil or aerosol chain lubricant suitable for O-ring chains
Steering head bearings . . . . Lithium-based multi-purpose grease
Swingarm pivot and bearings . . . . Lithium-based multi-purpose grease
Suspension linkage bearings . . . . Lithium-based multi-purpose grease
Bearing seals . . . . Lithium-based multi-purpose grease
Gearchange lever, clutch lever, front brake lever,
    rear brake pedal, sidestand pivots . . . . Lithium-based multi-purpose grease
Cables . . . . Engine oil or aerosol cable lubricant
Throttle twistgrip . . . . Lithium-based multi-purpose grease

Torque wrench settings

Cooling system drain plug . . . . 10 Nm
EXUP valve pulley cover bolts
    Front . . . . 8 Nm
    Rear . . . . 7 Nm
Fork clamp bolts (top yoke) . . . . 26 Nm
Handlebar positioning bolts . . . . 13 Nm
Handlebar clamp bolts . . . . 32 Nm
Oil drain plug . . . . 43 Nm
Oil filter . . . . 17 Nm
Rear wheel axle nut . . . . 110 Nm
Spark plugs . . . . 13 Nm
Steering head bearing adjuster nut
    Initial setting . . . . 52 Nm
    Final setting . . . . 14 Nm
Steering stem nut . . . . 115 Nm
Timing rotor cover bolts . . . . 12 Nm

Pre-ride

☐ See *Pre-ride checks* at the beginning of this manual.

After the initial 600 miles (1000 km)

Note: *This check is usually performed by a Yamaha dealer after the first 600 miles (1000 km) from new. Thereafter, maintenance is carried out according to the following intervals of the schedule.*

Every 500 miles (800 km)

☐ Check, adjust, clean and lubricate the drive chain (Section 1)

Every 6000 miles (10,000 km)

These items must be checked annually
☐ Check and adjust the spark plugs (Section 2)
☐ Check/adjust throttle body synchronisation (Section 5)*
☐ Check and adjust the throttle cables (Section 7)*
☐ Check and adjust the clutch cable (Section 8)
☐ Check the condition of the fuel lines (Section 6)*
☐ Lubricate the clutch lever pivot, gear lever pivot, brake lever pivot, brake pedal pivot, sidestand pivot and the throttle and clutch cables (Section 9)*
☐ Check the cooling system (Section 10)*
☐ Change the engine oil (Section 11)*
☐ Check the brake pads (Section 12)*
☐ Check the brake system and the operation of the brake light switches (Section 12)*
☐ Check the condition of the wheels and tyres (Section 13)*
☐ Check the wheel bearings (Section 13)
☐ Check the suspension (Section 14)
☐ Check and adjust the steering head bearings (Section 15)
☐ Check the sidestand and starter safety circuit (Section 16)*
☐ Check the tightness of all nuts, bolts and fasteners (Section 17)*
☐ Check the battery (Section 18)
☐ Check the EXUP system (Section 6)
☐ Check the air induction system – 2006 and 2007 models (Section 6)*

Every 12,000 miles (20,000 km)

Carry out all the items under the previous interval, plus the following:
☐ Fit new spark plugs (see Section 2)
☐ Fit a new engine oil filter (Section 11)
☐ Check the air induction system – 2008-on models (Section 6)*
☐ Re-grease the steering head bearings (Section 15)
☐ Re-grease the suspension linkage bearings (Section 14)

Every 24,000 miles (40,000 km)

Carry out all the items under the previous intervals, plus the following:
☐ Check and adjust the valve clearances (Section 19)
☐ Fit a new air filter element (see Section 3)

Every 30,000 miles (50,000 km)

☐ Re-grease the swingarm bearings (Section 14)

Every two years

☐ Change the brake fluid (Section 12)
☐ Fit new seals in the brake master cylinders and calipers (Section 12)

Every three years

☐ Change the coolant (Section 10)

Every four years

☐ Fit new brake hoses (Section 12)

Non-scheduled maintenance

☐ Fit new fuel hoses (Section 6)
☐ Change the front fork oil (Section 14)

Pre-ride
☐ See *Pre-ride checks* at the beginning of this manual.

After the initial 600 miles (1000 km)
Note: *This check is usually performed by a Yamaha dealer after the first 600 miles (1000 km) from new. Thereafter, maintenance is carried out according to the following intervals of the schedule.*

Every 500 miles (800 km)
☐ Check, adjust, clean and lubricate the drive chain (Section 1)

Every 4000 miles (6500 km) or 6 months
☐ Check and adjust the spark plugs (Section 2)
☐ Check the air filter element (Section 3)
☐ Check/adjust throttle body synchronisation (Section 5)
☐ Check the fuel system (Section 6)
☐ Check and adjust the throttle cables (Section 7)
☐ Check and adjust the clutch cable (Section 8)
☐ Lubricate the clutch lever pivot, gear lever pivot, brake lever pivot, brake pedal pivot, sidestand pivot and the throttle and clutch cables (Section 9)
☐ Check the cooling system (Section 10)
☐ Change the engine oil (Section 11)
☐ Check the brake pads (Section 12)
☐ Check the brake system and brake light switch operation (Section 12)
☐ Check the condition of the wheels and tyres (Section 13)
☐ Check the wheel bearings (Section 13)
☐ Check the suspension (Section 14)
☐ Check and adjust the steering head bearings (Section 15)
☐ Check the sidestand and starter safety circuit (Section 16)
☐ Check the tightness of all nuts, bolts and fasteners (Section 17)
☐ Check the battery (Section 18)
☐ Check the EXUP system (Section 6)

Every 8000 miles (13,000 km) or annually
Carry out all the items under the previous interval, plus the following:
☐ Fit new spark plugs (see Section 2)
☐ Fit a new engine oil filter (Section 11)
☐ Check the air induction system (AIS) (Section 6)
☐ Re-grease the suspension linkage bearings (Section 14)

Every 12,000 miles (20,000 km) or eighteen months
☐ Check the EVAP system (Section 6) – California models only
☐ Re-grease the steering head bearings (Section 15)

Every 16,000 miles (25,000 km) or two years
☐ Change the coolant (Section 10)

Every 24,000 miles (40,000 km)
☐ Check and adjust the valve clearances (Section 19)
☐ Fit a new air filter element (see Section 3)

Every 30,000 miles (50,000 km)
☐ Re-grease the swingarm bearings (Section 14)

Every two years
☐ Change the brake fluid (Section 12)
☐ Renew the seals in the brake master cylinders and calipers (Section 12)

Every four years
☐ Fit new brake hoses (Section 12)

Non-scheduled maintenance
☐ Fit new fuel hoses (Section 6)
☐ Change the front fork oil (Section 14)

Component locations on right side

1 Rear brake fluid reservoir
2 Engine oil filler cap
3 Front fork pre-load and damping adjuster
4 Front brake fluid reservoir
5 Brake lever span adjuster
6 Throttle cable upper adjuster

7 Radiator pressure cap
8 Coolant reservoir
9 Front fork compression damping
  adjusters
10 Front fork seals
11 Clutch cable lower adjuster

12 Coolant drain bolt
13 Engine oil level dipstick
14 EXUP valve pulley
15 Rear brake light switch
16 Rear brake pedal height adjuster
17 Drive chain adjuster

Component locations on left side

1 Clutch cable upper adjuster
2 Front fork pre-load and damping adjuster
3 Steering head bearing adjuster
4 Air filter element
5 Rear shock compression damping
  adjusters

6 Battery
7 Drive chain adjuster
8 Rear shock absorber rebound damping
  adjuster
9 Rear shock pre-load adjuster ring
10 Engine oil filter

11 Engine oil drain bolt
12 Engine oil pressure take-off point
13 Front fork seals
14 Front fork compression damping
   adjusters

1 This Chapter is designed to help the home mechanic maintain his/her motorcycle for safety, economy, long life and peak performance.

2 Deciding where to start or plug into the routine maintenance schedule depends on several factors. If the warranty period on your motorcycle has just expired, and if it has been maintained according to the warranty standards, you may want to pick up routine maintenance as it coincides with the next mileage or calendar interval. If you have owned the machine for some time but have never performed any maintenance on it, then you may want to start at the beginning and include all frequent procedures to ensure that nothing important is overlooked. If you have just had a major engine overhaul, then you should start the engine maintenance routines from the beginning. If you have a used machine and have no knowledge of its history or maintenance record, you should combine all the checks into one large initial service and then settle into the maintenance schedule prescribed.

3 Before beginning any maintenance or repair, the machine should be cleaned thoroughly, especially around the oil filter, drain plugs, spark plugs and valve cover. Cleaning will help ensure that dirt does not contaminate the engine and will allow you to detect wear and damage that could otherwise easily go unnoticed.

4 Certain maintenance information is sometimes printed on decals attached to the motorcycle. If any information on the decals differs from that included here, use the information on the decal.

 Warning: Read the Safety first! section of this manual carefully before starting work.

Maintenance procedures

1 Drive chain and sprockets

Chain slack check

1 A neglected drive chain won't last long and can quickly damage the sprockets. Routine chain adjustment and lubrication isn't difficult and will ensure maximum chain and sprocket life.

2 To check the chain, use a suitable stand to raise the bike so that the rear wheel is free. Shift the transmission into neutral.

3 Push up on the bottom run of the chain and measure the total up-and-down slack at a point midway between the two sprockets **(see illustrations)**, then compare your measurement to that listed in this Chapter's Specifications. As the chain stretches with wear, adjustment will periodically be necessary (see below). Since the chain will rarely wear evenly, rotate the rear wheel or roll the bike forward so that another section of chain can be checked (having an assistant to do this makes the task a lot easier); do this several times to check the entire length of chain, and mark the tightest spot.

Caution: Riding the bike with excess slack in the chain could lead to damage.

4 In some cases where lubrication has been neglected, corrosion and dirt may cause the links to bind and kink, which effectively shortens the chain's length and makes it tight

1.3a Chain freeplay is measured midway between the sprockets on the bottom run of the chain

1.3b Check the total up-and-down slack by pushing up on the chain and measuring with a ruler

1.4 Neglect has caused the links in this chain to kink

1.9 Slacken the axle nut (arrowed)

(see illustration). Thoroughly clean and work free any such links, then highlight them with a marker pen or paint. Take the bike for a ride.

5 After the bike has been ridden, repeat the measurement for slack in the highlighted area. If the chain has kinked again and is still tight, replace it with a new one (see Chapter 6). A rusty, kinked or worn chain will damage the sprockets and can damage transmission

bearings. If in any doubt as to the condition of a chain, it is far better to install a new one than risk damage to other components and possibly yourself.

6 Check the entire length of the chain for worn or damaged rollers and sideplates, loose links and pins, and missing O-rings and replace it with a new one if necessary. **Note:** *Never install a new chain on old sprockets, and never use the old chain if you install new sprockets – replace the chain and sprockets as a set.*

7 Inspect the drive chain slider on the front of the swingarm for excessive wear and damage and replace it with a new one if necessary.

Adjustment

8 Rotate the rear wheel until the chain is positioned with the tightest point at the centre of its bottom run. Support the bike upright as in Step 2.

9 Loosen the nut on the right-hand end of the rear axle **(see illustration)**.

10 Loosen the locknut on the adjuster bolt on each end of the swingarm, then turn the

adjuster bolts with an Allen key, evenly, a small amount at a time, until the specified chain tension is obtained – if the chain was slack turn the bolts anti-clockwise; if the chain was tight turn them clockwise, then move the wheel forwards in the swingarm to take up the gap between the adjustment plates and the adjuster bolt shoulders **(see illustrations)**. Following chain adjustment, check that the mark on each adjuster plate is in the same position in relation to the end of the swingarm **(see illustration)**. It is important that the same mark on each plate is used; if not, the rear wheel will be out of alignment with the front.

> **HAYNES HiNT** *Refer to Chapter 6 for information on checking wheel alignment.*

11 If there is a discrepancy in the position of the plates, correct it with the adjusters and then check the chain tension as described above. Also check that there is no clearance

1.10a Slacken the locknut on each side . . .

1.10b . . . and turn each adjuster (arrowed) by an equal amount . . .

1.10c . . . then check the alignment of the adjuster plate marks with the end of the swingarm as described

1.12 Tighten the axle nut to the specified torque

1.14 Apply the lubricant to the overlapping sections of the sideplates

between the adjuster bolt's shoulder and the rear of the adjuster – push the wheel forwards to eliminate any clearance.

12 Tighten the axle nut to the torque setting specified at the beginning of this Chapter, then tighten the adjuster locknuts securely **(see illustration)**. Recheck the adjustment.

Cleaning and lubrication

13 If required, wash the chain using a dedicated aerosol cleaner or in paraffin (kerosene), then wipe it off and allow it to dry, using compressed air if available. If the chain is excessively dirty, remove the rear wheel (see Chapter 6) and soak the chain in paraffin. *Caution: Don't use petrol (gasoline), solvent or other cleaning fluids which might damage the internal sealing properties of the chain. Don't use high-pressure water. The entire process shouldn't take longer than five to six minutes – if it does, the O-rings in the chain rollers could be damaged.*

14 The best time to lubricate the chain is after the motorcycle has been ridden. When the chain is warm, the lubricant will penetrate the joints between the sideplates better than when cold. **Note:** *Yamaha specifies engine oil or aerosol chain lube that is specifically for O-ring chains; do not use chain lube that is not specifically for O-ring chains, as it may contain solvents that could damage the O-rings.* Apply the lubricant

to the area where the sideplates overlap – not the middle of the rollers and protect the tyre from overspray with a rag **(see illustration)**.

> **HAYNES HINT** *Apply the lubricant to the top of the lower chain run, so centrifugal force will work it into the chain when the bike is moving. After applying the lubricant, let it soak in a few minutes before wiping off any excess.*

> ⚠ **Warning: Take care not to get any lubricant on the rear tyre or brake components. If any of the lubricant inadvertently contacts them, clean it off thoroughly using a suitable solvent or dedicated brake cleaner before riding the machine.**

Drive chain stretch and sprocket wear check

Note: *Over a period of time the drive chain will stretch and the sprocket teeth will wear, necessitating their replacement as a set. Chain stretch can be determined by measurement and sprocket wear by visual inspection.*

15 Check the entire length of the chain for worn or damaged rollers and side plates, loose links and pins, and missing O-rings. Fit a new chain if damage is found.

16 Remove the front sprocket cover (see Chapter 6). Check the teeth on the front sprocket and the rear sprocket for wear **(see illustration)**. If the sprocket teeth are worn excessively, replace the chain and both sprockets with a new set. Fit a new sprocket nut using thread locking compound and centre punch the nut's collar into the groove on the shaft. Check that the rear wheel sprocket nuts are tight (refer to Chapter 6 Specifications for the torque setting).

17 Inspect the drive chain slider on the front of the swingarm for excessive wear and damage and replace it with a new one if necessary.

18 Measure the amount of chain stretch as follows:

19 Loosen the nut on the right-hand end of the rear axle **(see illustration 1.9)**.

20 Slacken the adjuster bolt locknuts, then turn the adjuster bolts out evenly until all slack is taken up, but not so much that the chain is taut **(see illustrations 1.10a, 1.10b,1.10c)**. Measure a 15 link section along the bottom run of the chain **(see illustration)**. Rotate the rear wheel so that several sections of the chain can be measured, then calculate the average and compare it to the stretch limit specified at the beginning of the Chapter. If the chain stretch measurement exceeds the service limit it must be replaced with a new one (see Chapter 6).

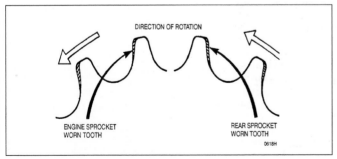

1.16 Check the sprockets in the areas indicated to see if they are worn excessively

1.20 Measure chain link sections as shown to determine chain stretch

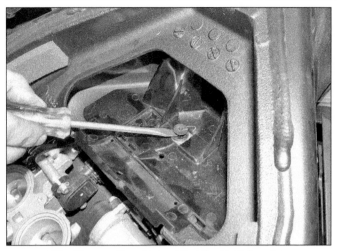

2.2a Remove the clip securing the blanking plate

2.2b Disconnect the fan wiring connectors . . .

2.2c . . . and remove the regulator/rectifier mounting

2.2d Make sure the bracket doesn't damaged the radiator

21 If the chain is good, reset the adjusters so that there is the correct amount of freeplay (see Steps 8 to 12).

Caution: Never install a new chain on old sprockets, and never use the old chain if you install new sprockets – replace the chain and sprockets as a set.

2 Spark plugs

Check and adjustment

1 You'll need a 16 mm hex size deep spark plug socket to remove the plugs – a special plug spanner is supplied in the motorcycle's tool kit which is stored under the passenger seat.

2 Raise the fuel tank (see Chapter 4) remove the air filter (see Section 3) and its housing (see Chapter 4) then depress the pin and remove the trim clip securing the blanking plate to the AIS **(see illustration)** and remove the blanking plate. If required for access remove the fairing side panels (see Chapter 7). Displace the radiator from its mounts and move it forwards and down as much as possible (see Chapter 3) – there is no need to drain the cooling system and the coolant hoses can remain connected, but you need to disconnect the fan wiring connectors **(see illustration)**, release all wiring ties, and displace the regulator/rectifier mounting plate from the left-hand side **(see illustration)**. Make sure the bracket for the bottom radiator mount does not dig into and damage the radiator fins **(see illustration)**. To improve access, or if as part of your service you are checking the valve clearances, remove the radiator (see Chapter 3).

3 Release the wiring tie on the air induction system (AIS) hose **(see illustration)**. Disconnect the cylinder identification sensor wiring connector, the AIS cut-off valve wiring

2.3a Release the wiring tie (arrowed) . . .

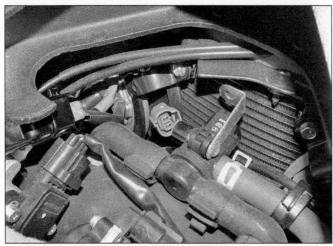

2.3b ... then disconnect the AIS valve wiring connector ...

2.3c ... and pull back the heat blanket

2.4 Pull the coil up off the plug

2.5 Unscrew the plug

connector (see illustration) and the AIS hose to the air filter housing. Remove the AIS hoses from the reed valves and withdraw the AIS assembly. Lift the heat blanket and fold it out of the way to expose the coils (see illustration).

4 Clean the area around each ignition coil to prevent any dirt falling into the spark plug channels. Pull the coil off each spark plug (see illustration). If compressed air is available blow away any accumulated dirt lying in the bottom of each spark plug well to prevent any falling into the engine when the plug is removed.

5 Using either a plug spanner or a deep socket type wrench, unscrew the plugs from the cylinder head (see illustration). Lay each plug out in relation to its cylinder so that, if any plug shows up a problem, it will be easy to identify the troublesome cylinder.

6 Inspect the electrodes for wear. Both the centre and side electrodes should have square edges and the side electrodes should be of uniform thickness. Look for excessive deposits and evidence of a cracked or chipped insulator around the centre electrode. Compare your spark plugs to the colour spark plug reading chart on the inside rear cover of this manual. Check the threads, the washer and the ceramic insulator body for cracks and other damage.

7 If the electrodes are not excessively worn, and if the deposits can be easily removed with a wire brush, and there are no cracks or chips visible in the insulator, the plugs can be re-used. If in doubt concerning the condition of the plugs, replace them with new ones, as the expense is minimal. Note that new spark plugs should be fitted at every second service interval.

8 Before installing the plugs, make sure they

are the correct type and heat range and check the gap between the side (earth) electrodes and the centre electrode (see illustration). Compare the gap to that specified and adjust

2.8a Using a wire type gauge to measure the spark plug electrode gap

2.8b The gaps between the two earth electrodes (A) and the centre electrode (B) must be equal and as specified

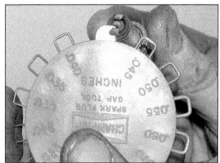

2.8c Adjust the electrode gap by bending the side electrodes only

HAYNES HiNT *Stripped plug threads in the cylinder head can be repaired with a thread insert – see Section 2 of 'Tools and Workshop Tips' in the Reference section.*

Renewal

12 At the prescribed interval, whatever the condition of the existing spark plugs, remove the plugs as described above and install new ones.

3 Air filter

as necessary **(see illustration)**. If the gap must be adjusted, bend the side electrodes only and be very careful not to chip or crack the insulator nose **(see illustration)**. Make sure the sealing washer is in place on the plug before installing it.

9 Since the cylinder head is made of aluminium, which is soft and easily damaged, thread the plugs into the head and turn the tool by hand. Once the plugs are finger-tight, the job can be finished with a spanner on the tool supplied or a socket drive **(see illustration 2.5)**. If a torque wrench is available, tighten the spark plugs to the torque setting specified at the beginning of this Chapter. Otherwise tighten them by 1/4 to 1/2 turn after they have been fully hand tightened and have seated. Do not over-tighten them.

HAYNES HiNT *As the plugs are quite recessed, you can slip a short length of hose over the end of the plug to use as a tool to thread it into place. The hose will grip the plug well enough to turn it, but will start to slip if the plug begins to cross-thread in the hole – this will prevent damaged threads.*

10 Install the coils, making sure they locate correctly onto the plugs **(see illustration 2.4)**. Reconnect the coil wiring connectors, making sure they are securely connected to the correct cylinder, and replace the heat blanket. Refit the AIS valve and its hoses, and reconnect the AIS and cylinder identification sensor wiring connectors **(see illustration 2.3b)**. Secure the wiring to the AIS hose with the tie.

11 Install the radiator (see Chapter 3). Locate the regulator/rectifier mounting and refit the wiring ties. Install the fairing panels (see Chapter 7).

3.2a Disconnect the secondary injector fuel hose

Note: *If the machine is continually ridden in dusty conditions, check, clean and replace the filter more frequently than specified.*

Cleaning

1 Raise and support the fuel tank, or remove it if required for better access (see Chapter 4).

2 Disconnect the secondary injector fuel hose **(see illustration)** and on 2006 and 2007 models disconnect and remove the atmospheric pressure sensor wires **(see illustration)**.

3 Undo the screws securing the cover and remove it **(see illustrations)**. On 2008-on

3.2b Disconnect the wiring connector on 2006/7 models

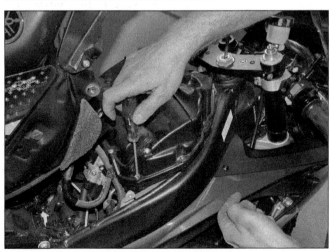

3.3a Undo the screws . . .

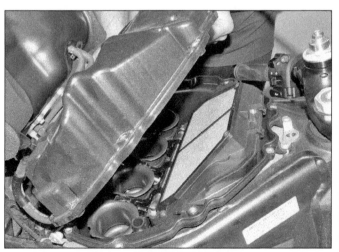

3.3b . . . and remove the cover

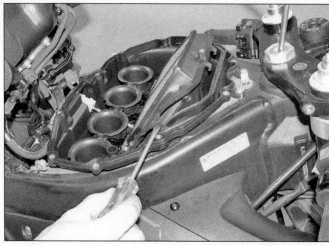

3.4a On 2006/7 models unscrew the filter element

3.4b Pry the element off its clips on 2008-on models

models equipped with YCC-I undo the front centre screw first.

4 On 2006 and 2007 models remove the screws securing the air filter element **(see illustration)**, on 2008-on models pry up the front edge to unclip the filter element and lift it to release the rear projections from the case **(see illustration)**.

5 The element in the air filter is made of an oil coated paper and should not be cleaned with compressed air.

6 Clean out any dirt from the filter housing and cover. Make sure the seals are in good condition and correctly seated.

7 Install the filter element and fit the cover, making sure they locate correctly. On 2008-on models the front centre screw securing the cover should be tightened last.

8 Check the crankcase breather hose between the engine and the rear of the air filter housing for loose connections, cracks and deterioration, and replace it with a new one if necessary **(see illustration)**. On 2006 and 2007 models reconnect the atmospheric pressure sensor coupling.

Renewal

9 Fit a new filter at the prescribed interval, whatever the condition of the existing filter element. In unusually wet or dusty conditions

3.8 Crankcase breather hose (arrowed)

the element may require replacement more often.

4 Idle speed

Note: *The idle speed is controlled by the ECU through the YCC-T system and there is no procedure for directly adjusting it.*

1 If the idle speed is incorrect then first check that the battery voltage is correct and that the battery is not flat or in need of replacement (see Chapter 8).

2 Then check if the air filter is dirty, incorrectly fitted, or damaged (see Section 3) and that the air intake is clear. Then check the throttle bodies for air leaks, poor synchronisation, wrongly adjusted cables, or flooding (see Sections 5 and 7, and Chapter 4)

3 Next check the AIS hoses, valve and reed valves for leaks and correct operation (see Section 6 and Chapter 4).

4 Then check the ignition coils and the spark plugs (see Section 2 and Chapter 4)

5 Check the valve clearances (see Section 19) and perform a compression check (see Chapter 2) to verify that the valves are not damaged.

5.2 Manometer (A) and vacuum gauges (B)

6 Check the crankshaft position sensor and cylinder identification sensor (see Chapter 4). Have a Yamaha dealer check the ECU.

5 Throttle body synchronisation

Warning: Petrol (gasoline) is extremely flammable, so take extra precautions when you work on any part of the fuel system. Don't smoke or allow open flames or bare light bulbs near the work area, and don't work in a garage where a natural gas-type appliance is present. If you spill any fuel on your skin, rinse it off immediately with soap and water. When you perform any kind of work on the fuel system, wear safety glasses and have a fire extinguisher suitable for a Class B type fire (flammable liquids) on hand.

Warning: Do not allow exhaust gases to build up in the work area; either perform the check outside or use an exhaust gas extraction system.

Special tool: *A set of vacuum gauges or a manometer is necessary for this job.*

1 Throttle body synchronisation ensures each throttle body passes the same amount of fuel/air mixture to each cylinder. This is done by measuring the vacuum produced in each cylinder. Throttle bodies that are out of synchronisation will result in increased fuel consumption, higher engine temperature, less than ideal throttle response and higher vibration levels. Before synchronising the throttle bodies, make sure that the valve clearances were checked at the previous prescribed interval.

2 To synchronise the throttle bodies you will need a set of vacuum gauges or a manometer **(see illustration)**. These instruments measure engine vacuum, and can be obtained from

5.4 The vacuum take-offs are located next to the intake rubbers

5.5 The air screws are to one side of the injectors

motorcycle dealers or mail order parts suppliers. The equipment used should be suitable for a four cylinder engine and come complete with the necessary adapters and hoses to fit the take-off points.

3 Start the engine and let it run until it reaches normal operating temperature, then shut it off. Support the machine upright on level ground using an auxiliary stand. Raise the fuel tank or temporarily remove it for best access (see Chapter 4).

4 Locate the vacuum take offs on the throttle bodies **(see illustration)** remove the blanking caps and connect the gauge hoses using suitable adapters if necessary. Make sure that the hose from No. 1 gauge is attached to No. 1 (left hand) throttle body, and so on.

5 Locate the throttle body air screws under the fuel rail **(see illustration)** and note that one is painted white. If removed, refit the fuel tank (see Chapter 4) and start the engine. Allow the engine to warm up to normal operating temperature and the idle speed to settle to normal. If the gauges are fitted with damping adjustment, set this so that needle flutter is just eliminated but so that they can still respond to small changes in pressure.

6 Unscrew the white painted screw slightly and then tighten it fully home. If necessary adjust the screws on the other throttle bodies so that their readings match the white painted screw's value or are at least within the maximum differences specified in the beginning of this Chapter. Should more than one screw have a white paint mark, use the one with the lowest vacuum reading as the benchmark.

7 After adjusting each screw open and close the throttle quickly two or three times and then recheck the vacuum reading. If an air screw is inadvertently removed, screw it in ¾ of a turn and make any fine adjustment to its setting according to the gauge readings.

8 If the above procedure fails to produce satisfactory results then screw all the air

screws fully home, check the readings to find the one with the lowest vacuum and adjust the others to match. When all the throttle bodies are synchronised, open and close the throttle quickly to settle the linkage, and recheck the gauge readings, readjusting if necessary.

9 When the adjustment is complete, check the idle speed (see Section 4). Remove the gauges and replace the blanking plugs and their clips **(see illustration 5.4)**. Lower the fuel tank (see Chapter 4).

6 Fuel system, AIS system, EVAP system and EXUP system

⚠️ **Warning: Petrol (gasoline) is extremely flammable, so take extra precautions when you work on any part of the fuel system. Don't smoke or allow open flames or bare light bulbs near the work area, and don't work in a garage where a natural gas-type appliance is present. If you spill any fuel on your skin, rinse it off immediately with soap and water. When you perform any kind of work on the fuel system, wear safety glasses and have a fire extinguisher suitable for a Class B type fire (flammable liquids) on hand.**

Fuel system

1 Raise the fuel tank (see Chapter 4) and check the tank, the fuel supply and return hoses, the tank overflow and breather hoses, and the throttle body vacuum hoses for signs of leaks, cracking, hardening, kinks or damage. In particular check that there are no leaks from the fuel hoses or hose unions. Replace any hose that has deteriorated with a new one (see Chapter 4).

2 If the joint between the fuel pump mounting plate and the tank is leaking, ensure the mounting bolts are tightened to the specified torque setting (see Chapter 4); if the leak

persists, remove the pump and fit a new gasket (see Chapter 4).

3 Inspect the joints between the fuel rail, the injectors and the throttle bodies. If there are any leaks, remove the fuel rail and fit new seals and O-rings to the injectors (see Chapter 4).

4 Make sure the air filter housing is securely mounted on the throttle bodies. Make sure the intake adapters between the throttle bodies and the cylinder head are in good condition and that the clamp screws securing them to the throttle bodies and the cylinder head are tight.

Air induction system (AIS)

5 To reduce the amount of unburned hydrocarbons released in the exhaust gases, an air induction system (AIS) is fitted. The system consists of the control valve (mounted above the valve cover), the reed valves (fitted in the valve cover) and the hoses linking them. The control valve is actuated electronically by the ECU.

6 Under certain operating conditions, a signal from the ECU opens up the AIS control valve which then allows filtered air to be drawn through the reed valves and cylinder head passages and into the exhaust ports. The air mixes with the exhaust gases, causing any unburned particles of the fuel in the mixture to be burnt in the exhaust port/pipes. This process changes a considerable amount of hydrocarbons and carbon monoxide into relatively harmless carbon dioxide and water. The reed valves in the valve cover are fitted to prevent the flow of exhaust gases back up the cylinder head passages and into the air filter housing.

7 The system is not adjustable and requires little maintenance. Raise the fuel tank (see Chapter 4) and remove the air filter (see Section 3) and its housing (see Chapter 4). Depress the pin and remove the trim clip securing the blanking plate to the AIS **(see illustration 2.2a)**. Check that the hoses are not kinked or pinched, are in good condition

6.7 Check the AIS system hoses

6.13a Unscrew the bolts and remove the cover . . .

and are securely connected at each end (see illustration). Replace any hoses that are cracked, split or generally deteriorated with new ones. Make sure the control valve wiring connector is securely connected and no wires or terminals are loose or corroded.

8 If the valve clearances are all correct and the throttle bodies have been synchronised and have no other faults, but the idle speed is erratic, it is possible that the AIS is faulty. Refer to Chapter 4 for further information on the system and for checks if it is believed to be faulty.

EVAP system (California models)

9 Raise the fuel tank (see Chapter 4). Visually inspect all the system hoses between the fuel tank, the roll-over valve, the purge control solenoid valve, and the canister for kinks and splits and any other damage or deterioration. Make sure that the hoses are securely connected with a clamp on each end. Replace any hoses that are damaged or deteriorated.

10 Check the EVAP canister and the valve for cracks or other damage.
11 Refer to your dealer for further information and tests on the system. Note that there is an emission control system hose routing diagram on a label under the passenger seat.

EXUP system check

12 When the ignition is first switched ON, the EXUP system performs its own self-diagnosis, and the servo can be heard turning the valve from fully closed to fully open and back again. If the servo does not turn refer to Chapter 4, Sections 7 and 15. Note that the motorcycle can be ridden even though a fault has been diagnosed, though a difference in performance will be noticed.
13 Unscrew the bolts securing the EXUP pulley cover on the exhaust and remove the cover (see illustrations). Turn the ignition ON and check that the pulley moves.
14 Measure the amount of freeplay in each cable as shown (see illustration) and check

6.13b . . . to access the EXUP cables

that it is as specified at the beginning of the Chapter. If the freeplay is incorrect then run the diagnostic check (see Chapter 4) and check that the stop on the pulley meets the stop cast into the silencer (see illustration). If it does not, and the cable adjustment is correct check the valve for free operation and the servo (see Chapter 4).

H48575

6.14a Cable freeplay is measured as total up-and-down play in cables (arrowed). Slacken locknuts (A) and adjust freeplay using threaded adjusters (B)

H48574

6.14b Check the pulley projection (A) contacts the stop (B)

7.4 Throttle cable freeplay is measured in terms of twistgrip rotation

7.5 Slacken the locknut and turn the adjuster (arrowed) as required

15 The EXUP pulley and valve are prone to corrosion, due to their location. The pulley cover and valve cover bolts can seize, the cable ends can seize in their sockets in the pulley, and the valve shaft can seize in its bushes. Keep the area well lubricated with WD40 or a suitable equivalent. It is highly advisable to disassemble the system as far as is possible from time to time (according to the conditions you ride in) and lubricate the shaft, bushes, cable ends and bolts with copper-based grease (see Chapter 4).

16 Apply some copper grease to the cover bolt threads. Install the cover **(see illustration 6.13)** and tighten the bolts to the torque setting specified at the beginning of the Chapter.

7 Throttle cables

1 Make sure the throttle twistgrip rotates easily from fully closed to fully open with the front wheel turned at various angles. The twistgrip should return automatically from fully open to fully closed when released.

2 If the throttle sticks, this is probably due to a cable fault. Remove the cables (see Chapter 4) and lubricate them (see Section 9). If the inner cables still do not run smoothly in the outer cables, replace the cables with new ones.

3 With the cables removed, check that the twistgrip turns smoothly around the handlebar – dirt combined with a lack of lubrication can cause the action to be stiff. If necessary, remove the handlebar end-weight and slide the twistgrip off the handlebar. Clean any old grease from the bar and the inside of the tube. Smear some new grease of the specified type onto the bar, then refit the twistgrip and end-weight. Install the lubricated or new cables, making sure they are correctly routed (see Chapter 4). If this fails to improve the operation of the throttle, the fault could lie in

the throttle cable pulley. Remove it and check the action of the linkage and throttle position sensor (see Chapter 4).

4 With the throttle operating smoothly, check for a small amount of freeplay in the cables, measured in terms of the amount of twistgrip rotation before the throttle opens, and compare the amount to that listed in this Chapter's Specifications **(see illustration)**.

5 If it is incorrect, adjust the cables using the adjuster in the throttle opening cable where it leaves the throttle/switch housing on the handlebar. Loosen the lock ring and turn the adjuster until the specified amount of freeplay is obtained, then retighten the lock ring **(see illustration)**. Turn the adjuster in to increase freeplay and out to reduce it.

6 If the cables cannot be adjusted as specified, replace them with new ones (see Chapter 4).

⚠️ **Warning: Turn the handlebars all the way through their travel with the engine idling. Idle speed should not change. If it does, the cables may be routed incorrectly. Correct this condition before riding the motorcycle.**

7 Check that the throttle twistgrip operates smoothly and snaps shut quickly when released.

8 Clutch cable

1 Check that the clutch lever operates smoothly and easily.

2 If the lever action is heavy or stiff, remove the cable (see Chapter 2) and lubricate it (see Section 9). If the inner cable still does not run smoothly in the outer cable, replace the cable with a new one. Install the lubricated or new cable (see Chapter 2).

3 If the lever itself is stiff, remove the lever from its bracket (see Chapter 5) and check for

damage or distortion, or any other cause, and remedy as necessary. Clean and lubricate the pivot and contact areas (see Section 9).

4 If the lever and cable are good, refer to Chapter 2 and check the release mechanism in the clutch cover and the clutch itself.

5 With the clutch operating smoothly, check that the clutch lever is correctly adjusted. Periodic adjustment is necessary to compensate for wear in the clutch plates and stretch of the cable. Check that the amount of freeplay at the clutch lever end is within the specifications listed at the beginning of this Chapter **(see illustration)**.

6 If adjustment is required, turn the adjuster in or out until the required amount of freeplay is obtained **(see illustration)**. To increase freeplay, turn the adjuster clockwise (into the lever bracket). To reduce freeplay, turn the adjuster anti-clockwise (out of the lever bracket). Tighten the locking ring securely.

7 If all the adjustment has been taken up at the lever, reset the adjuster to give the maximum amount of freeplay, then set the correct amount of freeplay using the adjuster on the lower end of the cable in the bracket on the right-hand side of the engine.

8 Slacken the rear adjuster nut, then turn

8.5 Measure the amount of freeplay at the clutch lever end as shown

8.6 Turn the adjuster in or out as required

8.8 Slacken nut (A) and adjust the nut (B) as described

the front nut as required to obtain the correct freeplay **(see illustration)**. To increase freeplay, thread the front nut towards the front of the motorcycle. To reduce freeplay, thread the front nut towards the back of the motorcycle. When the correct amount of freeplay has been achieved, locate the front nut against the bracket, then tighten the rear nut against the bracket.

9 Subsequent adjustments can now be made using the clutch lever adjuster only.

9 Stand, lever pivots and cable lubrication

Pivot points

1 Since the controls, cables and various other components of a motorcycle are exposed to the elements, they should be checked and lubricated periodically to ensure safe and trouble-free operation.

2 The footrest pivots, clutch and brake lever pivots, brake pedal and gearchange lever pivots and linkage and sidestand pivot should be lubricated frequently. In order for the lubricant to be applied where it will do the most good, the component should be disassembled (see Chapter 5). The lubricant recommended by Yamaha for each application is listed at the beginning of the Chapter. If aerosol chain or cable lubricant is being used, it can be applied to the pivot joint gaps and will usually work its way into the areas where friction occurs, so less disassembly of the component is needed (however it is always better to do so and clean off all corrosion, dirt and old lubricant first). If motor oil or light grease is being used, apply it sparingly as it may attract dirt (which could cause the controls to bind or wear at an accelerated rate). **Note:** *An alternative lubricant for the control lever pivots is a dry-film lubricant (available from many sources by different names).*

Cables

Special tool: *A cable lubricating adapter is*

necessary for this procedure **(see illustration 9.3c)**.

3 To lubricate the cables, disconnect the relevant cable at its upper end, then lubricate it with a pressure adapter and aerosol cable lubricant **(see illustrations)**. See Chapter 4 for throttle cable removal procedures, and Chapter 2 for the clutch cable.

9.3a Fit the cable into the adapter . . .

9.3b . . . and tighten the screw to seal it in . . .

9.3c . . . then apply the lubricant using the nozzle provided inserted in the hole in the adapter

10.2 Check the cooling system hoses as described

10.4 Check the oil cooler for water or oil leaks

10 Cooling system

Check

 Warning: The engine must be cool before beginning this procedure.

1 Check the coolant level in the reservoir (see *Pre-ride checks*).

2 Remove the fairing side panels and the lower fairing (see Chapter 7). Check the entire cooling system for evidence of leakage. Examine each rubber coolant hose along its entire length **(see illustration)**. Look for cracks, splits, abrasions and other signs of deterioration. Squeeze each hose at various points. They should feel firm, yet pliable, and return to their original shape when released. If they are cracked or hard, replace them with new ones.

3 Check for evidence of leaks at each cooling system joint. If necessary, tighten the hose clips carefully to prevent future leaks.

4 Examine the oil cooler inlet and outlet hoses for damage and signs of deterioration **(see illustration)** the cooler is on the front of the engine. Ensure that the hose clips are secure and that there is no sign of leakage of either coolant or oil at the oil cooler-to-crankcase joint. If there is, refer to Chapter 2 – if coolant is leaking replace the cooler with a new one, and if oil is leaking first make sure the cooler bolt is tightened to the specified torque (see Chapter 2 Specifications), and if it is, or if leakage persists, remove the cooler and replace the bolt sealing washer and the O-ring with a new one.

5 Check for leakage around the pump inlet and outlet hoses on the right-hand side and front of the engine **(see illustration)**. If there is leakage make sure the hose is seated properly and that the hose clips are secure..

6 Check the radiator for leaks and other damage. Leaks in the radiator leave tell-tale scale deposits or coolant stains on the outside of the core below the leak. If leaks are noted, remove the radiator (see Chapter 3) and have it repaired by a specialist.

Caution: Do not use a liquid leak stopping compound to try to repair leaks.

7 Check the radiator fins for mud, dirt and insects, which may impede the flow of air through the radiator. If the fins are dirty, remove the radiator (see Chapter 3) and clean it, using water or low pressure compressed air directed through the fins from the back. If the fins are bent or distorted, straighten them carefully with a screwdriver. Bent or damaged fins will restrict the airflow and impair the efficiency of the radiator causing the engine to overheat. Where there is substantial damage to the radiator's surface area, renew the radiator.

8 Remove the pressure cap from the radiator filler neck by turning it anti-clockwise until it reaches a stop. If you hear a hissing sound (indicating that there is still pressure in the system), wait until it stops. Now press down on the cap and continue turning until it can be removed **(see illustration)**.

10.5 Check around the water pump and its hoses for leaks

10.8 Remove the pressure cap as described

9 Check the condition of the coolant in the system. If it is rust-coloured or if accumulations of scale are visible, drain, flush and refill the system with new coolant (see below). Check the cap seal for cracks and other damage. If in doubt about the pressure cap's condition, have it tested by a Yamaha dealer or replace it with a new one.

10 Check the antifreeze content of the coolant with an antifreeze hydrometer (see Specifications). A mixture with less than 40% antifreeze (40/60 antifreeze to distilled water) will not provide proper corrosion protection. Sometimes coolant looks like it's in good condition, but might be too weak to offer adequate protection. If the hydrometer indicates a weak mixture, drain, flush and refill the system (see below). A higher than specified concentration of antifreeze decreases the performance of the cooling system and should only be used when additional protection against freezing is needed.

11 Install the cap by turning it clockwise until it reaches the first stop then push down on the cap and continue turning until it will turn no further.

12 Start the engine and let it reach normal operating temperature, then check for leaks again. As the coolant temperature increases beyond normal, the fans should come on automatically and the temperature should begin to drop. If they do not, refer to Chapter 8 and check the fuses, then refer to Chapter 3 and check the fan relay, fan motors, coolant temperature sensor and fan circuit carefully.

13 If the coolant level is consistently low, and no evidence of leaks can be found, have the entire system pressure-checked by a Yamaha dealer.

Change the coolant

Warning: Allow the engine to cool completely before performing this maintenance operation. Also, *don't allow antifreeze to come into contact with your skin or the painted surfaces of the motorcycle. Rinse off spills immediately with plenty of water. Antifreeze is highly toxic if ingested. Never leave antifreeze lying around in an open container or in puddles on the floor; children and pets are attracted by its sweet smell and may drink it. Check with local authorities (councils) about disposing of antifreeze. Many communities have collection centres where antifreeze can be disposed of safely. Antifreeze is also combustible, so don't store it near open flames.*

Draining

14 Secure the motorcycle upright on a level surface using an auxiliary stand. Remove the fairing side panels and the lower fairing (see Chapter 7).

15 Unscrew the bolts securing the reservoir to the radiator, remove the reservoir, and drain it into a suitable container, then rinse the inside with clean water – refer to *Pre-Ride checks* for access.

16 Remove the pressure cap from the radiator filler neck by turning it anti-clockwise until it reaches a stop **(see illustration 10.8)**. If you hear a hissing sound (indicating there is still pressure in the system), wait until it stops. Now press down on the cap and continue turning until it can be removed.

17 Position a suitable container beneath the drain bolt. Remove the bolt and allow the coolant to completely drain from the system **(see illustrations)**. Retain the old sealing washer for use during flushing.

Flushing

18 Flush the system with clean tap water by inserting a garden hose in the radiator filler neck. Allow the water to run through the system until it is clear when it flows out of the drain hole. If there is a lot of rust in the water, remove the radiator (see Chapter 3) and have it professionally cleaned. If the drain hole appears to be clogged with sediment, unblock it.

19 Install the drain bolt using the old sealing washer. Fill the system via the radiator with clean water mixed with a flushing compound. Make sure the flushing compound is compatible with aluminium components, and follow the manufacturer's instructions carefully. Install the pressure cap. Fill the coolant reservoir to the FULL mark with clean water.

20 Start the engine and allow it to reach normal operating temperature. Let it run for about ten minutes.

21 Stop the engine. Let it cool for a while, then cover the pressure cap with a heavy rag and turn it anti-clockwise to the first stop, releasing any pressure that may be present in the system. Once the hissing stops, push down on the cap and remove it completely.

22 Drain the system again.

23 Repeat Steps 19 to 22, filling the system with clean water only.

Refilling

24 Fit a new sealing washer onto the drain bolt and tighten it to the torque setting specified at the beginning of this Chapter **(see illustrations overleaf)**.

25 Fill the system via the radiator cap with the proper coolant mixture (see this Chapter's Specifications) Note: *Pour the coolant in slowly to minimise the amount of air entering the system.* When the system appears full, move the bike off its stand and shake it slightly to dissipate the coolant, then place the bike back on the auxiliary stand and top the system up.

26 When the system is full (all the way up to the top of the radiator filler neck), install the pressure cap. Now fill the coolant reservoir to

10.17a Unscrew the drain bolt . . .

10.17b . . . and allow the coolant to drain

10.24a Fit the drain bolt with a new sealing washer . . .

10.24b . . . and refit it

the FULL mark and fit the cap (see *Pre-ride checks*).

27 Start the engine and allow it to run for several minutes. Flick the throttle open 3 or 4 times, so that the engine speed rises to approximately 4000 – 5000 rpm, then stop the engine. Any air trapped in the system should bleed back to the top of the radiator, and the level will drop.

28 Wait a few minutes for the coolant to settle, then check the coolant level in both the radiator and the coolant reservoir. If necessary, top up the radiator to the base of the filler neck, then install the pressure cap. Also top up the coolant reservoir to the FULL mark.

29 Check the system for leaks.

30 Do not dispose of the old coolant by pouring it down the drain. Instead pour it into a heavy plastic container, cap it tightly and take it into an authorised disposal site or service station – see *Warning* at the beginning of this Section.

31 Install the fairing panels (see Chapter 7).

11 Engine oil and filter

> **Warning: Be careful when draining the oil, as the exhaust pipes, the engine, and the oil itself can cause severe burns.**

Engine oil

1 Regular oil changes are the single most important maintenance procedure you can perform on a motorcycle. The oil not only lubricates the internal parts of the engine, transmission and clutch, but it also acts as a coolant, a cleaner, a sealant, and a protector. Because of these demands, the oil takes a terrific amount of abuse and should be replaced often with new oil of the recommended grade and type. Saving a little money on the difference in cost between a good oil and a cheap oil won't pay off if the engine is damaged. The oil filter should be changed with every second oil change (see Steps 10 to 14).

2 Before changing the oil, warm up the engine so the oil will drain easily. Remove the lower fairing (see Chapter 7).

3 Position a clean drain tray below the engine. Unscrew the oil filler cap from the clutch cover to vent the engine and to act as a reminder that there is no oil in it **(see illustration)**.

4 Unscrew the oil drain plug from the underside of the engine and allow the oil to flow into the drain tray **(see illustration)**. Discard the sealing washer and replace it with a new one.

11.3 Unscrew the oil filler cap to act as a vent . . .

11.4 . . . then unscrew the oil drain plug

11.5a Fit a new sealing washer to the drain plug . . .

11.5b . . . before installing it in the sump

5 When the oil has completely drained, fit the plug with its new washer and tighten it to the torque setting specified at the beginning of the Chapter **(see illustrations)**. Avoid overtightening, as you will damage the threads.

6 Refill the engine to the proper level using

11.6a Refill the engine with new oil . . .

the recommended type and amount of oil (see *Pre-ride checks*) **(see illustration)**. With the motorcycle vertical, the oil level should lie between the maximum and minimum level lines on the dipstick, that is with the dipstick resting on the cover hole and not screwed fully into place **(see illustration)**. Install the filler cap, making sure the O-ring is in its groove and in good condition **(see illustration)**. Start the engine and let it run for two or three minutes. Stop the engine, wait a few minutes, then check the oil level. If necessary, add more oil to bring the level almost up to the maximum level line on the dipstick. Check that there are no leaks around the drain plug.

7 Every so often, and especially as Yamaha do not fit an oil pressure switch and warning light (the system fitted uses an oil level sensor), it is advisable to perform an oil pressure check (see Chapter 2, Section 3).

8 The old oil drained from the engine cannot be re-used and must be disposed of properly

at an oil disposal facility. Check with your local refuse disposal company, disposal facility or environmental agency to see whether they will accept the used oil for recycling – most will. Don't pour used oil into drains or onto the ground.

9 Install the lower fairing (see Chapter 7).

> **HAYNES HINT** *Check the old oil carefully – if it is very metallic coloured, then the engine is experiencing wear from break-in (new engine) or from insufficient lubrication. If there are flakes or chips of metal in the oil, then something is drastically wrong internally and the engine will have to be disassembled for inspection and repair. If there are pieces of fibre-like material in the oil, the clutch is experiencing excessive wear and should be checked.*

11.6b . . . to the correct level . . .

11.6c . . . then fit the filler cap

11.11a Using the correct size tool . . .

11.11b . . . remove the oil filter

11.11c Oil is likely to run onto the exhaust in this area

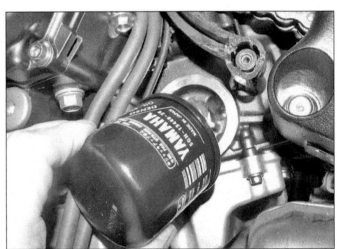

11.12 Thread the new filter on

Oil filter

Special tool: *A filter removing tool is necessary for this job* **(see illustration 11.11a)**.

10 The oil filter is on the left-hand side of the engine Drain the engine oil as described in Steps 2 to 5.

11 Place the drain tray below the oil filter. Clean the crankcase around the filter, then unscrew the filter using a dedicated removing tool. Several types are available, but the socket-type hex-wrench that is used with a ratchet is the best as it allows the new filter to be tightened to the correct torque – make sure you purchase the correct size as many are available **(see illustrations)**. Tip any residual oil into the drain tray. Clean off the oil that has dribbled over the exhaust **(see illustration)** to prevent excessive smoking when the engine is started.

12 Clean the sealing surface on the crankcase with a suitable solvent, then smear clean engine oil onto the rubber seal on the new filter, and screw the filter onto the engine until the seal just seats **(see illustration)**. If a

socket-type hex-wrench is being used, tighten the filter to the torque setting specified at the beginning of this Chapter. Otherwise, tighten the filter as tight as possible by hand, or by the number of turns specified on the filter or its packaging. **Note:** *Do not use a strap or chain wrench to tighten the filter as you will damage it.*

13 Refill the engine to the proper level (see Step 6).

14 Remember to drain all the old oil from the filter into the drain pan. Note that the old filter should be taken to an oil disposal facility rather than disposed of with the household rubbish.

Note: It is illegal and anti-social to dump oil down the drain. To find the location of your local oil recycling bank in the UK, call 08708 506 506 or visit www.oilbankline.org.uk

12 Brake system

Brake system check

1 A routine general check of the brake system will ensure that any problems are discovered and remedied before the rider's safety is jeopardised.

2 Check the brake lever and pedal for looseness, improper or rough action, excessive play, bends, and other damage. Replace any damaged parts with new ones (see Chapter 5). Clean and lubricate the lever and pedal pivots if their action is stiff or rough (see Section 9).

3 Make sure all brake fasteners are tight. Check the brake pads for wear (see Steps 9 to 13) and make sure the fluid level in the reservoirs is correct (see *Pre-ride checks*). Look for leaks at the hose connections and check for cracks in the hoses themselves **(see**

12.3 Check the hoses and all joints for leaks and deterioration

12.5a Turn the adjuster ring (arrowed) while holding the switch body

12.5b Rear brake light switch viewed from the inner side

12.6 Front brake lever span adjuster (arrowed)

illustration). If the lever or pedal is spongy, bleed the brakes (see Chapter 6). The brake fluid should be changed every two years (see Step 14) and the hoses replaced with new ones if they deteriorate, or every four years irrespective of their condition (see Step 17). The master cylinder and caliper seals should be replaced with new ones every two years, or if leakage from them is evident (see Step 15).

4 Make sure the brake light operates when the front brake lever is pulled in. The front brake light switch, mounted on the underside of the master cylinder, is not adjustable. If it fails to operate properly, check it (see Chapter 8).

5 Make sure the brake light is activated just before the rear brake takes effect. The switch is mounted behind the rider's right-hand footrest bracket. If adjustment is necessary, hold the switch and turn the adjuster nut on the switch body until the brake light is activated when required (see illustrations). If the brake light comes on too late, turn the nut clockwise. If the brake light comes on too soon or is permanently on, turn the nut anti-

clockwise. If the switch doesn't operate the brake light, check it (see Chapter 8).

6 The front brake lever has a span adjuster which alters the distance of the lever from the handlebar. Pull the lever away from the handlebar and turn the adjuster until the setting which best suits the rider is obtained (see illustration) – turning the adjuster clockwise increases the span, and anticlockwise reduces it. After making adjustment make sure the cut-outs in the adjuster locate on the block so it is seated in its position.

7 Check the position of the brake pedal (brake pedal height) – the pushrod end should be visible in the hole in the clevis (see illustration). If the pedal height is incorrect, or if the rider's preference is different, loosen the locknut on the master cylinder pushrod, then turn the pushrod using a spanner on the hex at the top of the rod until the pedal is at the desired height. After adjustment check that the pushrod end is still visible in the hole in the clevis. On completion tighten the locknut securely.

8 Adjust the rear brake light switch after adjusting the pedal height (see Step 5).

Brake pad wear check

⚠ *Warning: The dust created by the brake system may contain asbestos, which is harmful to your health. Never blow it out with*

12.7 Check that some of the pushrod is visible in the hole (arrowed)

12.10 Check the proximity of the turned in corners (arrowed) of the pad backing to the disc

12.11 Measure the amount of friction material remaining on each pad

compressed air and don't inhale any of it. An approved filtering mask should be worn when working on the brakes.

9 Each brake pad has wear indicators that can be viewed without removing the pads from the caliper.

10 On the front brake pads the turned-in corners of the pad backing material indicate the wear limit – when the corners are almost contacting the disc the pads must be replaced with new ones. The indicators are visible by looking up at the bottom corners of the pads **(see illustration)**.

Caution: Do not allow the pads to wear to the extent that the indicators contact the disc itself, as the disc will be damaged.

11 On the rear brake pads measure the distance between the metal backing of the pad and the disc **(see illustration)**.

12 If the pads are worn to the limit, new ones must be installed. If the pads are dirty or if you are in doubt as to the amount of friction material remaining, remove them for inspection (see Chapter 6). If required, measure the amount of friction material remaining – the minimum is 0.5 mm (front) and 1.0 mm (rear) although it is advisable to renew them well before these limits. **Note:** *It is not possible to degrease the friction material;*

if the pads are contaminated in any way they must be renewed.

13 Refer to Chapter 6 for details of pad removal and installation.

Brake fluid change

14 The brake fluid should be changed every two years, or whenever a master cylinder or caliper overhaul is carried out. Refer to Chapter 6 for details. Ensure that all the old fluid is be pumped from the hydraulic system and that the level in the fluid reservoir is checked and the brakes tested before riding the motorcycle.

Brake caliper and master cylinder seals

15 Brake system seals will deteriorate over a period of time and lose their effectiveness, leading to sticky operation of the brake master cylinders or the pistons in the brake calipers, or fluid loss. The seals should be replaced with new ones every two years or beforehand if fluid leakage or a sticking caliper action is apparent.

16 Replace all the seals in each caliper as a set – a rebuild kit for each caliper is available; master cylinder seals are supplied as a kit along with a new piston and spring (see Chapter 6).

Brake hoses

17 The hoses will deteriorate with age and should be replaced with new ones every four years regardless of their apparent condition (see Chapter 6).

18 Always replace the banjo union sealing washers with new ones when fitting new hoses. Refill the system with new brake fluid and bleed the system as described in Chapter 6.

13 Wheels, wheel bearings and tyres

Wheels

1 Cast wheels are virtually maintenance free, but they should be kept clean and checked periodically for cracks and other damage. Also check the wheel runout and alignment (see Chapter 6). Never attempt to repair damaged cast wheels; they must be replaced with new ones.

2 Check the tyre valve rubber for signs of damage or deterioration and have it replaced with a new one if necessary. Also, make sure the valve cap is in place and tight **(see illustration)**. Check that any wheel balance weights are fixed firmly to the wheel rim. If any weights have fallen off, have the wheel rebalanced by a motorcycle tyre specialist.

Tyres

3 Check the tyre condition and tread depth thoroughly – see *Pre-ride checks*.

Wheel bearings

4 Wheel bearings will wear over a period of time and result in handling problems.

5 Support the motorcycle upright using an auxiliary stand. Check for any play in the bearings by pushing and pulling the wheel against the hub **(see illustration)**. Also rotate the wheel and check that it rotates smoothly

13.2 Make sure there is a cap on each valve

13.5 Checking for play in the wheel bearings

and quietly, but do not mistake brake pad-to-disc noise for noisy bearings.

6 If any play is detected in the hub, or if the wheel does not rotate smoothly (and this is not due to brake or chain drag), the wheel must be removed for inspection of the bearings (see Chapter 6).

14 Suspension

1 The suspension components must be maintained in top operating condition to ensure rider safety. Loose, worn or damaged suspension parts decrease the motorcycle's stability and control.

Front suspension check

2 While standing alongside the motorcycle, apply the front brake and push on the handlebars to compress the forks several times **(see illustration)**. Check that the forks move up and down smoothly without binding. If binding is felt, the forks should be disassembled and inspected (see Chapter 5).
3 Inspect the fork inner tubes for signs of scratches, corrosion and pitting, and oil leakage **(see illustration)**. Carefully lever the dust seals out using a flat-bladed screwdriver and inspect the area around the fork seals (see Chapter 5). Any scratches, corrosion and pitting will cause premature oil seal failure. If the damage is excessive, new inner tubes should be installed (see Chapter 5). If oil leakage is evident, new oil seals must be fitted (see Chapter 5). If there is evidence of corrosion between the seal retaining ring and its groove in the fork outer tube spray the area with a penetrative lubricant, otherwise the ring will be difficult to remove if needed. Press the dust seal back into place on completion.
4 The forks are adjustable for spring pre-load, rebound damping and compression damping

14.2 Check the action of the front suspension as described

and it is essential that both fork legs are adjusted equally. Refer to Chapter 5 and check the settings on each fork if in doubt.
5 Check the tightness of all suspension nuts and bolts to be sure none have worked loose, referring to the torque settings specified at the beginning of Chapter 5.

Rear suspension check

6 Inspect the rear shock absorber for fluid leakage and tightness of its mountings, along with those of the suspension linkage. If leakage is found, a new shock should be installed (see Chapter 5).
7 With the aid of an assistant to support the bike, compress the rear suspension several times. It should move up and down freely without binding. If any binding is felt, the worn or faulty component must be identified and checked. The problem could be due to either the shock absorber, the suspension linkage components or the swingarm components (see Chapter 5).
8 Support the motorcycle using an auxiliary stand so that the rear wheel is off the ground. Grab the swingarm and rock it from side to side – there should be no discernible movement at the ends of the swingarm (Yamaha specify a maximum of 1 mm sideplay) **(see illustration)**.

14.3 Check for scratches, pitting and oil leakage on the fork inner tubes (arrowed)

If there is a little movement or a slight clicking can be heard, inspect the tightness of all the rear suspension mounting bolts and nuts, referring to the torque settings specified at the beginning of Chapter 5, and re-check for movement.
9 Next, grasp the top of the rear wheel and pull it upwards – there should be no discernible freeplay before the shock absorber begins to compress **(see illustration)**. Any freeplay felt in either check indicates worn bearings in the suspension linkage or swingarm, or worn shock absorber mountings. The worn components must be identified and checked (see Chapter 5).
10 To make an accurate assessment of the swingarm bearings it is necessary to remove the rear wheel (see Chapter 6) and the bolt securing the suspension linkage plates to the swingarm and shock absorber (see Chapter 5). Grasp the rear of the swingarm with one hand and place your other hand at the junction of the swingarm and the frame. Try to move the rear of the swingarm from side to side. Any wear (play) in the bearings should be felt as movement between the swingarm and the frame at the front. If there is any play, the swingarm will be felt to move forward and backward at the front (not from side-to-

14.8 Checking for play in the swingarm bearings

14.9 Checking for play in the rear shock mountings and suspension linkage bearings

side). Next, move the swingarm up and down through its full travel, holding the shock clear. It should move freely, without any binding or rough spots. If any play in the swingarm is noted or if the swingarm does not move freely, remove the swingarm for inspection of the bearings (see Chapter 5).

11 The rear shock is adjustable for spring pre-load, rebound damping and compression damping (see Chapter 5).

Front fork oil change

12 Although there is no set interval for changing the fork oil, note that the oil will degrade over a period of time and lose its damping qualities. Refer to Chapter 5 for details of front fork removal, oil draining and refilling. The forks do not need to be completely disassembled to change the oil.

Rear suspension bearing lubrication

13 Over a period of time the grease in the swingarm and suspension linkage bearings will be washed out (especially if pressure washers are used) or will harden allowing the ingress of dirt and water.

14 The suspension linkage and the swingarm should be disassembled at the specified mileage intervals and the bearings cleaned and re-greased as necessary (see Chapter 5).

15 Steering head bearings

Freeplay check and adjustment

1 Steering head bearings can become dented, rough or loose during normal use of the machine. In extreme cases, worn or loose steering head bearings can cause steering wobble – a condition that is potentially dangerous.

15.4 Steering head bearing pre-load check using a spring balance

Check

2 Support the motorcycle in an upright position using an auxiliary stand. Raise the front wheel off the ground either by having an assistant push down on the rear, or by placing a support under the engine, in which case remove the lower fairing first (see Chapter 7).

3 Point the front wheel straight-ahead, and slowly turn the handlebars from side to side. Any dents or roughness in the bearing races will be felt and if the bearings are too tight the bars will not move smoothly and freely. If the bearings are damaged or the action is rough, they should be replaced with new ones (see Chapter 5). If the bearings are too tight they should be adjusted as described below. Again point the wheel straight-ahead, and tap the front of the wheel to one side. The wheel should 'fall' under its own weight to the limit of its lock, indicating that the bearings are not too tight (take into account the restriction that cables and wiring may have). Check for similar movement to the other side.

4 If a spring balance graduated zero to 600 g is available, loosely fit a cable-tie around the end of one handlebar, then hook the end of the spring balance to the tie as shown (see illustration). With the steering straight-ahead and the balance at 90° to the handlebar, pull on the balance and check the reading at which the handlebars start to turn. Repeat on the other handlebar. If the reading on either side is below the minimum value specified in the range given in the Specifications at the beginning of the Chapter, the steering head is too loose, if the reading is above the maximum value specified the steering head is too tight. If the steering doesn't perform as described, and it's not due to the resistance of cables or hoses, then the bearings should be adjusted as described below.

5 Next, grasp the front forks and try to pull and push them forwards and backwards (see illustration). Any looseness in the steering head bearings will be felt as front-to-rear movement of the forks. If play is felt in the bearings, adjust them as follows.

> **HAYNES HiNT** *Freeplay in the fork due to worn fork bushes or rocking of the bike on its stand can be misinterpreted as steering head bearing play – do not get them mixed up.*

Adjustment

Special tool: *A suitably sized C-spanner is useful for this procedure (see illustration 15.11).*

6 Position the motorcycle in an upright position using an auxiliary stand. Raise or remove the fuel tank (see Chapter 4) and remove the fairing (see Chapter 7). **Note:** *Although it is not strictly necessary to remove the fuel tank and fairing, doing so will prevent the possibility of damage should a tool slip.*

7 Note the height of the fork legs above the top yoke (see illustration). Slacken the

15.5 Checking for play in the steering head bearings

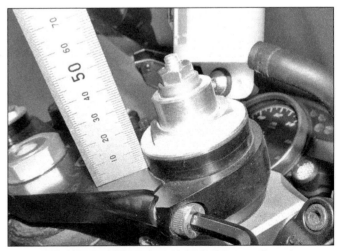

15.7a Measure the height of the fork legs to the yoke

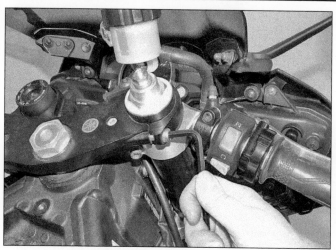

15.7b Slacken the top yoke clamp bolts . . .

15.7c . . . and the handlebar clamp bolts

handlebar clamp bolts and the fork clamp bolts in the top yoke **(see illustrations)**. Remove the blanking cap from each handlebar positioning bolt, then unscrew the bolts **(see illustrations)**. Undo the screw securing the reservoir bracket/cable guide to the top yoke if required.

8 Unscrew the steering stem nut and remove it along with its washer **(see illustrations)**. Ease the top yoke up off the forks and lay it to one side on some rag **(see illustration)**.

9 Remove the tabbed lockwasher, noting how it fits, then unscrew and remove the locknut using a C-spanner **(see illustrations)**. Remove the rubber washer **(see illustration)**.

15.7d Remove the blanking caps . . .

15.7e . . . then unscrew the handlebar positioning bolts

15.8a Unscrew the steering stem nut . . .

15.8b . . . and remove it with the washer

15.8c Ease the top yoke up and off the forks

15.9a Remove the tabbed lockwasher . . .

15.9b . . . then unscrew the locknut . . .

15.9c . . . and remove the rubber washer

15.10 Make sure the torque wrench arm is at right angles (90°) to the service tool

10 To adjust the bearings as specified by Yamaha, a special service tool (Pt. No. 90890-01403 for Europe, or YU-33975 for USA) and a torque wrench are required. If the tool is available, first slacken the adjuster nut slightly to take pressure off the bearing, then tighten the nut to the initial torque setting specified at the beginning of this Chapter. Make sure the torque wrench handle is at right-angles (90°) to the centre line between the adjuster nut and the service tool wrench socket **(see illustration)**. Now slacken the nut, then tighten it to the final torque setting specified.

11 If the Yamaha tool is not available, using a C-spanner slacken the adjuster nut slightly to take pressure off the bearing then tighten the nut until all freeplay is removed **(see illustration)**. Now tighten the nut a little more to pre-load the bearings. Now slacken the nut and retighten it, setting it so that all freeplay is just removed from the bearings, yet the steering is able to move freely from side to side. Tighten the nut only a little at a time, and after each adjustment repeat the checks outlined in Steps 3 to 5.

12 Turn the steering from lock to lock five times to settle the bearings, then recheck the

adjustment or the torque setting depending on your method used. The object is to set the adjuster nut so that the bearings are under a very light loading, just enough to remove any freeplay.

Caution: Take great care not to apply excessive pressure because this will cause premature failure of the bearings.

13 With the bearings correctly adjusted, install the rubber washer and the locknut **(see illustrations 15.9c and b)**. Tighten the locknut finger-tight, then tighten it further until its notches align with those in the adjuster nut, making sure the adjuster nut does not turn as well. Install the tabbed lockwasher so that the tabs fit into the notches in both the locknut and adjuster nut **(see illustration 15.9a)**. Recheck the bearing adjustment as described in Steps 3 to 5 to ensure the adjuster nut hasn't moved.

14 Fit the top yoke onto the steering stem and the forks **(see illustration 15.8c)**. Install the washer and steering stem nut and tighten it to the torque setting specified at the beginning of this Chapter **(see illustration 15.8b)**. Now tighten the fork clamp bolts in the top yoke to the specified torque –you may need to swivel the handlebars round on the fork to get a torque wrench onto the bolts **(see illustration 15.7d)**.

15 Locate the handlebars against the underside of the top yoke, align the bolt holes then fit the positioning bolts and tighten them to the specified torque **(see illustration 15.7e)**. Fit the blanking caps **(see illustration 15.7d)**. Now tighten the handlebar clamp bolts to the specified torque **(see illustration 15.7c)**. Fit the reservoir bracket onto the top yoke.

16 Recheck the bearing adjustment as described in Steps 3 to 5 and re-adjust if necessary. Install the fuel tank (see Chapter 4) and the fairing (see Chapter 7).

Lubrication

17 Over a considerable time the grease in

the bearings will be dispersed or will harden allowing the ingress of dirt and water.

18 At the specified interval the steering head should be disassembled and the bearings cleaned and re-greased (see Chapter 5).

16 Sidestand and starter safety circuit

1 The stand return spring must be capable of retracting the stand fully and holding it retracted when the motorcycle is in use. If a spring has sagged or broken, it must be replaced with a new one **(see illustration)**.

2 Lubricate the stand pivot regularly (see Section 9).

3 The sidestand switch prevents the motorcycle being started if the transmission is in gear and the stand is down, and cuts the engine if the stand is put down while the engine is running and in gear.

4 Check the operation of the safety circuit (which incorporates the sidestand, clutch and neutral switches, and the starter circuit cut-off relay and diodes) by shifting the transmission into neutral, retracting the stand and starting the engine. Pull in the clutch lever and select a gear. Extend the sidestand. The engine should stop as the sidestand is extended. Also make sure that the engine cannot be started while in gear unless the stand is up and the clutch lever is pulled in. If the circuit does not operate as described, check the incorporated components (see Chapter 8).

17 Nuts and bolts

1 Since vibration of the machine tends to loosen fasteners, all nuts, bolts, screws, etc. should be periodically checked for proper tightness.

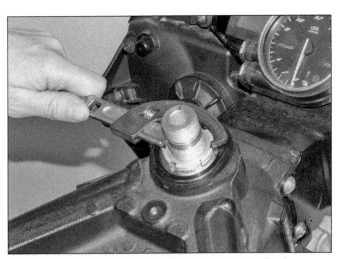

15.11 Alternately use a C-spanner as described

16.1 Check the spring (arrowed) is securely anchored and in good condition

2 Pay particular attention to the following:
Spark plugs
Engine oil drain plug
Coolant drain bolt
Lever and pedal bolts
Footrest and sidestand bolts
Engine mounting bolts
Shock absorber and suspension linkage
*   bolts; swingarm pivot bolt nut*
Handlebar positioning and clamp bolts
Front fork clamp bolts (top and bottom yoke)
*   and fork top bolts*
Steering stem nut
Front axle bolt and axle clamp bolts
Rear axle nut
Front and rear sprocket nuts
Chain adjuster bolt locknuts
Brake caliper and master cylinder mounting
*   bolts*
Brake hose banjo bolts and caliper bleed
*   valves*
Brake disc bolts
Exhaust system bolts/nuts

3 If a torque wrench is available, use it along with the torque specifications (where given) at the beginning of this and other Chapters.

18 Battery

1 All models are fitted with a sealed, gel-type maintenance-free battery. **Note:** *Do not attempt to open the battery as the resulting damage will render it unfit for further use.*
2 All that should be done is to check that the terminals are clean and tight and that the casing is not damaged or leaking. See Chapter 8 for further details.
Caution: Be extremely careful when handling or working around the battery. The electrolyte gel is very caustic and an explosive gas (hydrogen) is given off when the battery is charging.

19.5a Unscrew the bolts noting the clutch cable stop . . .

3 If the machine is not in regular use, disconnect the battery and give it a refresher charge every month to six weeks (see Chapter 8).

19 Valve clearances

1 The engine must be completely cool for this maintenance procedure, so let the machine sit overnight before beginning.
2 Remove the fairing side panels and the lower fairing (see Chapter 7). Remove the spark plugs (see Section 2). Remove the radiator (see Chapter 3). Remove the throttle bodies (see Chapter 4) and place some rag over the intake ports to prevent anything from falling in them.
3 Remove the valve cover (see Chapter 2). Each cylinder is referred to by a number. They are numbered 1 to 4 from left to right, viewed as normally seated on the bike.
4 Make a chart or sketch of all valve positions so that a note of each clearance can be made against the relevant valve.
5 Place an oil pan under the timing rotor cover on the right-hand side of the engine.

19.5b . . . the wiring clamp . . .

19.5c . . . and hose clamp positions

Unscrew the bolts and remove the cover, noting the wiring clamp, hose clamp, and clutch cable stop **(see illustrations)**. Discard the gasket as a new one must be used. If the cam chain guide blade pivot pin comes away with the cover, remove it, then realign the blade and slide the pin back into place **(see illustration)**.
6 Using a spanner or socket and ratchet on the timing rotor bolt and rotating in a clockwise direction only, turn the engine until the scribed line next to the T mark on the rotor faces to the rear and aligns with the crankcase mating surfaces and the camshaft lobes for

19.5d Check if the cam chain guide pivot pin comes with the cover . . .

19.5e . . . and if it does fit it back into the guide

19.6a Turn the engine clockwise using the bolt . . .

19.6b . . . until the line next to the T mark faces back and aligns with the crankcase mating surfaces . . .

19.6c . . . and the cam lobes for cylinder No. 1 are as shown

19.7a Insert the feeler gauge between the base of the intake cam lobe and the top of the follower . . .

19.7b . . . then between the base of the exhaust cam lobe and follower

19.8 T mark position for checking valves on Nos. 2 and 3 cylinders. Note use of rule to establish reference point on crankcase

19.13a Carefully lift out the follower using your fingers, grips, a lapping tool or a magnet . . .

19.13b . . . and retrieve the shim from the top of the valve using a magnet

the No. 1 (left-hand) cylinder face away from each other **(see illustrations)**. If the cam lobes are facing towards each other, rotate the engine clockwise 360° (one full turn) so that the T mark again faces back and aligns with the crankcase mating surfaces. The camshaft lobes will now be facing away from each other and the No. 1 cylinder will be at TDC (top dead centre) on the compression stroke **(see illustration 19.6c)**.

7 Check the clearances on the four No. 1 cylinder intake and exhaust valves. Insert a feeler gauge of the same thickness as the correct valve clearance (see Specifications) between the camshaft lobe and follower of each valve and check that it is a firm sliding fit – you should feel a slight drag when the you pull the gauge out **(see illustrations)**. If not, use the feeler gauges to measure the exact clearance. Record the measured clearance on your chart.

8 Now turn the engine clockwise 180° (half a turn) so that the mark faces forward and aligns with the crankcase mating surfaces (though you will not be able to see this as the cam chain guide blade blocks it – determine the angle using a steel rule **(see illustration)** and the camshaft lobes for the No. 2 cylinder are facing away from each other. The No. 2 cylinder is now at TDC on the compression stroke. Measure the clearances of the No. 2 cylinder valves using the method described in Step 7.

9 Now turn the engine clockwise 180° (half a turn) so that the mark faces to the rear and aligns with the crankcase mating surfaces and the camshaft lobes for the No. 4 cylinder are facing away from each other. The No. 4 cylinder is now at TDC on the compression stroke. Measure the clearances of the No. 4 cylinder valves using the method described in Step 7.

10 Now turn the engine clockwise 180° (half a turn) so that the 'T' mark faces forward and aligns with the crankcase mating surfaces

(see illustration 19.8) and the camshaft lobes for the No. 3 cylinder are facing away from each other. The No. 3 cylinder is now at TDC on the compression stroke. Measure the clearances of the No. 3 cylinder valves using the method described in Step 7.

11 When all clearances have been measured and recorded, identify whether the clearance on any valve falls outside that specified in the Specifications at the beginning of this chapter – note that the clearances are different for intake and exhaust valves. If it does, the shim between the cam follower and the valve must be replaced with one of a thickness which will restore the correct clearance.

12 Shim replacement requires removal of the camshafts (see Chapter 2). There is no need to remove both camshafts if shims from only one need replacing. Place rags over the spark plug holes and the cam chain tunnel to prevent a shim from dropping into the engine on removal.

13 With the camshaft removed, remove the cam follower of the valve in question, then retrieve the shim from inside the follower **(see illustrations)**. If it is not in the follower, pick it out of the top of the valve using either a magnet, a small screwdriver with a dab of

grease on it (the shim will stick to the grease), or a screwdriver and a pair of pliers. Do not allow the shim to fall into the engine.

14 A size should be marked on the upper face of the shim – a shim marked 175 is 1.75 mm thick **(see illustration)**. If the mark is not visible, the shim thickness will have to be measured. It is recommended that the shim is measured anyway, to check that it has not worn **(see illustration)**.

15 Calculate the required replacement shim by using the formula $a = (b - c) + d$, where a is the required replacement shim size, b is the measured valve clearance, c is the specified valve clearance, and d is the existing shim thickness. For example:

The measured clearance of an exhaust valve is 0.27 mm, so $b = 0.27$
The specified clearance range for an exhaust valve is 0.16 to 0.23 mm, the mid-point being 0.20 mm, so $c = 0.07$
The thickness of the existing shim is 1.80 mm, so $d = 1.8$
Therefore, the required replacement shim (a) $= 0.27 - 0.20 + 1.8$ ($a = 1.87$ mm). Round this to the nearest available shim size, which is 190.

19.14a The shim size is marked on one face . . .

19.14b . . . but check the thickness of the shim using a micrometer

19.18 Fit a new gasket then install the cover, making sure it locates correctly

Note: *If the existing shim is marked with a number not ending in 0 or 5, round it up or down as appropriate to the nearest number ending in 0 or 5. Shims are available in 0.05 mm increments from 1.50 mm to 2.40 mm.*

16 Obtain the replacement shim, then lubricate it with molybdenum disulphide grease and fit it into its recess in the top of the valve, with the size marking facing up **(see illustration 19.13b)**. Check that the shim is correctly seated, then lubricate the follower with molybdenum disulphide oil (a 50/50 mixture of molybdenum disulphide grease and engine oil) and fit it onto the valve **(see illustration 19.13a)**. Repeat the process for any other valves until the clearances are correct, then install the camshafts (see Chapter 2).

17 Rotate the crankshaft clockwise several turns to seat the new shim(s), then check the clearances again **(see illustration 19.6a)**.

18 Install the valve cover (see Chapter 2). Fit the timing rotor cover using a new gasket, locating the cam chain tensioner blade and guide blade pivot pins in the holes **(see illustration)**. Install the cover bolts, not forgetting the clamps for the wiring and hose and the clutch cable stop, and tighten the bolts to the torque setting specified at the beginning of this Chapter **(see illustration 19.5)**.

19 Install all remaining components (see Step 2). On completion, check the idle speed (see Section 4).

Chapter 2
Engine, clutch and transmission

Contents

Degrees of difficulty

Easy, suitable for novice with little experience	Fairly easy, suitable for beginner with some experience	Fairly difficult, suitable for competent DIY mechanic	Difficult, suitable for experienced DIY mechanic	Very difficult, suitable for expert DIY or professional

Specifications

General

Type	Four-stroke in-line four
Capacity	599 cc
Bore	67.0 mm
Stroke	42.5 mm
Compression ratio	12.8:1 (2006 and 2007), 13.1:1 (2008-on)
Cylinder numbering	1 to 4 from left to right
Cooling system	Liquid-cooled
Clutch	Wet multi-plate
Transmission	Six-speed constant mesh
Final drive	Chain

Cylinder head

Warpage (max)	0.05 mm

Camshafts

Intake lobe height
  Standard . . . . 33.725 to 33.875 mm
  Service limit (min) . . . . 33.675 mm
Intake base circle diameter
  Standard . . . . 25.225 to 25.325 mm
  Service limit (min) . . . . 25.175 mm
Exhaust lobe height
  Standard . . . . 32.925 to 333.075 mm
  Service limit (min) . . . . 32.875 mm
Exhaust base circle diameter
  Standard . . . . 25.082 to 25.182 mm
  Service limit (min) . . . . 25.032 mm
Journal diameter . . . . 22.459 to 22.472 mm
Holder diameter . . . . 22.500 to 22.521 mm
Journal oil clearance . . . . 0.028 to 0.062 mm
Runout (max) . . . . 0.03 mm
Cam chain type . . . . 98XRH201 – 118 links

Valves, guides and springs

Valve clearances . . . . see Chapter 1
Intake valves
  Stem diameter
    Standard . . . . 4.475 to 4.490 mm
    Service limit (min) . . . . 4.460 mm
  Guide bore diameter
    Standard . . . . 4.500 to 4.512 mm
    Service limit (max) . . . . 4.542 mm
  Stem-to-guide clearance
    Standard . . . . 0.010 to 0.037 mm
    Service limit (max) . . . . 0.08 mm
  Stem runout . . . . 0.04 mm
  Head diameter . . . . 26.90 to 27.10 mm
  Face width . . . . 1.410 to 2.550 mm
  Seat width
    Standard . . . . 0.9 to 1.1 mm
    Service limit (max) . . . . 1.6 mm
  Margin thickness
    Standard . . . . 0.90 to 1.10 mm
    Service limit (min) . . . . 0.80 mm
  Spring free length
    Standard . . . . 37.47 mm
    Service limit (min) . . . . 35.60 mm
  Spring bend (max) . . . . 1.6 mm
Exhaust valves
  Stem diameter
    Standard . . . . 4.460 to 4.475 mm
    Service limit (min) . . . . 4.445 mm
  Guide bore diameter
    Standard . . . . 4.500 to 4.512 mm
    Service limit (max) . . . . 4.542 mm
  Stem-to-guide clearance
    Standard . . . . 0.025 to 0.052 mm
    Service limit (max) . . . . 0.08 mm
  Stem runout . . . . 0.04 mm
  Head diameter . . . . 22.90 to 23.10 mm
  Face width . . . . 1.400 to 2.670 mm
  Seat width
    Standard . . . . 1.1 to 1.3 mm
    Service limit (max) . . . . 1.8 mm
  Margin thickness
    Standard . . . . 1.10 to 1.30 mm
    Service limit (min) . . . . 1.0 mm
  Spring free length
    Standard . . . . 37.67 mm
    Service limit (min) . . . . 35.79 mm
  Spring bend (max) . . . . 1.6 mm

Clutch
Friction plates
  Quantity
    Middle plates (black colour code)........................ 7
    Inner plate (purple colour code)...................... 1
    Outer plate (brown colour code)...................... 1
  Thickness
    Standard.. 2.92 to 3.08 mm
    Service limit (min)................................. 2.8 mm
Plain plates
  Quantity... 8
  Thickness.. 1.9 to 2.1 mm (for standard thickness plates)
  Warpage (max).. 0.1 mm
Clutch plate pack measurement .... 42.4 to 43.0 mm
Clutch springs
  Free length .... 55.00 mm
  Service limit (min).................................. 54.00 mm

Lubrication system
Engine oil pressure (engine hot)........................ 11.6 psi (0.8 Bar) @ 1300 rpm
Relief valve opening pressure .... 95.7 to 107.3 psi (6.6 to 7.4 Bars)
Bypass valve opening pressure .... 11.4 to 17.1 psi (0.78 to 1.18 Bars)
Oil pump
  Inner rotor tip-to-outer rotor clearance
    Standard.. Less than 0.12 mm
    Service limit (max)................................. 0.20 mm
  Outer rotor-to-body clearance
    Standard.. 0.09 to 0.15 mm
    Service limit (max)................................. 0.22 mm

Pistons
Piston diameter (measured 10 mm up from skirt
at 90° to piston pin axis).............................. 66.975 to 66.990 mm
Piston-to-bore clearance
  Standard... 0.010 to 0.035 mm
  Service limit .... 0.05 mm
Piston pin diameter
  Standard... 14.991 to 15.000 mm
  Service limit (min).................................. 14.971 mm
Piston pin bore diameter in piston
  Standard... 15.002 to 15.013 mm
  Service limit (max) .... 15.043 mm
Piston pin-to-piston pin bore clearance
  Standard... 0.002 to 0.022 mm
  Service limit (max) .... 0.022 mm

Piston rings
Top compression ring
  Type .... Barrel
  Ring width... 2.40 mm
  Ring thickness .... 0.8 mm
  Ring end gap (installed)
    Standard.. 0.25 to 0.55 mm
    Service limit .... 0.55 mm (0.6 mm 2008-on)
  Piston ring-to-groove clearance
    Standard.. 0.030 to 0.065 mm
2nd compression ring
  Type .... Taper
  Ring width... 2.50 mm
  Ring thickness .... 0.8 mm
  Ring end gap (installed)
    Standard.. 0.70 to 0.80 mm
    Service limit .... 1.00 mm (1.15 mm 2008-on)
  Piston ring-to-groove clearance
    Standard.. 0.020 to 0.055 mm
Oil ring
  Ring width... 2.00 mm
  Ring thickness .... 1.50 mm
  Side-rail end gap (installed) .... 0.10 to 0.35 mm

Cylinder bores

Bore	67.0 to 67.01 mm
Ovality (max).	0.05 mm
Cylinder compression	
Standard.	220.5 psi (15.2 Bars)
Maximum	227.6 psi (15.7 Bars)
Minimum.	184.9 psi (12.8 Bars)
Max. difference between cylinders.	14 psi (1 Bar)
Piston-to-bore clearance	
Standard.	0.010 to 0.035 mm
Service limit	0.120 mm

Crankshaft and bearings

Main bearing oil clearance	
Standard.	0.020 to 0.044 mm
Runout (max)	0.03 mm

Connecting rods

Big-end side clearance.	0.160 to 0.262 mm
Big-end oil clearance	
Standard.	0.037 to 0.061 mm

Transmission

Gear ratios (no. of teeth)	
Primary reduction.	2.073 to 1 (85/41T)
Final reduction	2.813 to 1 (45/16T)
1st gear.	2.583 to 1 (31/12T)
2nd gear.	2.000 to 1 (32/16T)
3rd gear	1.667 to 1 (30/18T)
4th gear	1.444 to 1 (26/18T)
5th gear	1.286 to 1 (27/21T)
6th gear	1.150 to 1 (23/20T)
Shaft runout (max)	0.02 mm

Gearchange mechanism

Gearchange linkage rod installed length	267.2 to 269.2 mm
Selector fork shaft runout (max).	0.050 mm

Torque wrench settings

Alternator cover bolts.	10 Nm
Alternator rotor bolt	70 Nm
Alternator stator bolts.	10 Nm
Cam chain tensioner bolts	12 Nm
Camshaft holder bolts	10 Nm
Camshaft sprocket bolts	18 Nm
Clutch nut.	115 Nm
Clutch cover bolts	12 Nm
Clutch spring bolts.	8 Nm
Connecting rod cap nuts	
Initial torque setting	15 Nm
Final angle setting (see Section 21)	+175° to 185°
Coolant inlet bolts	10 Nm
Crankcase 8 mm bolts Nos. 1 to 10 (2006 and 2007 models) – see Section 19	
Initial torque setting	20 Nm
Secondary torque setting.	25 Nm
Final torque setting.	27 Nm
Crankcase 8 mm bolts Nos. 1 to 10 (2008-on models) – see Section 19	
Initial torque setting	20 Nm
Secondary torque setting.	loosen, then 12 Nm
Final angle setting bolts Nos. 1 to 7 and 10	+50°
Final angle setting bolts Nos. 8 and 9	+75°
Crankcase 8 mm bolts Nos. 11 and 12 (All models)	24 Nm
Crankcase 6 mm bolts (All models)	10 Nm

Torque wrench settings (continued)

Cylinder head Allen-head nuts	
Stage 1	25 Nm
Stage 2	42 Nm
Cylinder head domed hex nuts	
Stage 1	30 Nm
Stage 2	60 Nm
Cylinder head bolts	12 Nm
Engine mounting bolts	
Front mounting bolts	45 Nm
Rear mounting bolt nuts.	65 Nm
External U-shaped oil pipe on front of crankcase bolts.	10 Nm
Front sprocket cover bolts	10 Nm
Oil baffle plate bolts	12 Nm
Oil cooler bolt	63 Nm
Oil level sensor bolts	10 Nm
Oil gallery bolt.	8 Nm
Oil pipe bolts	12 Nm
Oil pump drive chain guide bolts	12 Nm
Oil pump cover bolts and mounting bolts	12 Nm
Oil pump U-shaped pipe bolts.	12 Nm
Oil sump bolts	12 Nm
Selector drum/fork shaft retainer plate bolts	10 Nm
Starter idle/reduction gear shaft bolt	10 Nm
Stopper arm bolt	22 Nm
Thermostat housing bolts.	12 Nm
Timing rotor bolt.	35 Nm
Timing rotor cover bolts	12 Nm
Transmission input shaft bearing housing bolts.	12 Nm
Valve cover bolts	12 Nm

1 General information

The engine is a liquid-cooled in-line four cylinder, with four valves per cylinder (two intake and two exhaust). The valves are operated by double overhead camshafts which are chain driven off the right-hand end of the crankshaft. The engine assembly is constructed from aluminium alloy. The crankcase is divided horizontally.

The crankcase incorporates a wet sump, pressure-fed lubrication system which uses a chain-driven oil pump, an oil filter, a relief valve and an oil level sensor. The pump is chain-driven from the back of the clutch housing. The oil is circulated through a cooler which is located on the front of the crankcases.

The alternator is driven off the left-hand end of the crankshaft, and the starter clutch is on the back of the alternator.

Power from the crankshaft is routed to the transmission via the clutch. The clutch is of the wet, multi-plate type and is gear-driven off the crankshaft. The transmission is a six-speed constant-mesh unit. Final drive to the rear wheel is by chain and sprockets.

Read the *Safety first!* section of this manual carefully before starting work.

2 Component access

Operations possible with the engine in the frame

The components and assemblies listed below can be removed without having to remove the engine assembly from the frame. If however, a number of areas require attention at the same time, removal of the engine is recommended.

Valve cover
Cam chain tensioner
Camshafts
Cam chain and blades
Alternator
Clutch
Starter clutch
Gearchange mechanism
Starter motor
Cylinder identification and crankshaft position sensors
Oil filter and cooler
Oil sump, oil strainer and oil pressure relief valve
Oil pump
Water pump

Operations requiring engine removal

It is necessary to remove the engine from the frame to gain access to the following components.

Cylinder head
Cylinder bores
Pistons and rings
Crankshaft and bearings
Connecting rods and bearings
Transmission shafts
Selector drum and forks

3 Engine wear assessment

Cylinder compression check

Special tool: *A compression gauge with an M10 x 1.0 mm pitch adaptor is required for this test.*

1 Poor engine performance, exhaust smoke, heavy oil consumption and poor starting are indications of low compression. This may be caused by leaking valve stem seals, incorrect valve clearances, a leaking head gasket, or worn pistons, rings and/or cylinder walls.

2 Make sure the valve clearances are correctly set (see Chapter 1), then run the engine until it reaches normal operating temperature.

Stop the engine and remove all four ignition coils and spark plugs (see Chapter 1), taking care not to burn your hands on the hot components. Fit the plugs back into their coils and earth the metal body of each plug against the cylinder head to prevent sparking.

3 Install the adaptor and gauge into the No. 1 spark plug hole. Place a rag over the open spark plug holes of the other cylinders to prevent atomised fuel escaping.

4 Turn the ignition ON. Open the throttle grip fully and crank the engine over on the starter motor for a few seconds until the gauge reading stabilises. Take a note of the gauge reading, then turn the ignition OFF and transfer the compression gauge and adaptor to another cylinder. Continue until you have obtained a reading for all four cylinders.

5 Compare the readings obtained with those in the Specifications at the beginning of this Chapter. If they fall within the specified range and all are relatively equal, the engine is in good condition. If the readings are close to or below the minimum limit, or one cylinder differs markedly from the others, further investigation is required.

6 To distinguish between cylinder/piston wear and valve leakage, use a pump type oil can to inject a small quantity (teaspoonful) of oil into the suspect cylinder via the spark plug hole – this will serve to temporarily seal the piston rings. Repeat the compression test on that cylinder. If the result shows a noticeable increase in pressure this confirms that the cylinder bore, piston or rings are worn. If there is no change in reading, the cylinder head gasket or valves are leaking.

7 Although unlikely with the use of modern fuels, a high compression reading indicates excessive carbon deposits in the combustion chamber area.

Engine oil pressure check

Special tool: *An oil pressure gauge is required to perform this test.*

8 If there is any doubt about the performance of the engine lubrication system an oil pressure check must be carried out. The check provides useful information about the state of wear of the engine.

9 To check the oil pressure, a suitable pressure gauge (which screws into the crankcase) is

3.11 Oil gallery bolt (arrowed)

needed. Yamaha provide a gauge, Pt. No. 90890-03120 and gauge adapter Pt. No. 90890-03139 for this purpose.

10 Place the bike upright on level ground using an auxiliary stand. Remove the left-hand fairing side panels (see Chapter 7). Warm the engine up to normal operating temperature then stop it. Check the engine oil level and top up if necessary (see *Pre-ride checks*).

11 Unscrew the oil gallery bolt in the left-hand side of the crankcase **(see illustration)** and quickly screw the adapter into the crankcase threads. Connect the pressure gauge to the adapter. Discard the oil gallery bolt O-ring as a new one must be fitted on reassembly.

 Warning: Take great care not to burn your hand on the hot engine unit, exhaust pipe or with engine oil when accessing the gauge take-off point on the crankcase. Do not allow exhaust gases to build up in the work area; either perform the check outside or use an exhaust gas extraction system.

12 Start the engine take a pressure gauge reading at idle (1300 rpm). The oil pressure should be similar to that given in the Specifications at the beginning of this Chapter.

13 If the pressure is significantly lower than the standard, either the pressure relief valve is stuck open, the oil pump is faulty, the oil strainer or filter is blocked, or there is considerable engine wear. Begin diagnosis by checking the oil filter, strainer and relief valve, then the oil pump (see Sections 17 and 18). If those items check out okay, the engine bearing oil clearances are likely to be excessive and the engine needs to be overhauled.

14 If the pressure is too high, either an oil passage is clogged, the relief valve is stuck closed or the wrong grade of oil is being used.

15 Stop the engine and unscrew the gauge and adapter from the crankcase.

16 Lubricate the new oil gallery bolt O-ring with clean engine oil and fit it onto the bolt. Install the bolt and tighten it to the specified torque setting. Check the engine oil level (see *Pre-ride checks*).

17 Rectify any problems before running the engine again. Install the fairing panels (see Chapter 7).

4 Engine removal and installation

Caution: The engine is very heavy. Engine removal and installation should be carried out with the aid of at least one assistant. Personal injury or damage could occur if the engine falls or is dropped. An hydraulic or mechanical floor jack should be used to support and lower or raise the engine.

Removal

Note: *If you intend to remove the clutch with the engine removed from the frame, it is best to slacken the clutch nut while the engine is still in the frame – the nut is tight and the engine needs to be held securely while it is slackened. Refer to Section 13 for details.*

1 Support the motorcycle securely in an upright position using an auxiliary stand. Work can be made easier by raising the machine to a suitable working height on an hydraulic ramp or a suitable platform. Make sure the motorcycle is secure and will not topple over (see Section 1 of *Tools and Workshop Tips* in the *Reference* section). When disconnecting any wiring, cables and hoses, it is advisable to mark or tag them as a reminder of where they connect.

2 Disconnect the negative (–) lead from the battery, then disconnect the positive (+) lead (see Chapter 8).

3 Remove the fairing side panels, the lower fairing and the fairing trim panels (see Chapter 7).

4 If the engine is dirty, particularly around its mountings, wash it thoroughly before starting any major dismantling work. This will make work much easier and rule out the possibility of dirt falling inside.

5 Drain the engine oil and coolant (see Chapter 1).

6 Remove the fuel tank and the air filter housing (see Chapter 4) – when removing the air filter housing detach the crankcase breather hose from the engine rather than the housing and remove them together.

7 Remove the throttle bodies (see Chapter 4). Plug the intake manifolds with clean rag.

8 Remove the AIS control valve along with the hoses (see Chapter 4). Disconnect the green wiring connector for the coolant temperature sensor **(see illustration)**. Unscrew the bolt securing the crankcase earth (ground) leads and detach the leads **(see illustration)**.

4.8a Disconnect the coolant temperature sensor wire connector . . .

4.8b . . . and the engine earth leads

4.8c Remove the rubber heat shield

4.10a Disconnect the cylinder identification sensor . . .

4.10b . . . and draw the loom to one side

4.11 Note how the bracket fits

4.12a Unscrew the bolts and remove the bracket

4.12b Bend up the tag and free the cable

Secure the leads clear of the engine and remove the rubber heat shield, noting how it fits **(see illustration)**.

9 Remove the radiator along with the coolant hoses to the engine, water pump and oil cooler (see Chapter 3). Remove the thermostat housing and its hoses (see Chapter 3).

10 Remove the ignition coils (see Chapter 4). If not already done, disconnect the cylinder identification sensor wiring connector **(see illustration)** and draw the loom to one side **(see illustration)**.

11 Remove the exhaust downpipe assembly (see Chapter 4). If required unscrew the bolt securing the radiator mounting bracket to the front of the engine and remove the bracket, noting how it fits **(see illustration)**.

12 Unscrew the clutch cable holder bolt and free the holder, noting how it locates **(see illustration)**. Bend the retainer tag to free the cable in the release mechanism arm and detach the cable end from it **(see illustration)**.

13 Trace the oil level sensor wire from underneath the engine and disconnect it at the white/grey single pin connector **(see illustration)**. Trace the sidestand switch wiring from the switch and disconnect it at the two-pin connector **(see illustration)**. Release the wires from any ties and coil them so that they do not impede engine removal.

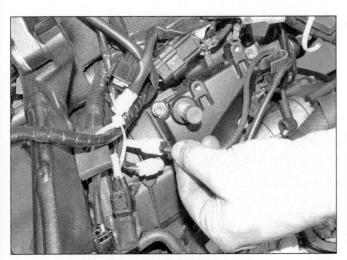

4.13a Disconnect the oil level sensor . . .

4.13b . . . and the sidestand switch wire connectors

4.14 Disconnect the alternator wiring connector

4.15a Disconnect the crankshaft position . . .

4.15b . . . and speed sensor wiring connectors

14 Disconnect the alternator wiring connector (white) from the regulator/rectifier **(see illustration)**. Coil the wiring on the crankcase so that it does not impede engine removal.

15 Disconnect the crankshaft position (CKP) sensor off-white, two-pin wiring connector and the speed sensor white three-pin wiring connector **(see illustrations)**.

16 Peel back the boot on the starter motor terminal, then unscrew the nut and detach the lead **(see illustrations)**.

17 Make sure the transmission is in neutral. Remove the gearchange arm with the linkage rod. Pass the linkage rod and gearchange arm underneath the gearchange lever and tie them to the sidestand spring.

18 Remove the front sprocket cover and front sprocket (see Chapter 6).

19 At this point, position an hydraulic or mechanical jack under the engine with a block of wood between the jack head and crankcase **(see illustration)**. Make sure the jack is centrally positioned so the engine will not topple in any direction when the last mounting bolt is removed and the engine is supported only by the jack. Take the weight of the engine on the jack.

20 Check around the engine and frame to make sure that all the necessary wiring, cables and hoses have been disconnected, and that any that remain connected to the engine are not retained by any clips, guides or brackets on the frame. When removing the engine mounting bolts note which fits where as there are different lengths.

21 Unscrew and remove the engine front mounting bolts on the right-hand side and remove the collars, (two pieces on 2006 and 2007 models, three pieces on 2008-on models) noting how they fit **(see illustrations)**.

22 Unscrew and remove the engine front

4.16a Peel back the rubber boot . . .

4.16b . . . and unscrew the nut

4.19 Support the engine using a jack

4.21a Unscrew the right-hand mounting bolts . . .

4.21b . . . and remove the collars

4.21c Early models have a two piece arrangement . . .

4.21d . . . later models a three piece one

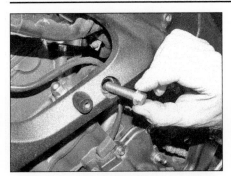

4.22 Unscrew and remove the left-hand mounting bolts

4.23a Unscrew the nuts from the upper . . .

4.23b . . . and lower rear mounting bolts

mounting bolts on the left-hand side **(see illustration)**.

23 Unscrew the nuts from the right-hand end of the upper and lower rear mounting bolts, but do not withdraw the bolts **(see illustrations)**. Make sure the engine is properly supported on the jack, and have an assistant support it as well, then withdraw the upper mounting bolt.

24 Remove the drive chain from the transmission shaft **(see illustration)**. Allow the front of the engine to drop sufficiently to allow access to the neutral light switch and disconnect it **(see illustration)**. Withdraw the lower mounting bolt **(see illustration)**.

25 Remove the collars from the right-hand

side of the frame noting their number and order **(see illustration)**.

26 Carefully lower the engine and bring it forward, then manoeuvre it out to the right-hand side.

Installation

27 Installation is the reverse of removal, noting the following points:

● With the aid of an assistant, place the engine unit onto the jack and block of wood and carefully raise it into position, looping the drive chain over the transmission output shaft as you do, so that the mounting bolt holes align. Make sure no

wires, cables or hoses become trapped between the engine and the frame. The engine mounting bolts are of different sizes and lengths. Make sure the correct bolt is installed in its correct location.

● Lubricate the threads of the upper and lower rear mounting bolts with lithium-based grease and slide the lower one into place **(see illustration 4.24c)** refit the neutral light lead **(see illustration 4.24b)**. Raise the front of the engine and fit the upper rear mounting bolt.

● Fit the collars and nuts and temporarily tighten first the upper rear, and then the lower rear mounting bolts.

● Install the front mounting bolts on the left-hand side and temporarily tighten them **(see illustration 4.22)**.

● Install the front mounting bolts on the right-hand side with their collars and temporarily tighten them **(see illustration 4.21a)**.

● Tighten the rear lower mounting bolt to the specified torque and then tighten the rear upper one to the specified torque

● Tighten the left and then the right front mounting bolts to the specified torque.

● Make sure all wires, cables and hoses are correctly routed and connected, and secured by any clips or ties.

● Refill the engine with oil and coolant to the

4.24a Remove the chain from the transmission shaft

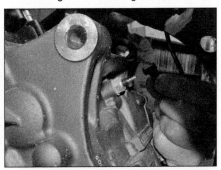

4.24b Drop the front of the engine and disconnect the neutral light switch

4.24c Remove the lower rear mounting bolt

4.25 Remove the collars from the right-hand side of the frame

correct levels (see Chapter 1 and *Pre-ride checks*).

● Check the throttle and clutch cable freeplay (see Chapter 1).
● Adjust the drive chain tension (see Chapter 1).
● Tighten all nuts and bolts to the specified torque settings where given.
● Start the engine and check that there are no oil or coolant leaks before installing the fairing panels.

5 Engine overhaul general information

1 Before beginning the engine overhaul, read through the related procedures to familiarise yourself with the scope and requirements of the job. Overhauling an engine is not all that difficult, but it is time consuming. Check on the availability of parts and make sure that any necessary special tools are obtained in advance.

2 Most work can be done with a decent set of typical workshop hand tools, although a number of precision measuring tools are required for inspecting parts to determine if they are worn.

3 To ensure maximum life and minimum trouble from a rebuilt engine, everything must be assembled with care in a spotlessly clean environment, using the correct lubricant where directed.

6.3a Unscrew the bolts . . .

Disassembly

4 Before disassembling the engine, thoroughly clean and degrease its external surfaces. This will prevent contamination of the engine internals, and will also make the job a lot easier and cleaner. A high flash-point solvent, such as paraffin (kerosene) can be used, or better still, a proprietary engine degreaser such as Gunk. Use old paintbrushes and toothbrushes to work the solvent into the various recesses of the casings. Take care to exclude solvent or water from the electrical components and intake and exhaust ports.

 Warning: The use of petrol (gasoline) as a cleaning agent should be avoided because of the risk of fire.

5 When clean and dry, position the engine on the workbench and support it as required using suitable blocks so that it is stable, leaving suitable clear area for working. Gather a selection of small containers, plastic bags and some labels so that parts can be grouped together in an easily identifiable manner. Also get some paper and a pen so that notes can be taken. You will also need a supply of clean rag, which should be as absorbent as possible.

6 Before commencing work, read through the appropriate section so that some idea of the necessary procedure can be gained. When removing components note that great force is seldom required, unless specified (checking the specified torque setting of the particular bolt being removed will indicate how tight it is, and therefore how much force should be needed). In many cases, a component's reluctance to be removed is indicative of an incorrect approach or removal method – if in any doubt, re-check with the text.

7 When disassembling the engine, keep 'mated' parts together (including gears, pistons, connecting rods, valves, etc, that have been in contact with each other during engine operation). These 'mated' parts must be reused or replaced as an assembly.

8 A complete engine disassembly should be done in the following general order with reference to the appropriate Sections (or Chapters, where indicated).

Remove the valve cover
Remove the cam chain tensioner
Remove the camshafts
Remove the cylinder head
Remove the clutch
Remove the alternator and starter clutch
Remove the starter motor (see Chapter 8)
Remove the gearchange mechanism
Remove the oil cooler
Remove the oil sump
Remove the water pump (see Chapter 3) and oil pump
Separate the crankcase halves
Remove the crankshaft
Remove the transmission output shaft
Remove the pistons and connecting rods
Remove the selector drum and forks
Remove the transmission input shaft

Reassembly

9 Reassembly is accomplished by reversing the general disassembly sequence.

6 Valve cover

Note: *This procedure can be carried out with the engine in the frame. If the engine has been removed, ignore the steps that do not apply.*

Removal

1 Remove the radiator (see Chapter 3).

2 Remove the AIS control valve along with the hoses (see Chapter 4). Remove the rubber heat shield and then remove the ignition coils (see Chapter 4).

3 Unscrew the bolts securing the valve cover and remove them with their sealing washers **(see illustration)**. Lift the cover off the cylinder head **(see illustration)** – if it is stuck, break the gasket seal by tapping gently around the edge with a soft-faced hammer or block of wood. Do not lever the cover off as this will damage the sealing surface.

4 Remove the gasket. Note the four AIS system air passage dowels and remove them if they are loose **(see illustration)**.

6.3b . . . and remove the valve cover

6.4 Note the AIS dowels (arrowed)

Installation

5 Examine the valve cover gasket rim and circular spark plug seals for signs of damage or deterioration and fit a new one if necessary. Similarly check the sealing washers on the cover bolts for cracks, hardening and deterioration and use new ones if necessary.

6 Clean the mating surfaces of the cylinder head and the valve cover with a suitable solvent.

7 Apply a smear of a suitable sealant to the cut-outs in the cylinder head **(see illustration)**. Make sure the AIS system dowels are pushed fully into place **(see illustration 6.4)**. Fit the gasket onto the valve cover, making sure it locates correctly, and using dabs of grease to hold it in place **(see illustration)**. If the gasket has a bridge piece between the cam chain end and the adjacent spark plug seal cut it away using a sharp knife.

8 Position the valve cover on the cylinder head, making sure the gasket stays in place **(see illustration 6.3b)**. Fit the sealing washers with the cover bolts and tighten the bolts to the torque setting specified at the beginning of this Chapter.

9 Install the remaining components in the reverse order of removal.

7 Cam chain tensioner

Note: *This procedure can be carried out with the engine in the frame. If the engine has been removed, ignore the steps that do not apply.*

7.3a Note the punch mark (arrowed) on the tensioner body

7.4b ... to release the plunger ...

6.7a Apply sealant to the cut outs in the head (arrowed) ...

Removal

1 Remove the lower fairing and the right-hand fairing side panel and trim panel (see Chapter 7).

2 Remove the valve cover (see Section 6). Remove the spark plugs (see Chapter 1). Place rags in the spark plug holes and the cam chain tunnel to prevent anything dropping into the engine. Refer to Section 8, Steps 2 to 5 and set the No. 1 cylinder at TDC (top dead centre) on the compression stroke.

3 Unscrew the tensioner mounting bolts and remove the tensioner – note the punch mark denoting the upper side of the tensioner **(see illustration)**. Discard the gasket as a new one must be used on reassembly **(see illustration)**.

Inspection

4 Hold the plunger and squeeze the ends

7.3b Renew the gasket

7.4c ... small spring, spring seat ...

6.7b ... before fitting the gasket

of the internal retaining clip together, then slowly release the plunger and remove it and the springs **(see illustrations)**. Clean all components and check them for wear and damage.

5 If the tensioner is worn or damaged, or if the plunger does not run smoothly in the body, the tensioner must be replaced with a new one – individual components are not available.

6 Make sure there is no oil in the tensioner body, then fit the large spring spring **(see illustration 7.4d)** followed by the smaller spring and its spring seat **(see illustration 7.4c)**. Fit the plunger into the body so that the pin on its top aligns with the external retaining clip on the body. Squeeze the ends of the internal retaining clip together and press the plunger all the way in **(see illustration 7.4a)**. Release the clip ends and flip the external clip up so that it hooks over the pin on the plunger,

7.4a Squeeze the ends of the clip together ...

7.4d ... and large spring

7.6 Flip the external clip up and over the pin

7.8 Fit the tensioner punch mark uppermost, and the gasket L mark to the lower left

8 Camshafts

Note: *This procedure can be carried out with the engine in the frame. If the engine has been removed, ignore the steps that do not apply.*

Removal

1 Remove the valve cover (see Section 6). Remove the spark plugs (see Chapter 1). Place rags in the spark plug holes and the cam chain tunnel to prevent anything dropping into the engine.

2 Place an oil pan under the timing rotor cover on the right-hand side of the engine. Unscrew the bolts and remove the cover, noting the hose clamps, and clutch cable stop **(see illustration)**. Discard the gasket, as a new one must be used. If the cam chain guide blade pivot pin comes away with the cover, remove it, then realign the blade and slide the pin back into place.

3 The engine must now be turned to position the No. 1 cylinder at TDC (top dead centre) on the compression stroke. To turn the engine, use a spanner on the timing rotor bolt and turn it in a clockwise direction only **(see illustration)**.

4 Turn the engine clockwise until the mark on the rotor faces to the rear and aligns with the crankcase mating surfaces **(see illustration)**. The camshaft lobes for the No. 1 (left-hand) cylinder should face away from each other; if the cam lobes are facing towards each other, rotate the engine clockwise 360° (one full turn) so that the mark again faces to the rear and aligns with the crankcase mating surfaces. The camshaft lobes should now be facing away from each other **(see illustration)** and the No. 1 cylinder will be at TDC (top dead centre) on the compression stroke.

5 Before disturbing the camshafts, identify and note the timing marks on the camshafts and holders – the relevant marks on the camshaft sprockets (I on the intake camshaft, E on the exhaust camshaft) line up with

making sure the pin is central in the clip **(see illustration)**. Check that this clip dislodges itself when the tensioner is positioned horizontally with the clip at the bottom and the plunger is pushed in slightly.

Installation

7 Ensure the tensioner and cylinder block surfaces are clean and dry. Lightly smear the new gasket with grease and fit it onto the tensioner **(see illustration 7.3)**.

8 Set the plunger in its fully retracted position and secure it with the external clip as in Step 6 **(see illustration 7.6)**. Fit the tensioner into

the cylinder block with the punch mark at the top and the L mark on the gasket to the lower left **(see illustration)**, then fit the bolts and tighten them to the torque setting specified at the beginning of this Chapter.

9 Turn the engine clockwise through two full turns and check again that all the timing marks still align (see Steps 4 and 5 of Section 8). If the cam chain has jumped a sprocket tooth with the tensioner removed it is vital that it is repositioned as described in Section 8. Install the valve cover and timing cover.

10 Install the remaining components in the reverse order of removal.

8.2 Unscrew the bolts and remove the timing cover

8.3 Turn the engine clockwise using a spanner

8.4a Align the line next to the T mark (A) with the crankcase join (B) . . .

8.4b . . . with No. 1 cylinder's camshaft lobes facing away from each other

8.5 Identify and note the camshaft timing marks

8.7a There are three holders for each camshaft . . .

the mating face of the cylinder head. **(see illustration)**. If you are in any doubt as to the alignment of the markings, or if they are not visible, make your own alignment marks between all components, and also between a tooth on each sprocket (including the timing sprocket) and its corresponding link on the chain, before disturbing them. These markings ensure that the valve timing can be correctly set up on assembly. As it is easy to be a tooth out on installation, marking between a tooth on each sprocket and its link in the chain is especially useful.

6 Remove the cam chain tensioner (see Section 7).

7 There are three camshaft holders for each camshaft **(see illustration)**. Each has an identity mark, and an arrow which points to the right-hand side of the engine **(see illustrations)**. Note the position of each holder for correct installation later. If the marks are unclear make your own. The small holders on the right-hand end are marked I1 and E1 for intake side and exhaust side respectively. The big holders for both intake and exhaust are marked I1, I2, E1 and E2 to denote their position on the left or right side of the engine.

8 Working on one camshaft at a time unscrew the camshaft holder bolts evenly and a little at a time in a criss-cross pattern, starting from the outside and working towards the centre.

8.7b . . . each marked with an arrow . . .

Slacken the bolts above any cam lobes that are pressing onto a valve last in the sequence so that the pressure from the open valves cannot cause the camshaft to bend.

Caution: If the bolts are loosened carelessly and the holders do not come away from the head squarely, a holder is likely to break. If this happens the complete cylinder head assembly must be replaced with a new one as the holders are matched to the head and cannot be obtained separately. Also, the camshaft could be damaged if the holder bolts are not slackened evenly and the pressure from a depressed valve causes a shaft to bend.

8.7c . . . and punched to identify it

9 Remove the bolts, then lift off the camshaft holders **(see illustration)**. Retrieve the dowels from either the holder or the cylinder head if they are loose.

10 Note the camshaft identification – the exhaust camshaft has a notched rib to trigger the cylinder identification sensor.

11 Disengage the chain from one camshaft sprocket at a time and lift the camshaft out of the head, then repeat for the other camshaft **(see illustrations)**. With both camshafts removed secure the cam chain to prevent it dropping into the crankcase, and avoid rotating the crankshaft in case the chain jams between the timing sprocket and the case.

8.9 Unscrew the bolts and remove the holders

8.11a Disengage the chain and lift out the exhaust camshaft . . .

8.11b . . . and then the intake camshaft

8.13a Remove the follower . . .

8.13b . . . and retrieve the shim

8.13c Noting that the size marking is uppermost

12 If required remove the cam chain front guide blade, the tensioner blade, timing rotor, and the cam chain (see Section 9).

13 If the followers and shims are being removed from the cylinder head, obtain a container which is divided into sixteen compartments, and label each compartment with the location of its corresponding valve in the cylinder head. If a container is not available, use labelled plastic bags (egg cartons also work very well). Remove the cam follower of the valve in question, then retrieve the shim from the inside of the follower **(see illustrations)**. If it is not in the follower, pick it out of the top of the valve using either a magnet, a small screwdriver with a dab of grease on it (the shim will stick to the grease), or a screwdriver and a pair of pliers. Do not allow the shim to fall into the engine.

Inspection

14 Inspect the bearing surfaces of the cylinder head and camshaft holders and the corresponding journals on the camshaft **(see illustration)**. Look for score marks, deep scratches and evidence of spalling (a pitted appearance). If damage is noted or wear is excessive, the relevant parts must be replaced with new ones. The cylinder head and holders must be replaced as a new matched set – individual parts are not available.

15 Check the camshaft lobes for heat discoloration (blue appearance), score marks, chipped areas, flat spots and spalling. Measure the height of each lobe and the

diameter of its base circle with a micrometer **(see illustrations)** and compare the results to the specifications listed in the beginning of this Chapter. If damage is noted or wear is excessive, the camshaft must be replaced with a new one. Also check the condition of the tops of the cam followers.

16 Check the amount of camshaft runout by supporting each end of the camshaft on V-blocks, and measuring any runout at the journals using a dial gauge. If the runout exceeds the specified limit the camshaft must be replaced with a new one.

 HAYNES HiNT *Refer to Tools and Workshop Tips (Section 3) in the Reference section for details of how to read a micrometer and dial gauge.*

17 The camshaft journal oil clearance should now be checked. There are two possible ways of doing this, either by direct measurement (see Steps 18 to 21) or by the use of a product known as Plastigauge (see Steps 22 to 27).

18 If the direct measurement method is to be used, make sure the camshaft holder dowels are fitted then install the holders in their correct location (see Step 7). Lubricate the threads of the holder bolts with clean engine oil, then tighten the bolts evenly and a little at a time in a criss-cross pattern to the torque setting specified at the beginning of this Chapter. Using telescoping gauges and a micrometer

8.14 Check all related bearing surfaces as described

(see *Tools and Workshop Tips*), measure the inside diameter of the holder journals.

19 Now measure the diameter of the corresponding camshaft journals with a micrometer **(see illustration)**. To determine the journal oil clearance, subtract the journal diameter from the holder diameter and compare the result to the clearance specified. If any clearance is greater than specified, it is an indication of wear on the camshaft, the holder, or both.

20 First check to see if the camshaft journals are worn below the service limit. If they are, a new camshaft must be fitted. However, since it is likely that the holders are also worn, ensure that the specified journal diameter for a new camshaft will restore the oil clearance to within specification before buying a new camshaft.

8.15a Measure the lobe height . . .

8.15b . . . and the base circle diameter

8.19 Measure the camshaft journal diameters

21 If the camshaft journals are good, or if fitting a new camshaft will not restore the oil clearance to within specification, the holders and cylinder head will have to be replaced as a new matched set.

22 If the Plastigauge method is to be used, clean the camshaft being checked (work on one at a time), the bearing surfaces in the cylinder head and camshaft holders with a suitable solvent and a clean, lint-free cloth, then lay the camshaft in place in the cylinder head, making sure the timing marks are correctly aligned (see Step 4 and 5).

23 Cut some strips of Plastigauge and lay one piece on each journal, parallel with the camshaft centreline **(see illustration 24.12)**. Make sure the camshaft holder dowels are fitted then install the holders in their correct location (see Step 7) **(see illustrations 8.7a, b, c and 8.9)**. Lubricate the threads of the holder bolts with clean engine oil, then tighten the bolts evenly and a little at a time in a criss-cross pattern to the torque setting specified at the beginning of this Chapter. Work from the centre of the camshafts outwards (i.e. starting with the bolts that are above valves that will be opened when the camshafts are tightened down). Whilst tightening the bolts, make sure each holder is being pulled down squarely and is not binding on the dowels, and make sure the camshaft does not rotate as this will distort the Plastigauge.

24 Now unscrew the bolts evenly and a little at a time in a criss-cross pattern, and carefully lift off the camshaft holders.

25 To determine the oil clearance, compare the crushed Plastigauge (at its widest point) on each journal to the scale printed on the Plastigauge container **(see illustration 24.16)**. Compare the results to this Chapter's Specifications. Carefully clean away all traces of Plastigauge using a fingernail or other object which will not score the bearing surfaces. If any clearance is greater than specified, it is an indication of wear on the camshaft, the holder, or both.

26 First check to see if the camshaft journals are worn below the service limit by measuring them with a micrometer **(see illustration 8.19)**. If they are, a new camshaft must be fitted. However, since it is likely that the holder is also worn, ensure that the specified journal diameter for a new camshaft will restore the oil clearance to within specification before buying a new camshaft.

27 If the camshaft journals are good, or if fitting a new camshaft will not restore the oil clearance to within specification, the holders and cylinder head will have to be replaced as a matched set.

> **HAYNES HINT** *Before fitting new camshafts, cylinder head or holders because of damage, check with local machine shops specialising in motorcycle engine work. In the case of the camshafts, it may be possible for cam lobes to be welded, reground and hardened, at a cost far lower than that of a new camshaft. Due to the cost of new components it is recommended that all options are explored!*

28 Inspect the cam chain guide blade, tensioner blade and cam chain (see Section 9).

29 Inspect the camshaft sprockets; if they show signs of wear, cracks or other damage replace them and the cam chain with a new set. If the clearance between the links of the cam chain and teeth of the sprocket is greater than one quarter of the width of the tooth then replace the camshaft sprockets and the chain as a set **(see illustration)**. The camshaft sprockets are retained by two bolts; unscrew the bolts and remove the sprockets, noting how they fit. Install the new sprockets taking care to align them correctly. Tighten the sprocket bolts to the specified torque setting.

30 Inspect the outer surfaces of the cam

followers for evidence of wear, scoring or other damage. If the side of a follower is in poor condition, it is probable that the bore in which it works is also damaged. Check for clearance between the followers and their bores. Whilst no specifications are given, if slack is excessive, replace the followers with new ones. If the bores are seriously out-of-round or tapered, then replace the cylinder head and followers with new ones.

Installation

31 If removed, lubricate each valve shim with molybdenum disulphide grease and fit it into its recess on the top of the valve, with the size marking on the shim facing up **(see illustration 8.13c)**. Make sure the shim is correctly seated, then lubricate each follower with molybdenum disulphide oil (a 50/50 mixture of molybdenum disulphide grease and engine oil) and fit it squarely into its bore **(see illustration 8.13a)**. **Note:** *It is most important that the shims and followers are returned to their original valves, otherwise the valve clearances will be inaccurate.*

32 Make sure the camshaft journals and the bearing surfaces in the cylinder head are clean, then apply molybdenum disulphide oil to them and to the camshaft lobes.

33 If removed, install the cam chain, the tensioner blade and the front guide blade (see Section 9).

34 Ensure that the mark on the timing rotor still faces back and aligns with the crankcase mating surfaces (see Step 4) **(see illustration 8.4a)**. Fit the exhaust camshaft, making sure the marks on the sprocket are aligned with the cylinder head cover mating face **(see illustration and 8.5)**. Fit the cam chain around the sprocket as you install the camshaft, pulling up on the chain to remove all slack in the front run between the crankshaft and the camshaft. If you made your own alignment marks prior to disassembly (see Step 5), check that they align.

35 Now fit the intake camshaft, making sure the marks on the sprocket align with

8.29 Check the camshaft sprockets for wear

8.34 Fit the exhaust camshaft

8.35a Fit the intake camshaft . . .

8.35b . . . noting the different coloured chain links. Sprocket timing marks arrowed

the cylinder head cover mating face **(see illustration and 8.5)**. Fit the cam chain around the sprocket, aligning the marks (if made) between sprocket and chain. When fitting the chain, pull it tight to make sure there is no slack between the two camshaft sprockets – any slack in the chain must lie in the rear run, so that it is taken up by the tensioner. If the chain has been removed, note that a genuine chain will have five of the links of a darker colour as a guide to the correct positioning of the chain **(see illustration)**.

36 Fit the camshaft holder dowels into the holders or cylinder head if removed. Make sure the bearing surfaces in the holders are clean, and then lubricate them with molybdenum disulphide oil.

37 Lubricate the threads of the holder bolts with clean engine oil and fit them into the holders. Install the holders in their correct location (see Step 7) **(see illustration)**. Tighten the bolts evenly and a little at a time in a criss-cross pattern to the torque setting specified at the beginning of this Chapter

(see illustration). Work from the centre of the holder outwards (i.e. starting with the bolts that are above valves that will be opened when the camshafts are tightened down). Whilst tightening the bolts, make sure each holder is being pulled down squarely and is not binding on the dowels.

Caution: The camshaft holder is likely to break if it is not tightened down evenly and squarely and the camshaft is likely to bend if it is tightened down onto the closed valves before the open ones.

38 Using a piece of wooden dowel, press on the back of the cam chain tensioner blade via the tensioner bore in the crankcase to take up any slack in the cam chain. Check that all the timing marks are still in **exact** alignment as described in Steps 4 and 5. If it is necessary to turn the engine slightly to align the marks with the engine mating surfaces, keep the wooden dowel pressed onto the tensioner blade as without the tensioner in place, the chain may slip on the sprockets. Note that it is easy to be slightly out (by one tooth on a sprocket)

without the marks appearing drastically out of alignment.

39 If the timing marks are out ensure there are five facing cam chain sideplates between the sprockets **(see illustration 8.35b)**, then release the tension on the chain and slip the chain around the relevant sprocket and turn the shafts as required to correct the alignment. Recheck the timing marks.

Caution: If the marks are not aligned exactly as described, the valve timing will be incorrect and the valves may strike the pistons, causing extensive damage to the engine.

40 With everything correctly aligned, install the cam chain tensioner (see Section 7). Turn the engine clockwise through two full turns and check again that all the timing marks still align (see Steps 4 and 5).

41 Check the valve clearances and adjust them if necessary (see Chapter 1). This is essential in new valve components have been fitted.

42 Fit the timing rotor cover using a new gasket, ensuring that the cam chain tensioner blade and guide blade pivot pins are correctly

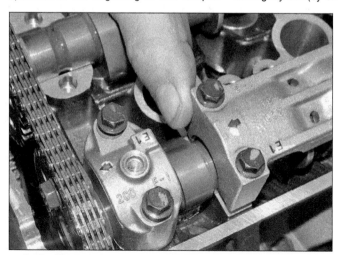

8.37a Fit the holders noting the alignment of the arrows and position marks

8.37b Tighten the bolts evenly in a criss-cross pattern to the specified torque

8.42a Refit the cover . . .

8.42b . . . noting the position of the water pump breather hose clamp . . .

8.42c . . . coolant reservoir breather hose clamp . . .

8.42d . . . and clutch cable stop

located **(see illustration)**. Install the cover bolts, not forgetting the clamps for the hoses, and the clutch cable stop **(see illustrations)**, and tighten the bolts to the torque setting specified at the beginning of this Chapter.
43 Install the valve cover (see Section 6).

9 Cam chain, tensioner blade and guides

Note: *This procedure can be carried out with the engine in the frame. If the engine has been removed, ignore the steps that do not apply.*

Tensioner blade and guides

Removal

1 Remove the valve cover (see Section 6), the

timing rotor cover (see Section 8, Step 2) and the cam chain tensioner (see Section 7). The cam chain top guide is fixed in the valve cover and should not be removed.

2 Remove the camshafts (see Section 8).
3 Withdraw the pivot pins, then draw the tensioner and guide blades out of the top of the engine, noting which way round they fit **(see illustrations)**.

Inspection

4 Check the sliding surfaces of the tensioner blade and guides for excessive wear, deep grooves, cracking and other obvious damage, and replace them with new ones if necessary.

Installation

5 Apply some clean engine oil to the pivot pins, then install the blades and insert the pins **(see illustrations 9.3d, c, b and a)**.
6 Install the camshafts (see Section 8).
7 Install the cam chain tensioner (see Section 7) and the valve cover (see Section 6) and timing rotor cover (see Section 8, Step 42).

Cam chain

Removal

8 Remove the tensioner blade and guides (see Steps 1 to 3).
9 Unscrew the bolt securing the timing rotor noting how it locates **(see illustration)**. To prevent the crankshaft turning, either select a gear and apply the rear brake (if the engine is in the frame), or remove the alternator cover and stator and counter-hold the bolt on the rotor. Remove the bolt, washer and the rotor, noting how they fit.

9.3a Withdraw the pin . . .

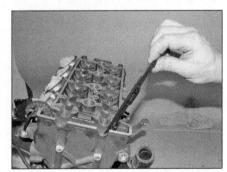

9.3b . . . and remove the front guide blade

9.3c Withdraw the pin . . .

9.3d . . . and remove the tensioner blade

9.9 Undo the bolt and remove the rotor, noting how it locates

10 Disengage the cam chain and draw it out of the engine **(see illustration)**

Inspection

11 Except in cases of oil starvation, the cam chain wears very little. If the chain is stiff or the links are binding, or if the links are loose, discard the chain. A chain in poor condition will wear the sprocket teeth and ideally the chain and sprockets should be replaced as a set.

Installation

12 Installation of the chain is the reverse of removal. Make sure the marked side of the ignition rotor faces out and that it locates correctly. Lubricate the rotor bolt threads with engine oil and tighten the bolt to the torque setting specified at the beginning of this Chapter ensuring the rotor is correctly located, counter-holding the crankshaft as on removal.

10 Cylinder head

Removal

1 Remove the engine from the frame (see Section 4).

9.10 Remove the cam chain from the engine

10.2 Remove the breather pipe

2 Remove the valve cover (see Section 6) and the camshafts and followers (see Section 8). Remove the breather pipe from the cylinder head **(see illustration)**.

3 The cylinder head is secured by two bolts and ten nuts, all with washers **(see illustration)**. First unscrew and remove the bolts on the right-hand end of the head **(see illustration)**. Now unscrew the nuts evenly and no more than a half turn at a time in a criss-cross pattern, starting from the outside

and working inwards in a reverse of the tightening sequence **(see illustrations)**. When all the nuts are loose remove them, then lift the washers off the studs, using a magnet if necessary **(see illustration)**.

4 Pull the cylinder head up off the cylinder block and the studs **(see illustration)**. If it is stuck, tap around the joint faces of the head with a soft-faced hammer or block of wood to free it. Do not attempt to free the head by inserting a lever between it and the cylinder

10.3a The head is secured by two bolts (A) and ten nuts (B)

10.3b Remove the bolts and their washers . . .

10.3c . . . and then evenly loosen the nuts and remove them . . .

10.3d . . . noting the Allen socket nuts . . .

10.3e . . . and retrieving their washers from the studs

10.4 Lift the head up off the studs

10.5a Remove and discard the head gasket

10.5b Check for the dowels (arrowed)

block you will damage the sealing surfaces. If the cam chain has not been removed pass it down the tunnel as you remove the head and drape it over the front of the block.

5 Remove the old cylinder head gasket and discard it as a new one must be fitted on reassembly **(see illustration)**. If they are loose, remove the dowels from the cylinder block **(see illustration)**. If they appear to be missing they are probably stuck in the underside of the cylinder head.

6 Check the cylinder head gasket and the mating surfaces on the cylinder head and block for signs of leakage from the cylinders, the oil or coolant passages, which could indicate that the head is warped. Refer to Section 11 and check the flatness of the cylinder head.

7 Lay a clean cloth over the cylinders and pistons while the head is off to prevent any dirt getting in.

Installation

8 Clean all traces of old gasket material from the cylinder head and block with a suitable solvent. If you need to use a scraper, take care not to scratch or gouge the soft aluminium. Be careful not to let any of the gasket material fall into the crankcase, the cylinder bores or the oil or coolant passages. Make sure all the studs are tight; if a stud is needs renewing, note that the new stud should be installed so that its length from the surface is 68.2 mm.

HAYNES HINT *Refer to Tools and Workshop Tips (Section 7) for details of gasket removal methods and Section 2 for stud removal/ installing methods.*

9 Lubricate the cylinder bores with clean engine oil. If removed, fit the dowels into the crankcase,

then lay the new head gasket in place, making sure it locates correctly over the dowels, and all the holes are correctly aligned **(see illustrations)**.

10 Carefully fit the cylinder head over the studs and onto the cylinder block – if the cam chain tensioner and guide blades are installed make sure they locate inside the head, and pass the cam chain up through the tunnel, and make sure the head locates correctly onto the dowels **(see illustration 10.4)**. Secure the cam chain to one of the exhaust studs using a piece of wire or a cable-tie.

11 Lubricate the threads and seating surfaces of the ten 10 mm cylinder head nuts and their washers with clean engine oil. Fit the washers onto the studs, using either a screwdriver shaft or rod as a guide or a magnetic tool **(see illustrations)**. Fit the nuts and tighten them finger-tight – the domed hex nuts fit on the left-hand end studs **(see**

10.9a Check that both the dowels . . .

10.9b . . . are in position . . .

10.9c . . . and that the gasket is correctly aligned

10.11a Fit the washers using a screwdriver . . .

10.11b . . . or a small magnet

10.11c The domed hex nuts go on the left-hand end studs

11.5 Valve components

1 Collets
2 Spring retainer
3 Spring
4 Spring seat
5 Oil seal
6 Valve

H28664

10.11d Cylinder head nut tightening sequence

illustration). Now tighten the nuts evenly and in two stages, working in a criss-cross pattern starting from the centre and moving outwards, to the Stage 1 and 2 torque settings specified at the beginning of this Chapter **(see illustration)**; note that the settings differ between Allen-head nuts and dome hex head nuts.

12 Install the bolts with their washers and tighten them to the specified torque setting **(see illustration 10.3b)**.

13 Install the remaining components in the reverse order of removal.

11 Valve overhaul

1 Because of the complex nature of this job and the special tools and equipment required, most owners leave servicing of the valves, valve seats and valve guides to a professional. However, you can make an initial assessment of whether the valves are seating correctly, and therefore sealing, by pouring a small amount of solvent into each of the valve ports. If the solvent leaks past any valve into the combustion chamber area the valve is not seating correctly and sealing.

2 With the correct tools (a valve spring compressor is essential – make sure it is suitable for motorcycle work), you can also remove the valves and associated components from the cylinder head, clean them and check them for wear to assess the extent of the work needed.

3 A dealer service department or engine specialist can replace the guides and re-cut the valve seats if needed.

4 After the valve service has been performed, be sure to clean the head very thoroughly before installation on the engine to remove any metal particles or abrasive grit that may still be present from the valve service operations. Use compressed air, if available, to blow out all the holes and passages.

Disassembly

5 Before proceeding, arrange to label and store the valves along with their related components in such a way that they can be returned to their original locations without getting mixed up **(see illustration)**. Either use the same container as the valve shims and followers are stored in (see Section 8), or obtain a separate container which is divided into sixteen compartments, and label each compartment with the identity of the valve which will be stored in it. Alternatively, labelled plastic bags will do just as well.

6 Clean all traces of old gasket material from the cylinder head with a suitable solvent. If you need to use a scraper, take care not to scratch or gouge the soft aluminium.

> **HAYNES HiNT** *Refer to Tools and Workshop Tips (Section 7) in the Reference section for details of gasket removal methods.*

7 Compress the valve spring on the first valve with a spring compressor, making sure it is correctly located onto each end of the valve assembly **(see illustrations)**. On the underside of the head, make sure the plate on the compressor only contacts the valve and not the soft aluminium of the head – if the plate is too big for the valve, use a spacer between them. Do not compress the spring any more than is absolutely necessary.

8 Remove the collets, using either needle-nose pliers, tweezers, a magnet or a screwdriver with a dab of grease on it **(see illustration)**. Carefully release the valve spring compressor and remove the spring retainer, noting which way up it fits, the spring and the valve **(see illustrations 11.5 and 11.30d, c and a)**. If the valve binds in the guide (won't pull through), push it back into the head and deburr the area

11.7a Make sure the valve spring compressor is a good fit on the bottom . . .

11.7b . . . and the top of the valve

11.8a Remove the collets taking care not to drop them into the engine

11.8b If the valve stem (2) won't pull through the guide, deburr the area above the collet groove (1)

11.9a Pull the oil seal off the valve guide . . .

11.9b . . . and remove the spring seat

11.15 Measure the valve seat width (arrowed)

11.16 Check the valve face (A), stem (B) and collet groove (C) for wear and damage

11.17 Measure valve stem runout with V-blocks and a dial gauge

around the collet groove with a very fine file or whetstone **(see illustration)**.

9 Pull the valve stem oil seal off the top of the valve guide with pliers and discard it (the old seals should never be reused) **(see illustration)**. Remove the spring seat, noting which way up it fits – using a magnet is the easiest way to lift the seat off the head **(see illustration)**.

10 Repeat the procedure for the remaining valves. Remember to keep the parts for each valve together and labelled so they can be reinstalled in the correct location.

11 Next, clean the cylinder head with solvent and dry it thoroughly. Compressed air will speed the drying process and ensure that all holes and recessed areas are clean.

12 Clean all the valve springs, collets, retainers and spring seats with solvent and dry them thoroughly. Clean the parts from one valve at a time so that no mixing of parts between valves occurs. Scrape off any deposits that may have formed on the valves. Again, make sure the valves do not get mixed up.

Inspection

13 Inspect the head very carefully for cracks and other damage. If cracks are found, a new head will be required. Check the cam bearing surfaces for wear and evidence of seizure. Check the camshafts for wear as well (see Section 8).

14 Using a precision straight-edge and a feeler gauge, check the head gasket mating surface for warpage. Refer to *Tools and Workshop Tips* (Section 3) in the *Reference* section for details of how to use the straight-edge. If the head is warped beyond the limit specified at the beginning of this Chapter, consult your Yamaha dealer or take it to an engineer for rectification.

15 Examine the valve seats in the combustion chamber. If they are pitted, cracked or burned, the head will require work beyond the scope of the home mechanic, although note that slight imperfections can be removed by grinding (see Step 24). Measure the valve seat width and compare it to this Chapter's Specifications **(see illustration)**. If it exceeds the service limit, or if it varies around its circumference, consult your Yamaha dealer or take the head to an engineer for rectification.

16 Examine each valve face for cracks, pits and burned spots **(see illustration)**. **Note:** *Grinding of the titanium valves is not possible (see Step 24).*

17 Rotate the valve and check for any obvious indication that it is bent. Using V-blocks and a dial gauge if available, measure the valve stem runout and compare the results to the specifications at the beginning of this Chapter **(see illustration)**. If the measurement exceeds the service limit specified, the valve must be replaced with a new one. Note that a slightly bent valve stem will prevent the valve from seating properly in the head.

18 Measure the various aspects of the valve head and compare them with the listed specifications **(see illustration)**. If the valve is worn it should be replaced with a new one.

11.18 Valve head measurement points
A Head diameter   B Face width   C Seat width   D Margin thickness

11.19a Measure valve stem diameter with a micrometer . . .

11.19b . . . and the valve guide diameter with a bore gauge

11.21 Measuring spring free length with a Vernier caliper

19 Measure the valve stem diameter **(see illustration)**. Clean the valve guides to remove any carbon build-up, then measure the inside diameters of the guides (at both ends and the centre of the guide) with a small hole gauge and micrometer (see *Tools and Workshop Tips* (Section 3) in the *Reference* section) **(see illustration)**. The guides are measured at the ends and at the centre to determine if they are worn in a bell-mouth pattern (more wear at the ends). Subtract the stem diameter from the valve guide diameter to obtain the valve stem-to-guide clearance. If the stem-to-guide clearance is greater than listed in this Chapter's Specifications, replace whichever components are worn beyond their specified limits with new ones. If the valve guide is within specifications, but is worn unevenly, it should be replaced with a new one.

20 Inspect the valve stem and collet groove area for scuffing and cracks **(see illustration**

11.16). Check the end of the stem for pitting and wear. The presence of any of the above conditions indicates the need for fitting new valves.

21 Check the end of each valve spring for wear. Measure the free length of each spring and compare it to that listed in the specifications **(see illustration)**. If any spring is shorter than specified it has sagged and must be replaced with a new one. Also place the spring upright on a flat surface and check it for bend by placing a ruler or engineer's square against it. If the bend in any spring exceeds the specified limit, it must be replaced with a new one.

22 Check the spring retainers and collets for obvious wear and cracks. Any questionable parts should not be reused, as extensive damage will occur in the event of failure during engine operation.

23 If the inspection indicates that no overhaul

work is required, the valve components can be reinstalled in the head.

Reassembly

24 The normal practice of grinding (lapping) the valves should not be attempted because the surface of the titanium valve face will be ruined in the process. It is permissble to grind the valve seats in the head using one of the existing intake and exhaust valves, but these valves must be renewed on assembly of the head. Note that titanium valves are expensive!

25 Working on one valve at a time, lay the spring seat in place in the cylinder head so that its shouldered side faces upwards **(see illustration 11.9b)**.

26 Coat the valve stem with molybdenum disulphide oil, then slide it into its guide **(see illustration)**. Fit a new valve stem oil seal onto the guide and use an appropriate size deep socket to press the seal over the end of the valve guide until it is felt to clip into place **(see illustration)** using the valve stem to keep it aligned to the guide. Don't remove it again or it will be damaged. Check that the valve moves up and down freely in the guide. Next, install the spring, with the closer-wound coils facing down into the cylinder head **(see illustration)**. Fit the spring retainer, with its shouldered side facing down so that it fits into the top of the spring **(see illustration)**.

27 Apply a small amount of grease to the inside of the collets – this will help to help hold them in place when fitting them on the valve stem **(see illustration)**. Compress the spring with the valve spring compressor **(see**

11.26a Lubricate the stem and fit the valve . . .

11.26b . . . and use it as a guide to fit the seals

11.26c Refit the spring . . .

11.26d . . . and the spring retainer

11.27a Apply a small amount of grease to the collets

11.27b Make sure the collets are securely located

illustrations 11.7a and b). When compressing the spring, do so only as far as is necessary to slip the collets into place. Make certain that the collets are securely located in the collet groove then release the spring compressor **(see illustration)**.

28 Repeat the procedure for the remaining valves. Remember to keep the parts for each valve together and separate from the other valves so they can be reinstalled in their original locations.

29 Support the cylinder head on blocks so the valves can't contact the workbench top, then very gently tap the top of each valve stem to seat the collets in the groove **(see illustration)**.

12 Clutch cable

Removal

1 Remove the right-hand fairing side panel and the lower fairing (see Chapter 7).

2 Bend up the tab in the cable retainer on the end of the arm **(see illustration 4.12b)**. Loosen the rear nut on the adjuster **(see illustration)**.

3 Slip the adjuster out of the bracket on the engine cover and release the cable end from the retainer, noting how it fits.

4 Screw the adjuster at the handlebar end of the cable fully into the lever bracket and align the slot in the adjuster with that in the lever bracket **(see illustration)**. Pull the outer

12.5a Release the cable-tie . . .

11.29 Tap the valve stem gently to seat the collets in the groove

cable end from the socket in the adjuster and release the inner cable nipple from the lever.

5 Release the cable-tie securing the cable to the coolant hose **(see illustration)**. Release the clip securing the cable to the cooling fan bracket **(see illustration)**. Remove the cable from the machine, noting its routing through the guide on the top yoke **(see illustration)**.

> **HAYNES HINT** *When fitting a new cable, tape the lower end of the new cable to the upper end of the old cable before removing it from the motorcycle. Slowly pull the lower end of the old cable out, guiding the new cable down into position. Using this method will ensure the cable is routed correctly.*

12.2 Loosen the rear nut on the adjuster (arrowed)

12.5b . . . and the clip

Installation

6 Installation is the reverse of removal. Apply grease to the cable ends and make sure the cable is correctly routed. Once the cable is installed, turn the adjuster on the lever bracket so that the slots are not aligned **(see illustration 12.4)** and bend the retainer tab on the release mechanism arm down to secure the cable end **(see illustration 4.12b)**. Adjust the clutch lever freeplay (see Chapter 1).

7 Check the clutch release mechanism for smooth operation and any signs of wear or damage. Remove it for cleaning and re-greasing if required (see Section 13). Install the fairing panels (see Chapter 7).

13 Clutch

Note: *This procedure can be carried out with the engine in the frame. If the engine has been removed, ignore the steps that do not apply.*
Special tool: *A clutch centre holding tool is useful, although not essential – see Step 7.*

Removal

1 Remove the right-hand fairing side panel and the lower fairing (see Chapter 7). Drain the engine oil (see Chapter 1). Detach the clutch cable from the release mechanism arm (see Section 12).

2 Remove the sump and oil strainer (see Section 17). Remove the water pump (see Chapter 3).

12.4 Screw in the adjuster and align the slot

12.5c Note the routing through the cable guide (arrowed)

13.3 Unscrew the bolts and remove the clutch cover

13.4a Note the position of the dowels . . .

13.4b . . . and remove them if they are loose

13.5a Unscrew the bolts in a criss-cross pattern . . .

13.5b . . . and remove the bolts, springs . . .

13.5c . . . and the spring seats

13.5d Note the alignment marks, then remove the pressure plate . . .

3 Working evenly in a criss-cross pattern, unscrew the clutch cover bolts and remove the cover, being prepared to catch any residual oil **(see illustration)**. If the cover will not lift away easily, break the gasket seal by tapping gently around the edge with a soft-faced hammer or block of wood. Note how the teeth on the clutch pull-rod engage on the actuating shaft in the clutch cover.

4 Remove the cover gasket and discard it as a new one must be fitted on reassembly. Note the position of the two locating dowels and remove them for safe-keeping if they are loose – they could be in either the cover or the crankcase **(see illustrations)**.

5 Working in a criss-cross pattern, gradually slacken the clutch spring bolts until the spring pressure is released, counter-holding the clutch using a rag **(see illustration)**. Remove the bolts, springs, spring seat washers, and outer pressure plate, noting the alignment marks between the outer clutch plate and the clutch housing **(see illustrations)**. Remove the pull-rod from the pressure plate, noting the bearing **(see illustration)**.

6 Remove the clutch friction and plain plates, hooking them out when necessary, noting how they fit and keeping them in order **(see illustration)**. In particular, note how the outer

13.5e . . . and separate it from the pull-rod

13.6 Remove the plates noting their alignment and order

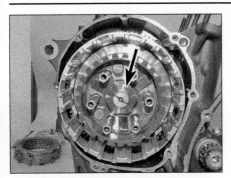

13.7a The staking on the centre nut (arrowed) . . .

13.7b . . . should be driven out of the slot . . .

13.7c . . . and the centre held so the nut can be unscrewed

friction plate, identified by a brown paint mark, has its tabs located in the shallow slots in the housing, while the rest, identified by a black paint mark, sit in the deep slots, along with the inner friction plate which has a purple paint mark. The two outermost plain plates may also vary in thickness and must be kept in their positions.

7 Unstake the rim of the clutch nut from the indent in the shaft end **(see illustrations)**. To remove the clutch centre nut, the transmission input shaft must be locked. This can be done

in several ways. If the engine is in the frame, engage 1st gear and have an assistant hold the rear brake on hard with the rear tyre in firm contact with the ground. Alternatively, the Yamaha service tool – Pt. No. 90890-04086 (Europe models) or YM-91042 (US models) – or a similar commercially available tool **(see illustration)**, can be used to stop the clutch centre from turning while the nut is loosened.

8 With the transmission input shaft locked, unscrew the nut and remove the three

diaphragm springs for the slipper mechanism, noting how their tabs fit into the slots in the clutch centre **(see illustration)**. Discard the nut as a new one must be fitted on reassembly.

9 Slide the clutch centre off the input shaft, noting how its dogs engage with the slots in the inner pressure plate. Slide the inner pressure plate off, followed by the conical spring washer and the thrust washer, noting which way round they fit **(see illustrations)**.

10 Using a suitably sized Allen key extract the clutch bearing sleeve and the needle

13.8 Note how the tabs on the diaphragm springs fit together

13.9a Remove the clutch centre (three reference dots arrowed) . . .

13.9b . . . inner pressure plate . . .

13.9c . . . conical spring washer . . .

13.9d . . . and the thrust washer

13.10a Use an Allen key to hook out the spacer . . .

13.10b . . . and remove the spacer and the bearing

13.10c Free the chain from the oil pump sprocket . . .

13.10d . . . and remove the chain with the housing . . .

13.10e . . . followed by the large thrust washer . . .

13.10f . . . and the smaller one

roller bearing **(see illustrations)**. Allow the clutch housing to drop on its shaft, and free the oil pump drive chain from the sprocket on the oil pump **(see illustration)**. Remove the clutch housing and the oil pump drive chain

13.11 Measure the thickness of the friction plates

(see illustration). Then remove the two thrust washers noting their order **(see illustrations)**.

Inspection

11 After an extended period of service the clutch friction plates will wear and promote clutch slip. Measure the thickness of each friction plate using a Vernier caliper **(see illustration)**. If any plate has worn to or beyond the service limit given in the Specifications at the beginning of this Chapter, the friction plates must be replaced with a new set. Also, if any of the plates smell burnt or are glazed, they must be replaced as a set.

12 The plain plates should not show any signs of excess heating (bluing). Check for warpage using a flat surface and feeler gauges **(see illustration)**. If any plate exceeds the maximum permissible amount of warpage, or shows signs of bluing, all the plain plates must be replaced as a set.

13 Using the original plates if they are reusable, or the new plates if necessary, assemble the clutch friction and plain plates together as a pack in their correct order of installation, making sure any oil is wiped off. Now measure the thickness of the assembled pack **(see illustration)**. It should be within the limits specified at the beginning of the Chapter. If not, replace either one or both of the outer two plain plates with thicker or thinner ones as required to bring the total thickness of the assembled plates within limits – adjust by replacing the outer plate first, only replacing the second plate if adjustment of the outer cannot bring the thickness within limits. The outer plate is available in thicknesses of 1.6 mm, 2.0 mm (standard) and 2.3 mm, and the second plate is available in thicknesses 2.0 mm (standard) and 2.3 mm.

14 Measure the free length of each clutch spring **(see illustration)**. If any spring is

13.12 Check the flatness of the plain plates with a feeler gauge

13.13 Measure the thickness of the assembled plates

13.14 Use a Vernier caliper to measure the free length of the springs

below the service limit specified, renew all the springs as a set. Check the slipper mechanism diaphragm springs for cracks and distortion and replace them with new ones if necessary, and irrespective of their apparent condition if you have noticed effectiveness of the slipper mechanism has reduced in use.

15 Inspect the clutch assembly for burrs and indentations on the edges of the protruding tangs of the friction plates and/or slots in the edge of the housing with which they engage **(see illustration)**. Similarly check for wear between the inner teeth of the plain plates and the slots in the clutch centre **(see illustration)**. Wear will cause clutch drag and slow disengagement during gear changes, as the plates will snag when the pressure plate is lifted. With care, a small amount of wear can be corrected by dressing with a fine file, but if it is excessive the worn components should be replaced with new ones. Also check the engagement dogs for the slipper mechanism on the inner face of the clutch centre and their slots in the inner pressure plate.

16 Inspect the needle roller bearing in conjunction with the internal bearing surface of the clutch housing and the external surface of the spacer **(see illustration 13.10b)**. If there are any signs of wear, pitting or other damage the affected parts must be replaced with new ones.

17 Check the teeth of the primary driven gear on the clutch housing and the corresponding teeth of the primary drive gear on the crankshaft. Replace the clutch housing with a new one if any teeth are worn or chipped. The primary drive gear is an integral part of the crankshaft (see Section 24 for removal of the crankshaft).

18 Check the teeth of the oil pump drive sprocket. If any are worn or chipped, replace the clutch housing with a new one and check the driven sprocket on the oil pump and the chain (see Section 18).

19 The primary driven gear on the back of the clutch housing incorporates a cush-drive mechanism – check that the springs are not loose and that there is no backlash between the centre of the housing and the primary driven gear.

13.15a Examine the clutch housing . . .

13.15b . . . and the centre for wear

13.21a If necessary remove the E-clip (arrowed) . . .

13.21b . . . noting the alignment marks before removing the arm

20 Check the outer pressure plate and its bearing for signs of wear or damage and roughness. Check the pull-rod for signs of wear or damage. Replace any parts, as necessary, with new ones.

21 Check the clutch release mechanism shaft pinion and the pull-rod teeth for signs of wear and damage. Check that the shaft turns smoothly in the clutch cover **(see illustration)**. If necessary, remove the E-clip and washer securing the shaft and withdraw it. Note the position of the return spring and the alignment marks on the clutch cover and release mechanism arm **(see illustration)**.

22 Check the condition of the shaft, oil seal and two bearings, and fit new parts if necessary. If the bearings need to be removed, first remove the oil seal, then warm the cover

to ease removal and drive the bearings out (see *Tools and Workshop Tips* (Sections 5 and 6) in the *Reference* section). Discard the oil seal as a new one must be fitted on reassembly.

23 If required, remove the circlip and washer securing the arm on the end of the shaft. Note the position of the arm and return spring, then slide the arm off the shaft and remove the spring.

24 Clean all components and lubricate the seal and bearings with grease. Installation is the reverse of removal.

Installation

25 Remove all traces of old gasket from the crankcase and clutch cover surfaces.
26 Fit the oil pump drive chain to the sprocket on the rear of the clutch housing **(see illustration)**. Fit the two thrust washers to the shaft **(see illustrations 13.10f and e)**. Slide the clutch housing onto the shaft and feed the oil pump drive chain into the lower crankcase checking that it is correctly located on the chain guide **(see illustration)**. Locate the chain onto the oil pump sprocket. Lubricate the bearing sleeve and the needle roller with clean engine oil and slide them onto the shaft and into the clutch basket. Check that the oil pump drive chain is correctly installed and that the clutch basket is engaged with the primary drive gear on the crankshaft,
27 Lubricate the thrust washer with clean engine oil and slide it onto the shaft, then

13.26a Fit the oil pump drive chain to the housing and refit it . . .

13.26b . . . making sure it locates correctly in the chain guide

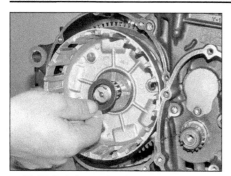

13.27 Lubricate the thrust washer and conical spring washer

13.29a Make sure the diaphragm springs have their tabs correctly located . . .

13.29b . . . and that the new nut locates correctly in the diaphragm springs . . .

13.29c . . . before tightening it to the specified torque . . .

13.29d . . . and restaking the thin rim

13.30 Fit the friction plates with the paint mark (A) next to the punch mark (B)

repeat for the conical spring washer **(see illustration)**.

28 Slide the inner pressure plate onto the shaft. Slide the clutch centre onto the inner pressure plate, engaging the dogs on the back with the slots in the inner pressure plate.

29 Fit the three diaphragm springs, locating the tab on each into a slot in the clutch centre, making sure each tab fits into a different slot so all three slots are taken up by the three tabs **(see illustration)**. Fit the new clutch nut, with its thin rim facing out **(see illustration)**. Ensure the shoulder on the rear of the nut

locates correctly in all three diaphragm springs. Tighten the nut to the torque setting specified at the beginning of this Chapter using the method employed on removal to lock the input shaft (see Step 7) **(see illustration)**. **Note:** *Check that the clutch centre rotates freely after tightening.* Stake the rim of the nut into one of the indents in the end of the shaft **(see illustration)**.

30 Lubricate the inner friction plate (purple paint mark) with clean oil, then fit the plate with the pink register mark to one side of the punch mark in the clutch drum **(see illustration)**.

31 Coat each clutch plate with clean engine oil prior to installation. Build up the plates as follows: first fit a plain plate, then a friction plate, then alternate plain plates and friction plates (black paint mark) until all are installed, making sure any adjusted plain plates (see Step 13) are correctly fitted as the outer two plain plates, and locating the tabs of the outer friction plate (brown paint mark) in the shallow slots in the housing **(see illustrations)**.

32 Lubricate the bearing in the outer pressure plate with clean engine oil. Fit the pull-rod into the back of the pressure plate

13.31a Lubricate the plain plates

13.31b Fit the last friction plate with its tabs (A) offset from the rest of the plates (B)

13.33a Align the mark on the pressure plate with a punch mark on the centre . . .

13.33b . . . to correctly position the spring retainers

13.34a Refit the spring seats . . .

13.34b . . . followed by the springs, washers and bolts . . .

13.34c . . . and them tighten them in a criss-cross pattern to the specified torque

13.35a Use a new gasket and refit the cover. Note the sealant applied across the crankcase joints (arrowed)

33 Line up the reference marks on the clutch outer pressure plate with one of the three dots on the clutch centre **(see illustration 13.9a)** and fit the pressure plate, making sure the castellations in its rim locate into the slots in the clutch centre **(see illustrations)**.
34 Fit the clutch spring seats **(see illustration)** and then install the clutch springs and bolts **(see illustration)**, and tighten the bolts evenly and a little at a time in a criss-cross sequence to the specified torque setting **(see illustration)**. Counter-hold the clutch housing to prevent it turning when tightening the spring

bolts. Set the pull-rod so that its teeth point towards the rear and are angled up slightly.
35 If removed, insert the dowels in the cover. Fit a new gasket over the dowels and apply sealant to the area which aligns with the crankcase join **(see illustration)**. When installing the clutch cover, getting the actuating shaft to engage correctly with the pull-rod teeth can be tricky. Set the release arm so that it is pointing diagonally out and back, then as the cover is installed and the teeth engage, the arm should turn in. With the cover fully installed, the alignment marks

on the cover and the clutch arm should be in line when the mechanism when it is at the full extent of the travel **(see illustration)**; if they are not, either pull the cover off, reposition the clutch arm and refit the cover or remove the circlip securing the arm and adjust it on the splines – note that the circlip should be renewed if it is disturbed. Check that both ends of the return spring are correctly located **(see illustration)**.
36 Install the cover bolts, applying a suitable thread locking compound to the two bolts nearest the front and either side of the

13.35b Check the dot on the clutch arm is aligned with the triangle on the cover . . .

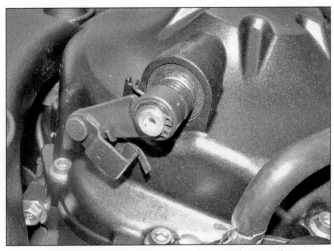

13.35c . . . and that the spring is seated correctly

13.36a Apply a suitable thread locking compound to the two front most bolts . . .

13.36b . . . the locations being marked by arrowheads on the cover (arrowed)

crankcase join, and tighten them evenly in a criss-cross sequence to the specified torque setting **(see illustrations)**.

37 Fit the clutch cable onto the release arm and adjust the cable as necessary (see Section 12).

38 Refit the oil strainer and sump (see Section 17). Refit the water pump (see Chapter 3). Refill the engine with oil to the correct level (see Chapter 1 and *Pre-ride checks*).

39 Install the fairing side panel and the lower fairing (see Chapter 7).

14 Starter clutch and alternator rotor

Note: *This procedure can be carried out with the engine in the frame. If the engine has been removed, ignore the steps which do not apply.*

Check

1 The operation of the starter clutch can be checked while it is in place. Remove the starter motor (see Chapter 8). Check that the starter idle/reduction gear is able to rotate freely anti-clockwise as you look at it from the right-hand side of the bike via the starter motor housing, but locks when rotated clockwise. If not, the starter clutch is faulty and should be removed for inspection.

Removal

2 Remove the left-hand fairing side panel and

the lower fairing (see Chapter 7). Drain the engine oil (see Chapter 1).

3 Locate the alternator wiring connector (white) behind the coolant pipe and disconnect it from the loom **(see illustration 4.14a)**. Feed the wiring through to the alternator cover, noting its routing and releasing it from any ties.

4 Unscrew and remove the bolts securing the alternator cover. If the cover gasket seal will not release easily, break it by tapping gently around the edge with a soft-faced hammer or block of wood, or by levering carefully with a screwdriver on the tabs **(see illustrations)** – do not try to lever between the cover/crankcases mating surfaces as they could be damaged. Discard the gasket as a new one must be used. Remove the dowels from either the cover or the crankcase if they are loose **(see illustration)**.

5 Unscrew and remove the alternator rotor

bolt. If the engine is in the frame, engage 1st gear and have an assistant hold the rear brake on hard with the rear tyre in firm contact with the ground. Alternatively, the Yamaha service tool – Pt. No. 90890-01701 (Europe models) or YS-01880-A (US models) – or a similar commercially available tool **(see illustration)** can be used to stop the rotor from turning while the bolt is loosened.

6 Remove the idle/reduction gear and its shaft **(see illustration)**.

7 Remove the rotor using the Yamaha service tool – Pt. No. 90890-01404 (Europe models) or YM-1404 (US models) – or a similar commercially available tool. Use a suitably sized socket between the puller's centre bolt and the end of the crankshaft to prevent damage.

Inspection

8 Inspect the teeth on the idle/reduction gear and the corresponding teeth on the starter motor shaft and the starter driven gear, and replace them with new ones if any are chipped or worn. Check the idle/reduction gear shaft bearing surfaces for signs of wear or damage, and replace with a new one if necessary. Check the plain bearing in the driven gear for signs of wear or damage, and replace with a new one if necessary.

9 With the rotor held in your hand, and the driven gear facing you, check that the starter driven gear rotates freely in an anti-clockwise direction and locks against the rotor in a clockwise direction.

10 If it doesn't, separate the driven gear from

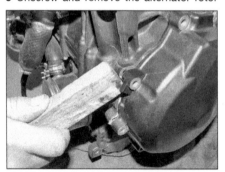

14.4a Remove the cover using the pry points at the front . . .

14.4b . . . and at the rear

14.4c Remove the dowels if they are loose

14.5 Use a suitable method hold the rotor and unscrew the bolt

14.6 Remove the reduction gear and its shaft

14.10a Remove the driven gear . . .

14.10b . . . and the circlip

14.11a Note the arrow mark faces away from the rotor

the rotor and remove the circlip retaining the starter clutch (see illustrations).

11 Inspect the condition of the sprags and their cage. If they are damaged or worn at any point, replace the sprag assembly with a new one. Fit the assembly back into the alternator rotor with the arrow mark facing away from the rotor and replace the circlip, making sure it locates correctly (see illustrations).

12 Inspect the starter driven gear bearing surfaces for signs of wear and scoring. If the bearing surfaces show signs of excessive wear, replace the gear with a new one and inspect the crankshaft for damage.

13 Refit the starter driven gear into the sprag, rotating it anti-clockwise. Check the operation as described in Step 9.

14 Check the alternator stator windings (see Chapter 8). If the windings need to be replaced, undo the screw from the wiring retainer and remove it. Ease the wiring grommet from the

cover, unscrew the three bolts retaining the stator in the cover and remove it noting the position of the wiring. Fit the new stator to the cover, apply thread lock to the bolts and tighten them to the torque given at the start of this chapter. Apply sealant to the wiring grommet and fit that into the cover. Fit the wiring retainer, apply thread lock to the bolt and tighten it to the same torque as the stator retaining bolt.

Installation

15 Clean the taper on the crankshaft and the one in the alternator rotor. Lubricate the starter driven gear bearing with clean engine oil and refit the rotor (see illustration). Using a new washer, lubricate the bolt threads and washer faces with clean engine oil, and tighten it to the torque setting specified at the beginning of this Chapter using the method employed on removal to lock the rotor (see illustration).

16 Lubricate the idle/reduction gear shaft with clean engine oil. Re-fit the shaft and gear, making sure the smaller pinion faces in and meshes with the starter motor diving gear and the teeth of the large pinion mesh with the starter driven gear.

17 If removed, fit the dowels into the crankcase, then locate a new gasket onto the dowels and refit the cover ensuring that it locates on the idle/reduction gear shaft (see illustration). Tighten the bolts in a criss-cross sequence to the torque specified at the beginning of this chapter (see illustration).

18 Feed the alternator wiring to the loom connector, making sure it is correctly routed, and reconnect it. Install the remaining components in the reverse order of removal.

19 Refill the engine with oil to the correct level (see Chapter 1 and Pre-ride checks).

15 Gearchange mechanism

Note: This procedure can be carried out with the engine in the frame. If the engine has been removed, ignore the steps which do not apply.

Removal

1 Remove the lower fairing and the fairing side panels (see Chapter 7). Drain the engine oil (see Chapter 1). Remove the clutch (see Section 13).

2 Make sure the transmission is in neutral.

14.11b Ensure the circlip is properly seated

14.15a Install the alternator rotor . . .

14.15b . . . and secure it with the washer and bolt

14.17a Locate a new gasket on the dowels and refit the cover

14.17b Tighten the screws in a criss cross sequence to the specified torque

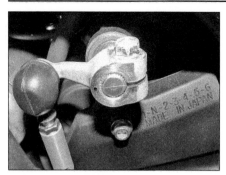

15.2a Note the alignment marks before ...

15.2b ... removing the arm

15.3a Remove the E-clip ...

15.3b ... and the washer

15.5a Unhook the spring

15.5b Collect the washer

Note the alignment mark for the linkage arm on the gearchange shaft **(see illustration)**. Unscrew the pinch bolt and slide the linkage arm off the shaft. Position the linkage arm and linkage out of the way **(see illustration)**. If required, the linkage can be removed by loosening the locknut at the gearchange lever and unscrewing it from the joint. Note the number of turns required to preserve the correct adjustment on re-fitting.

3 Release the E-clip and remove the washer from the shaft **(see illustrations)**.

4 On the right-hand side, stuff some clean lint-free rag into the bottom of the crankcase to prevent anything falling into the sump.

5 Note how the gearchange shaft centralising spring ends fit on each side of the locating pin, the pawls on the selector arm locate onto the pins on the end of the selector drum, and the stopper arm locates in the neutral detent on the selector drum. Release the stopper arm spring from its anchor pin **(see illustration)** and withdraw the gearchange shaft assembly. Ensure the washer is on the inner end of the shaft as you remove the assembly – it may stick to the crankcase wall **(see illustration)**.

6 If necessary, slide the washer off the shaft and remove the circlip **(see illustration)**, followed by the thrust washer, stopper arm, stepped collar and the centralising spring.

Inspection

7 Inspect the splines on the gearchange shaft and check that the shaft is straight; if the splines are worn or damaged, or if the shaft is bent, replace it with a new one. Check the shaft selector arm for cracks, distortion and wear of its pawls **(see illustration 15.6)**, and check for any corresponding wear on the selector pins on the selector drum **(see illustration)**.

15.6 Inspect the pawls (A), circlip (B), return spring (C), and detent roller (D)

15.7 Inspect the pins (arrowed) for wear

15.10a Pry out the seal . . .

15.10b . . . use an extractor to remove the left-hand . . .

15.10c . . . and right hand bearings

8 Check the stopper arm roller **(see illustration 15.6)** and the detents in the selector drum for any wear or damage, and make sure the roller turns freely. Make sure the arm is not bent. Check the stopper arm spring for signs of wear or damage.

9 Inspect the centralising spring, the pawl spring and the stopper arm return spring for fatigue, wear or damage. If any faults are found, replace the components with new ones.

10 Check the condition of the gearchange shaft oil seal and bearings in the crankcase. If the oil seal is damaged, deteriorated or shows signs of leakage it must be replaced with a new one. Lever out the old seal with a flat-bladed screwdriver **(see illustration)**. If the bearings are damaged or do not run smoothly and freely, they must be replaced with new ones (see Section 5 of *Tools and Workshop Tips* in the *Reference* section) **(see illustrations)**. Press or drive the new seal squarely into place with the marked side facing out using your fingers, a suitable socket or a seal driver **(see illustration)**.

Installation

11 If it has been removed stuff some clean and lint-free rag into the bottom of the

crankcase to prevent anything falling into the sump.

12 Fit the centralising spring onto the gearchange shaft with the straight leg outermost, and locate it on the stop on the gearchange shaft. Refit the shouldered collar, followed by the stopper arm. Ensure the stopper arm roller is facing in towards the selector drum. Fit the thrust washer and the circlip. Then fit the washer onto the shaft and attach the stopper arm spring to the stopper arm **(see illustration 15.6)**.

13 Use some lithium-based grease to lubricate the oil seal, and slide the gearchange shaft into place. Locate the ends of the centralising spring on each side of the pin and hook the stopper arm return spring onto its pin. Make sure the selector pawls are located correctly on the pins on the selector drum and that the stopper arm roller is located in the neutral detent **(see illustrations)**. Remove the rag.

14 Fit the washer and E-clip onto the left-hand end of the shaft **(see illustration 15.3b and a)**. If it was removed refit the linkage to the gear lever and slide the gearchange linkage arm on **(see illustration 15.2b and a)**, aligning the punch mark with the slit in the clamp, and tighten the bolt.

15.10d Fit a new seal

15 Install the clutch (see Section 13). Fill the engine with the correct type and amount of oil and check the level (see Chapter 1 and *Pre-ride checks*). Install the lower fairing and the fairing side panels (see Chapter 7).

16 Oil cooler

Note: *This procedure can be carried out with the engine in the frame. If the engine has been removed, ignore the steps that do not apply.*

15.13a Slide the gearchange shaft into place, having first set the transmission into neutral

15.13b Mesh the selector pawls with the drum pins and fit the spring ends over the pins (arrowed). Note the use of a screwdriver to engage the stopper arm roller in the neutral detent on the cam

16.3a Disconnect the feed hose from the cooler . . .

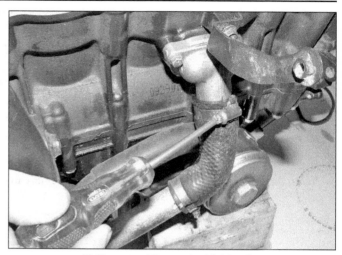

16.3b . . . and the coolant inlet union

 Warning: Allow the engine to cool completely before starting work.

Removal

1 The cooler is located on the front of the engine. Drain the engine oil and the coolant (see Chapter 1). Leave a drain tray under the cooler to catch residual oil and coolant as the cooler is removed.
2 Remove the exhaust system (see Chapter 4).
3 Release the clamp securing the hose to the bottom union on the oil cooler **(see illustration)** and the clip securing the hose

16.4a Disconnect the return hose from the cooler

16.4c . . . noting how it locates (arrowed)

to the coolant inlet union **(see illustration)** detach them both.
4 Release the clamp securing the return hose to the top union and detach it **(see illustration)**. Unscrew the oil cooler bolt and remove the washer **(see illustration)**. Note how the tab on the cooler body locates between the lugs on the crankcase **(see illustration)**.
5 Remove the O-ring from the cooler body **(see illustration)**. Discard the O-ring and the washer as new ones must be fitted on reassembly.
6 Check the cooler body for cracks and dents and any evidence of coolant leakage and

16.4b Unscrew the bolt and remove the cooler . . .

16.5 Remove the O-ring

replace it with a new one if necessary. Also check the hoses for splits, cracks, hardening and deterioration and fit new ones if required.

Installation

7 Installation is the reverse of removal, noting the following:
● Clean the mating surfaces of the crankcase and the cooler with a rag and solvent.
● Before reassembly, lubricate the new O-ring with clean engine oil and ensure it seats correctly on the cooler body **(see illustration 16.5)**.
● Use a new washer on the bolt and lubricate its threads, and tighten it to the torque setting specified at the beginning of this Chapter **(see illustration 16.4b)**.
● Make sure the coolant hoses are pressed fully onto their unions and tighten the clips securely.
● Refill the engine with oil and refill the cooling system, both to the correct levels (see Chapter 1 and Pre-ride checks).
● Start the engine and check that there are no leaks before taking the machine on the road.

17 Oil sump, strainer and pressure relief valve

Note: *This procedure can be carried out with the engine in the frame. If the engine has been removed, ignore the steps which do not apply.*

 Warning: Allow the engine to cool completely before starting work.

Removal

1 Drain the engine oil (see Chapter 1). Remove the exhaust system (see Chapter 4).
2 Raise or remove the fuel tank. Trace the wire from the oil level sensor underneath the sump and disconnect it at the connector **(see illustration 4.13a)**. Feed the wire through to

17.3a Do not overlook the bolt in the middle of the sump

17.3b Remove the sump and the gasket

17.4a Pull the strainer out of its socket

the underside of the engine, noting its routing and releasing it from any ties.

3 Unscrew the sump bolts (13 in all) ensuring that the one towards the middle of the sump is not overlooked **(see illustration)**, slackening them evenly in a criss-cross sequence to prevent distortion, and remove the sump **(see illustration)**. **Note:** *Do not unscrew the two bolts retaining the oil level sensor.* If necessary, break the gasket seal by tapping gently around the edge of the sump with a soft-faced hammer or block of wood; do not lever the sump off as this will damage the sealing surface. Note the position of the oil level sensor wiring clamp and bottom fairing brackets. Discard the gasket, as a new one must be used.

4 Pull the oil strainer out of its socket in the oil pump **(see illustration)**. Remove the seal and discard it as a new one must be used **(see illustration 17.9b)**. Pull the pressure relief valve out of the crankcase **(see illustration)**.

Remove the O-ring and discard it as a new one must be used.

Inspection

5 Remove all traces of gasket from the sump and crankcase mating surfaces, and clean the inside of the sump with a suitable solvent. Do not remove the oil level sensor unless it is necessary for testing the unit (see Chapter 8).
6 Clean the strainer in solvent, flushing it through from the inside, and remove any debris caught in the strainer mesh. Inspect the mesh for any signs of wear or damage and replace the strainer with a new one if necessary.
7 Push the relief valve plunger into the valve body and check that it moves smoothly and freely against spring pressure. If not, remove the circlip, noting that it is under spring pressure, and remove the spring seat, spring and plunger **(see illustration)**. Clean all the components in solvent and check them for scoring, wear or damage. If any is found,

replace the relief valve with a new one – individual components are not available. Otherwise, coat the inside of the valve body and the plunger with clean engine oil, then insert the plunger, spring and spring seat and secure them with the circlip. Check the action of the valve plunger again – if it is still suspect, replace the valve with a new one.

Installation

8 Lubricate the new seal for the oil strainer with grease and fit it onto the strainer **(see illustration)**. Fit the strainer onto the pump **(see illustration)**.
9 Fit a new O-ring onto the relief valve and smear it with grease **(see illustration)**. Push the valve into its socket in the crankcase **(see illustration 17.4b)**.
10 Lay a new gasket onto the sump (if the engine is in the frame) or onto the crankcase (if the engine has been removed and is upside down on the work surface) **(see illustration)**.

17.4b Pull the relief valve from the crankcase

17.7 Inspect the relief valve components

17.8a Fit a new seal to the strainer

17.8b Note how it locates in the oil pump

17.9 Fit a new O-ring to the relief valve

17.10 Fit a new sump gasket

17.11a Refit the sump noting where . . .

17.11b . . . the brackets for the fairing . . .

17.11c . . . and the cable clamp are positioned

17.11d Locate the oil level sender wires before tightening the clamp.

18.4a Unscrew the bolts . . .

18.4b . . . and pull out the U-shaped oil pipe

Make sure the holes in the gasket align correctly with the bolt holes.

11 Position the sump on the crankcase (see illustration). Install the bolts, not forgetting the oil level sensor wiring clamp and bottom fairing brackets (see illustrations). Tighten all bolts evenly and a little at a time in a criss-cross pattern to the specified torque setting (see illustration 17.3).

12 Connect the oil level sensor wire at the connector (see illustration 4.13a).

13 Install the exhaust system and the fuel tank (see Chapter 4).

14 Fill the engine with the correct type and quantity of oil (see Chapter 1 and *Pre-ride checks*).

15 Start the engine and check that there are no leaks around the sump before taking the machine on the road.

18 Oil pump

Note: *This procedure can be carried out with the engine in the frame. If the engine has been removed, ignore the steps which do not apply.*

 Warning: Allow the engine to cool completely before starting work.

Removal

1 Drain the engine oil and coolant (see Chapter 1).

2 Remove the sump and the oil strainer (see Section 17). If the engine is upside down on the bench, from here on take care not to drop any bolts as you remove them.

3 Remove the water pump (see Chapter 3). Remove the clutch (see Section 13).

4 Unscrew the Allen bolts retaining the U-shaped oil pipe and pull it out of its sockets (see illustrations). Discard the O-rings as new ones must be fitted on reassembly. Unscrew the bolt retaining the oil drain pipe and pull out the pipe (see illustrations).

18.4c Unscrew the bolt (arrowed) . . .

18.4d . . . and pull out the oil drain pipe

18.5a Note the rearmost bolt screws into the upper crankcase . . .

18.5b . . . and is longer than the foremost one

18.5c Collect the dowels if they are loose

18.7 Note the pins that locate the cover

18.8a Remove the rotors . . .

18.8b . . . noting how they fit

5 Unscrew and remove the bolts securing the oil pump and remove it, noting that the longer rearmost bolt screws into the upper crankcase and holds the crankcases together **(see illustrations)** and the position of the two locating dowels **(see illustration)**.

Inspection

6 Turn the oil pump sprocket and check for a tight or rough feeling. If any is found, disassemble and inspect the pump.
7 Unscrew the bolts securing the cover to the pump body and remove the cover, noting the position of the two locating pins **(see illustration)**.
8 Remove the outer and inner rotors, noting

how they fit **(see illustrations)**. It's a good idea to mark the outer face of each rotor with a felt-tipped marker pin so that the rotors can be fitted the same way round as before.
9 Withdraw the drive pin from the shaft, noting how it locates in the slots in the inner rotor **(see illustration)** and remove the drive sprocket and shaft **(see illustration)**.
10 Clean all components in solvent. Check that the oilways in the pump and the external pipes are clear by blowing them through with compressed air.
11 Inspect the components for scoring and wear. If any damage, scoring or uneven or excessive wear is evident, replace the relevant components with new ones – the rotors come

as a matched pair. Check the bearing in the pump housing and replace it with a new one if necessary.
12 Fit the outer rotor into the pump body and measure the clearance between them with a feeler gauge **(see illustration)**. Compare it to the maximum clearance listed in the specifications at the beginning of this Chapter. If the clearance measured is greater than the maximum listed, replace the rotors with a new pair.
13 Fit both rotors onto the shaft. Measure the clearance between the inner rotor tip and the outer rotor with a feeler gauge and compare it to the maximum clearance listed in the specifications at the beginning of the Chapter

18.9a Remove the inner rotor drive pin . . .

18.9b . . . and pull out the shaft

18.12 Check for wear between the outer rotor and the body . . .

18.13a . . . and between the rotors

18.13b **Check the clearance between the rotors and the cover**

18.15 **Refit the cover and tighten the bolts**

18.16 **Prime the pump with clean oil**

(see illustration). If the clearance measured is greater than the maximum listed, replace the rotors with a new pair. Place a straight-edge across the pump housing and measure the clearance between it and the rotors **(see illustration)** and compare it to the clearance listed in the specifications in the beginning of this Chapter. If the clearance measured is greater than the maximum listed, replace the pump.

14 Check the pump drive and driven sprockets and the chain for wear or damage, and replace them with new ones if necessary.

15 If the pump is good, make sure all the components are clean, then lubricate them

with clean engine oil. Fit the drive pin into the pump shaft **(see illustration 18.9a)**. Slide the outer and inner rotors onto the shaft, making sure that the slots in the inner rotor locate over the drive pin **(see illustrations 18.8b and a)**. Fit the locating pins **(see illustration 18.5c)**. Fit the cover, install the bolts and tighten them to the specified torque setting **(see illustration)**.

Installation

16 Before installing the pump, prime it with clean engine oil **(see illustration)**.

17 Install the pump, making sure the dowels are in place. Refit the oil drain pipe. Tighten the

bolts to the torque specified in the beginning of this Chapter.

18 Fit new O-rings smeared with grease to the U-shaped oil pipe and fit the pipe **(see illustration)**. Apply a suitable non permanent thread locking compound to the bolts **(see illustration)** and tighten them to the torque specified at the beginning of this Chapter.

19 Refit the clutch and the oil pump drive chain.

20 Install the water pump (see Chapter 3)

21 Install the oil strainer and the sump (see Section 17).

22 Fill the engine with the specified quantity and type of engine oil and coolant (see Chapter 1 and *Pre-ride checks*).

19 Crankcase separation and reassembly

Note: *To separate the crankcase halves, the engine must be removed from the frame.*

Separation

1 To gain access to the connecting rods, pistons and rings, crankshaft, bearings, transmission shafts and selector drum and forks, the crankcase must be split into two parts.

2 Remove the engine from the frame (see Section 4). **Note:** *To reduce the weight of the engine, where possible remove as many of the components listed below before removing the engine from the frame.*

3 If a full engine strip is being carried out remove all the following components. If you are only removing the crankshaft the cylinder head can remain in place, but the camshafts and cam chain must be removed. If you are only removing the transmission shafts and/ or selector drum and forks the top-end can remain intact. It is necessary to remove the clutch, oil sump and oil and water pumps whatever your procedure, and it is best to

18.18a **Refit the U-shaped oil pipe . . .**

18.18b **. . . and use a suitable thread locking compound on the screws**

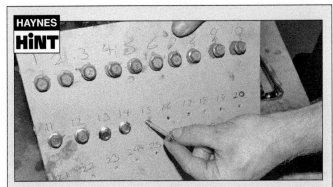

HAYNES HINT

Make a cardboard template of the crankcase and punch a hole for each bolt location. Number the holes according to the cast numbers in the crankcase. As each bolt is removed, store it in its relative position, with its washer where applicable, in the template. This will ensure all bolts are installed correctly on reassembly – this is important, as many bolts differ slightly in length.

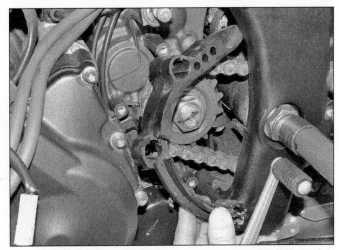

19.4 Ensure the final drive chain guide is removed

remove the alternator/starter clutch, and the starter motor. Remove the gearchange mechanism if the selector drum is being removed.

Camshafts and cam chain tensioner (Sections 7 and 8).
Cylinder head (Section 10).
Alternator rotor/starter clutch (Section 14).
Starter motor (Chapter 8).
Cam chain, tensioner blade and guide (Section 9).
Clutch (Section 13).
Gearchange mechanism (Section 15).
Oil cooler (Section 16) and filter (Chapter 1).
Oil sump, strainer and pressure relief valve (Section 17).
Water pump, oil pump and their drive chain (Chapter 3 and Section 18).
Crankshaft position (CKP) sensor (Chapter 4).

4 Ensure the final drive guide is removed **(see illustration)**.

5 Turn the engine upside down, taking care not to place undue strain on the cylinder head studs – use wood blocks to support the crankcase where necessary. The crankcases are joined by ten 8 mm crankshaft journal bolts (Nos. 1 to 10), two further 8 mm bolts (Nos. 11 and 12) and 17 (16 on early 2006 models) 6 mm bolts (Nos. 13 to 28 or 29 dependent on the model). Unscrew the bolts a quarter turn at

Bolts 1 to 7 – M8 x 85 mm
Bolts 8 and 9 – M8 x 115 mm
Bolt 10 – M8 x 85 mm
Bolts 11 and 12 – M8 x 65 mm
Bolts 13 and 14 – M6 x 65 mm
Bolt 15 – M6 x 55 mm
Bolt 16 – M6 x 65 mm
Bolts 17, 18 and 19 – M6 x 45 mm
Bolts 20 and 21 – M6 x 65 mm
Bolts 22 to 27 – M6 x 55 mm
Bolt 28 – M6 x 80 mm
Bolt 29 – M6 x 30 mm (except early 2006 model)

H48579

19.5a Crankcase bolt numbers indicate tightening sequence and are cast into the casing

a time in a reverse of the numerical sequence shown **(see illustrations)** and as marked on the crankcase (i.e. 10 down to 1), until they are finger-tight, then remove them and store them in the template to ensure correct installation (see *Haynes Hint*). Note the washers fitted to bolt Nos. 1 to 12 and that bolt Nos. 13 and 14 are shouldered **(see illustration)** and that bolt

number 28 is the rearmost bolt that secures the oil pump.

6 Carefully lift the lower crankcase half off the upper half, using a soft-faced hammer or block of wood to tap around the joint to initially separate the halves, if necessary **(see illustration)**. **Note:** *If the halves do not separate easily, make sure all fasteners*

19.5b Numbers cast into the crankcase indicate the bolt tightening sequence

19.5c Note the position of the shouldered bolts

19.6 Separate the crankcase halves

19.7a Note the position . . .

19.7b . . . of the three dowels . . .

19.7c . . . and collect them if they are loose

have been removed. *Do not try and separate the halves by levering between the sealing surfaces as they are easily damaged and will leak oil on reassembly.*

7 Remove the three locating dowels from the crankcase (they could be in either half) **(see illustrations)**.

8 Refer to Sections 20 to 28 for the removal and installation of the components housed within the crankcases.

Reassembly

9 Remove all traces of sealant from the crankcase mating surfaces.

10 Ensure that all components and their bearings are in place in the upper and lower crankcase halves. If the transmission shafts have not been removed, check the condition of the oil seal on the left-hand end of the output shaft and replace it with a new one if it is damaged, deformed or deteriorated – it is wise to fit a new seal whatever the perceived condition of the existing one (you wouldn't want to discover a leak after the engine has been rebuilt and put back in the frame) **(see illustration 25.3)**. Apply some grease to the inside of the new seal on installation. Check that the selector drum is in the neutral position.

11 Generously lubricate the crankshaft, transmission shafts and selector drum and forks, particularly around the bearings, with clean engine oil, then use a rag soaked in high flash-point solvent to wipe over the mating surfaces of both crankcase halves to remove all traces of oil.

12 Apply a small amount of suitable sealant (such as Yamaha Bond 1215) to the mating surface of one crankcase half in the areas shown **(see illustrations)**.

Caution: Do not apply an excessive amount of sealant as it will ooze out when the case halves are assembled and may obstruct oil passages. Do not apply the sealant on or too close (within 2 to 3 mm) to any of the bearing shells or surfaces.

13 Fit the three locating dowels into the crankcase **(see illustration 19.7a, b and c)**.

14 Check again that all components are in position, particularly that the bearing shells are located in their seats in the lower crankcase half, then fit the lower crankcase half onto the upper crankcase half, making sure the dowels locate correctly **(see illustration 19.6)**.

15 Check that the lower crankcase half is seated correctly. **Note:** *The crankcase halves should fit together without being forced. If the casings are not correctly seated, remove the lower crankcase half and investigate the problem. Do not attempt to pull them together using the crankcase bolts as the casing will crack and be ruined.* Rotate the transmission output shaft and turn the selector drum to ensure that the gears select correctly and investigate any problems before bolting the crankcase halves together.

16 Clean the threads of the crankcase bolts. Lubricate the underside of the heads and the washers of bolts 1 to 10, and the threads of all bolts with clean engine oil **(see illustration 19.5a)**.

17 Install the bolts in their correct locations and secure them finger-tight. Proceed according to model year:

2006 and 2007 models

First tighten the 8 mm bolts (Nos. 1 to 10) in the correct numerical sequence as cast into the crankcase (see illustration 19.5a) to the initial torque setting specified at the beginning of the Chapter. Now reverse the sequence (i.e. 10 down to 1) and loosen the bolts. Now tighten them in the correct sequence (1 to 10) to the secondary torque setting. Finally, reverse the sequence again and loosen the bolts, then tighten them in the correct sequence (1 to 10) to the final torque setting.

Next tighten the two 8 mm bolts (Nos. 11 and 12), followed by all 6 mm bolts to the specified torque settings. Again follow the numbers cast into the casing for tightening order.

2008-on models

First tighten the 8 mm bolts (Nos. 1 to 10) in the correct numerical sequence as cast into the crankcase (see illustration 19.5a) to the initial torque setting specified at the beginning of the Chapter. Now reverse the sequence (i.e. 10 down to 1) and loosen the bolts. Now tighten them in the correct sequence (1 to 10) to the secondary torque setting, then through the specified angle according to bolt number.

Next tighten the two 8 mm bolts (Nos. 11 and 12), followed by all 6 mm bolts to the specified torque settings. Again follow the numbers cast into the casing for tightening order.

18 With all crankcase bolts tightened, check that the crankshaft and transmission shafts rotate smoothly and easily. Check that all gears can be selected and that the shafts rotate freely in every gear. If there are any signs of undue stiffness, rough spots, or of any other problem, the fault must be rectified before proceeding further.

19 Install all the removed assemblies in the reverse order of removal, according to your procedure (see Step 3).

19.12a Apply a suitable sealant . . .

19.12b . . . only where arrowed

20 Main and big-end bearing information

1 Even though main and connecting rod bearings are generally replaced with new ones during an engine overhaul, the old bearings should be carefully examined as they can reveal valuable information about the condition of the engine.

2 Bearing failure occurs mainly because of lack of lubrication, the presence of dirt or other foreign particles, overloading the engine and/or corrosion. Regardless of the cause of bearing failure, it must be corrected before the engine is reassembled to prevent it from happening again.

3 When examining the bearings, match them with their corresponding journal on the crankshaft to help identify the cause of any problem.

4 Dirt and other foreign particles get into the engine in a variety of ways. They may be left in the engine during assembly or they may pass through filters or breathers, then get into the oil and from there into the bearings. Metal chips from machining operations and normal engine wear are often present. Abrasives are sometimes left in engine components after reconditioning operations, especially when parts are not thoroughly cleaned using the proper cleaning methods. Whatever the source, foreign objects often end up imbedded in the soft bearing material and are easily recognised. Large particles will not imbed in the bearing and will score or gouge the bearing and journal. The best prevention for this type of bearing failure is to clean all parts thoroughly and keep everything spotlessly clean during engine reassembly. Regular oil and filter changes are also essential.

5 Lack of lubrication or lubrication breakdown have a number of interrelated causes. Excessive heat (which thins the oil), overloading (which squeezes the oil from the bearing face) and oil leakage or throw off (from excessive bearing clearances, a worn oil pump or high engine speeds) all contribute to a breakdown of the protective lubricating film. Blocked oil passages will starve a bearing of lubrication and destroy it. When lack of lubrication is the cause of bearing failure, the bearing material is wiped or extruded from the steel backing of the bearing. Temperatures may increase to the point where the steel backing and the journal turn blue from overheating.

HAYNES HINT *Refer to Tools and Workshop Tips (Section 5) in the Reference section for bearing fault finding.*

6 Riding habits can have a definite effect on bearing life. Full throttle, low speed operation, or labouring the engine, puts very high loads on bearings, which tend to squeeze out the oil film.

These loads cause the bearings to flex, which produces fine cracks in the bearing face (fatigue failure). Eventually the bearing material will loosen in pieces and tear away from the steel backing. Short trip riding leads to corrosion of bearings, as insufficient engine heat is produced to drive off the condensed water and corrosive gases produced. These products collect in the engine oil, forming acid and sludge. As the oil is carried to the engine bearings, the acid attacks and corrodes the bearing material.

7 Incorrect bearing installation during engine assembly will lead to bearing failure as well. Tight fitting bearings which leave insufficient bearing oil clearances result in oil starvation. Dirt or foreign particles trapped behind a bearing shell result in high spots on the bearing which lead to failure.

8 To avoid bearing problems, clean all parts thoroughly before reassembly, double check all bearing clearance measurements and lubricate the new bearings with clean engine oil during installation.

21 Connecting rod assemblies and cylinder block

Note: *To remove the connecting rod assemblies and cylinder block the engine must be removed from the frame and the crankcases separated. On installation new rod bolts must be used, so it is wise to obtain them before commencing work.*

Removal

1 Remove the engine from the frame (see Section 4) and separate the crankcase halves (see Section 19).

2 Before separating the rods from the crankshaft, measure the big-end side clearance on each rod with a feeler gauge **(see illustration)**. If the clearance on any rod is greater than the service limit listed in this Chapter's Specifications, replace that rod with a new one.

3 Using paint or a marker pen, mark the cylinder identity on the top of each piston and on each connecting rod and cap. Cylinders are numbered 1 to 4 from the left-hand side of the motorcycle (as seated).

4 Unscrew the connecting rod cap nuts and separate the caps, complete with the lower bearing shells from the crankpins **(see illustrations)**. If a cap appears stuck, tap it on one end with a hammer while pulling it. Note the identification marks printed on the cap and rod.

5 Detach the connecting rods, complete with the upper bearing shells, from the crankpins and push the pistons up to the top (but not out) of the bores, then rest each rod against the bottom of its bore. Lift the crankshaft out of the upper crankcase half, taking care not to dislodge the main bearing shells **(see illustration 24.2)**. If required, remove the main bearing shells from the crankcase halves by pushing their centres to the side, then lifting them out **(see illustration 24.3)** – it is imperative that the shells are kept in order so that they can be returned to their original locations.

6 Remove the transmission output shaft (see Section 25).

7 Turn the engine on its side **(see illustration)**.

21.2 Measure the side clearance

21.4a Unscrew the nuts . . .

21.4b . . . and separate the caps

21.7 Remove the piston and connecting rod

21.12a Check the small-end for wear . . .

21.12b . . . and measure the diameter of the piston pin

8 If required push each piston/connecting rod assembly to the top end of its cylinder bore and remove it, making sure the connecting rod does not mark the bore walls **(see illustration 21.7)**. Note the 'Y' mark on each connecting rod that must face to the left-hand side of the engine, and the punch mark on the top of each piston which points to the front of the engine **(see illustration 22.15a)**. If this is not visible, mark the piston accordingly so that it can be installed the correct way round.

 HAYNES HiNT *To ease removal of the pistons, carefully remove any ridge of carbon built up on the top of each cylinder bore using a scraper. If there is a pronounced wear ridge, remove it using a ridge reamer.*

9 Fit the related bearing shells (if removed), bearing cap, and bolts/nuts on each piston/connecting rod assembly so that they are all kept together as a matched set. **Note:** *New big-end bolts and nuts must be used on final assembly, but do not discard the old ones yet as they are still needed.*
10 If required separate the pistons from the connecting rods (see Section 22).

Connecting rods

11 Check the connecting rods for cracks and other obvious damage.
12 Apply clean engine oil to the piston pin, insert it into its connecting rod small-end and

check for any freeplay between the two **(see illustration)**. If freeplay is excessive, measure the external diameter at the centre of the pin **(see illustration)**. Compare the result to the specifications at the beginning of this Chapter. Replace the pin with a new one if it is worn beyond its specified limits. If the pin diameter is within specifications, replace the connecting rod with a new one. Repeat the measurements for all the pins and rods.
13 Refer to Section 20 and examine the connecting rod bearing shells. If they are scored, badly scuffed or appear to have seized, new shells must be installed. Always renew the shells in the connecting rods as a set. If they are badly damaged, check the corresponding crankpin. Evidence of extreme heat, such as bluing, indicates that lubrication failure has occurred. Be sure to thoroughly check the oil pump and pressure relief valve as well as all oil holes and passages before reassembling the engine.
14 Have the rods checked by a Yamaha dealer if you are in doubt about their straightness.

Oil clearance check

Note: *It is essential that, throughout this procedure, the connecting rod does not rotate on the crankshaft. If the procedure is being carried out on a bench find some way of clamping the crankshaft so it cannot move, and also the connecting rod once it has been fitted onto its journal. The alternative is to assemble the cylinder block, rod and piston and lay the crankshaft in the crankcase to keep them held.*

15 Whether new bearing shells are being fitted or the original ones are being re-used, the connecting rod big-end bearing oil clearance should be checked prior to reassembly. Bearing oil clearance is measured with a product known as Plastigauge.
16 Remove the bearing shells from the rods and caps, keeping them in order **(see illustration)**. Clean the backs of the shells, the bearing locations in both the connecting rod and cap, and the crankpin journal with a suitable solvent.
17 Press the bearing shells into their locations, ensuring that the tab on each shell engages the notch in the connecting rod or cap and that the shell ends are flush with the rod and cap mating surfaces **(see illustration)**. Make sure the bearings are fitted in the correct locations and take care not to touch any shell's bearing surface with your fingers. Fit the caps onto the rods, making sure the cap is fitted the correct way around so the previously made markings align **(see illustration 21.35)**. Using the old connecting rod bolts and nuts, tighten the nuts first to the initial torque setting for bearing seating specified at the beginning of the Chapter, then through the specified angle – this ensures the bearings are correctly aligned and seated. Now unscrew the nuts and separate the caps from the rods.
18 Working on one rod at a time, cut an appropriate size length of Plastigauge (it should be slightly shorter than the width of the crankpin) and place it on the crankpin journal to be checked **(see illustration 24.12)**. Do not place Plastigauge over the oil holes in the journal.
19 Apply molybdenum disulphide grease to the flanged surface of the old nuts. Fit the connecting rod and cap onto the crankpin. Make sure the cap is fitted the correct way around so the previously made markings align (see Step 3), and that the 'Y' mark on the rod is facing to the left-hand end of the crankshaft (see Step 8) **(see illustration 22.15a)**. Fit the nuts and tighten them finger-tight. **Note:** *It is essential that, throughout this procedure, the connecting rod does not rotate on the crankshaft.*
20 Tighten the nuts to the initial torque setting for the oil clearance check specified at the beginning of this Chapter with a torque wrench, then through the specified angle **(see illustration 21.40a)**. Check that the side faces and thrust faces on the rods and caps are perfectly flush at the joints.
21 Slacken the nuts and remove the cap and rod from the crankshaft.
22 Compare the width of the crushed Plastigauge on the crankpin to the scale printed on the Plastigauge envelope to obtain the connecting rod bearing oil clearance **(see illustration 24.16)**. Compare the reading to the specifications at the beginning of this Chapter. If the clearance is within the range specified and the bearings are in perfect condition, they can be reused.

21.16 To remove a big-end bearing shell, push it sideways and then lift it out

21.17 Ensure tab (A) locates in notch (B)

21.27a Big-end bearing codes (A) and main bearing codes (B)

21.27b Connecting rod bearing housing size code (arrowed)

21.28 The colour code (arrowed) is on the side of the shell

23 Carefully clean away all traces of the Plastigauge from the crankpin journal and bearing shells using a fingernail or other object which will not score the bearing surfaces.

24 If the clearance is beyond the service limit, replace the bearing shells with new ones (see Steps 27 and 28) and check the oil clearance once again. Always renew all of the shells at the same time.

25 If the clearance is still greater than the service limit listed in this Chapter's Specifications, the big-end bearing journal is worn and the crankshaft should be replaced with a new one.

26 Repeat the procedure for the remaining connecting rods.

Bearing shell selection

27 Replacement bearing shells for the big-end bearings are supplied on a selected fit basis. Code numbers for the crankshaft journals are stamped on the outside of the crankshaft web on the left-hand end of the crankshaft (see illustration). The right-hand block of four numbers are the size codes for the big-end bearing journals (the left-hand block of five numbers are the size codes for the main bearing journals). The first number of the block is for the left-hand (No. 1 cylinder) journal, and so on. Each connecting rod size code number is marked in ink on the

flat face of the connecting rod and cap (see illustration).

28 A range of bearing shells are available. To select the correct shells for a particular journal, subtract the big-end bearing journal number from the connecting rod number and compare the result with the table below to find the colour coding of the replacement shells, e.g. connecting rod number 5 minus journal number 1 = 4; No. 4 bearing shells are colour-coded green. The colour code is marked on the side of each bearing shell (see illustration).

Number	Colour
1	blue
2	black
3	brown
4	green

Cylinder bores

29 Check the cylinder walls carefully for scratches and score marks. Note that damage to the plated cylinder walls is unlikely.

30 Using telescoping gauges and a micrometer (see Tools and Workshop Tips), check the dimensions of each cylinder to assess the amount of wear, taper and ovality (see illustration). Measure near the top (but below the level of the top piston ring at TDC), the centre and bottom (but above the level of

the oil ring at BDC) of the bore. Measure both parallel to and across the crankshaft axis in each case and calculate the average cylinder dimension at each point (see illustration). Compare the results to the specifications at the beginning of this Chapter.

31 If the precision measuring tools are not available, take the cylinder block to a Yamaha dealer or specialist motorcycle engineer for assessment and advice.

32 If the cylinders are worn beyond the service limit, or badly scratched, scuffed or scored, it may be possible to re-bore them to accept an after-market "big bore" piston kit, if not replace the crankcases with a new set. If new crankcases are used, new pistons and rings must be used.

Installation

Note: New big-end bolts and nuts must be used on reassembly.

33 Clean all traces of old gasket material from the cylinder block and crankcase mating surfaces with a suitable solvent. If you need to use a scraper, take care not to scratch or gouge the soft aluminium. Be careful not to let any of the gasket material fall into the crankcase, the cylinder bores or the oil or coolant passages. Make sure the cylinder studs are tight.

21.30a Measure the cylinder bores using a telescoping bore gauge . . .

21.30b . . . measuring in the directions shown

21.35a Align the markings (arrowed)

21.35b Use a hammer to drive the old bolts out of the rods

21.35c Insert the new bolts . . .

21.35d . . . lining up the head profile with that of the rod casting

21.35e Tap the bolt into place over a pre-drilled hole in a wood block . . .

21.35f . . . until the bolt is fully home and its head fully located

 HAYNES HINT *Refer to Tools and Workshop Tips (Section 7) for details of gasket removal methods.*

34 Fit the pistons onto the connecting rods (see Section 22).
35 Ensure that the backs of the bearing shells, the bearing seats in the caps and rods and the crankpin journals are clean. If new shells are being fitted, ensure that all traces of protective grease are removed using paraffin (kerosene). Dry the shells, caps, rods and journals with a clean, lint-free cloth. Install the shells, making sure the tab on each shell engages the notch in the cap or rod **(see illustration 21.17)**. Make sure the bearings are fitted in their correct locations and take care not to touch any bearing surfaces with your fingers. Fit the caps onto the rods, making sure the cap is fitted the correct way around so the previously

made markings align (see Step 3) **(see illustration)**. Fit the old connecting rod bolts and nuts and tighten them first to the initial torque setting for bearing seating specified at the beginning of the Chapter, then to the final setting – this ensures the bearings are correctly aligned and seated. Now unscrew the nuts, remove the bolts and separate the caps from the rods; the old bolts will require knocking out of the rods **(see illustration)**. Fit the new bolts to the rods, noting that the splined section of their shanks makes them an interference fit **(see illustrations)**. Lubricate the shells with clean engine oil.
36 Make sure the piston ring end gaps are correctly spaced (see Section 23). Lubricate the pistons, rings and cylinder bores with clean engine oil. Support the upper crankcase on the lower one. Insert each piston/connecting rod assembly into its bore **(see illustration)**. Make sure the punch mark on the piston is to the

front and the 'Y' mark on the rod faces to the left-hand side of the engine (see Step 8) **(see illustration)**. Using a piston ring compressor fit each piston into its bore. Note the oil ring expanders can easily overlap making it difficult to fit the piston in. If this happens DO NOT FORCE IT – remove the piston from the compressor and reset them so their ends butt against each other and try again.
37 Turn the engine over. Lower the crankshaft into position in the upper crankcase, making sure all the main bearing shells are in place (see Section 24) **(see illustration 24.2)**.
38 Working on one connecting rod at a time, lubricate the crankpin and the shells in the connecting rod and cap with clean engine oil. Pull the rod onto the crankpin and fit the cap onto the rod **(see illustration and 21.4b)**. Make sure the cap is fitted the correct way around so the previously made markings align (see Step 3).

21.36a Fit the piston assembly into the bore . . .

21.36b . . . with the Y mark (arrowed) to the left of the engine

21.38 Lubricate the bearings with clean engine oil

21.39 Lubricate the threads, faces and the washer with molybdenum disulphide oil

21.40a Mark the shoulder of the nut and the connecting rod 180° apart (arrowed) . . .

21.40b . . . and tighten until the marks align

39 Apply molybdenum disulphide oil to the flanged faces of the **new** big-end nuts, then fit them and tighten them finger-tight **(see illustration)**. Check that all components have been returned to their original locations using the marks made on disassembly.

40 Tighten the nuts to the initial torque setting specified at the beginning of this Chapter with a torque wrench. Now tighten each nut in turn and in one continuous movement through the final angle setting specified using a torque angle gauge (degree disc). If a degree disc is not available, mark the rod and one corner of the nut. Mark the opposite corner of the nut and its flange so the mark can be seen with the socket in place. Tighten the bolt in one movement until the marks align, at which point the bolt has been tightened through the specified angle **(see illustrations)**. If tightening is paused during the final settings, or if the angle is exceeded, obtain new bolts and nuts and repeat the procedure – do not repeat using the same ones. Check that the side faces and thrust faces on the rods and caps are perfectly flush at the joints. Fit the remaining rods onto the crankshaft in the same way.

41 Check that the crankshaft rotates smoothly and freely. If there are any signs of roughness or tightness, detach the rods and recheck the assembly. Sometimes tapping the bottom of the connecting rod cap will relieve tightness.

42 Reassemble the crankcase halves (see Section 19).

22 Pistons

Note: *To remove the pistons the engine must be removed from the frame.*

Removal

1 Remove the engine from the frame (see Section 4), then separate the crankcase halves (see Section 19). Remove the piston/connecting rod assemblies (see Section 21).

2 Before removing the piston from the connecting rod, ensure it is marked with its cylinder identity. If the piston is going to be cleaned, scratch the identity lightly on the inside of the piston skirt. Each piston must be installed in its original cylinder on reassembly. Note the punch mark on the top of each piston that points to the front of the engine. If this is not visible, mark the piston accordingly so that it can be installed the correct way round.

3 Carefully prise out the circlips on each side of the piston pin using needle-nose pliers or a small flat-bladed screwdriver inserted into the notch **(see illustration)**. Check for burring around the circlip grooves and remove any with a very fine file or knife blade, then push the piston pin out to free the piston from the connecting rod **(see illustration)**. Discard the circlips as new ones must be used on reassembly. When the piston has been removed from the rod, keep the piston and its pin together so that related parts do not get mixed up.

22.3a Insert a screwdriver into the notch and pry out the circlip

22.3b Press out the pin

> **HAYNES HiNT** *If a piston pin is a tight fit in the piston, heat the piston using a hot air gun to expand the alloy sufficiently to release its grip on the pin. If the piston pin is particularly stubborn, extract it using a drawbolt tool as well as heat, but be careful to protect the piston's working surfaces.*

4 Using your thumbs or a piston ring removal and installation tool, carefully remove the rings from the pistons **(see illustrations 23.11, 10b and a, and 8c, b and a)**. Do not nick or gouge the pistons in the process. Note which way up each ring fits and in which groove, as they must be installed in their original positions if being re-used. The upper surface of the two top rings (compression rings) should have a manufacturer's mark or letter at one end – if the mark on each ring is different, note which mark is for the top ring and which is for the second **(see illustration 23.2)**.

5 Scrape all traces of carbon from the tops of the pistons. A hand-held wire brush or a piece of fine emery cloth can be used once most of the deposits have been scraped away. Do not, under any circumstances, use a wire brush mounted in a drill motor; the piston material is soft and is easily damaged.

6 Use a piston ring groove cleaning tool to remove any carbon deposits from the ring grooves. If a tool is not available, a piece broken off an old ring will do the job. Be very careful to remove only the carbon deposits. Do not remove any metal and do not nick or gouge the sides of the ring grooves.

7 Once the carbon has been removed, clean the pistons with a suitable solvent and dry them thoroughly. Make sure the oil return holes at the back of the oil ring groove are clear. If the identification mark previously applied to the piston is cleaned off, be sure to re-mark it correctly.

Inspection

8 Inspect each piston for cracks around the skirt, at the pin bosses and at the ring lands. Normal piston wear appears as even, vertical wear on the thrust surfaces of the piston and

22.10 Use a micrometer to measure the piston

22.11 Measure the piston ring side clearance with feeler gauges

22.12a Check the pin for freeplay in the piston

22.12b Measure the ends of the pin . . .

22.12c . . . and the bore in the piston to check for wear

pin, insert it partway into the piston and check for any freeplay between the two **(see illustration)**. Measure the pin external diameter at each end, and the pin bores in the piston **(see illustrations)**. Subtract the pin diameter from the bore diameter to obtain the clearance. If it is greater than the specified figure, check whether it is the bore or pin that is worn beyond its service limit and replace them with new ones as required. Check for excessive play between the pin and the connecting rod small-end (see Section 21).

Installation

13 Inspect and install the piston rings (see Section 23).

14 Install a **new** circlip into one side of the piston (never re-use old circlips), then lubricate the piston pin, the piston pin bore and the connecting rod small-end bore with clean engine oil. Ensure that the ends of the circlip are at least 3 mm from the notch in the piston **(see illustration 22.15c)**.

15 Line up the piston on its connecting rod so that the punch mark on the top of the piston will point to the front and the 'Y' mark on the rod will face the left-hand side of the engine when they are installed **(see illustration)**. Insert the piston pin from the side without the circlip **(see illustration)**. Secure the pin with the other **new** circlip. When installing the circlips, compress them only just enough to fit them in the piston, and make sure they are properly seated in their grooves with the open end at least 3 mm away from the removal notch **(see illustration)**.

slight looseness of the top ring in its groove. If the skirt is scored or scuffed, the engine may have been suffering from overheating and/or abnormal combustion, resulting in excessively high operating temperatures.

9 A hole in the top of the piston (only likely in extreme circumstances), or burned areas around the edge of the piston crown, indicate that pre-ignition or knocking under load have occurred. If you find evidence of any problems the cause must be corrected or the damage will occur again (see *Fault Finding* in the *Reference* section).

10 Check the piston-to-bore clearance by measuring the bore (see Section 21) and the piston diameter. Make sure each piston is matched to its correct cylinder. Measure the piston the specified distance up from the bottom of the skirt and at 90° to the piston pin axis **(see illustration)**. Subtract the piston diameter from the bore diameter to obtain the clearance. If it is

greater than the figure specified at the beginning of this Chapter, check whether it is the bore or piston that is worn beyond its service limit. If the bores are good, install new pistons and rings. If the bore plating is worn then take the crankcase to a specialist motorcycle engineer for assessment and advice; oversize pistons are not available from Yamaha.

11 Measure the piston ring-to-groove clearance by laying each compression ring in its groove and slipping a feeler gauge in beside it **(see illustration)**. Make sure you have the correct ring for the groove (see Step 4). Check the clearance at three or four locations around the groove. If the clearance is greater than specified, replace both the piston and rings with a new set. If new rings are being used, measure the clearance using the new rings. If the clearance is greater than that specified, the piston is worn and must be replaced with a new one.

12 Apply clean engine oil to the piston

22.15a Align the punch mark (A) and the Y mark (B) correctly . . .

22.15b . . . before fitting the pin

22.15c Position the ends of the clip at least 3mm from the notch

16 Install the piston/connecting rod assemblies and cylinder block (see Section 21).

23 Piston rings

1 It is good practice to fit new piston rings when an engine is being overhauled. Before installing the rings on the pistons, the ring end gaps must be checked with the rings installed in the cylinder.

Inspection

2 Lay out each piston with its new ring set so the rings will be matched with the same piston and cylinder during the measurement procedure and engine reassembly. The two compression rings have different profiles, the top ring is barrelled in section and the second ring is tapered with its top surface being denoted by the letter T near one end **(see illustration)**.
3 To measure the ring end gap, fit the ring into the top of the cylinder and square it up with the cylinder walls by pushing it in with the top of the piston. The ring should be about 5 mm below the top edge of the cylinder. Slip a feeler gauge between the ends of the ring and compare the measurement to the specifications at the beginning of this Chapter **(see illustration)**.
4 If the gap is larger or smaller than specified, double check to make sure that you have the correct rings before proceeding.
5 Excess end gap is not critical unless it exceeds the service limit. Check that the bore is not worn (see Section 21).
6 Repeat the procedure for each ring and each cylinder in turn. Note that the end gaps differ between the top, second and oil ring. When checking the oil ring, only the side-rails can be checked as the ends of the expander ring should contact each other. Remember to keep the rings together with their matched pistons and cylinders.

23.2 Note the markings on the piston rings

Installation

7 Once the ring end gaps have been checked and corrected as necessary, the rings can be installed on the pistons.
8 Fit the oil control ring (lowest on the piston) first. It is composed of three separate components, namely the expander and the upper and lower side rails. Slip the expander into the ring groove, making sure the ends touch but do not overlap **(see illustration)**. Now fit the lower side rail **(see illustration)**. Do not use a piston ring installation tool on the oil ring side rails as they may be damaged. Instead, place one end of the side rail into the groove between the expander and the ring land. Hold it firmly in place and slide a finger around the piston while pushing the rail into

23.3 Measure the piston ring gap with a feeler gauge

the groove. Next, fit the upper side rail in the same manner **(see illustration)**.
9 After the three oil ring components have been installed, check to make sure that both the upper and lower side rails can be turned smoothly in the ring groove.
10 The upper surface of the second compression ring should have a T mark which must face up when the ring is installed on the piston (see Step 2). Fit the second ring into the middle groove in the piston. Do not expand the ring any more than is necessary to slide it into place **(see illustration)**. To avoid breaking the ring, use a piston ring installation tool, or pieces of old feeler gauge blades **(see illustration)**.
11 Finally, fit the top ring in the same manner into the top groove in the piston **(see**

23.8a First fit the oil control expander ring . . .

23.8b . . . followed by the lower side rail . . .

23.8c . . . and then the upper rail noting the position of the gaps

23.10a Carefully feed the second ring into its groove

23.10b Old pieces of feeler gauge blade can be used to guide the ring over the piston

23.11 Installing the top ring

23.12 Ensure that each ring has its end gap correctly positioned

A *Second ring end gap and lower oil ring side rail end gap*
B *Upper oil ring side rail end gap*
C *Top ring end gap and oil ring expander join*

24.2 Lift out the crankshaft

illustration). Note that the top ring is barrelled in section.

12 Once the rings are correctly installed, check they move freely without snagging and stagger their end gaps as follows **(see illustration)**. With the punch mark at the front of the piston between positions A and B, the lower oil ring side rail gap should be at position A. The ends of the oil ring expander should be at position C. The upper oil ring side rail should be at position B. The second ring gap should be at position A, and the top ring gap should be at position C.

24 Crankshaft and main bearings

Note: *To remove the crankshaft the engine must be removed from the frame.*

Removal

1 Remove the engine from the frame (see Section 4), separate the crankcase halves (see Section 19) and disconnect the piston/connecting rod assemblies from the crankshaft (see Section 21). There is no need to remove the cylinder head. Push the pistons up the bores so that the connecting rod ends are clear of the crankshaft and wrap clean rag around the rod ends to prevent damage to the bores. **Note:** *New big-end bolts and nuts must be used on reassembly.*

2 Lift the crankshaft out of the upper crankcase half, taking care not to dislodge the main bearing shells **(see illustration)**.

3 If required, remove the bearing shells from the crankcase halves by pushing their centres to the side, then lifting them out **(see illustration)**. Keep the shells in order so that they can be fitted in their original locations for the oil clearance check.

Inspection

4 Clean the crankshaft with a suitable solvent, paying particular attention to flush out the oil passages. If available, blow the crank dry with compressed air, and also blow through the oil passages. Check the primary drive gear for wear or damage **(see illustration)**. If any of the teeth are excessively worn, chipped or broken, the crankshaft must be replaced with a new one. Check the primary driven gear on the clutch housing for corresponding wear or damage. Also check the cam chain sprocket **(see illustration)**, the sprockets on the camshafts and the cam chain itself and replace them with new ones, if necessary.

5 Refer to Section 20 and examine the main bearing shells. If they are scored, badly scuffed or appear to have seized, new bearings must be installed. Always renew the main bearings as a set. If they are badly damaged, check the corresponding crankshaft journals. Evidence of extreme heat, such as bluing, indicates that lubrication failure has occurred. Be sure to thoroughly check the oil pump and pressure

relief valve as well as all oil holes and passages before reassembling the engine.

6 Give the crankshaft journals a close visual examination, paying particular attention where damaged bearings have been discovered. If the journals are scored or pitted in any way, a new crankshaft will be required. Note that undersized bearing shells are not available, precluding the option of re-grinding the crankshaft.

7 Place the crankshaft on V-blocks and check the runout at the main bearing journals using a dial gauge (see *Tools and Workshop Tips* in the *Reference* section). Compare the reading to the maximum specified at the beginning of this Chapter. If the runout exceeds the limit, the crankshaft must be replaced with a new one.

Oil clearance check

8 Whether new bearing shells are being fitted or the original ones are being re-used, the main bearing oil clearance should be checked before the engine is reassembled. Main bearing oil clearance is measured with a product known as Plastigauge.

9 If not already done, remove the bearing shells from the crankcase halves (see Step 3). Clean the backs of the shells and the bearing seats in both crankcase halves, and the main bearing journals on the crankshaft.

10 Press the bearing shells into their seats, ensuring that the tab on each shell engages in the notch in the crankcase **(see illustration)**. Make sure the bearings are fitted in the correct locations and take care not to touch the bearing surfaces with your fingers.

24.3 If required remove the bearings

24.4 Check the cam chain sprocket (A) and the primary drive gear (B) for wear

24.10 Ensure tab (A) locates in notch (B)

Engine, clutch and transmission 2•49

24.12 Place a strip of Plastigauge on each bearing journal

24.16 Measure the crushed Plastigauge using the scale on the pack

24.21 Main bearing size codes (arrowed)

11 Ensure the shells and crankshaft are clean and dry. Lay the crankshaft in position in the upper crankcase **(see illustration 24.2)**.

12 Cut five appropriate size lengths of Plastigauge (they should be slightly shorter than the width of the crankshaft journals). Place a strand of Plastigauge on each journal **(see illustration)**. Do not place Plastigauge over the oil holes in the crankshaft. Make sure the crankshaft is not rotated.

13 If removed, fit the dowels into the crankcase **(see illustration 19.7a, b and c)**. Carefully fit the lower crankcase half onto the upper half, making sure the dowels locate correctly and the Plastigauge is not disturbed **(see illustration 19.6)**. Check that the lower crankcase half is correctly seated. **Note:** *Do not tighten the crankcase bolts if the casing is not correctly seated.*

14 Clean and lubricate the threads and underside of the heads and washers of the crankcase bolts Nos. 1 to 10 **(see illustration 19.5a)** with clean engine oil. Install the bolts in their correct locations and secure them finger-tight. Now tighten the bolts according to the procedure for the model year of the bike (see Section 19) for details.

15 Unscrew the bolts a quarter turn at a time in a reverse of the numerical sequence (i.e. 10 to 1), until they are loose, then remove them. **Note:** *As each bolt is removed, store it in its relative position in the cardboard template of the crankcase halves.* Carefully lift off the lower crankcase half, making sure the Plastigauge is not disturbed.

16 Compare the width of the crushed Plastigauge on each crankshaft journal to the scale printed on the Plastigauge envelope to obtain the main bearing oil clearance **(see illustration)**. Compare the reading to the specifications at the beginning of this Chapter. If the clearance is within the range specified and the bearings are in perfect condition, they can be reused.

17 Carefully clean away all traces of the Plastigauge from the journals and bearing shells using a fingernail or other object which will not score the bearing surfaces.

18 If the clearance is beyond the service limit, replace the bearing shells with new ones (see Steps 20 to 22) and check the oil clearance once again. Replace all of the shells as a new set.

19 If the clearance is still greater than the service limit listed in this Chapter's Specifications, the crankshaft journal is worn and the crankshaft should be replaced with a new one.

Bearing shell selection

20 Replacement bearing shells for the main bearings are supplied on a selected fit basis. Code numbers for the crankshaft journals are stamped on the outside of the crankshaft web on the left-hand end of the crankshaft **(see illustration 21.27a)**. The left-hand block of five numbers are the size codes for the main bearing journals (the right-hand block of four numbers are the size codes for the big-end bearing journals). The first number of the block is for the left-hand (No. 1) journal, and so on.

21 The main bearing size codes are stamped into the back of the lower crankcase half **(see illustration)**. The first number of the five is for the left-hand (No. 1) bearing, and so on.

22 A range of bearing shells are available. To select the correct shells for a particular journal, subtract the crankshaft journal number from the crankcase number, and then subtract 1. Compare the result with the table below to find the colour coding of the replacement shells, e.g. crankcase number 5 minus crankshaft journal number 1 minus 1 = 3; No. 3 bearing shells are colour-coded brown. The colour code is marked on the side of each bearing shell **(see illustration 21.28)**.

Number	Colour
0	white
1	blue
2	black
3	brown
4	green

Installation

23 Ensure the backs of the bearing shells, the bearing seats in both crankcase halves, and the main bearing journals on the crankshaft are clean. If new shells are being fitted, ensure that all traces of the protective grease are cleaned off using paraffin (kerosene). Wipe the shells and crankcase halves dry with a lint-free cloth. Make sure all the oil passages and holes are clear, and blow them through with compressed air if available.

24 Press the bearing shells into their seats. Make sure the tab on each shell engages

in the notch in the casing **(see illustration 24.10)**. Make sure the bearings are fitted in the correct locations and take care not to touch any bearing surfaces with your fingers. Lubricate the shells with clean engine oil.

25 Lower the crankshaft into position in the upper crankcase, making sure all bearing shells remain in place **(see illustration 24.2)**.

26 Install the piston/connecting rod assemblies as required according to what has been removed (see Section 21).

27 Reassemble the crankcase halves (see Section 19).

25 Transmission shaft removal and installation

Note: *To remove the transmission shafts the engine must be removed from the frame.*
Special tool: *Although not strictly a tool, this procedure requires the use of two M6 x 1.0 bolts of 30 mm thread length – see Step 6.*

Removal

1 Remove the engine from the frame (see Section 4). Separate the crankcase halves (see Section 19).

2 Note how the bearing retainers locate in the grooves in the crankcase, and how the output shaft selector forks locate in the grooves of the 5th and 6th gear pinions and how the guide pins on the forks locate in the grooves in the selector drum. Lift the output shaft out of the crankcase **(see illustration)**; if it is stuck, use

25.2 Lift the output shaft out of the crankcase

25.3 Remove and discard the shaft oil seal

25.5 Unscrew the bolts (arrowed)

25.6a Displace the bearing housing by screwing in two bolts . . .

a soft-faced hammer and gently tap on the ends of the shaft to free it.

3 Remove the oil seal from the left-hand end of the shaft and discard it as a new one must be fitted on reassembly (see illustration).

4 Remove the selector drum and forks (see Section 27).

5 Undo the bolts securing the input shaft bearing housing, if necessary drilling the centre punched stakes (see illustration).

6 Obtain two 6 mm diameter bolts, 30 mm long excluding the bolt head, and with a 1 mm thread pitch, and screw them into the two holes in the bearing housing as shown (see illustration). Tighten the bolts until they contact the surface of the crankcase, then

continue tightening them evenly and a little at a time until the bearing housing is displaced (see illustration). Withdraw the input shaft from the crankcase.

7 To remove the input shaft bearing from the crankcase see *Tools and Workshop Tips* in the *Reference* section.

Installation

8 Slide the input shaft into the crankcase far enough for the left-hand end of the shaft to locate in its bearing (see illustration) – make sure the second gear pinion does not slide towards the end of the shaft as the tabbed lockwasher could disengage from the slotted

washer. Lightly tap the bearing housing home using a soft-face mallet (see illustration). The housing can be drawn fully home using the countersunk mounting bolts. When the housing is fully installed, unscrew and remove the bolts.

9 Apply a suitable thread locking compound to the bearing housing mounting bolts and tighten them to the torque setting specified at the beginning of this Chapter (see illustration). Using a centre punch, stake the bolts in position (see illustrations).

10 Install the selector drum and forks (see Section 27).

11 Smear the inside of the new output shaft seal with grease. Slide the seal onto the

25.6b . . . and turning them against the crankcase surface

25.8a Slide the shaft into the bearing . . .

25.8b . . . and lightly drive the housing home

25.9a Tighten the screws to the specified torque . . .

25.9b . . . and stake them with a centre punch . . .

25.9c . . . into the recess in the housing

25.11 Make sure the bearing retainer and pin are fitted

25.12a Ensure the selector forks . . .

25.12b . . . bearing retainer, and pin locate correctly

left-hand end of the shaft **(see illustration 25.3)**. Make sure the output shaft bearing retainer and pin are fitted **(see illustration)**.

12 Lower the output shaft into position in the upper crankcase **(see illustration 25.2)**, making sure the selector forks locate in their grooves in the pinions, and the bearing retainer and the pin locate in the crankcase **(see illustrations)**.

Caution: If the retainers are not correctly engaged, the crankcase halves will not seat correctly.

13 Make sure output shaft is correctly seated. Position the gears in the neutral position and check the shafts are free to rotate easily and independently (i.e. the input shaft can turn whilst the output shaft is held stationary) before proceeding further.

14 Reassemble the crankcase halves (see Section 19).

26 Transmission shaft overhaul

1 Remove the transmission shafts from the crankcase (see Section 25). Always disassemble the transmission shafts separately to avoid mixing up the components.

When disassembling the transmission shafts, place the parts on a long rod or thread a wire through them to keep them in order and facing the proper direction.

Input shaft disassembly

2 Slide the 2nd gear pinion off the left-hand end of the shaft, noting which way around it is fitted – mark its outer face with a marker pen as an aid to reassembly **(see illustration 26.26)**.

3 Note how the tabs on the lock washer fit into the slotted splined washer and remove the lockwasher **(see illustration 26.25c)**.

4 Turn the slotted splined washer to offset its splines with those on the shaft and slide it off **(see illustration 26.24)**.

5 Slide the 6th gear pinion and its splined bush off the shaft, followed by the splined washer **(see illustrations 26.23c, b and a)**.

6 Remove the circlip securing the combined 3rd/4th gear pinion, then slide the pinion off the shaft noting which way round it fits **(see illustrations 26.22b and a)**. Discard the circlip as a new one must be fitted on reassembly.

7 Remove the circlip securing the 5th gear pinion, then slide the splined washer, the pinion and its bush off the shaft **(see illustrations 26.21b and a and 26.20b and a)**. Discard the circlip as a new one must be fitted on reassembly.

8 The 1st gear pinion is integral with the shaft.

9 If required, remove the bearing and its housing from the right-hand end of the shaft, referring to *Tools and Workshop Tips* (Section 5) in the *Reference* section **(see illustration)**.

Shaft inspection

10 Wash all the components in solvent and dry them off.

11 Check the gear teeth for cracking, chipping, pitting and other obvious wear or damage. Any pinion that is damaged must be replaced with a new one.

12 Inspect the dogs and the dog holes in the gears for cracks, chips, and excessive wear especially in the form of rounded edges. Make sure mating gears engage properly. Replace mating gears as a set if necessary.

26.9 Remove the bearing and housing if required.

13 Check for signs of scoring or bluing on the pinions, bushes and shaft. This could be caused by overheating due to inadequate lubrication. Check that all the oil holes and passages are clear. Replace any worn or damaged parts with new ones.

14 Check that each pinion moves freely on the shaft or bush but without undue freeplay. Check that each bush moves freely on the shaft but without undue freeplay.

15 The shaft is unlikely to sustain damage unless the engine has seized, placing an unusually high loading on the transmission, or the machine has covered a very high mileage. Check the surface of the shaft, especially where a pinion turns on it, and replace the shaft with a new one if it has scored or picked up, or if there are any cracks. Check the shaft runout using V-blocks and a dial gauge and replace the shaft with a new one if the runout exceeds the limit specified at the beginning of this Chapter.

16 Check the washers and replace any that are bent or worn with new ones.

17 Check the bearings referring to *Tools and Workshop Tips* (Section 5) in the *Reference* section, and fit new ones if necessary. Do not forget the input shaft left-hand bearing, which is housed in the crankcase, and fits with its sealed side facing the outside of the engine.

Input shaft reassembly

18 During reassembly, apply clean engine oil or molybdenum disulphide oil (a 50/50 mixture of molybdenum disulphide grease and engine oil) to the mating surfaces of the shaft, pinions and bushes. Use **new** circlips and do not expand their ends any further than is necessary to slide them along the shaft. Install them so that their chamfered side faces the pinion they secure (see *Correct fitting of a stamped circlip* illustration in *Tools and Workshop Tips* (Section 2) in the *Reference* section).

19 If removed, fit the bearing and its housing onto the right-hand end of the shaft, referring to *Tools and Workshop Tips* (Section 5) in the *Reference* section **(see illustration 26.9)**.

20 Slide the 5th gear pinion bush onto the

26.20a Fit the fifth gear pinion bush . . .

26.20b . . . followed by the fifth gear pinion

26.21a Slide the splined washer onto the shaft. . .

26.21b . . .then fit the new circlip

26.22a Slide the 3rd/4th gear pinion onto the shaft . . .

26.22b . . . and secure it with the circlip

26.23a Fit the splined washer . . .

left-hand end of the shaft then fit the 5th gear pinion onto the bush with its dog holes facing away from the integral 1st gear **(see illustrations)**.

21 Slide the splined washer onto the shaft, then fit the **new** circlip, making sure that it locates correctly in the groove in the shaft **(see illustrations)**.

22 Slide the combined 3rd/4th gear pinion onto the shaft with the smaller 3rd gear pinion facing the 5th gear pinion **(see illustration)**. Ensure the oil hole in the pinion aligns with

the oil holes in the shaft. Fit the **new** circlip, making sure it locates correctly in its groove in the shaft **(see illustration)**.

23 Slide the splined washer onto the shaft, followed by the splined 6th gear pinion bush, aligning the oil hole in the bush with the hole in the shaft **(see illustrations)**. Fit the 6th gear pinion, making sure its dogs face the 3rd/4th gear pinion **(see illustration)**.

24 Slide the slotted splined washer onto the shaft and locate it in its groove, then turn it in the groove, so that the splines on the

26.23b . . . align the oil holes (arrowed) and fit the 6th gear pinion bush . . .

26.23c . . . and slide on the 6th gear pinion

26.24 Slide the slotted splined washer onto the shaft

26.25a Slide the lockwasher onto the shaft . . .

26.25b . . . then turn the slotted splined washer . . .

26.25c . . . to engage the tabs on the lockwasher

26.26 Slide the 2nd gear pinion onto the shaft

washer locate against the splines on the shaft and secure the washer in the groove **(see illustration)**.

25 Slide the lockwasher onto the shaft, and locate its tabs in the slots on the outside edge of the splined washer – note that there is a wide tab and corresponding slot so it can only fit one way **(see illustrations)**.

26 Slide the 2nd gear pinion onto the shaft, the correct way around as noted on removal **(see illustration)**.

27 Check that all components have been correctly installed. The assembled shaft should look as shown **(see illustration)**.

Output shaft disassembly

28 Slide the bearing off the right-hand end of the shaft **(see illustration 26.49)**.

29 Slide the thrust washer off the shaft, followed by the 1st gear pinion and its bush **(see illustrations 26.48c, b and a)**.

30 Slide the 5th gear pinion off the shaft **(see illustration 26.47)**.

31 Remove the circlip securing the 3rd gear pinion, then slide the splined washer, the pinion and its splined bush off the shaft **(see illustrations 26.46d, c, b and a)**. Discard the circlip as a new one must be fitted on reassembly.

32 Note how the tabs on the lock washer fit into the slotted splined washer and remove the lockwasher **(see illustration 26.45b and a)**.

33 Turn the slotted splined washer to offset its splines with those on the shaft and slide it off **(see illustrations 26.44a)**.

34 Slide the 4th gear pinion and its splined bush, followed by the splined washer, off the shaft **(see illustrations 26.43c, b and a)**.

35 Remove the circlip securing the 6th gear pinion, then slide the pinion off the shaft **(see illustrations 26.42b and a)**. Discard the circlip as a new one must be fitted on reassembly.

36 Remove the circlip securing the 2nd gear pinion, then slide the splined washer, the pinion and its bush off the shaft **(see illustrations 26.41d, c, b and a)**. Discard the circlip as a new one must be fitted on reassembly.

37 If required, remove the collar and bearing from the left-hand end of the shaft, referring to *Tools and Workshop Tips* (Section 5) in the *Reference* section **(see illustration)**. Only remove the bearing if a new one is being fitted. If a new shaft is being fitted fit a new bearing with it. Remove the retainer from the bearing.

26.27 The assembled gearbox input shaft

26.37 Remove the collar and bearing if required

26.41a Slide the 2nd gear pinion bush . . .

26.41b . . . the 2nd gear pinion . . .

26.41c . . . and the splined washer onto the shaft . . .

26.41d . . . and secure them with the circlip . . .

26.41e . . . making sure it locates in its groove

26.42a Align the oil holes and slide the 6th gear pinion onto the shaft . . .

Shaft inspection

38 Refer to Steps 10 to 17 above.

Output shaft reassembly

39 During reassembly, apply engine oil or molybdenum disulphide oil (a 50/50 mixture of molybdenum disulphide grease and engine oil) to the mating surfaces of the shaft, pinions and bushes. When installing the **new** circlips, do not expand their ends any further than is necessary to slide them along the shaft. Install them so that their chamfered side faces

the pinion they secure (see *Correct fitting of a stamped circlip* illustration in *Tools and Workshop Tips* (Section 2) in the *Reference* section).

40 If removed, fit the new bearing and collar onto the left-hand end of the shaft, making sure the bearing is fitted with the retainer groove to the outside, referring to *Tools and Workshop Tips* (Section 5) in the *Reference* section **(see illustration 26.37)**. Fit the retainer into its groove.

41 Slide the 2nd gear pinion bush onto the shaft, then slide on the 2nd gear pinion (dog

holes facing away from the bearing) and the splined washer **(see illustrations)**. Fit the **new** circlip, making sure it is locates correctly in its groove on the shaft **(see illustrations)**.

42 Align the oil holes in the shaft and the 6th gear pinion, and slide the pinion onto the shaft with its selector fork groove facing away from the 2nd gear pinion, then fit the **new** circlip, making sure it locates correctly in its groove on the shaft **(see illustrations)**.

43 Slide the splined washer and the splined 4th gear pinion bush onto the shaft, then fit the 4th gear pinion so that its dished side

26.42b . . . and secure it with the circlip . . .

26.42c . . . making sure it locates in its groove

26.43a Fit the splined washer . . .

26.43b . . . then the 4th gear pinion bush . . .

26.43c . . . and the 4th gear pinion

26.44a Slide the slotted splined washer onto the shaft . . .

26.44b . . . then turn it in its groove to lock the splines

26.45a Slide on the tabbed lockwasher . . .

and dog holes face the 6th gear pinion (see illustrations).

44 Slide the slotted splined washer onto the shaft and locate it in its groove, then turn it in the groove so that the splines on the washer align with the splines on the shaft and secure the washer in the groove (see illustrations).

45 Slide the lockwasher onto the shaft, so that the tabs on the lockwasher locate into the slots in the outer rim of the splined washer – note that there is a wide tab and corresponding slot so it can only fit one way (see illustrations).

46 Slide the splined 3rd gear pinion bush onto the shaft, then fit the 3rd gear pinion (dished side and dog holes facing away from the 4th gear pinion) and the splined washer (see illustrations). Fit the **new** circlip, making sure it locates correctly in its groove in the shaft (see illustration).

26.45b . . . and locate it against the slotted washer

26.46a Slide the 3rd gear pinion bush onto the shaft . . .

26.46b . . . followed by the 3rd gear pinion . . .

26.46c . . . and the splined washer . . .

26.46d . . . and secure them with the circlip making sure it locates in its groove

47 Slide the 5th gear pinion onto the shaft with its selector fork groove facing the 3rd gear pinion **(see illustration)**.
48 Slide the 1st gear pinion bush onto the shaft, followed by the 1st gear pinion (dished side facing the 5th gear pinion) and the thrust washer **(see illustrations)**.
49 Fit the bearing onto the end of the shaft **(see illustration)**.
50 Check that all components have been correctly installed. The assembled shaft should look as shown **(see illustration)**.

27 Selector drum and forks

Note: *To remove the selector drum and forks the engine must be removed from the frame.*

Removal

1 Position the transmission in neutral.

26.47 Slide the 5th gear pinion onto the shaft

26.48a Slide the 1st gear pinion bush onto the shaft . . .

Remove the engine from the frame (see Section 4). Separate the crankcase halves (see Section 19).
2 Note how the output shaft selector forks locate in the grooves on the 5th and 6th gear pinions and how the guide pins on the forks

locate in the grooves in the selector drum, then remove the output shaft (see Section 25).
3 Note the position of the neutral detent on the right-hand end of the selector drum as an aid for installation.
4 Note that each selector fork is lettered for

26.48b . . . followed by the 1st gear pinion . . .

26.48c . . . and the thrust washer . . .

26.49 . . . then fit the bearing

26.50 The assembled gearbox output shaft

27.6a Undo the bolts . . .

27.6b . . . and remove the retainer plates . . .

27.6c . . . and the output shaft selector fork shaft and the forks

identification. The right-hand fork has an 'R', the centre fork a 'C', and the left-hand fork an 'L' **(see illustration 27.18)**. These letters face the right-hand side (clutch side) of the engine. If no letters are visible, mark the forks using a felt pen before removing the forks.

5 Note how the input shaft selector fork locates in the groove on the 3rd/4th gear pinion and how the guide pin on the fork locates in the groove in the selector drum.

6 Unscrew the bolts securing the selector drum/fork shaft retainer plates and remove the plates, noting how they fit **(see illustrations)**. Support the output shaft selector forks (L and R), then withdraw the shaft from the crankcase and remove the forks **(see illustration)**. Note the springs in the ends of the shaft and remove them for safekeeping.

7 Slide the forks back onto the shaft in the correct order and the right way round **(see illustration)**.

8 Support the input shaft selector fork (C) and withdraw the fork shaft from the crankcase **(see illustration)**. Move the fork guide pin out of its track in the selector drum, then withdraw the selector drum from the left-hand side of the casing **(see illustrations)**.

9 Move the selector fork round in its groove in the 3rd/4th gear pinion and remove it **(see illustration)**. Slide the fork back onto the shaft.

Inspection

10 Inspect the selector forks for any signs of wear or damage, especially around the fork ends where they engage with the grooves in

the pinions **(see illustration)**. Check that each fork fits correctly in its pinion groove. Check closely to see if the forks are bent. If the forks are in any way damaged they must be replaced with new ones.

27.7 Reassemble the forks onto the shaft

27.8b . . . then disengage the fork guide pin . . .

11 Check that the forks fit correctly on their shaft **(see illustration)**. They should move freely with a light fit but no appreciable freeplay. Check that the fork shaft holes in the casing are neither worn nor damaged.

27.8a Withdraw the shaft for the input shaft selector fork . . .

27.8c . . . withdraw the selector drum . . .

27.9 . . . and remove the fork

27.10 Inspect the forks for wear

27.11 Check the fit of the forks on their shaft

27.13 Inspect the grooves (arrowed) for wear

27.15a Fit the selector fork . . .

27.15b . . . and position it out of the way

12 Check the selector fork shaft runout using V-blocks and a dial gauge and replace the shaft with a new one if the runout exceeds the limit specified at the beginning of this Chapter. A bent shaft will cause difficulty in selecting gears and make the gearchange action heavy.
13 Inspect the selector drum grooves and selector fork guide pins for signs of wear or damage **(see illustration)**. If either show signs of wear or damage they must be replaced with new ones.
14 Check the selector drum bearings, referring to *Tools and Workshop Tips* (Section 5) in the *Reference* section. If the bearing on the drum is worn a new selector drum will have to be fitted as the bearing is not available separately. The bearing in the crankcase can be replaced with a new one.

Also check that the neutral switch contact on the right-hand end of the drum is neither damaged nor worn away. If required, remove the contact and replace it with a new one.

Installation

15 Locate the input shaft selector fork (C) in its groove in the 3rd/4th gear pinion, making sure the letter faces the right-hand (clutch) side of the engine **(see illustration)**, then slide the fork round and below the input shaft so that it does not get in the way when installing the selector drum **(see illustration)**.
16 Lubricate the end of the selector drum and the drum bearings with clean engine oil, then align the selector drum so that the neutral detent points to the top of the engine and the neutral switch contact aligns with the switch

plunger, and slide the drum into the crankcase **(see illustrations)**. Make sure the drum end locates in its bearing in the crankcase, and that the neutral contact on the drum locates against the neutral switch contact.
17 Lubricate the shaft for the centre fork with clean engine oil. Move the input shaft selector fork round in its groove and locate the fork guide pin into its track in the selector drum, then slide the fork shaft into the crankcase and through the fork using an Allen key or similar as a hook to keep the fork in position **(see illustrations)**.
18 Make sure the springs are in the ends of the selector fork shaft for the R and L forks and lubricate the shaft with clean engine oil. Position the output shaft forks in the crankcase, making sure their letters face the

27.16a Lubricate the drum and bearings . . .

27.16b . . . slide the drum into the case . . .

27.16c . . . and into the bearing . . .

27.16d . . . aligning the neutral switch detent

27.17a Lubricate the shaft . . .

27.17b . . . and use a hook to align the fork with the shaft

27.18 Install the forks with the R and L marks correctly aligned

28.2a Withdraw the oil feed pipe from the crankcase . . .

28.2b . . . and inspect the O-rings

right-hand (clutch) side of the engine and the fork guide pins locate in their tracks in the drum **(see illustration)**. Slide the fork shaft into the crankcase and through the forks **(see illustration 27.6c)**.

19 Apply a suitable non-permanent thread locking compound to the selector drum/fork shaft retainer plate bolts. Install the plates with the OUT marks facing out and tighten the bolts to the torque setting specified at the beginning of this Chapter **(see illustration 27.6a and b)**.

20 Lower the transmission output shaft into the crankcase (see Section 25). Ensure that the fork marked 'R' locates in the groove in the 5th gear pinion, and that the fork marked 'L' locates in the groove in the 6th gear pinion (see Step 2).

21 Check that the output shaft is correctly

seated and that the transmission shafts rotate easily and independently when in neutral (see Section 25).

28 Crankcase inspection

1 After the crankcases have been separated, remove the crankshaft, connecting rods/ pistons and cylinder block, bearings, transmission shafts, selector drum and forks, and any other components or assemblies, referring to the relevant Sections of this and other Chapters (see Step 3 of Section 19).

2 Withdraw the oil feed pipe from the upper crankcase – it is a push-fit **(see illustration)**. Check the condition of the pipe O-rings and

replace them with new ones if they are in any way damaged, deformed or deteriorated **(see illustration)**. Remove the four oil jets from the upper crankcase and discard their O-rings **(see illustration)**.

3 Unscrew the oil gallery plugs from each side of the lower crankcase and discard the O-rings as new ones must be fitted on reassembly **(see illustrations)**. Unscrew the Allen bolts and remove the external oil pipe **(see illustration)**. Remove the O-rings as new one must be fitted.

4 Unscrew the bolts securing the oil baffle plate in the clutch housing and remove it noting how it fits **(see illustration)**. Unscrew the bolts securing the crankcase breather cover **(see illustration)**. Remove the cover and discard its gasket.

5 Unscrew the bolt securing the oil baffle plate

28.2c Poke out the oil jets

28.3a Remove the right hand . . .

28.3b . . . and left-hand oil gallery plugs

28.3c Unscrew the bolts (arrowed) and remove the oil pipe

28.4a Undo the screws (arrowed) and remove the baffle plate

28.4b Undo the screws and remove the breather cover

28.5 Undo the screw (arrowed) and remove the baffle plate

28.15 Align the tab with the cut-out

above the right hand end of the crankshaft **(see illustration)**.

6 Remove all traces of old gasket and sealant from all mating surfaces. Minor damage to the surfaces can be cleaned up with careful use of a fine sharpening stone.

7 Clean the crankcases thoroughly with solvent, and dry them with compressed air. Flush out all oil passages and pipes with solvent and blow compressed air through them.

Caution: Be very careful not to nick or gouge the crankcase mating surfaces, or oil leaks will result. Check both crankcase halves very carefully for cracks and other damage.

8 Check the various bearings, referring to *Tools and Workshop Tips* (Section 5) in the *Reference* section.

9 Small cracks or holes in aluminium castings can be repaired with an epoxy resin adhesive as a temporary measure. Permanent repairs can only be effected by argon-arc welding, and only a specialist in this process is in a position to advise on the economy or practical aspect of such a repair. Note that low temperature aluminium welding kits are available for minor repairs, such as Lumiweld. If any damage is found that can't be repaired, renew the crankcase halves as a set.

10 Damaged threads can be economically reclaimed by using a diamond section wire insert which is easily fitted after drilling and re-tapping the affected thread.

11 Sheared studs or screws can usually be removed with stud or screw extractors; if you are in any doubt consult your Yamaha dealer or specialist motorcycle engineer.

HAYNES HINT *Refer to Tools and Workshop Tips (Section 2) in the Reference section for details of installing a thread insert and using screw extractors.*

12 Install both the oil baffle plates, then apply a suitable non-permanent thread locking compound to the threads of the bolts and tighten them to the torque setting specified at the beginning of this Chapter **(see illustration 28.4a)**. Fit the crankcase breather cover using a new gasket and tighten its bolts **(see illustration 28.4b)**.

13 Lightly grease the new O-rings for the oil gallery plugs and install the plugs, tightening them to the specified torque setting.

14 Lightly grease the new O-rings for the external U-shaped oil pipe and install the pipe, then tighten the bolts to the specified torque setting.

15 Lightly grease the O-rings on the oil feed pipe and install the pipe **(see illustration 28.2a)**, locating the tab on the outer end in the cut-out in the crankcase **(see illustration)**. Ensure the outer end of the pipe is a flush fit with the crankcase; the pipe is retained by the lip of the input shaft bearing housing retainer plate.

16 Lightly grease the new O-rings for the oil jets. Install the jets, poking them into their bores with a suitable tool **(see illustration 28.2c)**.

17 Install the remaining components in the reverse order of removal.

29 Running-in procedure

1 Make sure the engine oil and coolant levels are correct with the engine cold (see *Pre-ride checks*).

2 Make sure there is fuel in the tank.

3 Turn the ignition 'ON' and check that the low oil level warning light, coolant temperature warning light and the low fuel warning light come on for a few seconds and then go off.

Ensure that the transmission is in neutral and that the neutral light is illuminated.

4 Start the engine, then allow it to run at a moderately fast idle until it reaches normal operating temperature.

5 As no oil pressure warning light is fitted, an oil pressure check is advised (see Section 3).

6 If a lubrication failure is suspected, stop the engine immediately and try to find the cause. If an engine is run without oil, even for a short period of time, severe damage will occur. Check carefully that there are no oil or coolant leaks and make sure the transmission and controls, especially the brakes and clutch, work properly before road testing the machine.

7 Treat the machine gently for the first few miles to allow the oil to circulate throughout the engine and any new parts installed to seat.

8 Great care is necessary if the engine has been extensively overhauled – the bike will have to be run in as when new. This means more use of the transmission and a restraining hand on the throttle until at least 600 miles (1000 km) have been covered. There is no point in keeping to any set road speed – the main idea is to keep from labouring the engine and to gradually increase performance up to the 1000 mile (1600 km) mark. These recommendations apply less when only a partial overhaul has been done, though it does depend to an extent on the nature of the work carried out and which components have been renewed. Experience is the best guide, since it is easy to tell when an engine is running freely. If in any doubt, consult a Yamaha dealer. The following maximum engine speed limitations, which Yamaha provide for new motorcycles, can be used as a guide.

Up to 600 miles (1000 km)
Do not exceed 8300 rpm

600 to 1000 miles (1000 to 1600 km)
Vary throttle position/speed. Do not exceed 9900 rpm for long periods

Over 1000 miles (1600 km)
Normal riding. Do not exceed tachometer red line

9 Upon completion of the road test check the engine oil level and top up if necessary. After the engine has cooled down completely, recheck the valve clearances (see Chapter 1) and check the coolant level.

10 After running the rebuilt engine for 1000 miles (1600 km), change the engine oil and filter (see Chapter 1).

Chapter 3
Cooling system

Contents

Degrees of difficulty

Easy, suitable for novice with little experience	**Fairly easy,** suitable for beginner with some experience	**Fairly difficult,** suitable for competent DIY mechanic	**Difficult,** suitable for experienced DIY mechanic	**Very difficult,** suitable for expert DIY or professional

Specifications

Coolant

Coolant type. . . . . 50% distilled water, 50% ethylene glycol anti-freeze with corrosion inhibitors for aluminium engines. **Note:** *Yamaha specify that soft tap water can be used, but NOT hard water. If in doubt use only distilled water.*

Coolant capacity
   Radiator . . . . 2.3 litres
   Reservoir. . . . . 0.25 litre

Radiator

Cap valve opening pressure. . . . . 15.6 to 19.9 psi (1.0 to 1.3 Bar)

Coolant temperature sensor

Resistance @ 80°C. . . . . 290 to 354 ohms

Thermostat

Opening temperature . . . . 71 to 85°C
Valve lift . . . . >8 mm @ 85°C

Water pump

Impeller shaft tilt (max.) . . . . 0.15 mm

Torque wrench settings

Coolant inlet pipe bolt . . . . 10 Nm
Coolant temperature sensor. . . . . 18 Nm
Oil cooler union bolt . . . . 63 Nm
Radiator mounting bolts. . . . . 10 Nm
Thermostat cover bolts . . . . 12 Nm
Water pump cover bolts. . . . . 10 Nm
Water pump mounting bolts. . . . . 12 Nm

1 General information

The cooling system uses a water/antifreeze mixture to carry excess heat away from the engine. The cylinders are surrounded by a water jacket, through which the coolant is circulated by thermo-syphonic action in conjunction with a water pump. The water pump driveshaft is keyed to that for the oil pump, both being driven by chain off the clutch housing.

Heated coolant rises through the system to a thermostat and then to the radiator. It flows across the radiator, where it is cooled by the air flow, then down to the water pump and back into the engine, where the cycle is repeated. The thermostat is fitted in the system to prevent the coolant flowing through the radiator when the engine is cold, therefore accelerating the speed at which the engine reaches normal operating temperature. Coolant is also routed around an oil cooler unit mounted on the front of the crankcase.

A coolant temperature sensor is fitted into the back of the water jacket. It provides information to the coolant temperature display on the instrument panel and to the ECU.

Two relay-controlled cooling fans are fitted behind the radiator, to aid cooling in extreme conditions. The relay is controlled by a signal from the ECU.

The complete cooling system is partially sealed and pressurised, the pressure being controlled by a spring-loaded valve contained in the radiator cap. By pressurising the coolant the boiling point is raised, preventing premature boiling in adverse conditions. The overflow hose from the system is connected to a reservoir mounted on the right-hand side of the radiator, into which excess coolant is expelled under pressure. The discharged coolant automatically returns to the radiator when the engine cools.

⚠️ **Warning: Do not remove the pressure cap from the radiator when the engine is hot. Scalding hot coolant and steam may be**

blown out under pressure and could cause serious injury. When the engine has cooled, place a thick rag such as a towel over the pressure cap; slowly rotate the cap anti-clockwise to the first stop. This procedure allows any residual pressure to escape. When the pressure has stopped escaping, press down on the cap while turning it anti-clockwise, and remove it.

⚠️ *Do not allow antifreeze to come into contact with your skin, or painted surfaces of the motorcycle. Rinse off any spills immediately with plenty of water. Antifreeze is highly toxic if ingested. Never leave antifreeze lying around in an open container or in puddles on the floor; children and pets are attracted by its sweet smell and may drink it. Check with the local authorities about disposing of used antifreeze. Many communities will have collection centres which will see that antifreeze is disposed of safely.*

Caution: At all times use the specified type of antifreeze, and always mix it with distilled water in the correct proportion. The antifreeze contains corrosion inhibitors which are essential to avoid damage to the cooling system. A lack of these inhibitors could lead to a build-up of corrosion which will block the coolant passages inside the engine, resulting in overheating and severe engine damage. Distilled water must be used as opposed to tap water to avoid a

build-up of scale which would also block the passages.

Read the *Safety first!* section of this manual carefully before starting work.

2 Radiator

Removal

⚠️ *Warning: The engine must be completely cool before carrying out this procedure.*

1 Remove the fairing side panels, the lower fairing, and the air ducts (see Chapter 7).
2 Drain the cooling system (see Chapter 1).
3 Remove the coolant reservoir and its breather hose disconnecting it from the clip on the clutch cable (see Section 3).
4 Unscrew the bolts securing the regulator/rectifier holder to the left-hand side of the radiator and tie it back out of the way **(see illustration)**.
5 Disconnect the cooling fan motor wiring at the black connectors **(see illustrations)**.
6 Release the clutch cable guide from the right-hand cooling fan bracket **(see illustration)**.
7 Unscrew the bolt on the radiator lower mounting bracket and remove the bolt and washer **(see illustration)**. Note the spacer that fits in the bush in the radiator mounting tab and remove it if it is loose.

2.4 Remove the regulator/rectifier mounting bracket

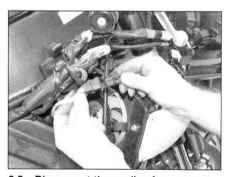

2.5a Disconnect the cooling fan connector on the right . . .

2.5b . . . and the left-hand sides

2.6 Release the clutch cable retaining clip

2.7 Unscrew the lower mounting bolt

2.8a Unscrew the upper and . . .

2.8b . . . lower hose clips

2.9 Remove the radiator

8 Release the clamps securing the radiator inlet and outlet hoses and detach them from the radiator, noting which fits where **(see illustrations)**.

9 Support the radiator then unscrew the upper mounting bolts and washers and remove the radiator **(see illustration)**. Note the spacers that fit in the bushes and remove them if loose.

10 If necessary, separate the cooling fans from the radiator (see Section 4). Check the radiator for signs of damage and clear any dirt or debris that might obstruct airflow and inhibit cooling. Radiator fins can be straightened carefully with a flat-bladed screwdriver, but if the fins are badly damaged or broken the radiator must be replaced with a new one. Also check the mounting bushes, and replace them with new ones if necessary.

Installation

11 Installation is the reverse of removal, noting the following.
● Make sure the spacers, bushes and washers are correctly installed with the mounting bolts. Tighten the bolts and nut to the torque setting specified at the beginning of this Chapter.
● Ensure the coolant hoses are in good condition (see Chapter 1), and are securely retained by their clamps, using new ones if necessary **(see illustration 2.7)**.
● Make sure that the wiring connectors are free of dirt and corrosion and all the wiring

is correctly connected and secured **(see illustrations 2.4 2.5a and b)**.
● Refill the cooling system as described in Chapter 1.

Radiator pressure cap

12 If problems such as overheating or loss of coolant occur, check the entire system as described in Chapter 1. The radiator cap opening pressure should be checked by a Yamaha dealer with the special tester required for the job. If the cap is defective, replace it with a new one.

3 Coolant reservoir

Removal

1 Remove the right hand side fairing panel.
2 Remove the reservoir cap and draw out the radiator overflow hose **(see illustration)**. Detach the breather hose from the clutch cable. **(see illustration)**.
3 Unscrew the reservoir mounting bolts and remove the reservoir **(see illustration)**. Tip the coolant out of the reservoir into a suitable container.

Installation

4 Installation is the reverse of removal, noting the following:

● Ensure the breather hose is correctly routed and secured.
● Fill the reservoir with the specified coolant up to the correct level (see *Pre-ride checks*).

4 Cooling fans and cooling fan relay

1 If the engine is overheating and the coolant temperature warning light is on, yet the cooling fans aren't cutting in, first check the fan circuit fuses (see Chapter 8) – note that if one fan works and the other doesn't, the fault is likely to be the fan fuse, motor or wiring, whereas if both fans don't work the fault is more likely to be the fan relay or the wiring between the relay and the battery.

2 If the fuses are good make sure there is battery voltage at the red wire to the fan relay with the ignition OFF, and to the red/white wire to the relay when the ignition is ON. If there is, the fault lies in either the fan relay or the cooling fan motors (see below), or the wiring and connectors between them. If not check the circuit between the cooling fan relay and the ignition switch, and between the relay and the ECU, referring to the wiring diagram for your model (see Chapter 8).

3.2a Remove the coolant reservoir cap

3.2b Detach the hose from the clutch cable

3.3 Unscrew the bolts (arrowed) and remove the reservoir

4.5 Fan mounting bolts (arrowed)

4.8a Cooling fan relay (arrowed)

Cooling fans

Check

3 To test the cooling fan motor(s), remove the left and/or right-hand rear cockpit trim panels as required (see Chapter 7). Trace the wiring from the fan motor and disconnect it at the connector **(see illustration 2.5a and b)**. Using a 12 volt battery and two jumper wires, connect the positive (+) battery lead to the blue wire terminal on the fan side of the wiring connector and the negative (–) lead to the black wire terminal. Once connected, the fan should operate. If it does not, and the wiring is all good, then the fan motor is faulty. Replace the fan assembly with a new one – individual components are not available.

Removal and installation

4 Remove the radiator (see Section 2).
5 Undo the screws securing each fan assembly to the radiator **(see illustration)**.
6 Installation is the reverse of removal.

Cooling fan relay

Check

7 Remove the left-hand fairing side panel (see Chapter 7). Refer to Step 2 if not already done and check the power to the relay.
8 If the voltage is good, disconnect the fan relay wiring connector **(see illustration)**. Set a multimeter to the ohms x 1 scale and connect the positive (+) probe to the red wire terminal on the relay, and the negative (-) probe to the brown/green wire terminal on the relay. Using a fully-charged 12 volt battery and two insulated jumper wires, connect the positive (+) terminal of the battery to the red/white wire terminal on the relay, and the negative (–) terminal to the green/yellow wire terminal on the relay **(see illustration)**. At this point the relay should be heard to click and the multimeter read 0 ohms (continuity). If this is the case the relay is proved good. If the relay does not click when battery voltage is applied and indicates no continuity (infinite

resistance) across its terminals, it is faulty and must be replaced with a new one. If the relay is good, and the wiring between the relay, the fan motors and the ECU is good, test the fan motors (if not already done), and the coolant temperature sensor (see Section 5).

Removal and installation

9 Remove the left-hand fairing side panel (see Chapter 7). The relay is mounted on the regulator/rectifier holder **(see illustration 4.8a)**.
10 Release the relay from its mounting, then disconnect the wiring connector.
11 Install the new relay and connect the wiring connector.

5 Coolant temperature display, warning light and sensor

Temperature display and warning light

Check

1 The circuit consists of the sensor mounted in the back of the cylinder head and the display and warning light mounted in the instrument cluster. The warning light should come on for a seconds when the ignition is switched ON, then go out – this serves as a check that the circuit is working correctly. If not, check the instrument cluster (see Chapter 8).
2 The temperature display should function as follows:

0 to 39°C	LO
40 to 116°C	Actual temperature of coolant
117 to 134°C	Actual temperature of coolant flashing and warning light on
Above 135°C	HI flashing and warning light on

Note: If the warning light comes on, stop the engine and allow it to cool.

4.8b Fan relay test terminal identification

A   Meter positive lead
B   Meter negative lead
C   Battery positive lead
D   Battery negative lead

3 If the system malfunctions, first check the fuses (see Chapter 8) and the sensor wiring and connections. Next check the temperature sensor as described below.
4 If no problems are found, take the instrument cluster to a Yamaha dealer for further assessment – Yamaha provide no specific test data for the instruments themselves. If there are any faults, even if just the warning light LED is faulty, a new cluster will have to be fitted, as no individual components are available.

Removal and installation

5 Refer to Chapter 8, Sections 16 and 17 for removal and installation details.

Coolant temperature sensor

Check

6 Raise or remove the fuel tank (see Chapter 4). Disconnect the coolant temperature sensor wiring connector, moving aside the wiring and hoses as required **(see illustration)**.
7 Using a jumper wire, connect between the terminals on the loom side of the temperature

5.6 Disconnect the wiring connector from the sensor (arrowed)

sensor connector, then turn the ignition ON. The temperature display and warning light should come on. If they don't, check the wiring between the connector and the instrument cluster (see the wiring diagrams at the end of this manual). If the wiring is good, the fault is likely to be in the instruments (see Step 4 above).

8 If the display and warning light do come on, it is likely that the sensor is faulty.

9 To check the operation of the sensor, remove it from the engine as described below, then fill a small heatproof container with cold coolant (see Specifications) and place it on a stove. Suspend the sensor in the coolant so that just the sensing portion and the threads are submerged – make sure the sensor terminals do not get wet. Using an ohmmeter, connect the probes to the terminals on the sensor. Place a thermometer capable of reading temperatures of up to 100°C in the water so that its bulb is close to the sensor **(see illustration)**. **Note:** *None of the components should be allowed to directly touch the container.*

 Warning: This must be done very carefully to avoid the risk of personal injury.

10 Heat the coolant, stirring it gently until the temperature exceeds 80°C, then turn off the heat and let it cool until the thermometer reads 80°C. Note the resistance at this point and compare it with that specified at the beginning of this Chapter. If the meter reading obtained is outside of the range specified then the sensor is faulty and must be replaced with a new one.

6.4a Unscrew the bolts . . .

H45560

5.9 Coolant temperature sensor test set-up

Removal and installation

 Warning: The engine must be completely cool before carrying out this procedure.

11 Partially drain the cooling system sufficient to avoid spilling coolant when the sensor is removed (see Chapter 1).

12 Remove the throttle bodies and the rubber heat shield (see Chapter 4).

13 Unscrew the sensor and remove it **(see illustration)**. Discard the sealing washer and obtain a new one.

14 On reassembly, apply a suitable sealant (Yamaha advise Three Bond Sealock 10) to the sensor threads, then install the sensor using a new sealing washer and tighten it to the torque setting specified at the beginning of this Chapter.

15 Top-up the cooling system (see Chapter 1 and *Pre-ride checks*) and install the remaining components in the reverse order of removal.

6 Thermostat

6.4b . . . and remove the thermostat

5.13 Unscrew and remove the sensor

1 The thermostat is automatic in operation and should give many years' service without requiring attention. In the event of a failure, the valve will probably jam open, in which case the engine will take much longer than normal to warm up. Conversely, if the valve jams shut, the coolant will be unable to circulate and the engine will overheat. Neither condition is acceptable, and the fault must be investigated promptly.

Removal

2 Partially drain the cooling system to a sufficient level to avoid spilling coolant when the thermostat housing is removed (see Chapter 1). Remove the fuel tank (see Chapter 4).

3 Remove the throttle bodies and the rubber heat shield (see Chapter 4).

4 Remove the hose from the thermostat housing and unscrew the bolts **(see illustration)**, being prepared to catch any residual coolant. Lift the thermostat out of the housing, noting how it fits **(see illustration)**.

5 Inspect the cover and housing for cracks and corrosion, especially around the hose unions. Clean off any corrosion with a wire brush or steel wool.

Check

6 Examine the thermostat visually before carrying out the test. If it remains in the open position at room temperature, it should be replaced with a new one.

7 To check the operation of the thermostat, suspend it in a container of cold water. Place a thermometer capable of reading temperatures up to 100°C in the water so that the bulb is close to the thermostat **(see illustration)**.

6.7 Thermostat test set-up

7.4a Remove the coolant hoses . . .

7.4b . . . and the breather hose

Heat the water whilst stirring it gently, noting the temperature when the thermostat opens, and compare the result with the specifications given at the beginning of this Chapter. Also check the amount the valve opens after it has been heated at 85°C for a few minutes and compare the measurement to the specifications. If the readings obtained differ from those given, the thermostat is faulty and must be replaced with a new one.

8 In the event of the thermostat jamming closed, *as an emergency measure only* it can be removed and the machine used without it. **Note:** *Take care when starting the engine from cold, as it will take much longer than usual to warm up.* Ensure that a new unit is installed as soon as possible.

Installation

9 Fit the thermostat into the housing, making sure that it seats correctly and that the breather hole is at the top **(see illustration 6.4b)**. Smear the new O-ring lightly with lithium-based grease and fit it into the cover.

10 Fit the housing and tighten the bolts to the specified torque setting **(see illustration 6.4a)**.

11 Make sure the hose is pushed fully onto the union and secured by the clamp. Fit the rubber strap around the main hose on the cover.

12 Install the throttle bodies and heat shield (see Chapter 4).

13 Top-up the cooling system (see Chapter 1 and *Pre-ride checks*) and install the remaining components in the reverse order of removal.

7 Water pump

Check

1 Remove the lower fairing (see Chapter 7). The water pump is located on the right side of the engine and is driven by the oil pump.

2 Check for signs of leakage from the pump or the hoses.

Removal

3 Disconnect the clutch cable and unscrew

and remove the bolts holding its stop (see Chapter 2). Drain the coolant (see Chapter 1).

4 Remove both coolant hoses and the breather hose from the pump **(see illustrations)**.

5 Unscrew the two Allen bolts, and remove the pump **(see illustration)**. Discard the O-ring as a new one must be fitted **(see illustration)**.

Inspection

6 Unscrew the two bolts and remove the cover **(see illustrations)**. To check the pump impeller bearing, wiggle the impeller back-and-forth and spin it by hand. If there is excessive movement, or the bearing is noisy or rough when turned, the bearing must be replaced with a new one. Also check the bearing referring to *Tools and Workshop Tips* (Section 5) in the *Reference* section.

7.5a Remove the Allen bolts (arrowed) . . .

7.5b . . . and remove the pump

7.5c Remove the O-ring and fit a new one

7.6a Unscrew the bolts . . .

7.6b . . . and remove the cover

7.7a Remove the circlip . . .

7.7b . . . and withdraw the shaft

7 Remove the circlip from the impeller shaft and withdraw the shaft **(see illustrations)**.
8 Check the condition of the rubber damper and its holder on the rear face of the impeller **(see illustration)**. Do not remove them from the shaft unnecessarily, as they cannot be reused. If they are damaged or deteriorated, fit a new impeller – Yamaha do not list the damper and holder as being available separately, though it is worth checking first. If they are available, lever off the old ones with a flat-bladed screwdriver. Apply coolant to the new ones and press them squarely down the shaft on to the back of the impeller. Check that they are in contact with the impeller
9 Inspect the pump body for corrosion or a build-up of scale and clean with steel wool

as necessary, then rinse the pump body in running clean water.
10 Lubricate the impeller shaft with coolant and slide it into the pump body **(see illustration 7.7b)**.

Seal and bearing removal and installation

11 Remove the pump from the engine and the cover from the pump (Steps 4, 5 and 6), then remove the circlip from the impeller shaft and withdraw the impeller/driveshaft from the pump body **(see illustrations 7.7a and b)**.
12 To remove the mechanical seal, tap it out from the back using a suitable punch or pull it out using an expanding internal puller – note which way round the seal fits **(see illustrations)**. Discard it, as a new one must be fitted.

13 To remove the oil seal, first remove the mechanical seal (see Step 12). Remove the oil seal with a seal pick and drive the bearing out from the front using a suitable socket as a drift and supporting the bearing housing on a second socket **(see illustrations)**. Note which way round the seal fits. Discard the seal and bearing, as new ones must be fitted.
14 Clean any traces of sealant from around the mechanical seal seat with a suitable solvent.
15 Press or drive the bearing into the pump body using a suitable driver or socket bearing on the outer race until it is properly seated **(see illustration)**.
16 Apply a smear of coolant to the outside of the new oil seal. Press or drive the seal into the body with the marked side facing out until it fits against the bearing.

7.8 Inspect the damper

7.12a Use a punch to drive out . . .

7.12b . . . the mechanical seal

7.13a Lever out the oil seal . . .

7.13b . . . and drive out the bearing

7.15 Mechanical seal (1), oil seal (2) and bearing (3)

17 Smear Yamaha Bond 1215 or a suitable equivalent to the mechanical seal seat. Press or carefully drive the new mechanical seal into the pump body using a suitable sized socket or seal driver which bears only on the outer rim of the seal and not on the centre. Yamaha produce a special tool for installing the seal, if required (Part Nos. 90890-04078 and 90890-04058 (European models) or YM-33221-A and YM-04058 (US models).

18 Lubricate the impeller shaft with coolant and slide it into the pump body and fit a new circlip.

Installation

19 Fit a new O-ring smeared with grease into the groove on the body **(see illustration 7.5c)**. Fit the cover using a new copper washer under the lower bolt **(see illustration)** and tighten the bolts to the specified torque setting **(see illustrations 7.6a)**.

20 Install the pump assembly and tighten the two Allen bolts **(see illustration 7.5a)** to the specified torque setting. Install the remaining components in reverse order of removal and refill the coolant system (see Chapter 1)

8 Coolant hoses, pipes and unions

Removal

1 Before removing a hose, pipe or union, drain the coolant (see Chapter 1). **Note:** *When removing components of the cooling system, be prepared to catch any residual fluids.*

7.19 Fit a new copper washer under the drain bolt

2 Use a screwdriver to slacken the larger-bore hose clamps, then slide them back along the hose and clear of the union spigot. The smaller-bore hoses are secured by spring clips which can be expanded by squeezing their ears together with pliers **(see illustration 7.4b)**.

Caution: The radiator unions are fragile. Do not use excessive force when attempting to remove the hoses.

3 If a hose proves stubborn, release it by rotating it on its union before working it off. If all else fails, cut the hose with a sharp knife then slit it at each union so that it can be peeled off in two pieces. Whilst this means renewing the hose, it is preferable to buying a new radiator.

4 Remove the inlet union on the front of the cylinder block by detaching the hose (see above), then unscrewing the two bolts, noting how the radiator mounting bracket fits **(see**

8.4 Unscrew the bolts (arrowed)

illustration). Discard the O-ring, as a new one must be fitted on reassembly.

Installation

5 Slide the clip onto the hose and then work the hose onto its union.

6 Rotate the hose on its union to settle it in position before sliding the clip into place and tightening it securely.

7 If the inlet union on the engine has been removed, fit a new O-ring and smear it with grease, then install the union and tighten the bolts to the torque setting specified at the beginning of the Chapter.

 HAYNES HiNT *If the hose is difficult to push onto its union, it can be softened by soaking it in very hot water, or alternatively a little soapy water can be used as a lubricant.*

Chapter 4
Engine management system

Contents

Degrees of difficulty

Easy, suitable for novice with little experience		Fairly easy, suitable for beginner with some experience		Fairly difficult, suitable for competent DIY mechanic		Difficult, suitable for experienced DIY mechanic		Very difficult, suitable for expert DIY or professional	

Specifications

General information

Cylinder numbering	1 to 4 from left to right
Ignition timing	10° BTDC @ 1300 rpm (determined by ECU)
Spark plugs	see Chapter 1

Component test data

AIS cut-off valve resistance	18 to 22 ohms @ 20°C
Atmospheric pressure sensor output voltage	3.15 to 4.15V
Camshaft position sensor output voltage	
On	0.8V or more
Off	4.8V or less
Crankshaft position sensor resistance	248 to 372 ohms @ 20°C
Coolant temperature sensor	
Resistance @ 80°C	290 to 354 ohms
Intake air pressure sensor output voltage	3.15 to 4.15V
Intake air temperature sensor resistance	290 to 390 ohms @ 80°C
Speed sensor output voltage	
On	4.8V or more
Off	0.6V or less
Throttle cable position sensor	
Resistance	2.0 to 3.0 K-ohms @ 20°C
Output voltage (2006 and 2007 models)	0.630 to 0.730V
Throttle body position sensor	
Resistance	2.0 to 3.0 K-ohms @ 20°C
Output voltage (2006 and 2007 models)	0.590 to 0.690V
Tip-over sensor output voltage	
Sensor upright	0.4 to 1.4V
Sensor tilted at specified angle	3.7 to 4.4V

Fuel

Grade	Premium unleaded, minimum 95 RON (Research Octane Number)
Fuel tank capacity (including reserve)	
2006 and 2007 models	17.5 litres
2008-on models	17.3 litres
Reserve (fuel light ON)	3.5 litres

Fuel level sensor

Fuel level sensor resistance	900 to 1050 ohms at 25°C

Throttle bodies

Type	
2006 and 2007 models	2 x Mikuni 41EIDW/1
2008-on models	2 x Mikuni 41EIDW
Throttle valve size	# 50
Intake vacuum	see Chapter 1

Fuel injector

Operating pressure	46.1 to 47.0 psi (3.18 to 3.24 Bar)

Ignition HT coils

Primary resistance	0.85 to 1.15 ohms @ 20°C
Secondary resistance	5.01 to 6.78 K-ohms @ 20°C
Minimum spark gap	6 mm

Torque wrench settings

Atmospheric pressure sensor screws	2 Nm
Cylinder identification sensor bolt	8 Nm
Crankshaft position sensor bolts	10 Nm
Exhaust catalyst section mounting bolts	20 Nm
Exhaust downpipe assembly flange nuts	20 Nm
Exhaust assembly mounting bracket bolts	30 Nm
EXUP cover bolt front	8 Nm
EXUP cover bolts rear	7 Nm
Fuel tank mounting bolts	7 Nm
Fuel tank cover screws	4 Nm
Fuel pump bolts	4 Nm
Oxygen sensor	45 Nm
Silencer mounting bolt	20 Nm
Silencer-to-catalyst section clamp bolt	10 Nm
Timing rotor cover bolts	12 Nm

1 General information and precautions

General information

All models are fitted with a fully electronic engine management system which controls both the fuelling and ignition from one engine control unit, or ECU.

Fuel system

The fuel system consists of the fuel tank, with an internal fuel pump, filter and pressure regulator integrated into one unit, the fuel supply hose, the primary fuel injectors located in the throttle bodies and the secondary fuel injectors located in the air filter housing, the throttle cables and cable position sensor, and the throttle body servo motor and position sensor. All models are equipped with YCC-T (Yamaha Chip Controlled Throttle) and the throttle bodies are under the direct control of

the ECU. Models from 2008 are equipped with YCC-I (Yamaha Chip Controlled Intake) and have intake funnels that adjust for length to enhance low speed torque under the control of the ECU.

In the event of the machine falling over, a lean angle sensor cuts power to the fuel and ignition systems.

The fuel injection system is controlled by the engine control unit (ECU) which monitors data sent from the various system sensors and adjusts fuel delivery to the engine and ignition timing accordingly. The ECU has its own fault diagnosis function and displays fault codes and diagnostic codes on the LCD display in the instrument cluster.

The exhaust is a four-into-two-into-one design and incorporates Yamaha's EXUP system The system consists of a servo actuated by the ECU and connected by cables to a valve in the exhaust that controls the flow of gasses through it according to engine speed. An air induction system (AIS)

introduces filtered air into the exhaust ports to promote the burning of excess fuel in the exhaust gases to reduce harmful emissions.

Ignition system

The ignition system comprises a timing rotor, crankshaft position sensor, the engine control unit (ECU) and ignition coils. All models are fitted with four 'stick' style HT coils which are integral with the spark plug caps.

The timing rotor on the right-hand end of the crankshaft generates a signal in the crankshaft position sensor as the crankshaft rotates. The crankshaft position sensor sends that signal to the ECU which, in conjunction with data sent from the various other system sensors, calculates the best ignition timing and supplies the ignition coils with the power necessary to produce a spark at the plugs. There is no provision for adjusting the ignition timing.

The system incorporates a starter safety circuit which will cut the ignition if the sidestand is extended whilst the engine is running and in gear, or if a gear is selected whilst the engine is running and the sidestand is extended. It also prevents the engine from being started if the engine is in gear unless the clutch lever is pulled in and the stand is up.

Models sold in certain markets are fitted with an immobiliser system which will not allow the engine to be started unless the correct key is used. The immobiliser system has its own fault diagnosis function. An alarm system is available as an optional extra.

Note: *Individual engine management system components can be checked but not repaired if faulty. If system troubles occur, and the faulty component can be isolated, the only cure for the problem in most cases is to replace the part with a new one. Keep in mind that most electronic parts, once purchased, cannot be returned. To avoid unnecessary expense, make very sure the faulty component has been positively identified before buying a new part.*

Precautions

⚠️ *Warning: Petrol (gasoline) is extremely flammable, so take extra precautions when you work on any part of the fuel system. Don't smoke or allow open flames or bare light bulbs near the work area, and don't work in a garage where a natural gas-type appliance is present. If you spill any fuel on your skin, rinse it off immediately with soap and water. When you perform any kind of work on the fuel system, wear safety glasses and have a fire extinguisher suitable for a class B type fire (flammable liquids) on hand.*

● Always perform service procedures in a well-ventilated area to prevent a build-up of fumes.

● Never work in a building containing a gas appliance with a pilot light, or any other form of naked flame. Ensure that there are no naked light bulbs or any sources of flame or sparks nearby.

● Do not smoke (or allow anyone else to smoke) while in the vicinity of petrol (gasoline), or of components containing petrol. Remember the possible presence of vapour from these sources and move well clear before smoking.

● Check all electrical equipment belonging to the house, garage or workshop where work is being undertaken (see the *Safety First!* section of this manual). Remember that certain electrical appliances such as drills, cutters, etc, create sparks in the normal course of operation and must not be used near petrol (gasoline) or any component containing it. Again, remember the possible presence of fumes before using electrical equipment.

● Always mop up any spilt fuel and safely dispose of the rag used.

● Any stored fuel that is drained off during servicing work must be kept in sealed containers that are suitable for holding petrol (gasoline), and clearly marked as such; the containers themselves should be kept in a safe place. Note that this last point applies equally to the fuel tank if it is removed from the machine; also remember to keep its filler cap closed at all times.

● Read the *Safety first!* section of this manual carefully before starting work.

2 Fuel tank

⚠️ *Warning: Refer to the precautions given in Section 1 before starting work.*

Raise

1 Make sure the fuel filler cap is secure. Remove the rider's seat (see Chapter 7).
2 Undo the screw securing each tank trim panel and remove the panels, noting how they fit **(see illustrations)**.
3 Unscrew the bolts securing the front and sides of the tank **(see illustrations)**.
4 Raise the tank at the front and support it using a prop or piece of wood as shown **(see illustration)**. Note the collar in the underside of the front mounting grommet and make sure it does not drop out.

Removal

Note: *To reduce the weight of the tank remove it when it is nearly empty, or if the tank is full siphon the fuel into a suitable container using a hand pump (available from tool suppliers) before removing the tank.*

5 Raise the tank (see Steps 1 to 4).

2.2a Undo the screws securing the trim (arrowed) . . .

2.2b . . . slide it forward and remove it . . .

2.2c . . . noting how it fits

2.3a Undo the bolts securing the front . . .

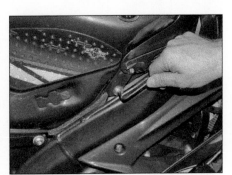

2.3b . . . and sides of the tank

2.4 Raise the front of the tank and prop it up

2.6 Disconnect the fuel pump and the fuel level sensor wiring connectors

2.7a Remove the security clip . . .

2.7b . . . press in the buttons . . .

2.7c . . . and remove the hose

2.8 Release the breather and overflow hoses

2.9a Unscrew the bolt . . .

6 Disconnect the fuel pump (green) and fuel level sensor (white) wiring connectors (see illustration).

7 Remove the security clip on the fuel supply hose connector, then press in the two tabs on the connector and pull it off the union (see illustrations). Have a rag ready to catch any residual fuel from the hose.

8 On all except California models release the clamp securing the breather/overflow hose to the hose joint and detach it (see illustration). On California models, release the clamps securing the overflow and EVAP system hoses

to their unions on the tank and detach the hoses, noting which fits where. Draw the hose out of the guide.

9 Remove the support and lower the tank. Unscrew the bolt securing the rear of the tank and then carefully lift the tank off the frame (see illustrations). Note: *Take care not to rest the tank directly on the fuel outlet pipe of the fuel pump.*

10 If required undo the screws, nuts and bolts securing the fuel tank cover and detach it from the front of the tank. Note the collars in the side mountings in the tank.

11 Inspect the tank support and mounting bolt rubbers for signs of damage or deterioration and replace them with new ones if necessary.

Installation

12 Installation is the reverse of removal, noting the following:
● Make sure the hoses are properly attached and secured by their clamps. Make sure the wiring connectors are secure.
● Tighten the mounting bolts to the torque settings specified at the beginning of the chapter.

2.9b . . . and remove it . . .

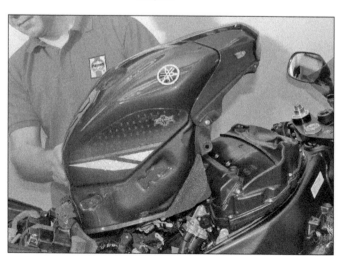

2.9c . . . before taking the tank off

● Start the engine and check that there are no signs of fuel leakage. If the tank has been emptied, ensure it is refilled before turning the ignition (main) switch ON.

Repair

13 All repairs to the fuel tank should be carried out by a professional who has experience in this critical and potentially dangerous work. Even after cleaning and flushing of the fuel system, explosive fumes can remain and ignite during repair of the tank.

14 If the fuel tank is removed from the bike, it should not be placed in an area where sparks or open flames could ignite the fumes coming out of the tank. Be especially careful inside garages where a natural gas-type appliance is located, because the pilot light could cause an explosion.

3 Fuel pump

⚠️ *Warning: Refer to the precautions given in Section 1 before starting work.*

Check

1 The fuel pump is located inside the fuel tank. When the ignition is switched ON, it performs its own self diagnosis, and in the event of a problem the fuel level warning light should flash eight times, then go out for three seconds, then repeat that cycle. Also it should

be possible to hear the pump run for a few seconds until the system is up to pressure. If you can't hear anything, first check that the battery is fully-charged, then check the main, ignition and fuel injection system fuses, the ignition and engine kill switches, and the pump relay which is contained within the relay assembly (see Section 8). If they are good, check the wiring and terminals in the circuit for physical damage or loose or corroded connections and rectify as necessary (see the *Wiring Diagrams* at the end of Chapter 8). If the pump still will not run, check the pump operates by performing a fuel delivery check.

2 If the pump is faulty replace it with a new one it. If the pump appears good, have the ECU checked by a Yamaha dealer.

Fuel delivery check

3 Raise the fuel tank, then disconnect the fuel hose from the fuel tank **(see illustration 2.7a, b and c)**.

4 Fit a suitable hose onto the pump outlet and place the open end in a suitable container.

5 Ensure the ignition is OFF, then disconnect the fuel pump (green) wiring connector **(see illustration 2.6)**. Using a fully-charged 12 volt battery and two insulated jumper wires, connect the battery positive (+) terminal to the pump's red/blue wire terminal, and the battery negative (-) terminal to the pump's black wire terminal. Fuel should flow from the pump into the container. If fuel does not flow, the pump is defective and must be replaced with a new one. If fuel flows but you suspect the flow rate to be insufficient, make sure all hoses are in

good condition and are not trapped or kinked and/or have the system operating pressure checked by a Yamaha dealer. If the filter is blocked a new pump will have to be installed as the filter is an integral component.

Removal and installation

6 Siphon the fuel from the tank into a suitable container using a hand-pump, available from good tool and DIY stores.

7 Remove the fuel tank (see Section 2), and lay it upside down on plenty of clean rag.

8 Unscrew the bolt securing the overflow and breather hose bracket **(see illustration)**. Unscrew the bolts securing the pump retaining ring and remove the ring, noting how it fits **(see illustrations)**.

9 Carefully lift the pump and manoeuvre it out of the tank, noting that there is little clearance and delicate bits can easily catch the rim **(see illustrations)**. Remove the pump O-ring and discard it as a new one must be fitted **(see illustration)**.

10 Install the pump using a new O-ring, fitting onto the pump base **(see illustration 3.9c)**. When inserting the pump, sit the wider diameter section of the rear on the rim of the aperture as shown so there is clearance for the protruding parts at the front **(see illustration 3.9a)**. Align the pump so the fuel supply hose union points to the right-hand side of the tank, and align the retaining ring over the peg at the front of the pump **(see illustration 3.8b)**. Tighten the bolts evenly and in a criss-cross sequence to the torque setting specified at the beginning of the Chapter.

3.8a Undo the screw holding the hose bracket . . .

3.8b . . . then unscrew the bolts securing the mounting ring (note the peg, arrowed) . . .

3.8c . . . and remove it noting how it fits

3.9a Remove the pump . . .

3.9b . . . being careful of projections . . .

3.9c . . . and remove the O-ring noting how it fits

4 Fuel level warning light and sensor

1 The circuit consists of the sensor mounted on the fuel pump inside the tank and the warning light mounted in the instrument cluster. The warning light should come on for a few seconds when the ignition is switched ON, then go out – this serves as a check that the circuit is working correctly. If not, check the instrument cluster (see Chapter 8). The warning light comes on and stays on when the level of fuel in the tank drops to approximately 3.5 litres.

2 If the system malfunctions, check first that the battery is fully-charged and that the fuses are good (see Chapter 8). If they are, remove the fuel pump from the tank (see Section 3). Make sure the wiring terminals and connectors are all secure (see illustration 2.6).

3 Using an ohmmeter or continuity tester,

check the resistance between the green/white and black wire terminals in the sensor wiring connector socket on the underside of the pump. The reading should be as specified at the beginning of the Chapter. If not, the sensor is faulty and a new pump will have to be fitted – individual components are not available.

4 If the sensor is good, disconnect the instrument cluster wiring connector (see Chapter 8), and check for continuity in the green/white wire between the level sensor and instrument cluster wiring connectors, referring to the *Wiring Diagrams* at the end of Chapter 8. Also check for continuity to earth in the black wire. If there is no continuity check the circuit and the connectors for faults.

5 Connect the instrument cluster wiring connector, then turn the ignition ON. Check for voltage at the level sensor connector green/white wire. If no voltage is present, and all other instrument functions are good, have the instrument cluster checked by a Yamaha dealer. If other instrument functions are not

working check the power input to the cluster (see Chapter 8).

5 Air filter housing

Removal

1 Remove the air filter (see Chapter 1).

2 Release the clip and pull the crankcase breather hose off its union at the rear of the housing (see illustration). Disconnect the YCC-I servo motor, if fitted, at the wiring connector (see illustration)

3 Undo the screws securing the intake funnels to the throttle bodies (see illustrations). Note that the screws are captive and should not be removed from the intake funnels on 2008-on models equipped with YCC-I.

4 Lift the housing up off the throttle bodies and when accessible release the clamp securing

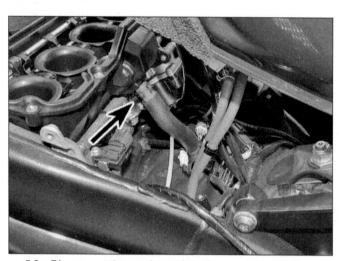

5.2a Disconnect the crankcase breather hose (arrowed) . . .

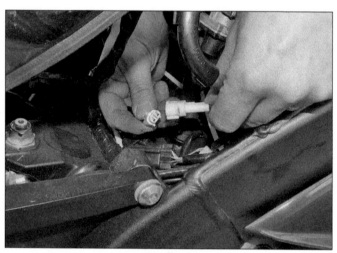

5.2b . . . and the YCC-I wiring connector if fitted

5.3a Intake funnel screws – 2006 and 2007 models

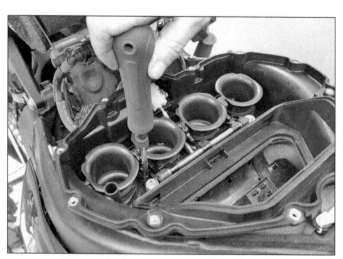

5.3b Intake funnel screws – 2008-on models

5.4a Remove the clamp on the AIS hose . . .

5.4b . . . and remove the housing

5.5 Check the sealing rings are seated correctly

the AIS hose and detach it from the housing, then remove the housing (see illustrations).

Installation

5 Installation is the reverse of removal. Check the condition of the hoses and their clamps and replace them with new ones if necessary. Check the condition of the sealing rings on the underside of the housing, making sure they are in good condition and are seated in their grooves (see illustration).

6 Fuel injection system description

1 The fuel injection system consists of two main component groups, the fuel circuit and the electronic control circuit.
2 The fuel circuit consists of the tank, pump which incorporates the fuel filter and pressure regulator, throttle bodies and injectors. Fuel is pumped under pressure from the tank to the fuel rails, from which the individual injectors are fed. Operating pressure is maintained by the pressure regulator. The injectors spray pressurised fuel into the throttle bodies where it mixes with air and vaporises, before entering the cylinder where it is compressed and ignited.

3 The electronic control circuit consists of the engine control unit (ECU), which operates and co-ordinates both the fuel injection and ignition systems, and the various sensors which provide the ECU with information on engine operating conditions.
4 The ECU monitors signals from the following sensors:

  Intake air temperature sensor
  Intake air pressure sensor
  Throttle position sensors
  Cylinder identification sensor (cam position)
  Crankshaft position sensor
  Coolant temperature sensor
  Atmospheric pressure sensor
  Speed sensor
  Tip-over sensor

5 Based on the information it receives, the ECU calculates the appropriate ignition and fuel requirements of the engine. By varying the length of the electronic pulse it sends to each injector, the ECU controls the length of time the injectors are held open and thereby the amount of fuel that is supplied to the engine. Fuel supply varies according to the engine's needs for starting, warming-up, idling, cruising and acceleration.
6 The engine management warning light should come on for 1.4 seconds when the ignition is switched ON, then go out – this serves as a check that the circuit is working correctly. If not, check the instrument cluster (see Chapter 8).
7 In the event of an abnormality in any of the sensor signals, the ECU will determine whether the engine can still be run safely. If it can, a back-up mode substitutes the sensor signal with a fixed signal, restricting performance but allowing the bike to be ridden home or to a dealer. When this occurs, the engine management warning light in the instrument cluster will come on and stay on. In some cases the engine will continue to run after the fault has been registered, but once stopped the engine will not be able to be restarted. If the fault is serious, the fuel injection system will be shut

down and the engine will not run. When this occurs, the engine management warning light will flash while the start switch is being pressed.
8 After the engine has been stopped, the appropriate self-diagnostic fault code will appear on the LCD. See Section 7 for fault diagnosis.

7 Fuel injection system fault diagnosis

1 The system incorporates a self-diagnostic function whereby most faults, when they occur, are identified by a fault code which is displayed on the LCD panel in the instruments after the engine has been stopped. The codes are stored in the ECU memory until a deletion operation is performed (see Step 9). In the case of a minor fault in the injection system, the engine management warning light in the instrument cluster will come on and stay on and the engine will continue to run, and may be able to be restarted, enabling the machine to be ridden, although performance will be significantly reduced. In the case of a major fault the warning light will flash and the engine will stop and not be able to be restarted. Certain faults will not activate the warning light and are not subject to a fault code, but will be recorded as a diagnostic code. If the engine does not run correctly but no warning light and fault code are shown, enter diagnostic mode (see Step 3 onwards), check the code given and refer to the table.
2 Compare the fault code displayed with those in Table 1 to identify the faulty component and the appropriate diagnostic code (where given), then follow the procedure in Steps 3 to 5 and set the instrument cluster to diagnostic mode to confirm the appropriate test procedure and specifications. If a diagnostic code is not given for a particular fault code (i.e. 11, 12 or 24), refer to Section 8 and check the component as described.

Table 1 Fuel system fault codes

Fault code	Faulty component – symptoms	Possible causes	Diagnostic code
11	Cylinder identification sensor – engine will continue to run but will not restart once turned OFF	Faulty wiring or wiring connector Damaged or improperly installed sensor Faulty ECU	-
12	Crankshaft position sensor – engine will not run and will not restart	Faulty wiring or wiring connector Damaged or improperly installed sensor or timing rotor Faulty ECU	-
13	Intake air pressure sensor – engine will run and start, air pressure signal fixed at 101.3 kpa	Faulty wiring or wiring connector Damaged or faulty sensor Faulty ECU	03
14	Intake air pressure sensor hose system – engine will run and start, air pressure signal fixed at 101.3 kpa	Hose system detached, pinched or blocked Faulty ECU	03
15	Throttle position sensors – engine may or may not start and run	Faulty wiring or wiring connector Damaged or improperly installed sensor Faulty ECU	01 or 13
17	EXUP servo – engine will start and run	Faulty wiring or wiring connector Faulty servo	53
18	EXUP motor is stuck – engine will run	Faulty wiring or wiring connector Servo or exhaust valve struck	53
19	Sidestand switch – engine will not run	Faulty wiring or wiring connector Faulty ECU Diode in the relay unit	20
20	Intake air pressure sensor/atmospheric pressure sensor – engine will start and run	Damaged air pressure sensor/atmospheric pressure sensor Sensor hose pinched or blocked Faulty ECU	03 or 02
21	Coolant temperature sensor – engine will start and run	Faulty wiring or wiring connector Damaged or improperly installed sensor Faulty ECU	06
22	Intake air temperature sensor – engine will start and run	Faulty wiring or wiring connector Damaged or improperly installed sensor Faulty ECU	05
23	Atmospheric pressure sensor – engine will start and run	Faulty wiring or wiring connector Damaged or improperly installed sensor Faulty ECU	02
24	O2 (oxygen sensor) out of normal range	Faulty wiring or wiring connector Damaged or improperly installed sensor Faulty ECU	-
30	Tip-over sensor – engine will not start or run, fuel system turned OFF	Machine overturned Faulty ECU	08
33	No. 1 cylinder ignition coil – engine will run on other 3 cylinders, fuel supply to No. 1 cylinder cut	Faulty wiring or wiring connector Damaged ignition coil Faulty ignition cut-off circuit Faulty ECU	30
34	No. 2 cylinder ignition coil – engine will run on other 3 cylinders, fuel supply to No. 2 cylinder cut	Faulty wiring or wiring connector Damaged ignition coil Faulty ignition cut-off circuit Faulty ECU	31
35	No. 3 cylinder ignition coil – engine will run on other 3 cylinders, fuel supply to No. 3 cylinder cut	Faulty wiring or wiring connector Damaged ignition coil Faulty ignition cut-off circuit Faulty ECU	32
36	No. 4 cylinder ignition coil – engine will run on other 3 cylinders, fuel supply to No. 4 cylinder cut	Faulty wiring or wiring connector Damaged ignition coil Faulty ignition cut-off circuit Faulty ECU	33
39	Primary injector fault – engine may start and run dependent on how many other injectors are faulty	Faulty wiring or wiring connector Damaged or wrongly fitted injector Faulty ECU	36, 37, 38 or 39

Fault code	Faulty component – symptoms	Possible causes	Diagnostic code
40	Secondary injector fault– engine may start and run dependent on how many other injectors are faulty	Faulty wiring or wiring connector Damaged or wrongly fitted injector Faulty ECU	40, 41, 42 or 43
41	Tip-over sensor – engine will not start or run, fuel system turned OFF	Faulty wiring or wiring connector Damaged sensor Faulty ECU	08
42	Speed sensor/neutral switch – engine will start and run	Damaged speed sensor Damaged neutral switch Faulty wiring or wiring connector Faulty ECU	07 21
43	Fuel pump and injector power supply abnormal– engine will start and run	Faulty wiring or wiring connector Faulty ECU	09
44	Carbon monoxide density in exhaust gas incorrect – engine will start and run	Faulty air induction system (AIS) Error writing CO to EPROM Faulty ECU	60
46	Abnormal power– engine will continue to run, and will restart	Faulty charging system (See Chapter 8)	-
50	ECU malfunction – fault code may not be displayed, engine may or may not run or start	Faulty wiring or wiring connector Damaged ECU	-
59	Throttle cable position sensor – engine may or may not run or start	Faulty wiring or wiring connector Damaged or wrongly fitted sensor Faulty ECU	14 or 15
60	Throttle body servo motor – engine may or may not run or start	Faulty wiring or wiring connector Damaged servo motor Faulty ECU	01
70	Idle shut off – engine will restart and run	The ECU shuts the engine down automatically after 20 minutes at idle speed.	-
Er-1	No ECU signals received by instrument cluster	Faulty wiring or wiring connector Damaged instrument cluster Faulty ECU	-
Er-2	No ECU signals received within the required time	Incorrectly connected wiring Damaged instrument cluster Faulty ECU	-
Er-3	ECU data incorrectly received	Incorrectly connected wiring Damaged instrument cluster Faulty ECU	-
Er-4	ECU data corrupt or unregistered	Incorrectly connected wiring Damaged instrument cluster Faulty ECU	-

Note: *The engine will not run when two or more ignition coils or fuel injectors fail.*

3 To set-up the diagnostic mode, first ensure that the ignition switch is OFF, that the engine stop switch is ON, then raise the fuel tank and disconnect the fuel pump wiring connector (see Section 2) **(see illustration 2.6)**.
4 Press the SELECT and RESET buttons on the instrument cluster simultaneously, then turn the ignition switch ON, keeping the SELECT and RESET buttons pressed for at least 8 seconds **(see illustration)**.
5 Select the diagnostic mode by pressing the SELECT button until dIAG appears on the LCD display. Confirm the selection by pressing the SELECT and RESET buttons simultaneously for 2 seconds. The diagnostic code d01 should be displayed.

6 Use the SELECT or RESET button to find the appropriate diagnostic code on the LCD. The SELECT button displays the code numbers in ascending order, the RESET button displays the numbers in descending order. The appropriate test specifications are displayed on the trip LCD. Compare the diagnostic code with Table 2 to identify the test action required. Compare the test results to any data displayed on the meter for that diagnostic code.
7 To test the actuator relevant to the code displayed, turn the engine kill switch to ON (if it is already on, turn it off then on again).
8 To cancel the diagnostic mode, turn the ignition switch OFF.

7.4 Press and hold the buttons and then turn the ignition ON

Table 2 Fuel system diagnostic codes and data

Diagnostic code	Action required	Data displayed
01	Throttle body sensor Check angle data displayed for signal 1 with throttle fully closed Check angle data displayed for signal 2 with throttle fully open	Fully closed – 12 to 21 Fully open – 97 to 106
02	Compare actual atmospheric pressure* with data displayed	-
03	Compare actual atmospheric pressure* with data displayed	Actual pressure with engine stopped
05	Check the temperature** in the air filter housing and compare with data displayed	-
06	Check the temperature*** of the coolant and compare with data displayed	-
07	Turn the rear wheel in the normal direction of rotation and check pulses are generated and displayed	0 to 999 (number of recorded pulses, returns to 0 on reaching 999)
08	Check the operation of the tip-over sensor	Machine upright – 0.4 to 1.4V Laid over – 3.7 to 4.4V
09	Turn the engine stop switch ON and check battery voltage (see Chapter 8)	0 to 18.7V. Normally 12V
13	Throttle body position sensor Check angle data displayed for signal 2 with throttle fully closed Check angle data displayed for signal 2 with throttle fully open	Fully closed – 9 to 23 Fully open – 94 to 108
14	Throttle cable position sensor Check angle data displayed for signal 1 with throttle fully closed Check angle data displayed for signal 1 with throttle fully open	Fully closed – 12 to 22 Fully open – 97 to 107
15	Throttle cable position sensor Check angle data displayed for signal 2 with throttle fully closed Check angle data displayed for signal 2 with throttle fully open	Fully closed – 10 to 24 Fully open – 95 to 109
20	Select a gear position other than neutral	Stand retracted – ON Stand down – OFF
21	Check the operation of the neutral switch	Gearbox in neutral – ON In gear – OFF
30 to 33	Check the operation of the appropriate ignition coil – setting the engine kill switch from OFF to ON will generate five sparks in the appropriate coil and the engine management warning light comes on. Check for the sparks by removing the plugs and checking as described in Section 18	-
34	Check the operation of the YCC-I system. Raises the funnels for three seconds and lowers them for three seconds the engine management light comes on.	-
36 to 39	Check the operation of the appropriate primary fuel injector – setting the engine kill switch from OFF to ON will generate five pulses in the appropriate injector and the engine management warning light comes on. Check for the pulses using a sounding rod as described in Section 10	-
40 to 43	Check the operation of the appropriate secondary fuel injector – setting the engine kill switch from OFF to ON will generate five pulses in the appropriate injector and the engine management warning light comes on. Check for the pulses using a sounding rod as described in Section 10	-
48	Check the operation of the AIS air cut-off valve – setting the engine kill switch from OFF to ON will actuate the valve five times and the engine management warning light comes on. You should be able to hear the valve – refer to Section 16 for access and further checks	-
50	Check the operation of the fuel injection system relay – setting the engine kill switch from OFF to ON will actuate the relay five times and the engine management warning light comes on. You should be able to hear the relay click – refer to Section 8 (fuel pump relay) for access and further checks	-
51	Check the operation of the fan relay – setting the engine kill switch from OFF to ON will actuate the relay five times and the engine management warning light comes on. You should be able to hear the relay – refer to Chapter 3 for access and further checks	-
52	Check the operation of the headlight ON/OFF relay – setting the engine kill switch from OFF to ON will actuate the relay five times and the engine management warning light comes on. You should be able to hear the relay and the light should come on – refer to Chapter 8 for access and further checks	-
53	Check the operation of the EXUP servo – setting the engine kill switch from OFF to ON will actuate the servo, opening then closing it	Exhaust valve angle
60	Check the carbon monoxide density in the exhaust gas Check the AIS cut-off valve	No fault – 00 Faulty cylinder – 01 to 04

Diagnostic code	Action required	Data displayed
61	Fault code history – cycles through one code every two seconds when more than one is present	11 to 60
62	Fault code history, total number of faults since last reset – setting the engine kill switch from OFF to ON will reset history	No fault – 00
63	Fault code reset for codes 24 and 40 only – setting the engine kill switch from OFF to ON will reset	No fault – 00 24 or 40
70	Programme control number displayed	00

* If an atmospheric pressure gauge is not available, use 101.3 kpa as the standard
** If possible, check the temperature next to the sensor, otherwise use the ambient temperature as the standard
*** Check the temperature of the coolant as close as possible to the sensor

9 Once the fault has been corrected, confirm that the fault code is no longer displayed by turning the ignition switch OFF and then ON again. If the code is no longer displayed on the clock LCD the repair is complete.

10 To delete the fault code from the ECU memory, follow the procedure in Steps 3 to 5 to set-up the diagnostic mode, then enter code 62 on the clock LCD. The total number of stored codes will be displayed on the trip LCD (00 to 21). Turn the engine stop switch ON to delete the stored codes – the LCD should display 00 codes.

8 Fuel injection system components

1 If a fault is indicated in any of the system components, first check the wiring and connectors between the appropriate component and the ECU (see *Wiring diagrams* at the end of Chapter 8). A continuity test of all wires will locate a break or short in any circuit. Inspect the terminals inside the wiring connectors and ensure they are not loose, bent or corroded. Spray the inside of the connectors with a proprietary electrical terminal cleaner before reconnection.

2 It is possible to undertake most checks on system components using a multimeter and comparing the results with the specifications at the beginning of the Chapter. **Note:**

Different meters may give slightly different results to those specified even though the component being tested is not faulty – do not consign a component to the bin before having it double-checked. However, some faults will only become evident when a component is tested with specialised equipment, in which case the checks should be undertaken by a Yamaha dealer.

3 If after a thorough check, the source of a fault has not been identified, it is possible that the ECU itself is faulty. Yamaha provides no test specifications for the ECU. In order to determine conclusively that the unit is defective it should either be taken to a Yamaha dealer or specialist repairer or substituted with a known good one along with its immobiliser, ignition switch and key where applicable.

Cylinder identification sensor

Check

4 Support the machine on an auxiliary stand with the rear wheel off the ground. Make sure the ignition is OFF. The sensor can be accessed either by removing the fairing side panels and lower fairing (see Chapter 7) and displacing the radiator (see Chapter 3), or by raising the fuel tank (see Section 2), removing the air filter housing (see Section 5) and AIS system (see Section 16) and then folding back the heat blanket **(see illustration)**.

5 Using a voltmeter or multimeter set to the volts (DC) scale, insert the positive (+)

probe of the meter into the white/black wire terminal in the back of the connector, with the connector still connected, and insert the negative (-) probe into the black/blue terminal **(see illustration)**. Turn the ignition switch ON, select a high gear and rotate the rear wheel by hand in its normal direction of rotation. As the engine turns, the output voltage should fluctuate between the two levels shown in the specifications at the beginning of the Chapter. Turn the ignition OFF.

6 If the voltage is not as specified, replace the sensor with a new one.

Removal and installation

7 Disconnect the sensor wiring connector (see Step 4 for access) **(see illustration 8.5)**. Unscrew the bolt securing the sensor to the valve cover and withdraw the sensor **(see illustration)**. On installation, smear the sensor O-ring with grease and apply a suitable thread lock to the bolt threads. Tighten the bolt to the torque setting specified at the beginning of the Chapter. Install all removed components.

Crankshaft position sensor

Check

8 Raise the fuel tank (see Section 2). Make sure the ignition is OFF.

9 The crankshaft position sensor is on the right-hand end of the crankshaft. Trace the wiring from below the timing rotor cover and disconnect it at the off-white 2-pin connector

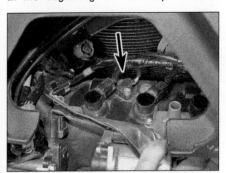

8.4 Fold back the heat blanket to access the sensor (arrowed)

8.5 Leave the connector block connected and test the sensor

8.7 Remove the bolt and withdraw the sensor

8.9 Uncouple the wiring connector for the crankshaft position sensor

8.11a Unscrew the bolts and remove the bracket

8.11b Bend up the tag and release the clutch cable

8.13 Unscrew the bolts, free both the wiring grommets and remove the sensor

(see illustration). Using an ohmmeter or multimeter set to the ohms x 100 scale, measure the resistance between the terminals on the sensor side of the connector. Connect the positive (+) probe to the grey wire terminal in the connector and the negative (-) probe to the black/blue wire terminal. If the result is not as specified, replace the sensor with a new one.

Removal and installation

10 Remove the lower fairing (see Chapter 7). Raise the fuel tank (see Section 2). Make sure the ignition is OFF.

11 Unscrew the clutch cable holder bolts and free the holder, noting how it locates **(see illustration)**. Bend down the retainer in the release mechanism arm and detach the cable end from it **(see illustration)**.

12 Trace the wiring from below the timing rotor cover and disconnect it at the off-white 2-pin connector **(see illustration 8.9)**. Feed the wiring back to the coil, noting its routing and releasing it from any clips.

13 Place an oil pan under the timing rotor cover on the right-hand side of the engine and then unscrew the bolts and remove it. Unscrew the bolts securing the crankshaft

position sensor, ease both wiring grommets from the crankcase and then remove the sensor **(see illustration)**.

14 Fit the sensor to the crankcase using a suitable non permanent thread locking compound on the bolts **(see illustration)**, then screw in the bolts and tighten them to the torque setting specified at the beginning of this Chapter **(see illustration 8.13)**.

15 Apply a suitable sealant such as Three Bond No1215 to the wiring grommets and locate them in the crankcase. Feed the wiring up to the connector and reconnect it **(see illustration 8.9)**.

16 Fit the timing rotor cover and the clutch cable holder. Screw in the bolts and tighten them to the torque setting specified at the beginning of this chapter. Fit the clutch cable into the release mechanism arm and bend the retainer to it **(see illustration 8.11b**

17 Install the fuel tank and the lower fairing. Check the engine oil level and replenish if necessary (see *Pre-ride checks*).

Intake air pressure sensor

Check

18 Make sure the ignition is OFF. Raise or remove the fuel tank (see Section 2) and remove the air filter housing (see Section 5).

19 The sensor is on the fuel rail **(see illustration)**. Check the condition of the vacuum hose between the underside of the sensor and the throttle bodies. If the hose is cracked or perished replace it with a new one. Ensure the hose is a tight fit on the sensor union, the hose connectors and the throttle bodies.

20 Using a voltmeter or multimeter set to the volts (DC) scale, insert the positive (+) probe of the meter into the pink/white wire terminal in the back of the connector, with the connector still connected, and insert the negative (-) probe into the black/blue terminal. Turn the ignition ON and measure the sensor output voltage. Turn the ignition OFF.

8.14 Apply a suitable thread locking compound to the bolts

8.19 The sensor (arrowed) is located on the fuel rail

8.22a Disconnect the vacuum hose . . .

8.22b . . . and uncouple the wiring connector

21 If the voltage is not as specified, replace the sensor with a new one.

Removal and installation

22 Raise or remove the fuel tank (see Section 2). Remove the air filter housing (see Section 5). Disconnect the wiring connector **(see illustration)** and the vacuum hose from the sensor **(see illustration)**. Undo the screw securing the sensor to the fuel rail and remove the sensor. On installation, ensure the wiring connector terminals are clean and that the vacuum hose is a tight fit on the sensor union.

Throttle position sensors and throttle servo

Check throttle body position sensor

23 Check the engine idle speed and make sure it is correct (see Chapter 1). Remove the sensor (see Step 27).

24 Using an ohmmeter or multimeter set to the K-ohms scale, connect the positive (+) probe to the blue wire terminal in the connector and the negative (-) probe to the black/blue wire terminal and measure the sensor maximum resistance **(see illustration)**. If the result is not as specified, replace the sensor with a new one.

Check throttle cable position sensor

25 Check the engine idle speed and make

sure it is correct (see Chapter 1). Remove the sensor (see Step 29).

26 Using an ohmmeter or multimeter set to the K-ohms scale, connect the positive (+) probe to the blue wire terminal in the connector and the negative (-) probe to the black/blue wire terminal and measure the sensor maximum resistance. If the result is not as specified, replace the sensor with a new one.

Removal, installation and adjustment – throttle body position sensor

27 Disconnect the sensor wiring connector using an Allen key to depress the tab on the connector **(see illustration)**. Remove the throttle bodies (see Section 9). Slacken the sensor screws and withdraw the sensor. When the sensor is removed check the actuating tab and the slot in the sensor for wear or damage.

28 Position the sensor and tighten the screws hand-tight **(see illustration)**. Reinstall the throttle bodies on the intakes. Connect the sensor wiring connector. Check that the throttle butterflies are closed. Perform the self diagnostic check (see Section 7). Tighten the sensor screws. Re-check the adjustment

Removal, installation and adjustment – throttle cable position sensor

29 Raise the fuel tank (see Section 2) and

8.24 Throttle body position sensor terminal identification – measure resistance between terminals arrowed

G Green   L Blue   B/L Black and blue

remove the air filter housing (see Section 5). Disconnect the sensor wiring connector **(see illustration)**. Slacken the sensor screws and withdraw the sensor. When the sensor is removed check the actuating tab and the slot in the sensor for wear or damage.

30 Position the sensor and tighten the screws hand-tight. Connect the sensor wiring connector. Check that the throttle butterflies

8.27 Use an Allen key to depress the tab and disconnect the wiring connector

8.28 Refit the screws and tighten them until they are hand-tight

8.29 Depress the tab and uncouple the wiring connector

8.33a Remove the front fairing to access the sensor on late models . . .

8.33b . . . or raise the fuel tank on early models

are closed. Perform the self diagnostic check (see Section 7). Tighten the sensor screws. Re-check the adjustment

Throttle servo motor

31 No service data is given for the throttle servo motor and Yamaha do not list it as separately available. The throttle bodies and servo motor have to be replaced as a unit if one or other is faulty.

Sidestand switch

32 Follow the procedure in Chapter 8 to check the operation of the switch.

Atmospheric pressure sensor

33 Make sure the ignition is OFF. On 2008-on models remove the fairing (see Chapter 7) to access the sensor (see illustration). On 2006 and 2007 models raise the fuel tank (see Section 2) to access the sensor (see illustration).
34 Using a voltmeter or multimeter set to the volts (DC) scale, insert the positive (+) probe of the meter into the pink wire terminal in the back of the connector, with the connector still connected, and insert the negative (-) probe into the black/blue terminal. Turn the ignition ON and measure the sensor output voltage. Turn the ignition OFF.
35 If the output voltage is not as specified, the sensor air passage may be clogged with dirt. Disconnect the wiring connector and undo the screws securing the sensor. Clean the outside of the sensor with a damp cloth and check the

air passage for any obstruction, then install the sensor and retest the output voltage.
36 If the voltage is still not as specified, replace the sensor with a new one.

Coolant temperature sensor

37 Follow the procedure in Chapter 3 to check the operation of the sensor.

Intake air temperature sensor

Check

38 To check the operation of the sensor, remove it from the machine as described below, then fill a small heatproof container with cold water (see Specifications) and place it on a stove. Suspend the sensor in the water so that just the sensing portion and the threads are submerged – make sure the sensor terminals do not get wet. Using an ohmmeter, connect the probes to the terminals on the sensor. Place a thermometer capable of reading temperatures of up to 100°C in the water so that its bulb is close to the sensor. Note: *None of the components should be allowed to directly touch the container.* Heat the water slowly, and then allow it to cool to 80°.
39 Using an ohmmeter or multimeter set to the ohms x 100 scale, measure the resistance between the terminals on the sensor side of the connector. Connect the positive (+) probe to the brown/white wire terminal in the sensor and the negative (-) probe to the black/blue wire terminal. If the result is not as specified replace the sensor with a new one.

 Warning: This must be done very carefully to avoid the risk of personal injury.

Removal and installation

40 Remove the headlight fairing (see Chapter 7). Disconnect the wiring connector and remove the screw (see illustrations). Withdraw the sensor. Refit the components in the reverse order.

Tip-over sensor

Check

41 Make sure the ignition is OFF. Remove the rider's seat and cowling (see Chapter 7), then displace the ECU.
42 Displace the sensor (see Step 45) leaving the wiring connected.
43 Using a voltmeter or multimeter set to the volts (DC) scale, insert the positive (+) probe of the meter into the yellow/green wire terminal in back of the connector, with the connector still connected, and insert the negative (-) probe into the black/blue terminal. Turn the ignition ON. Hold the sensor in its normal position when the bike is upright with the UP mark facing up, then tilt it more than 65° to one side and then the other. Turn the ignition OFF.
44 If the voltage is not as specified when the sensor is upright and tilted over, replace the sensor with a new one. Note the top surface of the sensor is marked UP.

Removal and installation

45 Make sure the ignition is OFF. Remove the rider's seat and cowling (see Chapter 7), displace the ECU. Undo the bolts securing the sensor, noting the washers (see illustration). Displace the sensor and disconnect the wiring connector. Note the top surface of the sensor is marked UP – make sure this mark is on top when installing the sensor.

Ignition coils

46 Follow the procedure in Section 19 to check the ignition coils.

Speed sensor

Check

47 Support the machine on an auxiliary stand with the rear wheel off the ground. Make sure

8.40a Disconnect the wiring connector . . .

8.40b . . . and remove the screw

8.45 Undo the screws and remove the sensor, noting the arrangement of the washers

8.50a Uncouple the 3-pin wiring connector (arrowed) for the sensor . . .

8.50b . . . undo the bolt (arrowed) . . .

the ignition is OFF. Raise or remove the fuel tank (see Section 2).

48 Locate the sensor white three-pin wiring connector on the right-hand side of the engine **(see illustration 8.50a)**. Using a voltmeter or multimeter set to the volts (DC) scale, insert the positive (+) probe of the meter into the white/yellow wire terminal in the back of the connector, with the connector still connected, and insert the negative (-) probe into the black/blue terminal. Turn the ignition switch ON, select a high gear and rotate the rear wheel by hand in its normal direction of rotation. As the engine turns, the output voltage should fluctuate between the two levels shown in the specifications at the beginning of the Chapter. Turn the ignition OFF.

49 If the voltage is not as specified, replace the sensor with a new one.

Removal and installation

50 Raise or remove the fuel tank (see Section 2). Disconnect the sensor white three-pin wiring connector and feed it back to the sensor, noting its routing **(see illustration)**. Carefully raise the rear of the heat blanket, removing the air filter housing (see Section 5) if necessary. Undo the bolt securing the sensor to the crankcase and withdraw the sensor **(see illustrations)**. On installation, apply grease to the O-ring, and make sure the wiring is correctly routed and the connector terminals are clean and the pins are not damaged.

Neutral switch

51 Follow the procedure in Chapter 8 to check the operation of the switch.

Fuel pump relay

52 Make sure the ignition is OFF. Remove the rider's seat (see Chapter 7). The relay assembly is mounted behind the battery and contains the fuel pump relay and starter circuit cut-off relay and diodes **(see illustration)**.

53 Disconnect the relay unit wiring connector. Using an ohmmeter or continuity tester, connect the positive (+) probe to the red

8.50c . . . and withdraw the sensor

wire terminal on the relay and the negative (-) probe to the red/blue wire terminal. There should be no continuity. Using a fully-charged 12V battery and some jumper leads, connect the positive (+) terminal of the battery to the red/black wire terminal on the relay, and the negative (–) terminal to the blue/yellow wire terminal. There should now be continuity between the red and red/blue wire terminals.

54 If the relay does not operate, replace the relay assembly with a new one.

Oxygen sensor

55 The sensor is in the right-hand side of the catalyst section of the exhaust **(see**

8.55a Oxygen sensor screws into top surface of catalyst section

8.52 The relay assembly (arrowed) is mounted behind the battery

illustration). Remove the right-hand fairing side panel and the lower fairing (see Chapter 7). Disconnect the sensor's wiring connector (raise the fuel tank for access), then free the sensor wiring from the cable-ties **(see illustrations 14.1a, b and c)**. Unscrew the sensor from the exhaust using either a cranked ring spanner which will fit over the wiring connector or an open-end spanner; the cutaway ring spanner and slotted socket are ideal for this job **(see illustration)**.

56 Apart from checking the wiring between the sensor and the ECU, the operation of the oxygen sensor itself cannot be checked

8.55b Slotted deep socket and cutaway ring spanner will fit over the sensor wiring

– if the sensor circuit is good (have this checked by a dealer for confirmation) remove the sensor and clean it with a wire brush or similar. Replace the sensor and clear the fault code (see diagnostic code 63 in the table). If the fault code reappears, replace the sensor.

9 Throttle bodies

  Warning: Refer to the precautions given in Section 1 before starting work.

Removal

1 Remove the air filter housing (see Section 5). Refer to Section 13, Steps 2 to 4 and detach the throttle cables from the throttle bodies noting that access to the bottom cable is restricted.
2 Disconnect the fuel injector wiring loom connector and both throttle position sensor wiring loom connectors **(see illustrations)**.
3 Disconnect the throttle servo motor wiring loom connector **(see illustration)**.
4 Place some rag under the fuel hose to catch any fuel, pull on the security clip and press in the two tabs to disconnect it from the fuel rail **(see illustrations)**.
5 Slacken the clamp bolts on the cylinder head intake rubbers, noting their orientation **(see illustration)**.
6 Ease the throttle body assembly up off the intakes and remove it **(see illustration)**.

9.2a Uncouple the connectors for the fuel injectors . . .

9.2c . . . and using an Allen key to depress the tab, the throttle body position sensor

7 Note how the clamps locate on the intake rubbers, and remove them if required **(see illustration)**.
8 If required remove the rubber heat shield,

9.2b . . . throttle cable position sensor . . .

9.3 Disconnect the wiring connector from the throttle servo motor

noting how it fits and how the wiring and hoses are routed **(see illustration)**.
Caution: Stuff clean rag (see illustration 9.7) or fit a plug (such as the top of an aerosol

9.4a Pull back the security clip . . .

9.4b . . . press on the buttons and disconnect the fuel hose

9.5 Slacken the clamp bolts (two arrowed) . . .

9.6 . . . and remove the throttle bodies

9.7 Note the position of the clamps

9.8 Remove the rubber heat shield if required

can) into each cylinder head intake to prevent anything from falling inside.

Disassembly

9 Remove the fuel rail and injectors (see Section 10). The throttle bodies should not be dismantled

10 Remove the throttle position sensors (see Section 8).

11 Note the arrangement of the vacuum hoses and where they connect on the throttle body, then pull them off their unions, leaving them connected to each other, and remove them **(see illustration 8.22b)**. On California models, detach the EVAP emission system hoses, noting how they fit. If required for cleaning the air screws may be removed (see Chapter 1, Section 5)

12 The throttle bodies should not be dismantled

Cleaning

Caution: Use only a petroleum-based solvent for cleaning. Do not use caustic cleaners.

13 Ensure that only metal components come into contact with the cleaning solvent and always follow manufacturer's recommendations as to cleaning time. If a spray cleaner is used, direct the spray into all passages.

14 After the cleaner has loosened and dissolved most of the varnish and other deposits, use a nylon-bristle brush to remove the stubborn deposits. Rinse the throttle bodies, then dry them with compressed air.

Caution: Never clean the jets or passages with a piece of wire or a drill bit, as they will be enlarged, causing the fuel and air metering rates to be upset.

15 Use compressed air to blow out all of the fuel and air passages.

Inspection

16 Check the throttle bodies for cracks, distorted sealing surfaces and other damage. If any defects are found, fit a new throttle body assembly.

17 Operate the throttle shaft to make sure the primary (lower) throttle butterfly valves open and close smoothly. If they don't, clean the throttle linkage, and also check the throttle bodies for wear where the butterfly valves close against them.

18 Check all the vacuum hoses for cracks, splits and kinks and replace them with new ones if necessary.

Reassembly

19 Reassemble the throttle bodies in a reverse of the disassembly procedure, referring to the relevant Sections. Make sure the vacuum and fuel hoses are all in good condition and replace them with new ones if necessary. Make sure they are pushed fully onto their unions and are secure. Make sure all wiring connectors are free from corrosion and that all terminals and wires are secure.

Installation

20 Installation is the reverse of removal, noting the following.

● Check for cracks or splits in the cylinder head intake rubbers, and replace them with new ones if necessary **(see illustration 9.7)**.

● Make sure the rubber heat shield is correctly positioned **(see illustration 9.8)**.

● Make sure the clamps on the cylinder head intake rubbers are correctly positioned **(see illustration 9.7)**. Make sure the throttle bodies are fully engaged with the rubbers – they can be difficult to engage, so a squirt of WD40 or a smear of grease will ease entry. Tighten the clamp bolts.

● Do not forget to connect the wiring loom connectors **(see illustrations 9.2a b and c and 9.3)**.

● Make sure all hoses are in good condition, correctly routed and secured and not trapped or kinked.

● Refer to Section 13 for installation of the throttle cables.

● Check idle speed and throttle body synchronisation and adjust as necessary (see Chapter 1).

10 Primary fuel rail and injectors

 Warning: Refer to the precautions given in Section 1 before proceeding.

Check

1 Refer to Section 7 and check for fault and diagnostic codes, and proceed accordingly.

2 To check the injectors, remove the fuel tank (see Section 2). If the engine runs, start it and allow it to idle. Check the operation of each injector in the throttle bodies using a stethoscope or sounding rod; an injector will emit a 'clicking' noise when functioning. If any injector is silent, either the injector or its wiring harness is faulty. If all injectors are silent refer to Section 7.

3 If the engine does not run, disconnect the wiring connector from each injector **(see illustration 10.6a)**. Connect an ohmmeter between the terminals of each injector in turn and measure the resistance – Yamaha do not specify a figure but it will be clear when comparing the four readings whether one is significantly different from the others. Using the wiring diagrams at the end of Chapter 8 check for continuity in the wiring and connectors between the injectors and the ECU, and between the injectors and earth.

Removal

4 Remove the air filter housing (see Section 5). If required remove the throttle bodies (see Section 9). Disconnect the vacuum hose and wiring connector from the inlet air pressure sensor **(see illustrations 8.22a and b)**.

5 Remove the screws securing the fuel rail to the throttle bodies **(see illustration)**. Carefully lift the fuel rail off the throttle bodies – the injectors will come away with the rail **(see illustration)**.

10.5a Undo the screw securing the fuel rail . . . **10.5b . . . and pull the fuel rail and injectors away from the throttle bodies**

10.6a Depress the tab and pull the wiring connector from the injector . . .

10.6b . . . then pull the injector from the fuel rail . . .

10.6c . . . and remove the O-ring . . .

10.6d . . . and the seals in the throttle body

6 Depress the tab and pull the wiring connector from each injector **(see illustration)** and then pull each injector out of the fuel rail, noting how it fits **(see illustration)**. Remove the O-rings from the injectors and the seals from the throttle bodies as new ones must be fitted on reassembly **(see illustrations)**.

7 Modern fuels contain detergents which should keep the injectors clean and free of gum or varnish from residue fuel. If an injector is suspected of being blocked, clean it through with injector cleaner. If the injector is clean but its performance is suspect, take it to a Yamaha dealer for assessment.

Installation

Note: *Apply a smear of clean engine oil to all new seals and O-rings before reassembly.*
8 Fit a new seal into each injector seat in the

throttle bodies, and a new O-ring onto the inlet end of each injector **(see illustration 10.6c and d)**. Carefully press the injectors into the fuel rail, making sure they are aligned so the wiring sockets face back **(see illustration 10.6a)**. **Note:** *Avoid twisting the injectors as this may damage the O-rings.*
9 Fit the fuel rail and injectors onto the throttle bodies, making sure each injector seats correctly in its seal **(see illustration 10.5b)**. Make sure the fuel rail is seated on its mounts with the screw holes aligned before installing the screws – do not use the screws to correctly seat and align them. Install the fuel rail screws and tighten them **(see illustration 10.5a)**.
10 If removed fit the intake air pressure sensor onto the fuel rail **(see illustration 8.22a)**.
11 Connect the individual injector wiring connectors and the intake air pressure sensor

connector **(see illustrations 10.6a and 8.22a)**. If necessary, secure the wiring to the fuel rail with new cable-ties **(see illustrations 10.5a and b)**.
12 Install the throttle bodies if removed (Section 9) and the air filter housing (Section 5). Run the engine with the fuel tank in the raised position and make sure there is absolutely no fuel leakage before riding the bike.

11 Secondary fuel rail and injectors

 Warning: Refer to the precautions given in Section 1 before proceeding.

Check

1 Refer to Section 7 and check for fault and diagnostic codes, and proceed accordingly.
2 Remove the secondary injector assembly as described below. Operate the injectors using the diagnostic code (see Section 7) and check their operation using a sounding rod or stethoscope; an injector will emit a 'clicking' noise when functioning. If any injector is silent, either the injector or its wiring harness is faulty. If all injectors are silent refer to Section 7.
3 Inspect each injector for signs of leaks or damage. Replace the O rings or injectors as necessary.

Removal

4 Raise the fuel tank (see Section 2). Place some rag under the fuel hose to catch any fuel, pull on the security clip and press in the two tabs to disconnect it from the fuel rail (see Chapter 1, Section 3). Trace the wiring for the secondary injectors from the air filter housing to the wiring loom connector and disconnect it noting the routing and any cable-ties.
5 Remove the top half of the air filter housing (see Chapter 1). Remove the grommet for the fuel rail, noting the position of the arrow mark **(see illustrations)**. Push the grommet for the injector wiring into the air filter housing **(see illustration)**.
6 Remove the Torx bolts that secure the

11.5a Remove the grommet . . .

11.5b . . . noting the arrow mark

11.5c Push the wiring grommet into the housing

11.6a Remove the screws securing the secondary injector assembly

11.6b Remove the rail feeding the fuel inlet through its hole . . .

secondary injector assembly to the top half of the air filter housing (see illustration). Remove the secondary injector assembly from the top half of the air filter housing feeding the fuel rail through its hole (see illustration). Feed the wiring connector through the hole in the top half of the filter housing (see illustration). Remove the rubber seal from the air filter housing as a new one must be used on reassembly.

7 If the injectors are to be removed loosen the screws securing the fuel rail to the plastic housing (see illustration) and remove it along with the injectors. Disconnect the wiring connector from the injectors to be removed (see illustration) and pull them from the fuel rail noting how they fit (see illustration). Remove the O rings from each injector as new ones must be fitted on reassembly (see illustration).

8 Modern fuels contain detergents which should keep the injectors clean and free of gum or varnish from residue fuel. If an injector is suspected of being blocked, clean it through with injector cleaner. If the injector is clean but its performance is suspect, take it to a Yamaha dealer for assessment.

Installation

Note: *Apply a smear of clean engine oil to all new seals and O-rings before reassembly.*

9 Fit a new O ring to each injector and carefully press them into the fuel rail making sure the wiring connectors are correctly aligned. **Note:** *Avoid twisting the injectors as this may damage the O-rings.*

10 Connect the wiring harness to the injectors. Check that the seals in the plastic housing are correctly located and replace any that are damaged (see illustration 11.7c). Carefully feed the injectors into the housing taking care not to displace the seals.

11 Ensure that the fuel rail is correctly seated and that the holes for the mounting screws line up; do not use the screws to draw the fuel rail into alignment. Apply a suitable non permanent thread locking compound to

the fuel rail screws and tighten them (see illustration 11.7a).

12 Fit a new rubber seal to the plastic housing and feed the wiring connector through the hole in the top half of the air filter housing (see illustration 11.6c). Refit the wiring grommet and feed the fuel rail through its aperture (see illustrations 11.6b and 11.5c). Refit the grommet for the fuel rail, ensuring that the alignment mark is pointing up (see illustration 11.5b).

13 Screw in the bolts that secure the secondary injector assembly to the top half of the air filter housing and tighten them. Refit the top half of the air filter housing and reconnect the fuel hose and wiring loom connector.

11.6c . . . and the wiring connector through its hole

11.7a Remove the screws securing the fuel rail

11.7b Detach the wiring connector . . .

11.7c . . . and remove the injector

11.7d Remove the O-ring as new ones must be fitted

12.1 Check the operation of the funnels

12.3 Remove the screws securing the pivot shaft

12.4a Pry the operating rod clip loose . . .

12.4b . . . and remove the funnels

13.3a Unscrew the nut and remove the adjuster

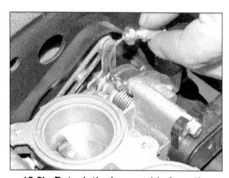

13.3b Detach the inner cable from the pulley

13.4a If necessary remove the throttle bodies to access the adjuster

13.4b Detach the inner cable from the pulley

12 YCC-I intake funnels

> **Warning:** *Refer to the precautions given in Section 1 before proceeding.*

Check

1 Refer to Section 7 for the diagnostic code and proceed accordingly. If the system fails to operate check the wiring loom connector for the servo motor and the wiring. Remove the funnels as described below, check for cracks or damage and that the operation is free and they will close under their own weight **(see illustration)**. Check the operating rod for damage. Replace any damaged components.

Removal

2 Raise the fuel tank (see Chapter 2) and remove the top half of the air filter housing (see Chapter 1).
3 Loosen the screws securing the intake funnel pivot shaft, and if the lower housing is still attached the screws securing the intake funnels to the throttle bodies **(see illustration)**. Note that the screws that secure the intake funnels to the throttle bodies are captive and should not be removed.
4 Pry the operating rod from its clip **(see illustrations)** and remove the intake funnels.

Installation

5 Installation is the reverse of removal noting that the intake funnels should be tightened to the throttle bodies before the pivot shaft is tightened and that the seals between the air filter housing and the throttle bodies should be checked and replaced if necessary.

13 Throttle cables

> **Warning:** *Refer to the precautions given in Section 1 before proceeding.*

Removal

1 Remove the air filter housing (see Section 5).
2 Mark each cable according to its location at both ends. If new cables are being fitted, match them to the old cables to ensure they are correctly installed.
3 Unscrew the hex on the throttle closing (top) cable and then slide the cable out of the bracket, noting how it locates **(see illustration)**. Detach the inner cable end from the throttle pulley **(see illustration)**.
4 It may be necessary to remove the throttle bodies to access the bottom cable (see Section 9 steps 2 to 6). Unscrew the hex on the throttle opening (bottom) cable, then slide the cable out of the bracket, noting how it locates **(see illustration)**. Detach the inner cable end from the throttle pulley **(see illustration)**.

13.5 Pull back the boot (A), then unscrew the bolts (B)

14.1a Uncouple the wiring connector

5 Pull the rubber boot back off the throttle housing on the handlebar **(see illustration)**. Remove the throttle housing bolts and separate the halves. Displace the cable elbows from the housing, noting how they fit, and detach the cable nipples from the pulley. Mark each cable to ensure it is connected correctly on installation.
6 Withdraw the cables from the machine, noting their correct routing.

Installation

7 Feed the cables from the handlebar through to the throttle bodies, making sure they are correctly routed. The cables must not interfere with any other component and should not be kinked or bent sharply.
8 Lubricate the cable nipples with multi-purpose grease and fit them into the throttle pulley at the handlebar, making sure the opening cable is at the front. Fit the cable elbows into the housing, making sure they locate correctly. Join the housing halves, making sure the pin locates in the hole in the handlebar, and tighten the screws **(see illustration 13.5)**. Fit the rubber boot.
9 Fit the throttle opening cable end into the pulley on the throttle body assembly, then fit the cable into the lower holder on the bracket **(see illustration 13.4b)**. Pull the cable to locate the nut against its lugs and

14.1b Remove any cable-ties and free the wiring . . .

tighten the hex against the bracket **(see illustration 13.4a)**.
10 Fit the throttle closing cable end into the pulley, then fit the cable into the upper holder on the bracket **(see illustration 13.3b)**. Pull the cable to locate the captive nut against its lugs and tighten the hex against the bracket **(see illustration 13.3a)**.
11 Refit the throttle bodies (see Section 9) if they were removed. Check and adjust the cable freeplay (see Chapter 1).
12 Install the air filter housing (Section 5). Start the engine, then turn the handlebars from lock to lock and check that the idle speed does not rise as you do. If it does,

14.1c . . . from the clip making a note of the routing

the throttle cables are routed incorrectly. Correct the problem before riding the motorcycle.

14 Exhaust system

⚠ *Warning: If the engine has been running the exhaust system will be very hot. Allow the system to cool before carrying out any work.*

Exhaust assembly
Removal

1 Remove the fairing side panels and the lower fairing (see Chapter 7). Remove the radiator (see Chapter 3) and raise the fuel tank (see Section 2). Detach the cables from the EXUP pulley (see Section 15). Trace the wires from the oxygen sensor to the wiring loom connection and disconnect it, removing any cable-ties and noting the routing **(see illustrations)**.
2 Slacken the bolt securing the silencer to the mounting, but do not remove it yet. Unscrew the mounting bolts that support the catalytic convertor section **(see illustration)**. Slacken the bolt securing the rubber mounting bush on the left hand side **(see illustration)**.

14.2a Slacken and remove the right-hand mounting bolt

14.2b Slacken and remove the left-hand mounting bolt (A) and loosen the bracket mounting bolt (B)

14.3 Undo the nuts and draw the flanges off of the studs

14.4a Support the system and withdraw the mounting bolt and washer

14.4b Detach the downpipes and remove the system

3 Unscrew the eight downpipe flange nuts and draw the flanges off the studs **(see illustration)**.
4 Supporting the system, remove the rear mounting bolt with its washer **(see illustration)**, then detach the downpipes from the cylinder head and remove the system **(see illustration)**. Note the collar in the rear mounting bush. Check the condition of the bush and replace it with a new one if necessary.
5 Remove the gasket from each port in the cylinder head and discard them, as new ones must be fitted **(see illustration 14.8)**.
6 If required undo the clamp bolt joining the silencer to the catalyst section and separate them **(see illustration)**. Discard the gasket as a new one must be used.

Installation

7 If necessary re-fit the silencer using a new gasket and ensuring that it is in the correct position to the catalytic convertor. Ensure the collar is in the rear mounting bush.
8 Fit a new gasket into each of the cylinder head ports **(see illustration)**. If necessary, apply a smear of grease to the gaskets to keep them in place whilst fitting the downpipe. If necessary fit a new sealing ring onto the end of the downpipe.
9 Manoeuvre the assembly into position so that the head of each downpipe is located in its port in the cylinder head and the catalytic convertor section is correctly positioned on the right hand mounting bracket. Screw in the silencer mounting bolt and its washer, but do not tighten them yet.
10 Loosely screw in the mounting bolts. Locate the downpipe flanges onto the studs, then fit the nuts and tighten them to the torque setting specified at the beginning of the

Chapter **(see illustration 14.3)**. Now tighten left-hand mounting bracket bolt and then the catalytic convertor section mounting bolts to the specified torque **(see illustration 14.2b and a)**.
11 Check the alignment of the silencer to its mounting and the catalyst section, slacken the clamp and adjust if necessary. Tighten the silencer mounting bolt to the torque specified at the beginning of this chapter and then tighten the clamp bolt to the specified torque. Install the EXUP cables (see Section 15). Install the radiator if removed (see Chapter 3). Route the wiring for the oxygen sensor, reconnect the wiring loom connector and replace the cable-ties.
12 Run the engine and check that there are no exhaust gas leaks. Install the fairing panels (see Chapter 7).

Silencer

Removal

13 To remove the silencer on its own, detach the EXUP cables (see Section 15).
14 Slacken the clamp bolt securing the silencer pipe to the catalyst section noting the locating tab on the clamp and the corresponding lugs on the silencer **(see illustration)**. Unscrew and remove the bolt and its washer from the silencer mounting **(see illustration 14.4a)**. Withdraw the bolt and release the silencer from the catalyst section **(see illustration)**. Remove the gasket as a new one must be fitted **(see illustration)**.

14.6 If required undo the clamp and separate the silencer from the system

14.8 Fit a new gasket into each port

14.14a Unscrew the bolt on the clamp noting the position of the locating lugs

14.14b Undo the clamp and remove the silencer

14.14c Remove the gasket

15.2 Unscrew the bolts and remove the cover

15.3a Unscrew the nut . . .

Installation

15 Check the condition of the silencer mounting rubber and replace it with a new one if damaged, deformed or deteriorated. Check that the collar is fitted into the inside of the mounting.

16 Fit a new gasket to the catalytic convertor.

17 Fit the silencer onto the catalyst piece, making sure it is pushed fully home. Align the silencer mounting bracket at the rear and install the bolt and washer, but do not yet tighten it **(see illustration 14.4a)**. Tighten the clamp bolt, then tighten the mounting bolt/nut to the torque setting specified at the beginning of the Chapter **(see illustration 14.14a)**.

18 Refit the EXUP cables (see section 15). Run the engine and check the system for leaks.

15 EXUP system

Cables

1 Remove the lower fairing (see Chapter 7).

2 Unscrew the bolts securing the EXUP pulley cover on the exhaust and remove the cover **(see illustration)**.

3 Slacken the hex securing each cable in its holder and release the cables, noting the adjusters for the opening and the closing cables are coloured differently and where each fits **(see illustrations)**. Unscrew the bolt securing the cable guide to the footrest mount **(see illustration)** and cut the cable-tie securing the oxygen sensor wire to the cables **(see illustration 14.1b)**.

4 Remove the servo (Step 13). Remove the rubber cover. Free the outer cables from their holders on the servo housing, noting which fits where, and detach the cable ends from the pulley **(see illustration)**.

5 Lubricate the cable nipples with

15.3b . . . and release the cable . . .

multi-purpose grease and fit them into the servo pulley **(see illustration 15.4)**. Fit the outer cable ends into their holders, making sure they locate correctly. Fit the rubber cover and install the servo (see below).

6 Route the cables correctly and refit the cable guide to the footrest mounting. Lubricate the cable ends with copper grease and fit them into the exhaust valve pulley **(see illustration 15.3b and c)**. Fit the cables into the holder and locate the nuts so they are captive, then tighten the other nut against it **(see illustration 15.3a)**, Check and adjust cable freeplay (see Chapter 1). Lubricate the cover bolt threads with copper grease. Install

15.3d Unscrew the bolt securing the cable guide

15.3c . . . noting where each fits

the cover and tighten the bolts to the specified torque setting specified at the beginning of the Chapter **(see illustration 15.2)**.

Check

7 When the ignition is first switched ON, the EXUP system performs its own self-diagnosis, and the servo can be heard turning the valve from fully closed to fully open and back again. If the servo does not turn refer to Section 7. Note that the motorcycle can be ridden even though a fault has been diagnosed, though a difference in performance will be noticed.

8 If the servo fails to operate and the fault code (see Section 7) indicates an electrical

15.4 Remove the rubber cover and free the cables

15.12 Unscrew the mounting bolt on each side (arrowed)

15.13 Disconnect the wiring connector (arrowed)

fault first check the wiring connector for loose or corroded terminals, then check the fuses and then the wiring between the connector and the ECU, referring to the test procedures and *Wiring Diagrams* in Chapter 8.

9 If the servo fails to operate and the fault code (see Section 7) indicates a mechanical problem, disconnect the EXUP cables and check that the valve is free to operate and that the cables are not seized or in need of lubrication.

10 If the servo is seized and doesn't respond to being operated by hand and lightly lubricated replace the servo with a new one.

11 If the operation of the valve is sticky, remove the silencer (see Section 14) clean off any visible dirt or corrosion and try to free it off. If the valve cannot be freed off, then a new silencer must be purchased.

Removal

12 Unscrew the bolts securing the mounting bracket and remove the bracket and servo **(see illustration)**.

13 Disconnect the wiring connector **(see illustration)**. Remove the rubber cover **(see illustration 15.4)**. Detach the cables as described above. If required unscrew the two bolts securing the mounting bracket and detach it from the servo.

14 The valve is integral with the silencer and replacement parts are not available.

16.4 Air should flow in through hose A and out of the two smaller-bore hoses when there is power to the valve

Installation

15 Installation is the reverse of removal.

16 Check the operation of the system and the cable freeplay (see Chapter 1). Install the pulley cover and tighten the bolts to the specified torque **(see illustration 15.2)**.

16 Air induction system (AIS)

Function

1 The air induction system uses exhaust gas pulses to suck fresh air into the exhaust ports, where it mixes with hot combustion gases. The extra oxygen causes continued combustion, allowing unburnt hydrocarbons to burn off, thereby reducing emissions. Reed valves control the flow of air into the ports, opening to allow fresh air to flow, and closing to prevent exhaust gases flowing back into the AIS. An air cut-off valve controlled by signals from the ECU shuts off the flow of air from the air filter housing when the engine reaches normal operating temperature. If the coolant temperature drops, the valve opens and air is added to aid combustion and raise the gas temperature inside the exhaust system.

2 Refer to Chapter 1, Section 6, for a check of the system.

16.8 Release the wiring connector from the cover

Testing

Air cut-off valve

3 Remove the valve from the motorcycle (see below).

4 Check the operation of the cut-off valve by blowing through the air filter housing hose union; no air should flow through the reed valve hose unions. Now connect battery voltage (12 volts) across the valve wiring connector terminals (positive to the red/white wire terminal and negative to the brown/red) and repeat the check; air should now flow freely through the valve if it is functioning correctly **(see illustration)**.

5 Check the resistance of the cut-off valve windings by connecting an ohmmeter to the connector terminals and compare the reading obtained to that given in the Specifications. Replace the valve with a new one if faulty.

Reed valves

6 Remove the AIS system (see below).

7 Attach a clean auxiliary hose of the correct bore and about 12 inches long to one of the unions **(see illustration 16.10a)**. Check the valve by blowing and sucking on the auxiliary hose end. Air should flow through the hose only when blown down it and not when sucked back up. If this is not the case the reed valve is faulty, though it is worth removing it (see below) and cleaning it in case it is just sticking due to a build-up of debris. Check the other valve in the same way.

Removal and installation

Air cut-off valve

8 Remove the fuel tank (see Chapter 2) and the air filter housing (see Section 5). Free the plastic cover from the frame by depressing the centre pin of the clip (see Chapter 7). Release the cover for the wiring connector from the plastic cover by squeezing its sides together **(see illustration)**. Remove the plastic cover,

9 Disconnect the wiring connector for the AIS cut-off valve and release the wiring tie

16.9 Disconnect the wiring connector (A) and release the wiring tie (B)

16.10a Pull the hose off each reed valve housing

on the air induction system (AIS) hose **(see illustration)**.

10 Disconnect the hose from each reed valve housing **(see illustration)**. Remove the cut-off valve and its bracket with its hoses attached **(see illustration 16.4)**. Detach the hoses if required. Note the protective sleeves over the spring clips **(see illustration)**.

11 Installation is the reverse of removal.

Reed valves

12 Remove the cut-off valve and its hoses (see Steps 8 to 10).

13 Carefully pull back the heat blanket and unscrew the bolts securing the reed valve cover and remove the cover **(see illustration)**. Remove the reed valve and the base plates, noting which way around they are fitted **(see illustrations)**.

14 Installation is the reverse of removal. Make sure the reed valve components and housings are clean and correctly fitted. Use a suitable thread locking compound when fitting the cover screws **(see illustration)**.

17 Catalytic converter

General information

1 A catalytic converter is incorporated in the exhaust system to minimise the level of exhaust pollutants released into the atmosphere.

2 The catalytic converter consists of a canister containing a fine mesh impregnated with a catalyst material, over which the hot exhaust gases pass. The catalyst speeds up the oxidation of harmful carbon monoxide, unburned hydrocarbons and soot, effectively reducing the quantity of harmful products released into the atmosphere via the exhaust gases.

3 The catalytic converter is of the closed-loop design, the oxygen sensor providing feedback to the ECU.

Precautions

4 The catalytic converter is a reliable and simple device which needs no maintenance in itself, but there are some facts of which an owner should be aware if the converter is to function properly for its full service life.

● DO NOT use leaded or lead replacement petrol (gasoline) – the additives will coat the precious metals, reducing their converting efficiency and will eventually destroy the catalytic converter.

● Always keep the ignition and fuel systems well-maintained in accordance with the manufacturer's schedule – if the fuel/air

16.10b Protective sleeves fit over spring clips

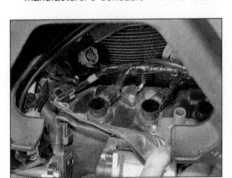

16.13a Carefully pull back the heat blanket to expose the covers

16.13b Remove the reed valves . . .

16.13c . . . and the base plates

16.14 Use a suitable thread locking compound

mixture is suspected of being incorrect have the exhaust gas CO content checked by a Yamaha dealer.

● If the engine develops a misfire, do not ride the bike at all (or at least as little as possible) until the fault is cured.

● DO NOT use fuel or engine oil additives – these may contain substances harmful to the catalytic converter.

● DO NOT continue to use the bike if the engine burns oil to the extent of leaving a visible trail of blue smoke.

● Remember that the catalytic converter is FRAGILE – handle the silencer carefully if removing it from the machine.

18 Ignition system check

 Warning: The energy levels in electronic systems can be very high. On no account should the ignition be switched on whilst the plugs or coils are being held. Shocks from the HT circuit can be most unpleasant. Secondly, it is vital that the plugs are soundly earthed (grounded) when the system is checked for sparking. The ignition system components can be seriously damaged if the HT circuit becomes isolated.

1 As no means of adjustment is available, any failure of the system can be traced to failure of a system component or a simple wiring fault. Of the two possibilities, the latter is by far the most likely. In the event of failure, check the system in a logical fashion, as described below.

2 Disconnect the wiring connector on the coil for No. 1 cylinder and pull the coil off the spark plug (see Section 19). Reconnect the wiring connector and fit a spare spark plug into the coil (preferably use a new plug, properly gapped – see Chapter 1). Connect the plug threads to a good earth (such as an engine mounting bolt) using an auxiliary wire with a crocodile clip on each end to give more freedom of movement. If necessary, hold the spark plug with an insulated tool. Do not lay the plug against the valve cover.

Warning: Do not remove any of the spark plugs from the engine to perform this check – atomised fuel being pumped out of the open spark plug hole could ignite, causing severe injury!

3 Check that the kill switch is in the RUN position and the transmission is in neutral, then turn the ignition switch ON and turn the engine over on the starter motor. If the system is in good condition a regular, fat blue spark should be evident at the plug electrodes. If the spark appears thin or yellowish, or is non-existent, further investigation will be necessary. Turn the ignition off and repeat the test for each coil in turn.

4 The ignition system must be able to produce a spark which is capable of jumping a particular size gap. Yamaha specify that a healthy system should produce a spark capable of jumping at least 6 mm. An ignition spark gap tester tool can be purchased to test the minimum gap across which the spark will jump **(see illustration)**.

5 Set the tool gap to 6 mm, following the manufacturer's instructions. Connect the coil of No. 1 cylinder to the test tool, and contact the tool to a good earth (ground) on the engine or frame as in Step 2. Check that the kill switch is in the RUN position, turn the ignition switch ON and turn the engine over on the starter motor. If the system is in good condition a regular, fat blue spark will be seen to jump the gap between the electrodes. Repeat the test for the other coils. If the test results are good the entire ignition system can be considered good. If the spark appears thin or yellowish, or is non-existent, further investigation will be necessary.

6 Ignition faults can be divided into two categories, namely those where the ignition system has failed completely, and those which are due to a partial failure. The likely faults are listed below, starting with the most probable source of failure. Work through the list systematically, referring to the appropriate Section of this Chapter and/or the specified Chapter for full details of the necessary checks and tests. **Note:** *Before checking the following items ensure that the battery is fully charged and that all fuses are in good condition.*

Loose, corroded or damaged wiring connections; broken or shorted wiring between any of the component parts of the ignition system (see 'fault finding' in Chapter 8).

Faulty spark plug, dirty, worn or corroded plug electrodes, or incorrect gap between electrodes (Chapter 1).

Faulty ignition switch or engine kill switch (see Chapter 8).

Faulty neutral, clutch or sidestand switch (see Chapter 8).

Faulty tip-over sensor (see Section 8).

Faulty starter circuit cut-off relay (see Chapter 8).

Faulty crankshaft position sensor (Section 8) or damaged timing rotor trigger (Chapter 2).

Faulty ignition coil(s) (Section 19).

Faulty ECU (Section 20).

7 If the above checks don't reveal the cause of the problem, have the ignition system tested by a Yamaha dealer.

19 Ignition coils

Check

1 Remove each coil (see Steps 5 to 7) and check them visually for cracks and other damage. Inspect the wiring terminals and the spark plug terminal.

2 Measure the primary circuit resistance with a multimeter as follows. Set the meter to the ohms x 1 scale and measure the resistance between the terminals on the coil **(see illustration)**. If the reading obtained is not within the range shown in the Specifications, it is likely that the coil is defective.

3 Measure the secondary circuit resistance with a multimeter as follows. Set the meter to the K-ohm scale. Connect one meter probe to one primary circuit terminal and the other probe to the spark plug terminal **(see illustration)**. If the reading obtained is not within the range shown in the Specifications, it is likely that the coil is defective.

4 If a coil is confirmed to be faulty, it must be replaced with a new one: the coils are sealed units and cannot therefore be repaired.

18.4 An adjustable spark gap testing tool

19.2 Coil primary resistance test connections

19.3 Coil secondary resistance test connections

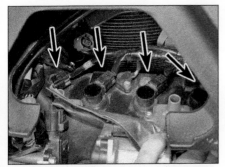

19.6 Disconnect the coil wiring connectors (arrowed)

Removal and installation

5 Raise the fuel tank (see Chapter 2), remove the air filter housing (see Section 5), and remove the AIS valve and hoses (see Section 16).
6 Carefully pull back the heat blanket and disconnect coil wiring connectors **(see illustration)**.
7 Clean the area around each coil to prevent any dirt falling into the spark plug channels. Pull the coil off each spark plug **(see illustration)**.
8 Installation is the reverse of removal. Make sure the coils are pushed down firmly onto the spark plugs and that the wiring connectors are securely connected.

20 ECU (Engine Control Unit)

1 If the tests shown in the preceding Sections have failed to isolate the cause of an ignition fault, it is possible that the ECU itself is faulty. No details are available with which the unit can be tested using home workshop equipment and it is recommended to take the unit to a Yamaha dealer for assessment. Note that checking whether the ECU is faulty by substituting it with a known good one is not feasible on machines equipped with an immobiliser; to do so would require the immobiliser system components to be re-registered to the different ECU.
2 Remove the rider's seat (see Chapter 7). Disconnect the battery negative (–) lead.

20.3 Ease back the clips (arrowed)

19.7 Pull the coil off the spark plug

3 Ease back the clips to the left and right of the ECU and raise the front of it up **(see illustration)**.
4 Disconnect the ECU wiring connectors **(see illustration)**.
5 Withdraw the ECU towards the front of the machine.
6 Installation is the reverse of removal. Make sure the wiring connector is correctly and securely connected.

21 Immobiliser system (Europe models)

General information

1 The immobiliser system will only allow the machine to be started if a correctly registered key is used to turn the ignition ON. The system consists of a transponder which is part of the ignition key, a receiver which is fitted around the ignition switch **(see illustration 21.27)**, and the engine control unit (ECU).
2 When the ignition is switched ON, the ECU sends power through the receiver to the transponder. The transponder sends a coded signal back through the receiver to the ECU. If the signal sent by the transponder matches the signal stored in the ECU memory, the immobiliser indicator light in the instrument cluster (marked by a key symbol and located in the tachometer face) comes on for about a second, then goes out, and the ECU allows the engine to be started. If the key code signal is not recognised, or if there is a fault

20.4 Disconnect the wiring connectors

in the system, the indicator light flashes. If the light flashes, refer to the fault diagnosis and troubleshooting Sections below. Likewise if the light does not come on at all. When the ignition is switched OFF the immobiliser light will start to flash after thirty seconds, indicating the system is enabled. The light will stop flashing after 24 hours but the system remains enabled.
3 The ECU can store the codes for up to three registered keys, two of which are standard use keys with black casings, and one is a code re-registering key with a red casing. The keys should be stored separately (i.e. not on the same key-ring) as the proximity of another key to the one being used in the switch can lead to the signal from it being jammed, and the bike will not start. The key has a built in transponder which can be damaged if the key is dropped or knocked, gets too hot, is too close to a magnetic object, or is submerged in water. If all the keys are lost, the ECU must be replaced with a new one, so always make sure you have one spare key. If a new key is obtained, it must be registered into the system before the bike can be started.

> **HAYNES HINT** *If you lose a key, or suspect it has been stolen, immediately re-register your code re-registering key and your remaining key – this will cancel the registration of the key that has been lost (or possibly stolen) which means that it will not be possible to start the bike using that key.*
> *If all three keys are lost, or if the ignition switch is faulty, a new ECU, immobiliser unit and lock set must be fitted. If either the immobiliser or ECU is faulty either unit can be replaced on its own.*

Standard key registration procedure

Note: *This must be done when a key is lost and a new one is obtained, or when a new 'code re-registering key' has been registered.*
4 Obtain a new key from a Yamaha dealer, and have it cut to match the original key.
5 Turn the ignition switch ON using the code re-registering key, then turn it OFF and within 5 seconds turn it ON with the key you wish to register. The immobiliser indicator light should flash on and off every half second. This indicates that the system is in registration mode. At this point the registration of the other existing standard key will have been cancelled, so this will also have to be registered.
6 To register the second key, turn the ignition OFF and remove the first key, placing it well away from the receiver, and within 5 seconds insert the second key into the switch and turn it ON. Turn the ignition OFF and remove the key. If the light stops flashing, more than 5 seconds have elapsed and the system is no

4•28 Engine management system

longer in registration mode, in which case start again.

7 On completion turn the ignition OFF and remove the key. After five seconds the light will stop flashing and the system is no longer in registration mode.

8 Check that both registered keys can start the motorcycle.

Code re-registering key registration procedure

Note: *This must be done when a new ECU or immobiliser receiver is fitted.*

9 Obtain a new key from a Yamaha dealer, and have it cut to match the original key.

10 Turn the ignition switch ON using the new code re-registering key. The immobiliser light will come on for about one second, then go out, indicating that the key has been registered.

11 Check that the key can start the motorcycle.

12 Now register the standard keys as described in Steps 4 to 8.

Installing a new ECU

13 Install the ECU (see Section 20).

14 Turn the ignition switch ON using the code re-registering key. This registers the key to the new ECU.

15 Check that the key can start the motorcycle.

16 Now register the standard keys as described in Steps 4 to 8.

Installing a new immobiliser

17 Remove the old immobiliser receiver from the ignition switch and fit the new one (see Step 27).

18 Turn the ignition switch ON using the code re-registering key. This registers the key to the new immobiliser.

19 Check that the key can start the motorcycle.

20 Now register the standard keys as described in Steps 4 to 8.

H48577

21.24 Immobiliser pin identification

R/G	Red/green	B2	Black (to alarm)
Lg	Light green	Y/L	Yellow/blue
R/W	Red/white	B	Black (to earth)

Fault code	Symptoms	Possible causes
51	Signal from key not being received by immobiliser	Interference from other keys or magnet Faulty key transponder Faulty immobiliser receiver
52	Code from key not recognised by receiver	Interference from other key Unregistered key being used
53	Signal from immobiliser not being received by ECU	Faulty wiring or wiring connector Faulty immobiliser receiver Faulty ECU
54	Code from immobiliser not recognised by ECU	Faulty wiring or wiring connector Immobiliser unregistered to ECU – code re-registering key not registered Faulty immobiliser receiver Faulty ECU
55	Key registration error	Same key being registered twice
56	Code from immobiliser not recognised by ECU	Faulty wiring or wiring connector Faulty immobiliser receiver Faulty ECU

Fault diagnosis

21 If there is a fault in the system, the immobiliser indicator light in the instrument cluster (marked by a key symbol and located in the tachometer face) flashes and a fault code is shown in the LCD display.

Troubleshooting procedure

22 If fault code 51 or 52 is shown, first check that none of the other registered keys are close to the receiver. If they are, remove them and try the ignition again.

23 If any fault code is shown, first check the fuses and the wiring and connectors between the immobiliser receiver, ignition switch and the ECU (see *Wiring diagrams* at the end of Chapter 8). A continuity test of all wires will locate a break or short in any circuit. Inspect the terminals inside the wiring connectors and ensure they are not loose, bent or corroded. Spray the inside of the connectors with a proprietary electrical terminal cleaner before reconnection. Also make sure the battery is in good condition and that the ignition switch is not faulty (see Chapter 8).

24 Remove the fuel tank (see Chapter 2) and the air filter housing (see Section 5). Free the plastic cover from the frame by depressing the centre pin of the clip (see Chapter 7). Release the cover for the wiring connector

21.27 Undo the screws (arrowed) and remove the immobiliser

from the plastic cover by squeezing its sides together **(see illustration 16.8)**. Disconnect the immobiliser off-white 6-pin wiring connector. Using a voltmeter, connect the positive (+) probe to the red/white (R/W) wire terminal on the loom side of the connector and the negative (–) probe to the black (B) wire terminal indicated **(see illustration)**. Turn the ignition ON – there should be battery voltage. Now repeat the test with the positive (+) probe connected to the red/green (R/G) wire terminal. If no voltage was recorded in either test refer to the wiring diagrams and check the red/white and red/green circuits to their power sources, and check the black wire for continuity to earth. If there is voltage the immobiliser receiver is probably faulty and must be replaced with a new one.

25 If the immobiliser LED or the LCD display in the instrument cluster does not come on, refer to Chapter 8 and check the instrument cluster.

26 If all indications are that either the immobiliser or the ECU are faulty, it is worth having them checked by a Yamaha dealer before buying replacements. Note that the immobiliser receiver, ignition switch, fuel filler cap, seat lock and ECU are available as a kit.

Replacement

27 Remove the fuel tank (see Chapter 2) and the air filter housing (see Section 5). Free the plastic cover from the frame by depressing the centre pin of the clip (see Chapter 7). Release the cover for the wiring connector from the plastic cover by squeezing its sides together **(see illustration 16.8)**. Disconnect the immobiliser off-white 6-pin wiring connector. Feed the wiring back to the receiver, freeing it from any ties and noting its routing. Undo the screws and remove the receiver, noting how it fits **(see illustration)**. If you don't have the correct tools to easily access the screws, removing the fairing will help (see Chapter 7), otherwise follow the procedure for removing the top yoke in the ignition switch replacement Section in Chapter 8.

28 To replace the ECU see Section 20.

Chapter 5
Frame and suspension

Contents

Degrees of difficulty

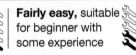

Easy, suitable for novice with little experience	**Fairly easy,** suitable for beginner with some experience	**Fairly difficult,** suitable for competent DIY mechanic	**Difficult,** suitable for experienced DIY mechanic	**Very difficult,** suitable for expert DIY or professional

Specifications

Front forks

Fork oil type
   All models . . . . Öhlins fork oil R&T 43
Fork oil capacity (per leg)
   2006 and 2007 models . . . . 465 cc
   2008-on models . . . . 482 cc
Fork oil level*
   2006 and 2007 models. . . . . 108 mm
   2008-on models . . . . 103 mm
Fork spring free length
   2006 and 2007 models
      Standard. . . . . 247 mm
      Service limit . . . . 242 mm
   2008-on models
      Standard. . . . . 254 mm
      Service limit . . . . 248.9 mm

*Oil level is measured from the top of the tube with the fork spring removed and the leg fully compressed.

Torque wrench settings

Clutch lever bracket clamp bolt . . . . 11 Nm
Footrest bracket bolts (rider's and passenger's) . . . . 28 Nm
Fork clamp bolts
    Bottom yoke . . . . 23 Nm
    Top yoke . . . . 26 Nm
Fork damper cartridge . . . . 35 Nm
Fork damper cartridge rod-to-top bolt locknut . . . . 25 Nm
Fork top bolt . . . . 20 Nm
Front brake master cylinder clamp bolts . . . . 13 Nm
Handlebar clamp bolts . . . . 32 Nm
Handlebar positioning bolts . . . . 13 Nm
Rear master cylinder mounting bolts . . . . 13 Nm
Rear shock absorber upper mounting bolt nut . . . . 44 Nm
Rear shock absorber top mounting bracket nut . . . . 52 Nm
Rear shock absorber lower mounting bolt nuts . . . . 44 Nm
Rear sub-frame to main frame bolts . . . . 37 Nm
Rear suspension linkage plate and linkage arm nuts . . . . 40 Nm
Sidestand bracket bolts . . . . 26 Nm
Steering stem nut . . . . 115 Nm
Swingarm pivot bolt nut . . . . 70 Nm
Swingarm pivot bolt . . . . 16 Nm
Swingarm pivot bolt locknut . . . . 95 Nm

1 General information

All models use a twin spar box-section Deltabox aluminium frame, with the beams above the angled cylinders so allowing a narrower design. As such the engine is not used as a fully stressed member, but the design provides good torsional rigidity without sacrificing weight. The narrow frame allows a slim line fuel tank.

Front suspension is by upside-down oil-damped 41 mm forks which have cartridge type dampers. The forks are adjustable for spring pre-load and both rebound and compression damping.

At the rear, an aluminium alloy truss-type swingarm acts on a single shock absorber via a three-way linkage. The shock absorber is adjustable for spring pre-load and for both rebound and compression damping.

2 Frame inspection and repair

1 The frame should not require attention unless accident damage has occurred. In most cases, fitting a new frame is the only satisfactory remedy for such damage. A few frame specialists have the jigs and other equipment necessary for straightening the frame to the required standard of accuracy, but even then there is no simple way of assessing to what extent the frame may have been over-stressed.
2 After the machine has covered a high mileage, the frame should be examined closely for signs of cracking or splitting at the welded joints. Loose engine mount bolts can cause ovaling or fracturing of the mounts themselves. Minor damage can often be repaired by welding, depending on the extent and nature of the damage, but this is a task for an expert.
3 Remember that a frame which is out of alignment will cause handling problems. If misalignment is suspected as the result of an accident, first check the wheel alignment (see Chapter 6). To have the frame checked thoroughly it will be necessary to strip the machine completely.

3 Brake pedal and footrests

Brake pedal and rider's right-hand footrest

Removal

1 Remove the split pin and washer from the clevis pin connecting the brake pedal to the master cylinder pushrod **(see illustration)**. Remove the clevis pin and separate the pushrod from the pedal. Discard the split pin, as a new one must be used on reassembly.
2 Unhook the pedal return spring and brake light switch spring from the lug on the back of the pedal **(see illustration)**. Undo the screw

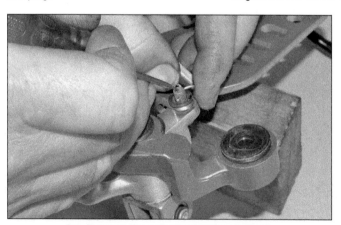

3.1 Remove the split pin and the clevis pin

3.2 Unscrew the switch bracket (A) unhook the switch spring (B) unhook the return spring (C) and undo the bolt (D)

securing the switch bracket and displace the switch. Cut the cable-tie securing the brake light switch wiring. Note the collar fitted in the rubber grommet and take care it doesn't drop out.

3 Unscrew the bolts securing the rear brake master cylinder to the footrest bracket **(see illustration)**.

4 Unscrew the bolts securing the EXUP cable guide. Unscrew and remove the silencer mounting bolt and washer.

5 Unscrew the bolts securing footrest bracket to the frame and remove the bracket **(see illustration)**. Unscrew the footrest bolt, then draw the footrest from the bracket and remove the pedal. Note the washer fitted between the pedal and the bracket. If required unscrew the two bolts securing the heel plate and the inner bracket and remove them.

Installation

6 Installation is the reverse of removal. Apply grease to the brake pedal pivot. Use a new split pin on the clevis pin securing the brake pedal to the master cylinder pushrod. **Note:** *See Chapter 1, Section 12 for details of adjusting the pedal height and brake light switch setting.* Tighten the footrest bracket bolts and the master cylinder bolts to the torque settings specified at the beginning of this Chapter. Use a new cable-tie to secure the brake light switch wiring.

Rider's left-hand footrest

7 Unscrew the bolts securing the footrest bracket to the frame and remove the bracket **(see illustration)**.

8 Unscrew the two bolts securing the heel plate and remove the plate. Depress the pin and remove the clips securing the chain guard plate.

9 The footrest can be obtained separately from the bracket. Remove the split pin to free the cotter pin and spring.

10 Installation is the reverse of removal.

Passenger footrests

11 Unscrew the footrest pivot bolt and nut, then withdraw the bolt and remove the footrest. Note the fitting of the detent plate, ball, spring and bolt spacer – take care that they do not fall out when removing the footrest.

12 To remove the footrest brackets, remove

3.3 Unscrew the bolts securing the master cylinder

3.7 Unscrew the bolts securing the left-hand footrest bracket to the frame (arrowed)

the seat cowling (see Chapter 7). Unscrew the bolts securing the footrest brackets to the rear sub-frame and remove the brackets **(see illustration)**.

13 Installation is the reverse of removal. Tighten the bracket bolts to the torque setting specified at the beginning of the Chapter.

4 Gearchange lever and sidestand

Gearchange lever

1 Support the motorcycle securely in an upright position using an auxiliary stand. Remove the lower fairing (see Chapter 7).

3.5 Unscrew the bolts securing the right-hand footrest bracket to the frame (arrowed)

3.12 Passenger footrest brackets bolt to rear sub-frame

2 Unscrew and remove the bolt securing the gearchange arm to the gearchange shaft and remove it noting the alignment marks **(see illustrations)**. Unscrew the pivot bolt for the gearchange lever and remove it along with the three washers, noting their order **(see illustration)**.

3 Installation is the reverse of removal, noting the following points:
● Apply lithium-based grease to the pivot contact areas.
● Use the alignment marks to return the gearchange arm to its orignal position on the shaft.

Sidestand

4 Remove the lower fairing (see Chapter 7).

4.2a Unscrew the bolt securing the gearchange arm . . .

4.2b . . . noting the alignment marks

4.2c Unscrew the bolt and remove the gearchange lever

4.4 Remove the plastic cover

4.5 Disconnect the spring from its posts and remove the nut (arrowed)

4.6 Bolt and large washer on inside of stand (arrowed)

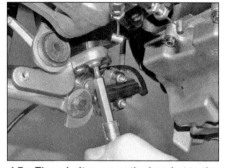

4.7a Three bolts secure the bracket to the frame

4.7b Disconnect the sidestand switch wiring connector and free the wiring from cable-ties

actuates the switch when the stand is lowered.
● Check the spring tension – it must hold the stand up when it is not in use. If the spring has sagged, replace it with a new one.
● Ensure the plastic cover tabs locate correctly into the cut-outs in the sidestand switch bracket.
● Check the operation of the sidestand switch (see Chapter 1).

5 Handlebars and levers

Handlebars

Removal – right-hand bar

1 Disconnect the brake light switch wiring connectors **(see illustration)**. Unscrew the bolt securing the reservoir bracket to the top yoke **(see illustration)**. Unscrew the master cylinder clamp bolts and remove the clamp, noting how it fits, then displace the master cylinder and reservoir away from the handlebar **(see illustration)**. There is no need to disconnect the hydraulic hoses. Keep the reservoir upright to prevent fluid spillage and make sure no strain is placed on the hoses.
2 Detach the throttle cables (see Chapter 4). Undo the switch housing screws and

Unclip the plastic cover from the inside of the frame **(see illustration)**.
5 With the stand in the raised position unhook the spring, noting how it fits, and remove it. Undo the nuts and withdraw the washer from the end of the stand pivot **(see illustration)**.
6 Press the threaded end of the pivot inwards so that it is withdrawn from the inside of the stand bracket. If resistance is felt, remove the end bolt and large washer from the inner side of the pivot and work the stand off the pivot shank **(see illustration)**. As the stand is removed from its bracket note the location of any thrust washers.
7 The sidestand mounting bracket can

be detached from the frame if required by removing its three mounting bolts **(see illustration)**. Note that the gearchange lever must first be disconnected from the bracket as described above and the sidestand switch wiring disconnected **(see illustration)**.
8 Installation is the reverse of removal, noting the following points:
● Apply a suitable thread locking compound to the bracket bolts before installation and tighten the bolts to the specified torque setting.
● Apply lithium-based grease to the pivot contact areas.
● Ensure the stand contact plate

5.1a Disconnect the wiring connectors (arrowed)

5.1b Unscrew the bolt (arrowed)

5.1c Unscrew the master cylinder clamp bolts (arrowed) and displace the assembly

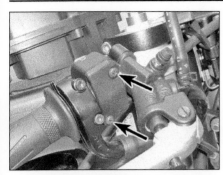

5.2 Undo the screws (arrowed) and displace the switch housing

5.4a Remove the blanking caps . . .

5.4b . . . then unscrew the bolts (arrowed)

displace the housing from the handlebar **(see illustration)**.

3 Unscrew the handlebar end-weight screw and remove the weight, then slide the twistgrip off the handlebar.

4 Remove the blanking cap from the head of each handlebar positioning bolt using a small flat-bladed screwdriver, then unscrew the bolts **(see illustrations)**.

5 Slacken the fork clamp bolts in the top yoke **(see illustration)**. Unscrew the steering stem nut and remove the washer **(see illustrations)**. Ease the top yoke up and off the forks **(see illustration)**.

6 Slacken the handlebar clamp bolt **(see illustration)**. Ease the handlebar up and off the fork.

Removal – left-hand bar

7 Disconnect the clutch switch wiring connectors **(see illustration)**. Undo the switch housing screws and detach the housing from the handlebar **(see illustration)**.

8 Unscrew the handlebar end-weight screw and remove the weight. Pull the grip off the bar – push a screwdriver between the grip and the bar and blow compressed air or spray lubricant inside the grip to loosen it. If the grip has been bonded in place you may need to cut it free.

9 Detach the clutch cable from the lever (see Chapter 2), then slacken the lever bracket

5.5a Slacken the fork clamp bolt on each side of the top yoke

5.5b Unscrew the nut . . .

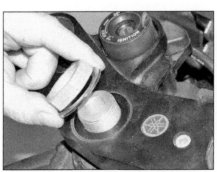

5.5c . . . removing it and the washer . . .

5.5d . . . then ease the top yoke up off the forks

5.6 Slacken the handlebar clamp bolt

5.7a Disconnect the wiring connectors

5.7b Undo the screws (arrowed) and detach the switch housing

5.9 Slacken the lever bracket clamp bolt (arrowed)

5.14 Thread the adjuster in, then unscrew the locknut on the bottom of the pivot bolt (arrowed)

5.16 Unscrew the locknut (A), then the pivot bolt (B)

pinch bolt and slide the lever off the bar end **(see illustration)**.

10 Remove the blanking cap from the head of each handlebar positioning bolt using a small flat-bladed screwdriver, then unscrew the bolts **(see illustrations 5.4a and b)**. Remove the bolt securing the reservoir bracket to the top yoke **(see illustration 5.1b)**.

11 Slacken the fork clamp bolts in the top yoke **(see illustration 5.5a)**. Unscrew the steering stem nut and remove the washer **(see illustration 5.5b)**. Ease the top yoke up and off the forks **(see illustration 5.5c)**.

12 Slacken the handlebar clamp bolt **(see illustration 5.5a)**. Ease the handlebar up and off the fork.

Installation

13 Installation is the reverse of removal, noting the following.

● Locate the handlebar on its fork and leave it loose, then fit the top yoke.

● Tighten the steering stem nut to the torque setting specified at the beginning of the Chapter, then tighten the fork clamp bolts – the handlebars need to be swivelled round on the forks to get a torque wrench on the clamp bolts, so do not fit the handlebar positioning bolts before doing so.

● Tighten the handlebar positioning bolts and handlebar clamp bolts, in that order, to the torque settings specified at the beginning of this Chapter.

● Align the master cylinder clamp mating

surfaces with the punch mark on the top of the handlebar, and fit the clamp with the UP mark facing up **(see illustration 5.1c)**. Make sure there is 2 mm between the switch housing and the master cylinder clamp. Tighten the clamp bolts to the specified torque, tightening the top bolt first.

● Slide the clutch lever bracket on before the grip. Align the slit in the clutch lever bracket with the punch mark on the underside of the handlebar, and tighten the clamp bolt to the specified torque.

● Lubricate the right-hand bar before sliding on the throttle twistgrip. Tighten the end-weight screws to the specified torque.

● Do not forget to reconnect the front brake light switch and clutch switch wiring connectors **(see illustrations 5.1a and 5.7a)**.

● Apply grease to the clutch and throttle cable ends. Refer to Chapter 4 for the installation of the throttle cables and Chapter 2 for the clutch cable.

● Locate the peg on each switch housing in its hole in the handlebar.

● Check and adjust throttle and clutch cable freeplay (see Chapter 1).

● Check the operation of all switches and the front brake and clutch before taking the machine on the road.

Clutch lever

14 Thread the clutch cable adjuster fully into the bracket to provide maximum freeplay in

the cable **(see illustration)**. Unscrew the lever pivot bolt locknut, then push the pivot bolt out of the bracket and remove the lever, detaching the cable nipple as you do so. Note the bush inside the lever and remove it if it is loose.

15 Installation is the reverse of removal. Apply grease to the pivot bolt shaft, the bush and the contact areas between the lever and its bracket, and to the clutch cable nipple. Adjust the clutch cable freeplay (see Chapter 1).

Front brake lever

16 Unscrew the lever pivot bolt locknut, then unscrew the pivot bolt and withdraw it from the bracket, and remove the lever **(see illustration)**.

17 Installation is the reverse of removal. Apply grease to the pivot bolt shaft and the contact areas between the lever and its bracket.

6 Fork removal and installation

Removal

1 Support the motorcycle with an auxiliary stand so that the front wheel is off the ground. Remove the fairing side panels and the fairing (see Chapter 7).

2 Remove the front mudguard (see Chapter 7).

3 Remove the front wheel (see Chapter 6).

4 Work on each fork leg individually. Note the routing of the various hoses and wiring around the forks. If removing the right-hand fork cut the cable-tie securing the brake hose **(see illustration)**. If removing the left-hand fork, cut the cable-tie for the horn wiring. Measure the amount the fork leg protrudes above the top yoke so it can be installed to the same position **(see illustration)**. Note that the model photographed has the forks set 10 mm above the surface of the top yoke, but the standard setting is flush with the top yoke, i.e. no protrusion.

5 If the fork legs are to be dismantled loosen the fork top bolt at this stage, but don't

6.4a Cut the cable-tie securing the wiring

6.4b Note the amount that the fork leg protrudes above the yoke – in this case 10 mm

6.5 Slacken the fork top bolt if the fork leg is to be dismantled

6.6a Slacken the clamp bolts in the lower yoke . . .

6.6b . . . then draw the fork leg down and out of the yokes

remove it **(see illustration)**. Slacken the fork clamp bolt in the top yoke and the handlebar clamp bolt **(see illustration 5.5a)**.

6 Support the fork leg, then loosen the fork clamp bolts in the bottom yoke **(see illustration)**. Remove the fork leg by twisting it and pulling it downwards out of the yoke and handlebar clamp **(see illustration)**. Note which fork leg fits on which side.

> **HAYNES HINT**
> *If the fork legs are seized in the yokes, spray the area with penetrating oil and allow time for it to soak in before trying again.*

Installation

7 Remove all traces of corrosion from the fork tubes and the yokes.

8 Slide the fork leg up through the bottom yoke and into the handlebar and top yoke, making sure the wiring, cables and hoses are the correct side of the leg as noted on removal **(see illustration 6.4a)**. Set the forks so the top edge of the outer tube (not the top bolt) is flush with the upper surface of the top yoke – this is the standard setting. The forks shown in photograph 6.4b have been set higher in the yokes by a previous owner.

9 Tighten the fork clamp bolts in the bottom yoke to the torque setting specified at the beginning of this Chapter **(see illustration 6.6a)**. If the fork leg has been dismantled or if the oil

has been changed, tighten the top bolt to the specified torque setting **(see illustration 6.5)**. Tighten the fork clamp bolt in the top yoke to the specified torque setting **(see illustration 5.5a)** – if access for your torque wrench is restricted, remove the blanking cap from the head of the handlebar positioning bolt using a small flat-bladed screwdriver, then unscrew the bolt and swivel the handlebar round on the fork **(see illustrations 5.4a and b)**. Afterwards align the handlebar and tighten the positioning bolt to the specified torque. Tighten the handlebar clamp bolt 7to the specified torque.

10 Fit new cable-ties to secure the brake hose to the right-hand fork and the horn wiring to the left-hand fork **(see illustration 6.4a)**, but be careful not to distort the brake hose. Install the remaining components in the reverse order of removal.

11 Check the operation of the front forks and brakes before taking the machine out on the road.

7 Fork oil change

Special Tool: *A special tool is needed to disassemble the forks – see Step 4.*

1 After a high mileage the fork oil will deteriorate and its damping and lubrication qualities will be impaired. Always change the oil in both fork legs.

2 Remove the fork leg; ensure that the top bolt is loosened **(see illustration 6.5)** and the spring pre-load set to the minimum while the leg is still clamped in the bottom yoke (see Section 13).

3 Support the fork leg in an upright position and unscrew the fork top bolt from the top of the fork tube **(see illustration)**. Note that a new O-ring should be fitted on refitting. Slide the fork outer tube down onto the inner tube.

4 With the aid of an assistant, pull up on the fork top bolt, then press down on the spacer to compress the spring and expose the locknut on the bottom of the damping adjuster. **Note:** *Yamaha service tools are available for this purpose – spacer holder Pt. No. 90890-01441 (YM-01441 in the US) and stopper plate Pt. No. 90890-01434 (YM-01434 in the US). Alternatively, use the home-made set-up shown using a piece of threaded rod, some nuts and some steel strap, and a washer with a slot cut in, making sure the tool is wide enough to fit over the tube. Do not insert the handle pieces too far into the spacer as they could foul the top bolt. Insert the stopper plate or slotted washer under the locknut* **(see illustrations)**. Carefully release pressure on the spacer and allow the plate or slotted washer to rest against the underside of the locknut under spring pressure.

5 Counter-hold the locknut and loosen the top bolt, then thread the top bolt assembly off the damper cartridge rod and remove it **(see**

7.3 Unscrew the fork top bolt

7.4a Fit the tool onto the spacer . . .

7.4b . . . then compress the spring and slide the slotted washer under the nut

7.5 Counter-hold the locknut and unscrew the top bolt from the rod

7.6a Withdraw the damping adjuster rod . . .

7.6b . . . and collect the washer

7.7a Remove the slotted washer and the spacer

7.7b On later models remove the spring seat

illustration). It may be necessary to reduce the thickness of a tool by grinding it to avoid damage to the protrusions on the top bolt assembly. **Note:** *The top bolt assembly should not be disassembled.*

6 Withdraw the damping adjuster rod from inside the damper cartridge rod **(see illustration)** and collect the washer from the locknut **(see illustration)**.

7 Compress the spacer and remove the plate or slotted washer, then carefully allow the spring to relax and remove the spacer with the tool still attached **(see illustration)**. Unscrew the locknut from the damper rod. Note that 2008-on models have a separate seating washer for the spring which was incorporated into the spacer on earlier models **(see illustration)**. Withdraw the spring from the tube, noting which way up it fits **(see illustration)**. The spring seating washer under the spring will probably remain in the leg but will come out when the oil is being drained.

8 Invert the fork leg over a suitable container **(see illustration)**. The damper cartridge rod will slide out of the fork when it is inverted **(see illustration)**. Pump the fork and rod to expel as much oil as possible. Collect the lower spring seating washer if necessary **(see illustration)**.

9 Support the leg and allow it to drain for several minutes. Wipe any excess oil off the

7.7c Withdraw the spring noting which way up it fits

7.8a Invert the fork leg over a suitable container to drain the oil . . .

7.8b . . . and so that the damper cartridge slides out

7.8c Collect the lower spring seat

7.10 Pour the oil into the top of the tube and distribute and bleed it as described . . .

7.11 Measure the level of oil and adjust if necessary

spring and spacer. If the fork oil contains metal particles inspect the fork components for signs of wear (see Section 8).

10 Slowly pour in the correct quantity and type of fork oil as specified at the beginning of this Chapter, keeping a hold on the damper rod to prevent it sinking **(see illustration)**. Secure the fork leg upright and if required fit a slotted washer under the locknut **(see illustration 7.6b)** to prevent the rod sinking into the tube, and allow it to stand for several minutes to allow all the air to escape. Now pump the rod again – once all the air is expelled you should feel stiff resistance when pumping the rod.

Take great care to ensure that all air is expelled from the damper cartridge at this stage.

11 Fully compress the fork outer tube and damper cartridge rod onto the inner tube and measure the oil level from the top of the tube **(see illustration)**. Add or subtract oil until it is at the level specified at the beginning of this Chapter.

12 Install the lower spring seat and then the spring in the correct orientation, sliding them over the damper rod **(see illustrations)**.

13 Draw out the damper rod **(see illustration)**. On 2008-models fit the loose spring seat **(see illustration)**. Position the

damper cartridge rod locknut all the way onto the rod, then fit a piece of thin wire around the rod under the locknut to help keep it extended **(see illustration)**. Fit the spacer sliding it over the wire or holding tool if being used **(see illustration)**.

14 Keeping the damper rod fully extended, press down on the spacer to compress the spring using the spacer holding tool (see Step 4), then insert the stopper plate or slotted washer under the locknut **(see illustration 7.4c)**. Remove the wire.

15 Fit the damping adjuster rod inside the damper rod **(see illustration 7.6a)**.

7.12a Install the lower spring seat . . .

7.12b . . . followed by the spring close-coiled end first

7.13a Withdraw the damper cartridge rod . . .

7.13b . . . fit the spring seat (where fitted) . . .

7.13c . . . then screw the locknut all the way onto the rod and use some wire . . .

7.13d . . . to hold it up while fitting the spacer

7.16a Fit a new O-ring to the top bolt . . .

7.16b . . . fit the washer to the locknut . . .

7.16c . . . and screw the top bolt all the way onto the damper cartridge rod

16 Fit a new O-ring to the top bolt **(see illustration)**, then fit the washer onto the locknut **(see illustration)** and thread the top bolt onto the damper rod screwing it all the way down to the locknut **(see illustration)**. Counter-hold the top bolt and tighten the locknut securely against it, to the specified torque if the correct tools are available **(see illustration 7.5)**.
17 Press down on the spacer to compress the spring and remove the plate or slotted washer, then carefully release the spring pressure, making sure the spacer is seated correctly onto the top bolt assembly **(see illustration)**. Remove the holding tool.
18 Pull the outer tube all the way up from the inner tube and carefully screw the top bolt into the outer tube making sure it is not cross-threaded **(see illustration 7.3)**. **Note:** *The top bolt can be tightened to the specified torque setting at this stage but a better method is*

to tighten the top bolt when the fork leg has been installed and is securely clamped in the bottom yoke (see Section 6).
19 Install the forks (see Section 6).

8 Fork overhaul

Special Tool: *Yamaha service tools are available for removing the damper cartridge and installing the fork seal, although alternatives are discussed in the procedure.*

Disassembly

1 Remove the fork legs as described in Section 6. Always dismantle the fork legs separately to avoid interchanging parts and store all components in separate, clearly marked containers.

2 Refer to Section 7, Steps 3 to 9 and drain the oil from the fork.
3 Separate the fork tubes **(see illustration)**.
4 Carefully clamp the inner tube in a vice using some rag to protect it **(see illustration)**, or alternatively fit the front wheel spindle and get an assistant to hold the inner tube. Unscrew the damper cartridge **(see illustration)**. **Note:** *A Yamaha service tool is available for this purpose – Pt. No. 90890-01506 (YM-01506 in the US). Alternatively a tool can be fashioned from a suitable piece of steel tube* **(see illustration)**.
5 Withdraw the damper cartridge assembly from inside the inner tube **(see illustration)**.
6 Carefully prise the dust seal from the bottom of the outer tube to gain access to the oil seal retaining clip and then remove the retaining clip **(see illustrations)**.
7 Carefully prise out the oil seal using either a seal hook or an internal puller with

7.17 Make sure the spacer is correctly seated

8.3 Separate the inner and outer tubes

8.4a Use some rag as protection and clamp the inner tube in a vice

8.4b Unscrew the damper cartridge

8.4c A home-made tool for unscrewing the damper cartridge

8.5 Withdraw the damper cartridge

8.6a Prise out the dust seal . . .

8.6b . . . remove the retaining clip . . .

8.7 . . . and use a suitable tool to remove the seal (arrowed) and washer

slide-hammer attachment, taking great care not to damage the rim of the tube, then remove the oil seal washer **(see illustration)**. Discard the seals as new ones must be fitted on reassembly.

Inspection

Note: *The fork bushes cannot be replaced with new ones. If, upon inspection, the bushes are found to be worn, new fork tubes will have to be fitted. Do not remove the compression damping adjusters.*

8 Clean all parts in solvent and blow them dry with compressed air, if available. Check the fork inner tube for score marks, scratches, flaking or pitted finish and excessive or abnormal wear. Look for dents in the inner tubes and replace them in both forks if necessary. Check the fork seal seat for nicks, gouges and scratches. If damage is evident, leaks will occur. Also check the oil seal washer

for damage or distortion; replace damaged or worn parts with new ones as necessary.
9 Check the fork inner tube for runout (bending) using V-blocks and a dial gauge, or have it done by a Yamaha dealer or suspension specialist **(see illustration)**. Yamaha specify a runout limit of 0.2 mm, so if the inner tube is bent beyond that seek the advice of a suspension specialist – straightening is sometimes possible but it is advisable to fit a new one.
10 Check the spring for cracks and other damage. Measure the spring free length and compare the measurement to the specifications at the beginning of this Chapter **(see illustration)**. If a spring is defective or has sagged below the service limit, replace the springs in both fork legs with new ones. Never replace only one spring.
11 Examine the working surfaces of the two bushes; if worn or scuffed (the grey Teflon surface will have worn away and the copper

underneath will be visible) the fork tube must be replaced with a new one.
12 Check the damper cartridge for damage and wear, and replace it with a new one if necessary.

Reassembly

13 Fit the oil seal washer into the fork tube **(see illustration)**. Fit the new oil seal into the tube and press or tap it into place until it seats and the retaining clip groove is visible – if necessary tap it in using a suitable socket with walls thin enough so it sits only on the hard outer rim of the seal and not on the seal's spring rim – you can use the old seal as an interface between the socket and the new seal, especially if the socket is not the ideal size **(see illustrations)**. Alternatively obtain the Yamaha service tool (Pt. No. 90890-01442 (YM-01442 in the US)).
14 Fit the retaining clip, making sure it locates

8.9 Check for any runout using V-blocks and a dial gauge

8.10 Measure the free length of the spring

8.13a Fit the seal washer . . .

8.13b . . . then lubricate the seal and fit it . . .

8.13c . . . using a suitable socket if necessary

8.13d Check that the seal is seated fully

8.14a Fit the retaining clip . . .

8.14b . . . and then the new dust seal

8.15 Fit the outer tube onto the inner tube

correctly in its groove **(see illustration)**. Press the dust seal into the tube **(see illustration)**.
15 Lubricate the inner surfaces of the new seals with the specified fork oil. Lubricate the inner tube and bushes inside the outer tube with fork oil, then carefully insert the inner tube fully into the outer tube **(see illustration)**.

16 Re-fit the damper cartridge assembly into the fork leg using either the Yamaha service tool or a home-made version to thread it into place **(see illustration 8.5 and 8.4b)**.
17 Refer to Section 7, Steps 10 to 18 and fill the fork with oil and finish reassembly.
18 Install the fork (see Section 6).

9 Steering stem

Removal

1 Remove the fairing side panels and fairing (see Chapter 7). It is also advisable to raise the fuel tank to avoid the possibility of scratching it (see Chapter 4).
2 Remove the front forks (see Section 6).
3 Disconnect the horn wiring connectors Unscrew the bolts securing the brake hose splitter, horn and trim piece to the bottom yoke and tie the front calipers to one side – cover them in rag to prevent scratching **(see illustration)**.
4 Unscrew the bolt securing the reservoir bracket to the top yoke **(see illustration 5.1b)**. Remove the blanking cap from the head of each handlebar positioning bolt using a small flat-bladed screwdriver, then unscrew the bolts **(see illustrations 5.4a and b)**.
5 Unscrew the steering stem nut and remove it and its washer, then lift the top yoke up off the steering stem **(see illustrations)**. Cable-tie the right handlebar to the right-hand mirror mount on the fairing stay, and the top yoke and left handlebar to the left-hand mirror mount. Free the throttle cables from the cable guide **(see illustration)**.
6 Remove the tabbed lockwasher, noting how it fits **(see illustration)**. Unscrew and remove the locknut using a C-spanner and remove the rubber washer **(see illustrations)**.
7 Supporting the bottom yoke, unscrew the

9.3 Unscrew the bolts securing the brake splitter and horn to the bottom yoke

9.5a Unscrew the nut and remove the washer . . .

9.5b . . . then lift off the top yoke

9.5c Free the throttle cables from the guide

9.6a Remove the lock washer noting how it fits . . .

9.6b . . . then unscrew the adjuster nut . . .

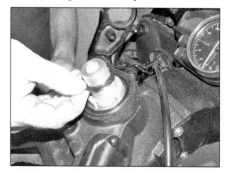

9.6c . . . and remove the rubber washer

9.7 Support the yoke and unscrew the adjuster nut

9.11 Remove the lower bearing and the dust seal (arrowed)

9.12a Coat the bearing with grease and refit it . . .

9.12b . . . followed by the bearing race . . .

9.12c . . . and the bearing cover

9.16 Align the handlebars then fit the positioning bolts

adjuster nut using a C-spanner if necessary **(see illustration)**. Gently lower the bottom yoke and steering stem out of the frame .

8 Remove the bearing cover, inner race and bearing from the top of the steering head **(see illustrations 9.12c, b, and a)**.

9 Remove the bearing and dust seal from the base of the steering stem **(see illustration 9.11)**. Discard the dust seal as a new one must be fitted on reassembly. Use a suitable solvent to remove all traces of old grease from the bearings and races and check them for wear or damage as described in Section 10. **Note:** *Do not remove the races from the steering head or the steering stem unless they are to be replaced with new ones – do not re-use the races if they have been removed.*

Installation

10 Smear a liberal quantity of lithium-based grease onto the bearing races and work some grease well into both the upper and lower bearings.

11 Fit the new dust seal over the lower bearing inner race on the steering stem, then fit the bearing **(see illustration)**.

12 Carefully lift the bottom yoke and steering stem up through the steering head and support it. Install the upper bearing and the inner race into the top of the steering head **(see illustrations)**. Fit the bearing cover **(see illustration)**. Thread the adjuster nut onto the steering stem by hand, making sure it is tight enough to hold the stem in the head without any play **(see illustration 9.7)**.

13 Install the forks, fitting the handlebars

onto them, and the front wheel, as their leverage and inertia need to be taken into account to properly set the bearings. Refer to the procedure in Chapter 1, Section 15, and adjust the bearings as described, noting that you may need to carry out the procedure several times if new bearings have been fitted to allow them to settle.

14 Fit the rubber washer and the locknut **(see illustration 9.6c and b)**. Tighten the locknut finger-tight, then tighten it further until its notches align with those in the adjuster nut. If necessary, counter-hold the adjuster nut to prevent it turning. Install the tabbed lockwasher so that the tabs fit into the notches in both the locknut and adjuster nut **(see illustration 9.6a)**.

15 Fit the top yoke onto the steering stem, then install the washer and steering stem nut and tighten it to the torque setting specified at the beginning of this Chapter **(see illustrations 9.5b and a)**. Now tighten the fork clamp bolts in the top yoke to the specified torque **(see illustration 5.5a)**.

16 Locate the handlebars against the underside of the top yoke and align the bolt holes, then fit the positioning bolts and tighten them to the specified torque **(see illustration)**. Fit the blanking caps **(see illustration 5.4a)**. Now tighten the handlebar clamp bolts to the specified torque **(see illustration 5.5a)**.

17 Install the remaining components in the reverse order of removal.

18 Carry out a check of the steering head bearing freeplay as described in Chapter 1, and if necessary re-adjust.

10 Steering head bearings

Inspection

1 Remove the steering stem (see Section 9). Using a suitable solvent remove all traces of old grease from the bearings and races.

2 Check for wear or damage – the races should be polished and free from indentations **(see illustration)**. Inspect the bearing balls for signs of wear, damage or discoloration, and examine their retainer cages for cracks or splits. Spin the bearing balls by hand. They should spin freely and smoothly. If there are signs of wear on any of the above components, both upper and lower bearing assemblies must be replaced with a new

10.2 Check the races for wear and damage

10.3a Drive the race out . . .

10.3b . . . locating the end of the drift as shown

10.5 Drawbolt arrangement for fitting steering stem bearing races

1 Long bolt or threaded bar
2 Thick washer
3 Guide for lower race

set. **Note:** *Do not remove the races from the steering head or the steering stem unless they are to be replaced with new ones – do not re-use the races if they have been removed.*

Renewal

3 The outer races are an interference fit in the steering head and can be tapped out using a suitable drift located on the exposed inner rim of the race **(see illustrations)**. Move the drift around the race so that it is driven out squarely.

4 Alternatively, the races can be removed using a slide-hammer type bearing extractor – these can often be hired from tool shops.

5 The new outer races can be installed in the head using a drawbolt arrangement **(see illustration)**, or by using a large diameter tubular drift. Ensure that the drawbolt washer or drift (as applicable) bears only on the outer

edge of the race and does not contact the bearing surface.

> **HAYNES HINT** *Installation of new bearing outer races is made much easier if the races are left overnight in the freezer. This causes them to contract slightly making them a looser fit. Alternatively, use a freeze spray.*

6 To remove the lower bearing race from the steering stem, first thread the steering stem nut onto the top of the stem to protect the threads, they lay the stem over and drive a chisel between the base of the race and the bottom yoke **(see illustration)**. Work the chisel around the race to ensure it lifts

squarely. Once there is clearance beneath the race, use two levers placed on opposite sides of the race to work it free, using blocks of wood to improve leverage and protect the yoke **(see illustration)**. If the race is firmly in place it will be necessary to use a bearing puller **(see illustration)**. Alternatively, take the steering stem to a Yamaha dealer.

7 Fit the new lower race onto the steering stem. A length of tubing with an internal diameter slightly larger than the steering stem will be needed to tap the new race into position **(see illustration)**.

8 Install the steering stem (see Section 9).

10.6a Dislodge the lower bearing race . . .

10.6b . . . and remove it as described . . .

11 Rear shock absorber

> ⚠ **Warning: Do not attempt to disassemble the shock absorber. It is nitrogen-charged under high pressure. Improper disassembly could result in serious injury. Take the shock to a Yamaha dealer or suspension specialist for servicing and disposal.**

Removal

1 Support the motorcycle so that no weight is transmitted through any part of the rear suspension – tie the front brake lever to the handlebar to ensure the bike can't roll forward. Position a support under the swingarm so that it does not drop when the suspension linkage

10.6c . . . or using a puller if necessary

10.7 Drive the new race on using a suitable driver or a length of tubing

11.1a Support the motorcycle so no weight is on the back wheel . . .

11.1b . . . using a suitably-sized wooden block as a packer

is removed **(see illustrations)**. Remove the fuel tank (see Chapter 4).

2 Remove the rear suspension linkage (see Section 12). Remove the swingarm support and allow it to rest at its lowest point.

3 Slacken the nut holding the top mounting bracket in the frame **(see illustration)**. Support the shock then thread the nut off. Draw the shock absorber down, then manoeuvre it out between the swingarm and the rear sub-frame **(see illustration)**. Collect the spacer washer from the top mounting bracket **(see illustration)**.

Inspection

4 Inspect the body of the shock absorber for obvious physical damage and the coil spring for looseness, cracks or signs of fatigue.

5 Inspect the damper rod for signs of bending, pitting and oil leakage **(see illustration)**.

6 Inspect the gas cylinder for damage.

7 Unscrew the nut and withdraw the bolt securing the top mounting bracket to the shock body **(see illustration)**. Inspect the pivot bush in the top mounting for wear – it is not available as a spare part so if worn a new shock absorber must be fitted. If the bush is good, or after obtaining a new shock, smear

some grease inside it, then fit the top mounting bracket and tighten the top mounting bolt nut to the torque setting specified at the beginning of the chapter.

8 Ensure that the spring pre-load adjusting ring is clean and free to rotate; inspect the indents on the ring for wear.

9 Ensure that the rebound damping and compression damping adjusters are clean and free to rotate.

10 The shock absorber cannot be dismantled for the replacement of parts. If it is worn or damaged, it must be replaced with a new one.

11.3a Support the shock absorber and remove the nut

Installation

11 Installation is the reverse of removal noting that the spacer washer for the top mounting bracket must be installed the correct way round with the coloured dot and UP mark facing upwards **(see illustration 11.3c)** and the tab facing to the rear **(see illustration 11.3a)**. Tighten the shock absorber lower mounting bolt nut and the top mounting bracket nut to the torque settings specified at the beginning of this Chapter.

11.3b Lower the shock absorber to clear the stud and manoeuvre it out

11.3c Collect the washer from the stud

11.5 Check around the rod (arrowed) for signs of pitting or leakage

11.7 Unscrew the nut (arrowed), withdraw the bolt and remove the bracket

12.2 Unscrew the bolt and remove the mounting bracket

12.3a Unscrew the nuts and collect the washers then . . .

12.3b . . . withdraw the bolts from the swinging arm . . .

12.3c . . . and the suspension linkage

12.3d Remove the collar from the swinging arm

12 Rear suspension linkage

Removal

1 Support the motorcycle so that no weight is transmitted through any part of the rear suspension (see illustrations 11.1a and b) – tie the front brake lever to the handlebar to ensure the bike can't roll forward. Position a support under the swingarm so that it does not drop when the linkage is removed.

2 Remove the lower fairing (see Chapter 7). Remove the rear wheel (see Chapter 6). Remove the exhaust (see Chapter 4) and unscrew the bolt securing the left-hand exhaust mounting bracket to the frame and remove the bracket (see illustration).

3 Unscrew the nuts, remove the washers, and withdraw the bolts securing the linkage plates to the swingarm and linkage arm (see illustrations). Remove the collar from swingarm (see illustration).

4 Unscrew the nut on the bolt securing the linkage arm to the bottom of the shock absorber (see illustration). Raise the swingarm if required, then withdraw the bolt.

5 Unscrew the nut and withdraw the bolt securing the linkage arm to the frame (see illustrations). Remove the collar from the frame and remove the linkage arm (see illustration). Withdraw the collars from the linkage arm, noting their positions (see illustration).

12.4 Unscrew the nut and withdraw the bolt securing the shock absorber to the linkage arm

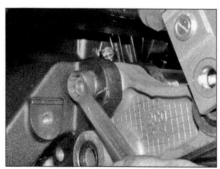

12.5a Unscrew the nut . . .

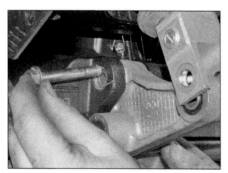

12.5b . . . and withdraw the bolt . . .

12.5c . . . and the collar then remove the linkage arm

12.5d Withdraw the collars from the linkage arm noting their positions

12.6 Lever out the bearing seals

12.8a Check the condition of the bearings (arrowed) in the linkage arm . . .

12.8b . . . and the linkage arm mount in the swinging arm

Inspection

6 Lever out the bearing seals **(see illustration)**. Thoroughly clean all components with a suitable solvent, removing all traces of dirt, corrosion and grease.

7 Inspect all components closely, looking for obvious signs of wear such as heavy scoring, or for damage such as cracks or distortion. Inspect the bolt holes in the linkage plates for elongation.

8 Check the condition of the needle roller bearings in the linkage arm and in the linkage plate mounting in the swingarm **(see illustrations)**. Refer to *Tools and Workshop Tips* (Section 5) in the Reference section for more information on bearings. Slip each collar back into its bearing and check that there is not an excessive amount of freeplay between the two components.

9 Worn bearings can be driven or drawn out of their bores, but note that removal will destroy them; new bearings should be obtained before work commences. The new bearings should be pressed or drawn into their bores rather than driven into position. In the absence of a press, a suitable drawbolt tool can be made up as described in *Tools and Workshop Tips* in the Reference section. When fitting the new bearings to the front and rear pivot points of the linkage arm make sure they are central in their bores. Measure the installed depth of the bearings and seals before removal and install the new ones to the same specification.

Yamaha specify the following installed depths.

Linkage arm needle roller bearings
Single bearing at the shock absorber and frame mounting points – 4.5 mm on each side Dual bearings at the linkage plate mounting point – 3.5 mm on each side

10 Lubricate the needle bearings, collars and seals with grease. Press the new seals squarely into place with their marked side facing out **(see illustration)**. Note that the seals on each side of the linkage plate mounting in the linkage arm should be installed to a depth of 1 mm.

Installation

11 Installation is the reverse of removal, noting the following:
● If not already done, withdraw the collars from the arm and the linkage plate mounting in the swingarm and linkage arm then clean the seals and needle bearings and apply lithium-based grease. Tighten the linkage plate and linkage arm nuts to the specified torque setting (see Specifications).

13 Suspension adjustment

Note: *Refer to the Owner's Manual supplied with the machine for recommended front and rear suspension settings to suit loading.*

Caution: Never attempt to turn an adjuster beyond the minimum or maximum setting.

Front forks

1 The front forks are adjustable for spring pre-load, rebound damping, and fast and slow compression damping.

2 **Spring pre-load** is adjusted using a suitable spanner on the adjuster hex flats on the top of the forks; the amount of pre-load is indicated by lines on the adjuster **(see illustration)**. There are five lines. The standard position is with the 2nd line visible above the fork top bolt **(see illustration)**. Turn the adjuster clockwise to increase pre-load, and anti-clockwise to decrease it. Always make sure both adjusters are set equally.

3 **Rebound damping** is adjusted using a screwdriver in the slot in the adjuster protruding from the spring pre-load adjuster **(see illustration 13.2a)**. Turn the adjuster clockwise to increase damping and anti-clockwise to decrease it. There are twenty-five positions. To establish the current setting, turn the adjuster in (clockwise) until it stops, counting the number of clicks, then reset it as required by turning it out (anti-clockwise). The standard position is twenty clicks out. The maximum damping is one click out and the minimum is twenty five clicks out. Always make sure both adjusters are set equally.

4 **Fast Compression damping** is adjusted by turning the hex on the adjuster on the

12.10 Press the new seals into place

13.2a Fork spring pre-load adjuster (A) and rebound damping adjuster (B)

13.2b Pre-load adjuster settings

13.4 Fast compression adjuster (A) and slow compression adjuster (B)

13.7 Spring pre-load (A) rebound damping (B) fast (C) and slow (D) compression damping adjusters

base of each fork **(see illustration)**. Turn the adjuster clockwise to increase damping and anti-clockwise to decrease it. The adjuster will move through four turns, screw the adjuster in (clockwise) counting the number of turns. This is the hardest setting, the standard setting is two turns out, and the softest setting is four turns out. Always make sure both adjusters are set equally

5 **Slow compression damping** is adjusted by using a screwdriver in the slot in the adjuster on the base of each fork **(see illustration 13.4)**. There are twenty positions. To establish the current setting, turn the adjuster in (clockwise) until it stops, counting the number of clicks, then reset it as required by turning it out (anti-clockwise). The standard position is fifteen clicks out. The maximum damping is one click out and the minimum is twenty five clicks out. Always make sure both adjusters are set equally.

Rear shock absorber

6 The rear shock absorber is adjustable for spring pre-load, rebound damping, and fast and slow compression damping.
7 **Spring pre-load** is adjusted with the C-spanner from the bike's toolkit **(see illustration)**. Turning the adjuster clockwise reduces the spring preload, turning it anti-

clockwise increase the spring preload. There are nine settings, the standard one is the fourth from the softest setting.
8 **Rebound damping** is adjusted by turning the adjuster on the base of the shock absorber **(see illustration 13.7)**. Turn the adjuster clockwise to increase damping and anti-clockwise to decrease it. There are twenty positions. To establish the current setting, turn the adjuster clockwise until it stops, counting the number of clicks, then reset it as required by turning it anti-clockwise. The standard position is sixteen clicks anti-clockwise, the maximum position is three clicks anti-clockwise and the minimum is twenty clicks anti-clockwise.
9 **Fast compression damping** is adjusted using a spanner on the adjuster hex on the back of the shock absorber top **(see illustration 13.7)**. Turn the adjuster nut clockwise to increase damping and anti-clockwise to decrease it. The adjuster moves through four turns. To establish the current setting turn it clockwise counting the number of turns. This is the hardest setting, the standard setting is two turns out, and the softest setting is four turns out.
10 **Slow compression damping** is adjusted using a screwdriver in the slot in the adjuster on the shock absorber top **(see illustration**

13.7). Turn the adjuster screw clockwise to increase damping and anti-clockwise to decrease it. There are twenty positions. To establish the current setting, turn the adjuster in (clockwise) until it stops, counting the number of clicks, then reset it as required by turning it out (anti-clockwise). The standard position is sixteen clicks out, the maximum position is one click out and the minimum is twenty clicks out.

14 Swingarm removal and installation

Special Tool: *A special tool is needed to remove the swingarm – see Step 5.*

Removal

1 Remove the exhaust system (see Chapter 4). Remove the front chain guide (see Chapter 6). Remove the rear wheel (see Chapter 6). Now support the motorcycle using a jack under the engine. Make sure the bike is properly supported and that there is no danger of it tipping back – tie the front down, and tie the brake lever to the handlebar to ensure the bike can't roll forward.
2 Remove the suspension linkage and shock absorber (see Sections 11 and 12).
3 Release the brake hose from its guides on the swingarm and hugger **(see illustration)**. Disconnect the stop light switch wiring connector, unscrew the bolts and remove the right-hand footrest assembly and rear caliper as one unit.
4 Before removing the swingarm it is advisable to check for play in the bearings (see Chapter 1). Any problems which were not evident with the other suspension components attached may now show up.
5 Loosen the locknut on the right-hand side of the frame using the Yamaha service tool (Pt. No. 90890-01507 or YM-01507 in the US) or a homemade equivalent **(see illustrations)**.

14.3 Release the rear brake hose from the guides

14.5a Head of special tool is 41.5 mm diameter, with 5 mm wide tabs spaced at 120°

14.5b Unscrew the locknut from the right side

14.5c Remove the nut and washer from the left side . . .

14.5d . . . then unscrew the pivot bolt from the right side

Unscrew the nut on the left-hand end of the swingarm pivot bolt, if necessary counter holding the pivot bolt, and remove the washer **(see illustration)**. Unscrew the pivot bolt using either the Yamaha service tool (Pt. No. 90890-01328 or YM-01328 in the US) or a 24 mm hex sump plug removal tool **(see illustration)**.

6 Support the swingarm, then withdraw the pivot bolt from the right-hand side and remove the swingarm, freeing the chain from the front sprocket and bringing it with the swingarm **(see illustrations)**. Knock the pivot bolt through using a large drift if required, but be careful not to damage the threaded end.

7 If required unscrew the two bolts and depress the pin in the clip securing the chainguard and remove it, then depress the pin and remove the clip securing the chain slider and remove it, noting how they fit **(see illustrations)**. Retrieve the collars and spring nuts for safekeeping. If the slider is badly worn or damaged, it should be replaced with a new one.

8 If required unscrew the three bolts securing the mudguard (hugger) to the swingarm and remove it **(see illustration)**.

9 Inspect all components for wear and damage as described in Section 15.

Installation

10 Remove the bearing cover from each side of the swingarm and check the condition of

14.6a Support the swingarm and remove the pivot bolt . . .

14.6b . . . to allow the swingarm to be lifted free

14.7a Undo the screws at the rear . . .

14.7b . . . and front of the chainguard . . .

14.7c . . . and depress the pin in the centre of the clip to remove the chainguard . . .

14.7d . . . before depressing the pin and removing the clip to free the chain slider

14.8 Undo the three screws (arrowed) to remove the rear mudguard

14.10 Remove the bearing cover from each side of the swingarm . . .

14.11 . . . and slide out the inner sleeve

15.7 A needle roller bearing is located in each side of the swingarm pivot

the seal inside the cover **(see illustration)**. If the seal is in good condition, the covers can be re-used, otherwise discard them and fit new ones.

11 Withdraw the long inner sleeve **(see illustration)**. Wipe all old grease from the inner sleeve and bearings, then apply fresh lithium-based grease to their surfaces. Slide the sleeve back through the bearings. Grease the suspension linkage bearing on the underside of the swingarm (see Section 12).

12 If removed, install the hugger, the chain slider and chainguard, making sure the collars are in the mounts **(see illustrations 14.7a, b, c d and 14.8)**.

13 Grease the inside of the bearing covers and fit them **(see illustration 14.10)**. Grease the swingarm pivot bolt and its threads.

14 Loop the drive chain over the slider at the front, then manoeuvre the swingarm into a position that allows the chain to be engaged over the front sprocket. Slide the pivot bolt through from the right-hand side **(see illustration 14.6a)** and using the same tool used for removal tighten it to the torque specified at the beginning of this chapter.

15 Grease the threads and then fit the washer and the locknut onto the right-hand end of the pivot bolt and tighten the nut to the torque setting specified at the beginning of this chapter using the same tool used for removal **(see illustration 14.5b)**. Grease the threads and fit the washer and nut to the left-hand end of the pivot bolt then tighten the nut to the torque specified in the beginning of this chapter.

16 Install the remaining components in the reverse order of removal. Check and adjust the drive chain slack (see Chapter 1), and

check the operation of the rear suspension before taking the machine on the road.

15 Swingarm and bearing inspection

Inspection

1 Remove the swingarm (see Section 14).

2 Thoroughly clean the swingarm, removing all traces of dirt and grease. Pay particular attention to the area covered by the chain slider and the slots for the rear axle and the chain adjuster plates. Unscrew the chain adjusters and check the condition of the threads in the swingarm; if they are damaged consult a specialist engineer or a Yamaha dealer to have them repaired. Note that if the chain is to be separated from the swingarm it must be split at its soft link (see Chapter 6).

3 If not already done, remove the bearing cover from each side of the swingarm and withdraw the long inner sleeve **(see illustrations 14.10 and 14.11)**. Clean all old grease off the bearings.

4 Inspect all components for signs of wear such as heavy scoring, and cracks or distortion due to accident damage. Any damaged or worn component must be replaced with a new one.

5 Remove any corrosion from the swingarm pivot bolt and the inner sleeve with steel wool. Check they are straight by rolling them on a flat surface such as a piece of plate glass. If available, measure the runout with V-blocks and replace either component with a new one if it is bent.

Bearing check and replacement

6 Remove the swingarm (see Section 14). Remove the bearing cover from each side of the swingarm and withdraw the long inner sleeve **(see illustrations 14.10 and 14.11)**. Clean all old grease off the bearings.

7 Refer to Tools and Workshop Tips in the Reference section and check the bearings – there is a needle bearing in each side **(see illustration)**. Clean and inspect them for wear and damage. If the bearings do not run smoothly and freely or if there is excessive freeplay in them or between them and the sleeve, they must be replaced with new ones – refer to the Reference Section for removal and installation methods. The needle bearings must be replaced with new ones if removed – they cannot be reused.

8 Inspect the bearing seats and remove any scoring or corrosion carefully with steel wool or a suitable scraper.

9 The new bearings must be pressed or drawn into their bores, rather than driven into position. In the absence of a press, a suitable drawbolt arrangement can be made up as described in Tools and Workshop Tips (Section 5) in the Reference section. Yamaha specify an installed depth of 0 to 1 mm for the swingarm pivot bearings. Lubricate the bearings with lithium-based grease before fitting the covers.

10 If the suspension linkage pivot bearing in the underside of the swingarm are to be replaced, note that Yamaha specify an installed depth of 4 mm from the outer edge for each bearing. When fitting the new grease seals install them to a depth of 1 mm.

Chapter 6
Brakes, wheels and final drive

Contents

Degrees of difficulty

Easy, suitable for novice with little experience 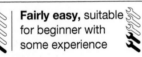 | **Fairly easy,** suitable for beginner with some experience | **Fairly difficult,** suitable for competent DIY mechanic | **Difficult,** suitable for experienced DIY mechanic | **Very difficult,** suitable for expert DIY or professional

Specifications

Brakes

Brake fluid type	DOT 4
Brake pad friction material wear limit	see Chapter 1
Front caliper bore ID	
Upper bore	30.2 mm
Lower bore	27.0 mm
Front disc thickness	
2006 and 2007 models	
Standard	4.5 mm
Service limit	4.0 mm
2008-on models	
Standard	5.0 mm
Service limit	4.5 mm
Front disc maximum runout (all models)	0.1 mm
Front master cylinder bore ID	16.0 mm
Rear caliper bore ID	38.1 mm
Rear disc thickness	
Standard	5.0 mm
Service limit	4.5 mm
Rear disc maximum runout	0.15 mm
Rear master cylinder bore ID	12.7 mm

Wheels

Rim size

Front . . . .   17 x MT3.50

Rear . . . .   17 x MT5.50

Wheel runout (max)

Axial (side-to-side) . . . .   0.5 mm

Radial (out-of-round) . . . .   1.0 mm

Tyres

Tyre pressures . . . .   see *Pre-ride checks*

Tyre sizes*

Front 120/70-ZR17 (58W)

Rear 180/55-ZR17 (73W)

Refer to the owners manual or your Yamaha dealer for approved tyre brands.

Final drive

Chain type . . . .   DAIDO 525V8

Length   . . . .   114 links

Chain slack and stretch limit . . . .   see Chapter 1

Sprocket sizes . . . .   Front 16T, Rear 45T

Torque wrench settings

Brake caliper bleed valves

Front caliper . . . .   5 Nm

Front master cylinder . . . .   6 Nm

Rear caliper . . . .   5 Nm

Brake hose banjo bolts. . . . .   30 Nm

Front brake caliper mounting bolts . . . .   35 Nm

Front brake disc bolts . . . .   18 Nm

Front brake master cylinder clamp bolts . . . .   13 Nm

Front sprocket cover bolts . . . .   10 Nm

Front sprocket nut . . . .   85 Nm

Front wheel axle bolt . . . .   91 Nm

Front wheel axle pinch bolts . . . .   21 Nm

Rear brake caliper front slider pin . . . .   27 Nm

Rear brake caliper rear mounting bolt/slider pin . . . .   22 Nm

Rear brake pad retaining pin . . . .   17 Nm

Rear brake disc bolts . . . .   30 Nm

Rear brake master cylinder mounting bolts . . . .   13 Nm

Rear sprocket nuts. . . . .   100 Nm

Rear wheel axle nut . . . .   110 Nm

1 General information

All models are fitted with cast alloy wheels designed for tubeless tyres only.

Both front and rear brakes are hydraulically-operated disc brakes.

The front brakes are twin floating discs with twin, opposed-piston calipers, radially mounted. The rear brake is a single disc with a single-piston sliding caliper.

Drive from the gearbox to the rear wheel is by chain and sprockets.

Caution: Disc brake components rarely require disassembly. Do not disassemble components unless absolutely necessary. If a hydraulic brake line is loosened, the entire system must be disassembled, drained, cleaned and then properly filled and bled upon reassembly. Do not use solvents on internal brake components. Solvents will cause the seals to swell and distort. Use only clean brake fluid or denatured alcohol for cleaning. Use care when working with brake fluid as it can injure your eyes and it will damage painted surfaces and plastic parts.

2 Front brake pads

 Warning: The dust created by the brake system may contain asbestos, which is harmful to your health. Never blow it out with compressed air and don't inhale any of it. An approved filtering mask should be worn when working on the brakes.

1 The pads can be removed with the caliper in situ, although if fitting new pads it may be easier to remove the caliper in order to retract the pistons – note that the hydraulic hose can remain connected (see Section 3). Removal of the caliper will also enable cleaning of the exposed heads of the pistons. **Note:** *Yamaha recommend that a new pad spring is fitted whenever new pads are fitted.*

2 Remove the R-clip from each end of the pad retaining pin **(see illustration)**. If the clips are distorted or corroded, discard them and fit new ones on reassembly.

3 Withdraw the pin, noting how it fits through

2.2 Remove the R-clips (arrowed) . . .

2.3a . . . then pull out the pin . . .

2.3b . . . remove the pad spring (note the arrow) . . .

2.3c . . . and lift the inner pad . . .

2.3d . . . then the outer pad out

2.9a Press the pistons in as described to make clearance for new pads

2.9b A piston pushing tool

the pad spring **(see illustration)**. Remove the pad spring, noting which way round it fits, and withdraw the pads from the caliper, noting how they fit **(see illustrations)**. **Note:** *Do not operate the brake lever while the pads are out of the caliper.*

4 Inspect the surface of each pad for contamination and check that the friction material has not worn to or beyond its wear limit (see Chapter 1, Section 12). If either pad is worn down to or beyond the limit, is fouled with oil or grease, or is heavily scored or damaged by dirt and debris, both pads in each caliper must be replaced with new ones. Note that it is not possible to degrease the friction material; if the pads are contaminated in any way, new ones must be fitted.

5 Check that each pad has worn evenly at each end, and that each has the same amount of wear as the other. If uneven wear is noticed, one of the pistons is probably sticking in the caliper, in which case the caliper must be overhauled (see Section 3).

6 If the pads are in good condition clean them carefully, using a fine wire brush which is completely free of oil and grease, to remove all traces of road dirt and corrosion. Using a pointed instrument, clean out the groove in the friction material and dig out any embedded particles of foreign matter. Spray the caliper with a dedicated brake cleaner to remove any dust and remove any traces of corrosion which might cause sticking of the caliper/pad operation.

7 Check the condition of the brake disc (see Section 4).

8 Remove all traces of corrosion from the pad retaining pin. Check it for signs of wear and replace it with a new one if necessary.

9 Clean around the exposed section of each piston to remove any dirt or debris that could cause the seals to be damaged. If new pads are being fitted, push the pistons all the way back into the caliper to create room for them; if the old pads are still serviceable push the pistons in a little way. To push the pistons back, use finger pressure or a piece of wood as leverage, or place the old pads back in the caliper and use a metal bar or a screwdriver inserted between them, or use grips and a piece of wood, with rag or card to protect the caliper body **(see illustration)**. Alternatively obtain a proper piston-pushing tool from a good tool supplier **(see illustration)**. As the pistons are pushed in brake fluid will be displaced back into the brake fluid reservoir so depending on the initial level it may be necessary to remove the master cylinder reservoir cap, plate and diaphragm and siphon out some fluid (see *Pre-ride checks*). If the pistons are difficult to push back, remove the bleed valve cap, then attach a length of clear hose to the bleed valve and place the open end in a suitable container, then open the valve and try again (see Section 11). Take great care not to draw any air into the system. If in doubt, bleed the brake afterwards.

10 If any of the pistons appear seized, first

block or hold the other pistons using wood or cable-ties, then apply the brake lever and check whether the piston in question moves at all. If it moves out but can't be pushed back in, the chances are there is some hidden corrosion stopping it. If it doesn't move at all, or to fully clean and inspect the pistons, disassemble the caliper and overhaul it (see Section 3).

11 Smear the backs of the pads and the pad pin lightly with copper-based grease, making sure that none gets on the front or sides of the pads.

12 Insert the pads into the caliper so that the friction material faces the middle **(see illustration 2.3c and d)**. Fit the new pad spring onto the pads, making sure the arrow points in the direction of normal disc rotation **(see illustration 2.3b)**. Insert the pad retaining pin through the hole in the outer pad, then press down on the pad spring and push the pin through the spring and the hole in the inner pad **(see illustration 2.3a)**. Install the R-clips, using new ones if necessary **(see illustration 2.2)**.

13 Install the calipers if they were removed (see Section 3).

14 Operate the brake lever several times to bring the pads into contact with the discs. Check the fluid level in the reservoir (see *Pre-ride checks*). Check the operation of the front brake before riding the motorcycle.

3 Front brake calipers

⚠️ **Warning:** *If a caliper is in need of an overhaul all old brake fluid should be flushed from the system. Also, the dust created by the brake system may contain asbestos, which is harmful to your health. Never blow it out with compressed air and do not inhale any of it. An approved filtering mask should be worn when working on the brakes. Overhaul must be done in a spotlessly clean work area to avoid contamination and possible failure of the brake hydraulic system components. Do not, under any circumstances, use petroleum-based solvents to clean brake parts. Use clean DOT 4 brake fluid, dedicated brake cleaner or denatured alcohol only, as described. To prevent damage from spilled brake fluid, always cover paintwork when working on the braking system.*

Note: *If the calipers are being overhauled (usually due to sticking pistons or fluid leaks) read through the entire procedure first and make sure that you have obtained all the new parts required, including some new DOT 4 brake fluid.*

Removal

1 Unscrew and remove the bolt securing the brake hose guide, noting it threads into a nut on the inside of the mudguard **(see illustration)**.
2 If the caliper is just being displaced, do not disconnect the brake hose. If the caliper is being completely removed or overhauled, unscrew the brake hose banjo bolt and detach the banjo fitting, noting its alignment with the caliper – if standard brake hoses are fitted a hose clamp can be used to prevent fluid loss, but be prepared with a rag to catch any drops **(see illustrations)**. Secure the hose in an upright position to minimise fluid loss and

3.1 Unscrew the brake hose guide bolt

3.2b Fit a hose clamp to prevent fluid loss . . .

3.2a Brake hose banjo bolt (arrowed)

3.2c . . . then unscrew the bolt and detach the hose, catching any fluid with a rag

wrap clingfilm around its end to prevent the entry of dirt. Obtain new sealing washers for use on reconnection.
3 If the pads have not been removed stick some protective tape to the section of wheel rim behind the caliper – there is very little clearance for the caliper, especially with the pads installed, and it is easy to knock it against the rim and damage the paint (removing the pads makes things easier – see Section 2). Unscrew the caliper mounting bolts and slide the caliper off the disc, twisting it so that it clears the wheel rim **(see illustrations)**. If the caliper is just being displaced, secure it to the motorcycle with a cable-tie to avoid straining

the brake hose. **Note:** *Do not operate the brake lever while either caliper is off its disc.*
4 If required remove the brake pads (see Section 2).

Overhaul

5 Clean the exterior of the caliper with denatured alcohol or brake system cleaner. **Note:** *The pistons are of different sizes (differing in diameter by 3 mm). Mark each piston head and the caliper body with a suitable marker to ensure that the pistons can be matched to their original bores on reassembly.*
6 Due to the construction of these calipers it is easier to overhaul one side of the caliper

3.3a Unscrew the caliper bolts . . .

3.3b . . . and slide the caliper off the disc, taking care not to knock the wheel rim

3.6a Using wood to block the pistons on one side while applying compressed air to expel the opposite pistons

3.6b Using a tool and brake pad to block the pistons on one side while applying compressed air to expel the opposite pistons

3.6c Remove each piston from its bore

3.8a Remove the dust seals . . .

3.8b . . . and the piston seals

completely and refit the components and then do the other side, rather than removing all components in both sides. Push the pistons on one side of the caliper fully into their bores until they are flush with the body **(see illustration 2.9a or b)**. Hold the pistons in place using a piece of wood that is between 10 and 14 mm thick, or use a retracting tool as shown and one of the brake pads to provide the extra thickness **(see illustrations)**. Apply compressed air to the brake fluid inlet until the pistons on the other side contact the piece of wood or tool. Remove the wood or tool, then remove the pistons from their bores **(see illustration)**. Have some clean rag ready to catch the shower of hydraulic fluid. **Note:** *Use only low pressure air to ease the pistons out – if the air pressure is too high and the pistons are forced out, the caliper and/ or pistons may be damaged.*

⚠️ **Warning: Never place your fingers in front of the pistons in an attempt to catch or protect them when applying compressed air, as injury could result.**

7 If a piston sticks in its bore and cannot be displaced, the caliper will have to be replaced with a new one.
Caution: Do not try to remove the pistons by levering them out, or by using pliers or any other grips. Do not attempt to remove the coloured caliper bore plugs on the outside of the caliper.
8 Remove the dust seals and the piston seals from the piston bores, preferably using a soft

wooden or plastic tool to avoid scratching the bores **(see illustrations)**. Discard the seals as new ones must be fitted on reassembly.
9 Clean the pistons and bores with clean DOT 4 brake fluid. If compressed air is available, blow it through the fluid galleries in the caliper to ensure they are clear and use it to dry the parts thoroughly (make sure it is filtered and unlubricated).
Caution: Do not, under any circumstances, use a petroleum-based solvent to clean brake parts.
10 Inspect the caliper bores and pistons for signs of corrosion, nicks and burrs and loss of plating. If surface defects are present, the caliper assembly must be replaced with a new one. If the caliper is in bad shape the master cylinder should also be checked.
11 Lubricate the new piston seals with the

brake grease supplied in the rebuild kit, or with clean DOT 4 brake fluid if none was supplied, and carefully fit them into the lower grooves in the caliper bores **(see illustration 3.8b)**. Compare the seals and measure them if necessary to ensure that the correct seals are fitted in the correct bores (see Specifications). The same applies when fitting the new dust seals and pistons.
12 Lubricate the new dust seals and fit them into the upper grooves in the caliper bores **(see illustration 3.8a)**.
13 Lubricate the pistons and fit them, closed-end first, into the caliper bores **(see illustration)**. Using your thumbs, push the pistons all the way in, making sure they enter the bores squarely and do not displace the seals **(see illustration)**. Wipe away any excess lubricant as it will attract dirt.

3.13a Lubricate the pistons . . .

3.13b . . . and fit them into their bores

14 Now block the side of the caliper that has been overhauled and displace the pistons from the other side, repeating steps 6 to 13.

Installation

15 If removed, install the brake pads (see Section 2).

16 Slide the caliper onto the brake disc, taking care not to contact the wheel rim **(see illustration 3.3b)**. Make sure the pads sit squarely each side of the disc **(see illustration)**. Make sure the caliper locates correctly onto its bracket.

17 Install the caliper mounting bolts and tighten them to the torque setting specified at the beginning of this Chapter **(see illustration 3.3a)**.

18 If removed, connect the brake hose to the caliper, using **new** sealing washers on each side of the banjo fitting **(see illustration)**. Align the fitting as noted on removal. Tighten the banjo bolt to the torque setting specified at the beginning of this Chapter.

19 Fit the brake hose guide and tighten the nut/bolt **(see illustration 3.1)**.

20 Top-up the hydraulic reservoir with new DOT 4 brake fluid (see *Pre-ride checks*) and bleed the system as described in Section 11. Check that there are no fluid leaks and thoroughly test the operation of the brake before riding the motorcycle.

4 Front brake discs

Inspection

1 Inspect the surface of the discs for score marks and other damage. Light scratches are normal after use and will not affect brake operation, but deep grooves and heavy score marks will reduce braking efficiency and accelerate pad wear. If a disc is badly grooved it must be replaced with a new one.

2 The disc must not be allowed to wear down to a thickness less than the service limit listed in this Chapter's Specifications. The thickness of the disc can be checked with a micrometer or Vernier caliper **(see illustration)**. If the thickness of the disc is less than the service limit, a new one must be fitted.

3.16 Make sure the disc fits between the pads

3 To check disc runout, position the bike on an auxiliary stand and support it so that the front wheel is raised off the ground. Mount a dial gauge to a fork leg, with the plunger on the gauge touching the surface of the disc about 10 mm (1/2 in) from the outer edge **(see illustration)**. Rotate the wheel and watch the gauge needle, comparing the reading with the limit listed in the Specifications at the beginning of this Chapter. If the runout is greater than the service limit, check the wheel bearings for play (see Chapter 1). If the bearings are worn, install new ones (see Section 16) and repeat this check. If the disc runout is still excessive, new discs will have to be fitted; never renew just one brake disc and always fit new pads and pad springs with new discs.

Removal

4 Remove the wheel (see Section 14).
Caution: Don't lay the wheel down and allow it to rest on either disc – the disc could become warped. Set the wheel on wood blocks so the wheel rim supports the weight of the wheel.

5 If you are not replacing the disc with a new one, mark the relationship of the disc to the wheel so that it can be installed in the same position. Unscrew the disc retaining bolts, loosening them evenly and a little at a time in a criss-cross pattern to avoid distorting the disc, then remove the disc from the wheel **(see illustration)**.

Installation

6 Before installing the disc, make sure there is no dirt or corrosion where the disc seats

3.18 Always use new sealing washers

on the hub, particularly right in the angle of the seat. If the disc does not sit flat when it is bolted down, it will appear to be warped when checked or when the front brake is used.

7 Install the disc on the wheel; align the previously applied register marks if you are reinstalling the original disc.

8 Clean the threads of the disc mounting bolts, then apply a suitable non-permanent thread locking compound. Install the bolts and tighten them evenly and a little at a time in a criss-cross pattern to the torque setting specified at the beginning of this Chapter. Clean the brake disc using acetone or brake system cleaner. If a new brake disc has been installed, remove any protective coating from its working surfaces. **Note:** *If new discs have been fitted, also fit new brake pads and new pad springs.*

9 Install the front wheel (see Section 14).

10 Operate the brake lever several times to bring the pads into contact with the disc. Check the operation of the brake carefully before riding the motorcycle.

5 Front brake master cylinder

⚠️ *Warning: If the brake master cylinder is in need of an overhaul all old brake fluid should be flushed from the system. Overhaul of the brake master cylinder must be done in a spotlessly clean work area to avoid contamination and possible failure of the brake hydraulic*

4.2 Measure disc thickness with a micrometer

4.3 Checking disc runout with a dial gauge

4.5 The disc is secured by five bolts (arrowed)

5.1 Disconnect the brake light switch wires (arrowed)

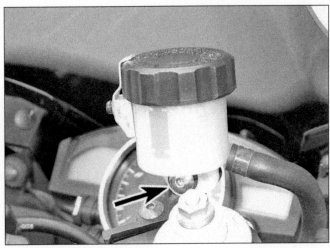

5.2a Unscrewing the reservoir mounting bolt . . .

system components. Do not, under any circumstances, use petroleum-based solvents to clean brake parts. Use clean DOT 4 brake fluid, dedicated brake cleaner or denatured alcohol only, as described. To prevent damage from spilled brake fluid, always cover paintwork when working on the braking system.

Note: *If the master cylinder is being overhauled (usually due to sticking or poor action, or fluid leaks) read through the entire procedure first and make sure that you have obtained all the new parts required, including some new DOT 4 brake fluid.*

Removal

Note: *If the master cylinder is just being displaced and not completely removed from the motorcycle, unscrew the bolt securing the fluid reservoir to its bracket on the top yoke and follow Step 5. Secure the master cylinder to the motorcycle with a cable-tie to avoid straining the hydraulic hose. Keep the reservoir upright to prevent air entering the system.*

1 Disconnect the brake light switch wiring connectors **(see illustration)**. Remove the front brake lever (see Chapter 5).

2 Remove the fluid reservoir cap clamp and loosen the cap, then unscrew the bolt

securing the reservoir to its bracket on the top yoke **(see illustrations)**.

3 Remove the reservoir cap and lift off the diaphragm plate and the diaphragm **(see illustration)**. Drain the brake fluid into a suitable container. Release the clip securing the reservoir hose to the union on the master cylinder and detach the hose **(see illustration)**. Wipe any remaining fluid out of the reservoir with a clean rag and replace the diaphragm, diaphragm plate and cap temporarily.

4 Unscrew the brake hose banjo bolt and separate the hose banjo fitting from the

master cylinder, noting the alignment **(see illustration)**. Obtain new sealing washers for use on reconnection. Wrap clingfilm tightly around the end of the hose to prevent dirt entering the system and secure the hose in an upright position and catch any fluid from the master cylinder with rag – the objective is to prevent fluid spills and system contamination.

5 Unscrew the master cylinder clamp bolts and remove the clamp, noting how it fits, then lift the master cylinder away from the handlebar **(see illustration)**.

6 If required, undo the screw securing the

5.2b . . . then remove the clamp which retains the cap

5.3a Remove the cap, plate and diaphragm and drain the reservoir

5.3b Detach the hose (arrowed) from its union and remove the reservoir

5.4 Unscrew the brake banjo bolt (arrowed) and detach the hose

5.5 Unscrew the bolts (arrowed) and remove the master cylinder and its clamp

5.6 Front brake light switch screw (arrowed)

5.7a Remove the pushrod and boot . . .

5.7b . . . then release the circlip . . .

brake light switch and remove the switch (see illustration).

Overhaul

7 Remove the pushrod and rubber boot, then release the circlip and remove the piston assembly, spring and spring guide (see illustrations). Lay the parts out in order as they are removed to prevent confusion during reassembly.

8 Clean all parts with clean DOT 4 brake fluid. If compressed air is available, blow it through the fluid galleries to ensure they are clear and use it to dry the parts thoroughly (make sure the air is filtered and unlubricated).

Caution: Do not, under any circumstances, use a petroleum-based solvent to clean brake parts.

9 Check the master cylinder bore for corrosion, scratches, nicks and score marks (see

5.7c . . . and remove the piston assembly, spring and guide

5.9 Check the bore for damage

illustration). If damage or wear is evident, the master cylinder must be replaced with a new one. If the master cylinder is in poor condition, then the calipers should be checked as well.

10 The pushrod, dust boot, circlip, piston assembly (including the seal and cup, which should come fitted), spring and spring guide are all included in the master cylinder rebuild kit. Use all of the new parts, regardless of the apparent condition of the old ones. Fit them according to the layout of the old piston assembly.

11 Fit the guide into the inner end of the spring, then fit them into the master cylinder, locating the end of the guide into the well in the end of the cylinder (see illustrations). Lubricate the cup and seal on the piston with brake grease or clean brake fluid and fit the assembly into the master cylinder, making sure it is the correct way round (see illustrations). Make sure the lips on the cup do not turn inside out when they are slipped into the bore. Depress the piston and install the new circlip, making sure it is properly located in the groove (see illustration). Fit the pushrod

5.11a Fit the guide into the spring . . .

5.11b . . . then fit them into the master cylinder so the end of the guide locates in the well

5.11c Lubricate the cup and seal . . .

5.11d . . . then slide the piston into the bore . . .

5.11e . . . and secure it with the circlip

into the dust boot if not already assembled, locating the boot lips in the groove, then locate the pushrod against the outer end of the piston and press the boot into place **(see illustration 5.7a)**.

12 Inspect the fluid reservoir cap, diaphragm plate and diaphragm and replace them with new ones if they are damaged or deteriorated. Inspect the reservoir hose for cracks or splits and replace it with a new one if necessary. Check the hose clips and replace them with new ones if they are distorted or corroded.

Installation

13 If removed, fit the brake light switch onto the bottom of the master cylinder, making sure the pin locates in the hole, and tighten the screw **(see illustration 5.6)**.

14 Attach the master cylinder to the handlebar, aligning the clamp mating surfaces with the punch mark in the handlebar, then fit the clamp with its UP mark facing up and tighten the upper bolt to the torque setting specified at the beginning of this Chapter, followed by the lower bolt **(see illustration 5.5)**.

15 Connect the brake hose to the master cylinder, using **new** sealing washers on each side of the banjo fitting **(see illustration 5.4)**. Align the hose as noted on removal. Tighten the banjo bolt to the torque setting specified at the beginning of this Chapter.

16 Fit the reservoir onto its bracket and tighten the bolt **(see illustration 5.2b)**. Connect the hose to the master cylinder and secure it with the clamp **(see illustration 5.3b)**.

17 Install the brake lever (see Chapter 5). Connect the brake light switch wiring **(see illustration 5.1)**.

18 Fill the fluid reservoir with new DOT 4 brake fluid (see *Pre-ride* checks). Refer to Section 11 and bleed the air from the system.

19 Check the operation of the brake before riding the motorcycle.

6 Rear brake pads

Warning: The dust created by the brake system may contain asbestos, which is harmful to your health. Never blow it out with compressed air and don't inhale any of it. An approved filtering mask should be worn when working on the brakes.

1 Unscrew the pad retaining pin plug, then unscrew the pin **(see illustrations)**. Unscrew the caliper rear mounting bolt/slider pin **(see illustration)**.

2 Pivot the back of the caliper up off the disc and remove the pads, noting how they fit **(see illustration)**. Note the pad spring in the top of the caliper and the pad guide on the caliper bracket and remove them if required for cleaning or replacement, noting how they fit. Yamaha specify fitting a new pad spring if new brake pads are being fitted. **Note:** *Do not*

6.1a Unscrew the plug . . .

operate the brake pedal while the pads are out of the caliper.

3 Remove the shims from the back of each pad, noting how they fit – new pads should come with new shims where applicable, but make sure they do, especially if fitting after-market pads, before discarding the old ones.

4 Inspect the surface of each pad for contamination and check that the friction material has not worn beyond its service limit (see Chapter 1, Section 12). If either pad is worn down to, or beyond, the service limit, is fouled with oil or grease, or heavily scored or damaged, fit a set of new pads. **Note:** *It is not possible to degrease the friction material; if the pads are contaminated in any way they must be replaced with new ones.*

5 If the pads are in good condition clean them carefully, using a fine wire brush which is completely free of oil and grease to remove all traces of road dirt and corrosion. Using a pointed instrument, dig out any embedded particles of foreign matter. If required, spray with a dedicated brake cleaner to remove any dust.

6 Check the condition of the brake disc (see Section 8).

7 Remove all traces of corrosion from the pad pin and check it for wear and damage. Also check the slider pins and boots (see Section 7, Step 10) – slide the caliper off its bracket to do this.

8 Clean around the exposed section of the piston to remove any dirt or debris that could cause the seals to be damaged. If new pads

6.2 Pivot the caliper up and remove the pads

6.1b . . . then unscrew and remove the pad pin . . .

6.1c . . . and the rear bolt/slider pin

are being fitted, now push the piston all the way back into the caliper to create room for them; if the old pads are still serviceable push the piston in a little way. To push the piston back use finger pressure, or place the old pads back in the caliper and push the caliper against the disc, or use grips and a piece of wood, with rag or card to protect the caliper body **(see illustration)**. Alternatively obtain a proper piston-pushing tool from a good tool supplier **(see illustration 2.9b)**. As the piston is pushed in, brake fluid will be displaced back into the fluid reservoir so depending on the initial level it may be necessary to remove the master cylinder reservoir cover, plate and diaphragm and siphon out some fluid (see *Pre-ride checks*). If the piston is difficult to push back, remove the bleed valve cap, then attach a length of clear hose to the bleed valve and place the open end in a suitable container, then open the valve and try again (see Section 11). Take great care not to draw

6.8 Push the piston back into its bore

6.10 Make sure the shim tabs locate correctly all around

6.11 Seat the pads against the disc and bracket

6.13a Push up on the outer pad and insert the pin . . .

any air into the system. If in doubt, bleed the brakes afterwards.

9 If the piston appears seized, apply the brake pedal and check whether the piston moves at all. If it moves out but can't be pushed back in the chances are there is some hidden corrosion stopping it. If it doesn't move at all, or to fully clean and inspect the piston, overhaul the caliper (see Section 7).

10 Where applicable fit the shims onto the back of each pad **(see illustration)**. Lightly smear the back of the pad backing material or shim and the edges of the backing material where it contacts the caliper body with copper-based grease, making sure that none gets on the friction material. Also smear the pad pin.

11 Seat the pads in the caliper bracket so that the friction material of each pad faces the disc, making sure the leading edges locate correctly against the guide **(see illustration)**.

12 Clean the rear mounting bolt/slider pin and apply some silicone based grease to the section of the shank the caliper slides on, then tighten it to the torque setting specified at the beginning of the Chapter **(see illustration 6.1c)**.

13 Push up on the end of each pad so the pads compress the spring and insert the

pad pin when the holes are aligned **(see illustrations)**. Tighten the pad pin to the specified torque setting, then fit the pin plug **(see illustrations 6.1b and a)**.

14 Operate the brake pedal until the pads contact with the disc. Check the level of fluid in the hydraulic reservoir and top-up if necessary (see *Pre-ride checks*).

15 Check the operation of the rear brake before riding the motorcycle.

7 Rear brake caliper

> ⚠ *Warning: If the caliper is in need of an overhaul all old brake fluid should be flushed from the system. Also, the dust created by the brake system may contain asbestos, which is harmful to your health. Never blow it out with compressed air and do not inhale any of it. An approved filtering mask should be worn when working on the brakes. Overhaul of the brake caliper must be done in a spotlessly clean work area to avoid contamination and possible failure of the brake hydraulic system components. Do not, under any circumstances, use petroleum-based*

solvents to clean brake parts. Use clean DOT 4 brake fluid, dedicated brake cleaner or denatured alcohol only, as described. To prevent damage from spilled brake fluid, always cover paintwork when working on the braking system.

Removal

Note: *If the caliper is being overhauled (usually due to a sticking piston or fluid leaks) read through the entire procedure first and make sure that you have obtained all the new parts required, including some new DOT 4 brake fluid.*

1 If the caliper is being completely removed or overhauled, unscrew the brake hose banjo bolt and detach the banjo union, noting its alignment with the caliper – if standard brake hoses are fitted a hose clamp can be used to prevent fluid loss **(see illustration)**. Wrap clingfilm around the banjo union and secure the hose in an upright position to minimise fluid loss. Obtain new sealing washers for use on reconnection.

2 If the caliper is being overhauled, remove the brake pads (see Section 6). Pivot the caliper up and draw it away from the bike so the front slider pin comes out of the bracket. If required remove the pad spring from the caliper and the guide from the bracket, noting how they fit **(see illustrations 7.15a and b)**.

3 If the caliper is just being displaced, free

6.13b . . . then push up on the inner pad and thread the pin into the caliper

7.1 Brake hose banjo bolt (arrowed)

7.3a Release the hose from its guides (arrowed) as required

7.3b Unscrew the bolts (arrowed) . . .

the brake hose from its guide or guides (as required) on the swingarm **(see illustration)**. Unscrew the caliper rear mounting bolt/slider pin and the front slider pin, then lift the caliper off its bracket and the disc **(see illustrations)**. If required, remove the pad spring from the caliper and the guide from the bracket, noting how they fit **(see illustrations 7.15a and b)**.

Overhaul

4 Clean the exterior of the caliper with denatured alcohol or brake system cleaner. Have some clean rag ready to catch any spilled brake fluid.

5 Place a piece of wood between the piston and the caliper body – it should be just thick enough to stop the piston leaving the bore

entirely **(see illustration)**. Apply compressed air gradually and progressively, starting with a fairly low pressure, to the fluid inlet on the caliper body and allow the piston to ease out of its bore, controlling it with the wood **(see illustration)**.

6 If the piston is stuck in its bore due to corrosion, the caliper should be replaced with a new one. Do not try to remove a piston by levering it out or by using pliers or other grips.

7 Remove the dust seal and the piston seal from the piston bore preferably using a soft wooden or plastic tool to avoid scratching the bores **(see illustration)**. Discard the seals as new ones must be fitted on reassembly.

8 Clean the piston and bore with clean DOT 4 brake fluid. Blow compressed air through the fluid passages in the caliper to ensure

they are clear (make sure it is filtered and unlubricated).

Caution: Do not, under any circumstances, use a petroleum-based solvent to clean brake parts.

9 Inspect the caliper bore and piston for signs of corrosion, nicks and burrs and loss of plating. If surface defects are present, the piston and/ or the caliper assembly must be replaced with new ones. If the caliper is in poor condition, the master cylinder should also be checked.

10 Remove the collar from the rear rubber boot in the caliper **(see illustration)**. Clean off all traces of corrosion and hardened grease from the collar, boots and pins – the boot for the front pin may be on the pin but more likely will remain in the bracket **(see illustration)**.

7.3c . . . and lift the caliper off

7.5a Fit the wood, then apply compressed air as described . . .

7.5b . . . until the piston is displaced

7.7 Remove the seals and discard them

7.10a Remove the collar

7.10b The boot (arrowed) for the front pin will be in the bracket if it wasn't on the pin

7.11a Lubricate the new piston seal with brake fluid . . .

7.11b . . . then fit it into its groove . . .

7.12 . . . followed by the new dust seal

Replace the rubber boots with new ones if they are damaged, deformed or deteriorated, making sure they locate correctly. Apply a smear of silicone-based grease to the collar, boots and slider pins. Fit the collar into the rear boot.

11 Lubricate the new piston seal with brake grease or clean DOT 4 brake fluid and fit it into the lower groove in the caliper bore **(see illustrations)**.

12 Lubricate the new dust seal with brake grease or clean DOT 4 brake fluid and fit it into the upper groove in the caliper bore **(see illustration)**.

13 Lubricate the piston with clean DOT 4 brake fluid and fit it, closed-end first, into the caliper bore, taking care not to displace the seals **(see illustration)**. Using your thumbs,

push the piston all the way in, making sure it enters the bore squarely **(see illustration)**.

Installation

14 If the caliper has not been overhauled, refer to Step 10 and clean, check and re-grease the slider pin boots and collar.

15 Make sure that the pad spring and pad guide are correctly fitted **(see illustrations)**.

16 If the caliper is overhauled, slide it onto the bracket and leave it with the rear pivoted up, then install the brake pads (see Section 6).

17 If the caliper was just displaced, fit it onto the disc and bracket **(see illustration 7.3c)**, making sure the pads locate on each side of the disc, and the front edges locate correctly against the guide. Install the front

slider pin and the rear mounting bolt/slider pin and tighten them to the torque settings specified at the beginning of the Chapter **(see illustrations)**. Fit the brake hose into its guide(s) **(see illustration 7.3a)**.

18 If detached, connect the brake hose to the caliper, using **new** sealing washers on each side of the fitting **(see illustration 7.1)**. Align the hose as noted on removal. Tighten the banjo bolt to the torque setting specified at the beginning of the Chapter.

19 Top up the hydraulic reservoir with DOT 4 brake fluid (see *Pre-ride checks*) and bleed the system as described in Section 11. Check that there are no fluid leaks and test the operation of the rear brake before riding the motorcycle.

7.13a Fit the piston . . .

7.13b . . . and push it all the way in

7.15a Make sure the spring (arrowed) in the caliper . . .

7.15b . . . and the guide (arrowed) on the bracket are correctly fitted

7.17a Fit the front slider pin . . .

7.17b . . . and the rear bolt/slider pin

8.3 The disc is secured by five bolts

9.1a Undo the screw . . .

9.1b . . . then remove the cap assembly and drain the reservoir

8 Rear brake disc

Inspection

1 Refer to Section 4 of this Chapter, noting that the dial gauge should be attached to the swingarm.

Removal

2 Remove the rear wheel (see Section 15). *Caution: Don't lay the wheel down and allow it to rest on the disc or the sprocket – they could become warped. Set the wheel on wood blocks so the wheel rim supports the weight of the wheel.*

3 If you are not replacing the disc with a new one, mark the relationship of the disc to the wheel so that it can be installed in the same position. Unscrew the disc retaining bolts, loosening them evenly and a little at a time in a criss-cross pattern to avoid distorting the disc, then remove the disc from the wheel **(see illustration)**.

Installation

4 Before installing the disc, make sure there is no dirt or corrosion where the disc seats on the hub, particularly right in the angle of the seat. If the disc does not sit flat when it is bolted down, it will appear to be warped when checked or when the rear brake is used.

5 Install the disc on the wheel; align the previously applied register marks if you are reinstalling the original disc.

6 Clean the threads of the disc mounting bolts, then apply a suitable non-permanent thread locking compound. Install the bolts and tighten them evenly and a little at a time in a criss-cross pattern to the torque setting specified at the beginning of this Chapter **(see illustration 8.3)**. Clean the brake disc using acetone or brake system cleaner. If a new brake disc has been installed, remove any protective coating from its working surfaces. *Note: If a new disc is fitted, also fit new brake pads and a new pad spring.*

7 Install the rear wheel (see Section 15).

8 Operate the brake pedal several times to bring the pads into contact with the disc. Check the operation of the rear brake carefully before riding the motorcycle.

9 Rear brake master cylinder

 Warning: If the brake master cylinder is in need of an overhaul all old brake fluid should be flushed from the system. Overhaul of the brake master cylinder must be done in a spotlessly clean work area to avoid contamination and possible failure of the brake hydraulic system components. Do not, under any circumstances, use petroleum-based solvents to clean brake parts. Use clean DOT 4 brake fluid, dedicated brake cleaner or denatured alcohol only, as described. To prevent damage from spilled brake fluid, always cover paintwork when working on the braking system.

Note: *If the master cylinder is being overhauled (usually due to sticking or poor action, or fluid leaks) read through the entire procedure first and make sure that you have obtained all the new parts required, including some new DOT 4 brake fluid.*

Removal

Note: *If the master cylinder is just being displaced and not completely removed from the motorcycle, remove the screw securing the fluid reservoir to the frame and follow Steps 3 and 4. Secure the master cylinder to the frame with a cable-tie to avoid straining the hydraulic hose and keep the reservoir upright to prevent air entering the system.*

1 Undo the screw securing the fluid reservoir, then remove the reservoir cap, diaphragm plate and diaphragm **(see illustrations)**. Drain the brake fluid into a suitable container. Release the clip securing the reservoir hose to the union on the master cylinder and detach the hose, catching any residual fluid in a rag **(see illustration)**. Wipe any remaining fluid out of the reservoir with a clean rag and refit the diaphragm, diaphragm plate and cap temporarily.

2 Unscrew the brake hose banjo bolt and separate the hose banjo fitting from the master cylinder, noting its alignment **(see illustration)**. If standard brake hoses are fitted a hose clamp can be used to prevent fluid loss. If you haven't got the correct tools to access the bolt with the master cylinder mounted on its bracket, follow Steps 3 and 4 then unscrew the bolt. Obtain new sealing washers for use on reconnection. Wrap clingfilm tightly around the end of the hose to prevent dirt entering the system and secure it in an upright position. The objective is to prevent excessive

9.1c Reservoir hose clamp (A) and brake hose banjo bolt (B)

9.2 Unscrew the banjo bolt noting the alignment of the banjo with the lug (arrowed)

9.3 Remove the split pin and washer (arrowed) and withdraw the pin

9.4 Unscrew the master cylinder bolts

1 Clevis
2 Locknut
3 Rubber boot
4 Circlip
5 Pushrod
6 Seal
7 Piston
8 Cup
9 Spring
10 Master cylinder
11 Seal
12 Hose union

9.5 Rear brake master cylinder components

loss of brake fluid, fluid spills and system contamination.

3 Remove the split pin and washer from the clevis pin connecting the brake pedal to the master cylinder pushrod **(see illustration)**. Remove the clevis pin and separate the pushrod from the pedal. Obtain a new split pin for use on reassembly.

4 Unscrew the two bolts securing the master cylinder to the footrest bracket and remove the master cylinder **(see illustration)**.

Overhaul

5 If required, carefully remove the reservoir hose union from its seal in the master cylinder **(see illustration)**. Remove the seal and discard it as a new one must be used on reassembly.

6 Note the position of the clevis on the pushrod and that the pushrod is visible through the inspection hole **(see illustration)**, then slacken the locknut and thread the clevis and nut off the pushrod **(see illustration)**.

7 Carefully remove the dust boot from the end of the master cylinder to reveal the pushrod retaining circlip **(see illustrations)**. Depress the pushrod and use circlip pliers to remove the circlip, then slide out the pushrod, piston assembly and spring, noting how they fit

9.6a Check that the pushrod is visible through the inspection hole (arrowed)

9.6b Slacken the locknut and undo the clevis

9.7a Carefully pull off the rubber boot . . .

9.7b . . . remove the circlip . . .

9.7c . . . and withdraw the piston assembly

9.11a Fit the spring to the piston assembly . . .

(see illustration). Lay the parts out in order to prevent confusion during reassembly **(see illustration 9.5).**

8 Clean all of the parts with clean DOT 4 brake fluid. If compressed air is available, blow it through the fluid galleries to ensure they are clear and use it to dry the parts thoroughly (make sure the air is filtered and unlubricated).

Caution: Do not, under any circumstances, use a petroleum-based solvent to clean brake parts.

9 Check the master cylinder bore for corrosion, scratches, nicks and score marks. If damage or wear is evident, the master cylinder must be replaced with a new one. If the master cylinder is in poor condition, then the caliper should be checked as well.

10 The dust boot, circlip, pushrod, piston

assembly (including the cup and seal) and spring are included in the master cylinder rebuild kit. Use all of the new parts, regardless of the apparent condition of the old ones. Fit them according to the layout of the old piston assembly. If the cup and seal are not already on the piston lubricate them with brake grease or clean brake fluid before fitting them to make it easier, and fit them with their wider sides facing the inner end of the piston.

11 Fit the spring to the piston assembly. Lubricate the piston assembly with brake grease or clean brake fluid and fit the assembly into the master cylinder, making sure it is the correct way round **(see illustrations).** Make sure the lips on the cup and seal do not turn inside out when they are slipped into the bore.

12 Grease the pushrod cup and then fit

the pushrod **(see illustration).** Push it in to compress the spring and fit the new circlip, making sure it is properly located in its groove **(see illustrations).**

13 Fit the dust boot, making sure it seats correctly in the master cylinder and locates correctly around the pushrod **(see illustration).**

14 Thread the clevis locknut and the clevis onto the pushrod. Position the clevis as noted on removal **(see illustration 9.6a)**, then tighten the locknut securely **(see illustration 9.6b).** Note that the clevis position controls brake pedal height and can be set after installation as described in Chapter 1, Section 12.

15 If removed fit a new seal onto the reservoir hose union, then press the union into the master cylinder, making sure it is positioned correctly.

9.11b . . . lubricate the new seals with clean brake fluid . . .

9.11c . . . and fit the piston into the master cylinder

9.12a Grease the end of the piston . . .

9.12b . . . depress the pushrod against the spring . . .

9.12c . . . and fit the circlip making sure it is correctly seated

9.13 Fit the dust boot and make sure it is seated correctly

16 Inspect the fluid reservoir cap, diaphragm plate and diaphragm and replace any damaged or deteriorated parts with new ones. Inspect the reservoir hose for cracks or splits and replace it with a new one if necessary. Check the hose clips and replace them if they are strained or corroded.

Installation

17 Installation is the reverse of removal, noting the following points:
● Fit the master cylinder onto the footrest bracket and tighten its mounting bolts to the torque setting specified at the beginning of this Chapter **(see illustration 9.4)**.
● Secure the master cylinder pushrod clevis pin with a **new** split pin **(see illustration 9.3)**.
● Connect the brake hose banjo fitting to the master cylinder, using **new** sealing washers on each side of the banjo fitting, and aligning the fitting so it locates between against the lug **(see illustration 9.2)**. Tighten the banjo bolt to the specified torque setting.
● Attach the fluid reservoir in position temporarily; ensure that the hose is correctly routed, then connect it to the union on the master cylinder and secure it with the clip **(see illustration 9.1a and c)**.
● Fill the fluid reservoir with new DOT 4 brake fluid (see *Pre-ride checks*). Refer to Section 11 of this Chapter and bleed the air from the system.
● Ensure the reservoir diaphragm is correctly seated, and that the cap is tightened securely **(see illustration 9.1b)**.
● Set the brake pedal height and check the

rear brake light switch setting as described in Chapter 1, Section 12.
● Check the operation of the rear brake before riding the motorcycle.

10 Brake hoses and unions

Inspection

1 Brake hose condition should be checked regularly and the hoses replaced with new ones at the specified interval (see Chapter 1).
2 Twist and flex the hoses while looking for cracks, bulges and seeping hydraulic fluid. Check extra carefully around the areas where the hoses connect with the banjo fittings, as these are common areas for hose failure.
3 Check the banjo fittings connected to the brake hoses. If the fittings are rusted, scratched or cracked, fit new hoses.

Removal and installation

4 The brake hoses have banjo fittings on each end. Cover the surrounding area with plenty of rags and unscrew the banjo bolt at each end of the hose, noting the alignment of the fitting with the master cylinder or brake caliper **(see illustrations 3.2a, 5.4, 7.1 and 9.2)**. Free the hose from any clips or guides and remove it, noting its routing. Discard the sealing washers.
5 Position the new hose, making sure it is not twisted or otherwise strained, and ensure that it is correctly routed through any clips or

guides and is clear of all moving components.
6 Check that the fittings align correctly, then install the banjo bolts, using **new** sealing washers on both sides of the fittings **(see illustration 3.18)**. Tighten the banjo bolts to the torque setting specified at the beginning of this Chapter.
7 Flush the old brake fluid from the system, refill with new DOT 4 brake fluid (see *Pre-ride checks*) and bleed the air from the system (see Section 11).
8 Check the operation of the brakes before riding the motorcycle.

11 Brake system bleeding and fluid change

Special Tool: *In its simplest form, the brake bleeding equipment described in Step 2 will be required. A quicker alternative would be a 'one-man' brake bleeding kit consisting of a non-return valve in the pipe which prevents air being drawn back into the caliper. If, however, either set-up fails to bleed the brake effectively, use of a vacuum-type brake bleeding tool **(see illustration 11.18)** is advised.*

Bleeding air from the system

1 Bleeding the brakes is simply the process of removing air from the brake fluid reservoirs, the hoses and the brake calipers. Bleeding is necessary whenever a brake system hydraulic connection is loosened, after a component or hose is removed, or when the master cylinder or caliper is overhauled. Leaks in the system may also allow air to enter, but leaking brake fluid will reveal their presence and warn you of the need for repair.
2 To bleed the brakes, you will need some new DOT 4 brake fluid, a length of clear vinyl or plastic hose, a small container partially filled with clean brake fluid, some rags and a spanner to fit the brake caliper bleed valve **(see illustration)**.
3 Cover the fuel tank and other painted components to prevent damage in the event that brake fluid is spilled.
4 When bleeding the rear brake, remove the screw securing the fluid reservoir to the frame to allow it to be manoeuvred for topping up **(see illustration 9.1a)**.
5 Refer to *Pre-ride checks* at the start of this manual and remove the reservoir cap, diaphragm plate and diaphragm. Slowly pump the brake lever (front brake) or pedal (rear brake) a few times, until no air bubbles can be seen floating up from the holes in the bottom of the reservoir. This bleeds the air from the master cylinder end of the line. Temporarily refit the reservoir cap. Note that the front master cylinder is fitted with a bleed valve – if there is evidence of air in the system bleed the master cylinder as well, both before and after bleeding the calipers, as described below.
6 Pull the dust cap off the bleed valve **(see illustrations)**. Attach one end of the clear vinyl

11.2 Set-up for bleeding the brakes

11.6a Front brake caliper bleed valve (arrowed)

11.6b Front master cylinder bleed valve (arrowed)

11.6c Rear brake caliper bleed valve (arrowed)

or plastic hose to the bleed valve – it must be an air-tight fit – and submerge the other end in the clean brake fluid in the container **(see illustration 11.2)**. **Note:** *To avoid damaging the bleed valve during the procedure, loosen it and then tighten it temporarily with a ring spanner before attaching the hose. With the hose attached, the valve can then be opened and closed with an open-ended spanner.*

7 Remove the reservoir cap and check the fluid level. Do not allow the fluid level to drop below the lower mark during the procedure.

8 Carefully pump the brake lever or pedal three or four times and hold it in (front) or down (rear) while opening the bleed valve. When the valve is opened, brake fluid will flow out into the clear tubing, and the lever will move toward the handlebar, or the pedal will move down. If there is air in the system you will see air bubbles in the brake fluid coming out.

9 Retighten the bleed valve, then release the brake lever or pedal gradually. Top-up the reservoir as required and repeat the process until no air bubbles are visible in the brake fluid, and the lever or pedal is firm when applied. On completion, disconnect the hose, then tighten the bleed valve to the torque setting specified at the beginning of this Chapter and fit the dust cap. When bleeding the front brake system, both calipers must be bled.

 HAYNES HiNT *If it is not possible to produce a firm feel to the lever or pedal, the fluid may be aerated. Let the brake fluid in the system stabilise for a few hours and then repeat the procedure when the tiny bubbles in the system have settled out.*

10 Top-up the reservoir, install the diaphragm, diaphragm plate and cap, and wipe up any spilled brake fluid. Tighten the rear brake fluid reservoir screw. Check the entire system for fluid leaks.

11 Check the operation of the brakes before riding the motorcycle.

Changing the fluid

12 Changing the brake fluid is a similar process to bleeding the brakes and requires the same materials plus a suitable tool for siphoning the fluid out of the hydraulic reservoir. Also ensure that the container is large enough to take all the old fluid when it is flushed out of the system.

13 Follow Steps 3, 4 and 6, then remove the reservoir cap, diaphragm plate and diaphragm and siphon the old fluid out of the reservoir. Fill the reservoir with new brake fluid, then follow Step 8.

14 Retighten the bleed valve, then release the brake lever or pedal gradually. Keep the reservoir topped-up with new fluid to above the LOWER level at all times or air may enter

11.18 Vacuum-operated bleeding tool

the system and greatly increase the length of the task. Repeat the process until new fluid can be seen emerging from the bleed valve.

 HAYNES HiNT *Old brake fluid is invariably much darker in colour than new fluid, making it easy to see when all old fluid has been expelled from the system.*

15 Disconnect the hose, then tighten the bleed valve to the specified torque setting and install the dust cap.

16 Top-up the reservoir, install the diaphragm, diaphragm plate and cap, and wipe up any spilled brake fluid. Attach the rear brake fluid reservoir to the frame and tighten the retaining screw securely. Check the entire system for fluid leaks.

17 Check the operation of the brakes before riding the motorcycle.

Draining the system for overhaul

18 Draining the brake fluid is again a similar process to bleeding the brakes. The quickest and easiest way is to use a commercially available vacuum-type brake bleeding tool **(see illustration)** – follow the manufacturer's instructions. Otherwise follow the procedure described above for changing the fluid, but quite simply do not put any new fluid into the reservoir – the system fills itself with air instead.

12 Wheel inspection and repair

1 In order to carry out a proper inspection of the wheels, it is necessary to support the bike upright so that the wheel being inspected is raised off the ground. Position the motorcycle on an auxiliary stand. Clean the wheels thoroughly to remove mud and dirt that may interfere with the inspection procedure or mask defects. Make a general check of the wheels (see Chapter 1) and tyres (see *Pre-ride checks*).

2 Attach a dial gauge to the fork or the swingarm and position its tip against the side of the wheel rim **(see illustration)**. Spin the

12.2 Check the wheel for radial (out-of-round) runout (A) and axial (side-to-side) runout (B)

wheel slowly and check the axial (side-to-side) runout at the rim.

3 In order to accurately check radial (out of round) runout with the dial gauge, remove the wheel from the machine, and the tyre from the wheel. With the axle clamped in a vice and the dial gauge positioned on the top of the rim, the wheel can be rotated to check the runout.

4 An easier, though slightly less accurate, method is to attach a stiff wire pointer to the fork or the swingarm and position the end a fraction of an inch from the edge of the wheel rim where the wheel and tyre join. If the wheel is true, the distance from the pointer to the rim will be constant as the wheel is rotated. **Note:** *If wheel runout is excessive, check the wheel bearings very carefully before renewing the wheel.*

5 The wheels should also be inspected for cracks, flat spots on the rim and other damage. Look very closely for dents in the area where the tyre bead contacts the rim. Dents in this area may prevent complete sealing of the tyre against the rim, which leads to deflation of the tyre over a period of time. If damage is evident, or if runout in either direction is excessive, the wheel will have to be replaced with a new one. Never attempt to repair a damaged alloy wheel.

13 Wheel alignment check

1 Misalignment of the wheels due to a bent frame or forks, or simply a cocked rear wheel due to incorrect drive chain adjustment, can cause strange and possibly serious handling problems. If the frame or forks are at fault, repair by a frame specialist or replacement with new parts are the only options.

2 To check wheel alignment you will need an assistant, a length of string or a perfectly

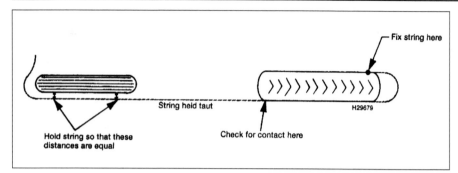

13.5 Wheel alignment check using string

straight piece of wood and a ruler. A plumb bob or spirit level for checking that the wheels are vertical will also be required.

3 In order to make a proper check of the wheels it is necessary to support the bike in an upright position, using an auxiliary stand. First ensure that the chain adjuster markings coincide on each side of the swingarm (see Chapter 1, Section 1). Next, measure the width of both tyres at their widest points. Subtract the smaller measurement from the larger measurement, then divide the difference by two. The result is the amount of offset that should exist between the front and rear tyres on both sides of the machine.

4 If a string is used, have your assistant hold one end of it about halfway between the floor and the rear axle, with the string touching the back edge of the rear tyre sidewall.

5 Run the other end of the string forward and pull it tight so that it is roughly parallel to the floor **(see illustration)**. Slowly bring the string into contact with the front edge of the rear tyre sidewall, then turn the front wheel until it is parallel with the string. Measure the distance from the front tyre sidewall to the string.

6 Repeat the procedure on the other side of the motorcycle. The distance from the front tyre sidewall to the string should be equal on both sides.

7 As previously mentioned, a perfectly straight length of wood or metal bar may be substituted for the string **(see illustration)**.

8 If the distance between the string and tyre is greater on one side, or if the rear wheel appears to be out of alignment, have your machine checked by a Yamaha dealer.

9 If the front-to-back alignment is correct, the wheels still may be out of alignment vertically.

10 Using a plumb bob or spirit level, check the rear wheel to make sure it is vertical. To do this, hold the string of the plumb bob against the tyre upper sidewall and allow the weight to settle just off the floor. If the string touches both the upper and lower tyre sidewalls and is perfectly straight, the wheel is vertical. If it is not, adjust the stand until it is.

11 Once the rear wheel is vertical, check the front wheel in the same manner. If both wheels are not perfectly vertical, the frame and/or major suspension components are bent.

14 Front wheel

Removal

1 Using an auxiliary stand, support the motorcycle securely in an upright position with the front wheel off the ground.

2 Displace the front brake calipers (see Section 3).

3 Slacken the axle clamp bolts on the bottom of each fork, then unscrew the axle bolt, which is on the left-hand end of the axle **(see illustrations)**.

4 Push the axle out from the left-hand side, making sure the internal threads are not damaged, until you can grasp it from the other side, then support the wheel, withdraw the axle, and remove the wheel from between the forks **(see illustration)**.

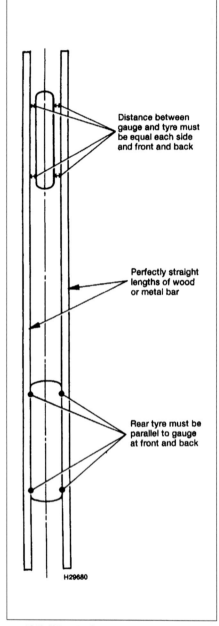

Distance between gauge and tyre must be equal each side and front and back

Perfectly straight lengths of wood or metal bar

Rear tyre must be parallel to gauge at front and back

13.7 Wheel alignment check using a straight-edge

14.3a Slacken the axle clamp bolts on each side . . .

14.3b . . . then unscrew the axle bolt

14.4 Withdraw the axle and remove the wheel

14.5 Remove the shouldered spacer and dust seal from each side

14.9 Fit the spacer and dust seal into each side

5 Remove the shouldered spacers with the dust covers from both sides of the wheel, noting how the spacers fit inside the bearing seals **(see illustration)**.

Caution: Don't lay the wheel down and allow it to rest on either brake disc – the disc could become warped. Set the wheel on wood blocks so the wheel rim supports the weight of the wheel, or keep the wheel upright. Don't operate the brake lever with the wheel removed.

6 Clean the axle and remove any corrosion using steel wool. Check the axle for straightness by rolling it on a flat surface such as a piece of plate glass. If available, place the axle in V-blocks and check for runout using a dial gauge. If the axle is bent, replace it with a new one.

7 Wipe any old grease off the bearing seals and check the condition of the seals and the wheel bearings (see Section 16).

8 Clean the axle spacers and remove any corrosion with steel wool. The spacers should be perfectly smooth where they locate in the seals.

Installation

9 Apply lithium-based grease to the insides of the bearing seals, then fit the spacers with the dust covers into the seals so that the shouldered end of the spacers faces out **(see illustration)**.

10 Apply a thin coat of lithium-based grease to the axle. Position the wheel between the forks, making sure the directional arrows on the wheel point in the direction of normal rotation. Lift the wheel into position, making sure the spacers remain in place, and slide the axle in from the right-hand side **(see illustration 14.4)**.

11 Check that the axle is correctly located then fit the axle bolt **(see illustration 14.3b)**. Tighten the bolt to the torque setting specified at the beginning of the Chapter **(see illustration)**.

12 Install the brake calipers, making sure the pads sit squarely on each side of the discs (see Section 3). Apply the front brake to bring the pads back into contact with the discs. Take the bike off its auxiliary stand and compress the forks by applying the brake and

pressing down on the handlebars to align the wheel and the suspension.

13 Tighten the pinch bolts on the bottom of each fork to the specified torque setting **(see illustration 14.3a)**.

14 Check the operation of the front brake before riding the motorcycle.

15 Rear wheel

Removal

1 Using an auxiliary stand, support the motorcycle securely in an upright position with the rear wheel off the ground.

2 Displace the rear brake caliper (see Section 7).

3 Loosen the axle nut and the chain adjuster locknuts, then turn the adjusters fully in and slide the wheel forwards in the swingarm to provide some slack in the chain **(see illustration)**.

14.11 Tighten the axle bolt to the specified torque

15.3 Slacken the axle nut (A) and the locknut (B), then turn the adjuster (C) on each side in

15.4 Unscrew the axle nut and remove the washer

15.5 Disengage the chain

left-hand side wheel bearing **(see illustration 16.22)**.

10 Clean the axle spacers and remove any corrosion with steel wool. The spacers should be perfectly smooth where they locate in the seals.

Installation

11 If removed fit the sprocket coupling **(see illustration 16.22)**. Apply lithium-based grease to the insides of the bearing seals, then fit the plain spacer and dust cover into the right-hand side of the wheel and the shouldered spacer with the dust cover into the left-hand side **(see illustrations)**.

12 Manoeuvre the wheel into place in the swingarm and engage the drive chain on the sprocket **(see illustration 15.5)**.

13 Locate the brake caliper bracket on the swingarm.

14 Apply a thin coat of lithium-based grease to the axle.

15 Lift the wheel into position, making sure the spacers and caliper bracket remain in place, and slide the axle through from the left-hand side **(see illustration 15.6a)**. Engage the flat head of the axle against the left-hand chain adjuster **(see illustration)**, and ensure the axle passes through the caliper bracket and right-hand chain adjuster, then fit the washer and the axle nut **(see illustrations 15.4)**.

16 Adjust the chain tension as described in Chapter 1, then tighten the axle nut to the

4 Unscrew the axle nut and remove the nut and washer **(see illustration)**.

5 Disengage the chain from the rear wheel sprocket **(see illustration)**.

6 Support the wheel, then withdraw the axle and lower the wheel to the ground **(see illustration)**. Note how the caliper bracket locates between the wheel and the swingarm and remove the bracket **(see illustration)**. Remove the wheel from the swingarm.

7 Remove the plain spacer and dust cover from the right-hand side of the wheel and the shouldered spacer with the dust cover from the left-hand side, noting how the spacers fit inside the bearing seals **(see illustrations 15.11a, b and c)**.

Caution: Don't lay the wheel down and

allow it to rest on the disc or the sprocket – they could become warped. Set the wheel on wood blocks so the wheel rim supports the weight of the wheel, or keep the wheel upright. Don't operate the brake pedal with the wheel removed.

8 Clean the axle and remove any corrosion using steel wool. Check the axle for straightness by rolling it on a flat surface such as a piece of plate glass. If available, place the axle in V-blocks and check for runout using a dial gauge. If the axle is bent, replace it with a new one.

9 Wipe any old grease off the bearing seals and check the condition of the seals and the wheel bearings (see Section 16). Lift the sprocket coupling out of the hub to check the

15.6a Withdraw the axle and lower the wheel . . .

15.6b . . . then remove the caliper bracket

15.11a Fit the plain spacer into the right-hand side . . .

15.11b . . . then fit the dust cover . . .

15.11c . . . and fit the shouldered spacer and the cover into the left side

15.15 Locate the flat side of the axle head against the chain adjuster as shown

15.16 Tighten the axle nut to the specified torque

16.2 Lever out the bearing seals

16.4 Using an expanding puller with slide-hammer attachment to remove the bearings

torque setting specified at the beginning of this Chapter **(see illustration)**.

17 Install the brake caliper (see Section 7).

18 Apply the rear brake to bring the pads into contact with the disc. Check the operation of the rear brake before riding the motorcycle.

16 Wheel and sprocket coupling bearings

Front wheel bearings

Note: *Fit new wheel bearings in sets, never individually. Avoid using a high pressure cleaner on the wheel bearing area.*

1 Remove the wheel (see Section 14).

2 Lever out the bearing seals from both sides of the hub using a seal hook or a large, flat-bladed screwdriver and a piece of wood, taking care not to damage the hub **(see illustration)**. Discard the seals as new ones must be fitted on reassembly.

3 Inspect the bearings (see *Tools and Workshop Tips (Section 5)* in the Reference Section) – a caged ball bearing is fitted in each side of the hub. **Note:** *Do not remove the bearings unless they are going to be replaced with new ones.*

4 If the bearings are worn, remove them using an internal expanding puller with slide-hammer attachment, which can be obtained commercially (see *Tools and Workshop Tips*) **(see illustration)**. Remove the spacer which fits between the bearings.

5 Turn the wheel over and remove the remaining bearing using the same procedure.

6 Thoroughly clean the hub area of the wheel with a suitable solvent and inspect the bearing seats for scoring and wear. If the seats are damaged, consult a Yamaha dealer before reassembling the wheel.

7 The new bearings can be installed in the hub using a drawbolt arrangement or by using a bearing driver or suitable socket (see *Tools and Workshop Tips*) **(see illustration)**. Ensure that the drawbolt washer or driver (as applicable) bears only on the outer edge of the race and does not contact the bearing seat.

8 Install the bearings with the marked or sealed side facing outwards. Ensure the bearing is fitted squarely and all the way into its seat. Turn the wheel over then install the bearing spacer and the other new bearing.

9 Apply a smear of grease to the new seals, then press them into the hub **(see**

16.7 Using a socket to drive the bearing in

illustration). Level the seals with the rim of the hub using a hammer and a small block of wood if necessary.

10 Clean the brake discs using acetone or brake system cleaner, then install the wheel (see Section 14).

Rear wheel bearings

11 Remove the rear wheel (see Section 15) and lift the sprocket coupling out of the hub **(see illustration 16.22)**. Remove the collar from the centre of the left-hand bearing, then draw out the bearing spacer – if it is difficult to get out remove it after removing the bearing **(see illustrations)**.

12 Set the wheel on wooden blocks with the disc (right-hand side) facing up, then lever out the bearing seal using a seal hook or a large flat-bladed screwdriver and a piece of wood, taking care not to damage the hub **(see illustration)**. Discard the seal as a new one must be fitted on reassembly.

16.9 Press the seal into place

16.11a Remove the collar . . .

16.11b . . . then withdraw the spacer

16.12 Lever out the bearing seal

16.14a Remove the circlip from the right-hand side . . .

16.14b . . . then drive the bearing out from the left using a drift

16.15 Driving the left-hand bearing out using a drift

13 Inspect the bearings (see *Tools and Workshop Tips (Section 5)* in the Reference Section) – a caged ball bearing is fitted in the right-hand side of the hub and a needle roller bearing is fitted in the left-hand side. **Note:** *Do not remove the bearings unless they are going to be replaced with new ones – they will be destroyed by the removal method.*

14 If the bearings are worn, remove the circlip securing the caged ball bearing in the right-hand side **(see illustration)**. Turn the wheel over and rest it on the wooden blocks. Using a metal rod (preferably a brass punch) inserted through the centre of the needle bearing, tap evenly around the outer race of the caged ball bearing to drive it from the hub **(see illustration)**.

15 Turn the wheel over and drive the left-hand bearing out of the hub using the same

procedure **(see illustration)**. Alternatively use a bearing puller **(see illustration 16.4)**.

16 Thoroughly clean the hub area of the wheel with a suitable solvent and inspect the bearing seats for scoring and wear. If the seats are damaged, consult a Yamaha dealer before reassembling the wheel.

17 First fit the caged ball bearing into its recess in the right-hand side of the hub, with its marked side facing outwards. Using an old bearing (if new ones are being fitted), a bearing driver or a socket large enough to contact the outer race of the bearing, drive it in squarely until it is completely seated **(see illustration)**. Fit the circlip, making sure it locates correctly in its groove **(see illustration 16.14a)**.

18 Lubricate the right-hand bearing seal with lithium-based grease and press it into the hub, using a bearing driver or a suitable socket with a small block of wood to level the

seal with the inner rim of the hub if necessary **(see illustration)**.

19 Turn the wheel over. Fit the bearing spacer **(see illustration 16.11b)**. Fit the new needle bearing, which must be pressed or drawn (not driven) into position in the left-hand side **(see illustration)**. In the absence of a press, a suitable drawbolt arrangement can be made up as described in *Tools and Workshop Tips (Section 5)* in the Reference section. Fit the collar into the needle bearing **(see illustration 16.11a)**.

20 Clean the brake disc using acetone or brake system cleaner.

21 Check the sprocket coupling/rubber dampers (see Section 20). Fit the sprocket coupling then install the wheel (see Section 15).

Sprocket coupling bearing

22 Remove the rear wheel (see Section 15) and lift the sprocket coupling out of the hub **(see illustration)**.

23 Lever out the bearing seal using a seal hook or a large flat-bladed screwdriver and a piece of wood, taking care not to damage the rim of the coupling **(see illustration)**. Discard the seal as a new one must be fitted on reassembly.

24 Inspect the bearing (see *Tools and Workshop Tips (Section 5)* in the Reference Section). **Note:** *Do not remove the bearing unless it is going to be replaced with a new one.*

25 Support the coupling on blocks of wood

16.17 Using a socket to drive the bearing in

16.18 Press the seal into place

16.19 The needle bearing (arrowed) must be drawn or pressed into place

16.22 Lift the sprocket coupling off the wheel

16.23 Lever out the bearing seal

16.25 Drive the bearing out from the inside

16.27 Using a socket to drive the bearings in

16.28 Fit the grease seal and press or tap it into place

and drive the bearing out from the inside using a bearing driver or socket **(see illustration)**.
26 Thoroughly clean the bearing seat with a suitable solvent and inspect the seat for scoring and wear. If the seat is damaged, consult a Yamaha dealer before reassembling the wheel.
27 Fit the bearing into the coupling with its marked side facing out. Using the old bearing (if a new one is being fitted), a bearing driver or a socket large enough to contact the outer race of the bearing, drive it in until it is completely seated **(see illustration)**.
28 Lubricate the new seal with lithium-based grease and press it into the coupling, using a bearing driver or a suitable socket to tap it in if necessary **(see illustration)**.

29 Check the sprocket coupling rubber dampers (see Section 20).
30 Clean the brake disc using acetone or brake system cleaner, then install the sprocket coupling assembly and install the wheel (see Section 15).

17 Tyre fitting

General information

1 The wheels fitted on all models are designed to take tubeless tyres only. Tyre sizes are given

in the Specifications at the beginning of this chapter.
2 Refer to *Pre-ride checks* at the beginning of this manual for tyre maintenance and pressures.

Fitting new tyres

3 When selecting new tyres, refer to the tyre information in the Owner's Manual. Ensure that front and rear tyre types are compatible, and of the correct size and speed rating; if necessary, seek advice from a Yamaha dealer or motorcycle tyre specialist **(see illustration)**.
4 It is recommended that tyres are fitted by a motorcycle tyre specialist and that this is not attempted in the home workshop. This

17.3 Common tyre sidewall markings

18.2 The soft link is identified by its punched pin ends (arrowed)

19.2a Unscrew the bolt securing the gearchange arm and remove it . . .

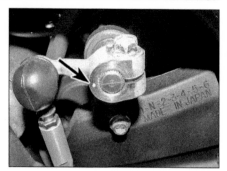

19.2b . . . noting the alignment mark (arrowed)

is particularly relevant in the case of tubeless tyres because the force required to break the seal between the wheel rim and tyre bead is substantial, and is usually beyond the capabilities of an individual working with normal tyre levers. Additionally, the specialist will be able to balance the wheels after tyre fitting.

5 Note that punctured tubeless tyres can in some cases be repaired. Seek the advice of a Yamaha dealer or a motorcycle tyre specialist concerning tyre repairs.

18 Drive chain

Special tool: *A chain breaking/joining tool is required to remove the drive chain – if you do not have access to such tools or do not have the skill to operate them correctly, have the old chain removed and a new one fitted by a Yamaha dealer.*

Removal

1 Remove the front sprocket cover (see Section 19).

2 Place the soft link in a suitable position for working on, by rotating the back wheel **(see illustration)**. The soft link can be recognised by the identification marks on its sideplate (and usually its different colour), as well as its two deeply centre-punched pins.

3 Slacken the drive chain as described in Chapter 1.

4 Split the chain at the soft link using the chain tool, following the manufacturer's operating instructions carefully (see also Section 8 in *Tools and Workshop Tips* in the *Reference* Section). Remove the chain from the bike, noting its routing through the swingarm.

Installation

⚠️ **Warning: NEVER install a drive chain which uses a clip-type master (split) link.**

5 Route the drive chain through the swingarm sections and around the front and rear sprockets, leaving the two ends in a convenient position to work on.

6 Refer to Section 8 in *Tools and Workshop Tips* in the *Reference* Section. Fit an O-ring onto each pin of the **new** soft link, then slide the link through from the inside and fit the other two O-rings. Install the new sideplate with its identification marks facing out and use the chain tool to press the sideplate into position. Rivet the link pin ends using the chain tool, following the instructions of both the chain manufacturer and the tool manufacturer carefully. DO NOT re-use old soft link components.

7 After riveting, check the soft link and pin ends for any signs of cracking. If there is any evidence of cracking, the soft link, O-rings and sideplate must be replaced with new ones.

8 Install the sprocket cover (see Section 19).

9 On completion, adjust and lubricate the chain following the procedures described in Chapter 1.

19 Sprockets

Front sprocket cover

1 Remove the lower fairing (see Chapter 7).

2 Unscrew the bolt securing the gearchange arm to the shaft, noting the alignment marks **(see illustrations)**. Tie the gearchange linkage out of the way.

3 Unscrew the bolts securing the front sprocket cover and remove the cover **(see illustrations)**.

4 Installation is the reverse of removal. To adjust the gearchange lever position, first loosen both locknuts on the linkage rod. Rotate the rod in one direction or the other to either raise or lower the lever height. Tighten both locknuts on completion.

Front sprocket

5 Remove the front sprocket cover (see Steps 1 to 3). Remove the front chain guide **(see illustration)**.

6 Have an assistant apply the rear brake hard, then unscrew the nut and remove

19.3a Unscrew the bolts (arrowed) . . .

19.3b . . . and remove the cover

19.5 Remove the front chain guide

19.6a Have an assistant hold the back brake while loosening the nut . . .

19.6b . . . then unscrew the nut . . .

19.6c . . . and remove the washer

19.7 Draw the sprocket off the shaft and disengage the chain

19.9 Punch the shoulder of the nut into the indent in the shaft

19.13 Rear sprocket nuts

the washer (see illustrations); note that it may be necessary to relieve the staking on the nut shoulder applied on tightening (see illustration 19.9). Obtain a new nut for use on refitting. Adjust the chain so that it is fully slack (see Chapter 1, Section 1).

7 Slide the sprocket and chain off the shaft and slip the sprocket out of the chain (see illustration). If there is not enough slack in the chain to disengage the sprocket, slip the chain off the rear wheel sprocket. Note: If the sprocket is not being replaced with a new one, mark its outside face with a scratch, or dab of paint, so that it can be installed the same way round.

8 Engage the new sprocket with the chain and slide it on the shaft. If removed, install the chain on the rear sprocket and take up the slack in the chain (see Chapter 1, Section 1).

9 Install the new nut with its shouldered side facing out (see illustration 19.6b) and tighten it to the torque setting specified at the beginning of this Chapter, applying the rear brake to prevent the sprocket from turning (see illustration 19.6a). Use a centre punch to drive the nut's shoulder into the register on the transmission shaft (see illustration).

10 Install the front sprocket cover.

11 Install the remaining components in the reverse order of removal.

Rear sprocket

12 Remove the rear wheel (see Section 15).
Caution: Don't lay the wheel down and

allow it to rest on the disc – it could become warped. Set the wheel on wood blocks so the wheel rim supports the weight of the wheel. Don't operate the brake pedal with the wheel removed.

13 Unscrew the nuts securing the sprocket to the hub assembly and remove the washers (see illustration). Remove the sprocket, noting which way round it fits. Note: The size of the sprocket (i.e. its number of teeth) should be stamped on the outside face of the sprocket.

14 Install the sprocket onto the hub with the stamped mark facing out. Fit the washers and tighten the nuts evenly and in a criss-cross sequence to the torque setting specified at the beginning of this Chapter.

15 Install the rear wheel (see Section 15).

20 Rear sprocket coupling/ rubber dampers

1 Remove the rear wheel (see Section 15). Set the wheel on wood blocks with the sprocket facing up
Caution: Don't lay the wheel down and allow it to rest on the disc – it could become warped. Set the wheel on wood blocks so the wheel rim supports the weight of the wheel. Don't operate the brake pedal with the wheel removed.

2 Lift the sprocket coupling out of the hub, leaving the rubber dampers in position (see illustration 16.22). Check the coupling for cracks or any obvious signs of damage. Also check the sprocket studs for looseness, wear or damage.

3 Lift the rubber damper segments from the hub and check them for cracks, hardening, wear and general deterioration (see illustration). Replace the rubber dampers as a set, if necessary.

4 Checking and replacement procedures for the sprocket coupling bearing are described in Section 16.

5 Installation is the reverse of removal.

6 Install the rear wheel (see Section 15).

20.3 Check the rubber dampers as described

Chapter 7
Bodywork

Contents

Degrees of difficulty

Easy, suitable for novice with little experience	**Fairly easy,** suitable for beginner with some experience	**Fairly difficult,** suitable for competent DIY mechanic	**Difficult,** suitable for experienced DIY mechanic	**Very difficult,** suitable for expert DIY or professional

1 General information

1 This Chapter covers the procedures necessary to remove and install the body parts. Since many service and repair operations on these motorcycles require the removal of the body parts, the procedures are grouped here and referred to from other Chapters.

2 In the case of damage to the body parts, it is usually necessary to remove the broken component and replace it with a new (or used) one. The material from which the body panels is made does not lend itself to conventional repair techniques. There are, however, some shops that specialise in 'plastic welding', so it may be worthwhile seeking the advice of one of these specialists before consigning an expensive component to the bin. There are

also fairing repair kits available for DIY use.

3 When attempting to remove any body panel, first study it closely, noting any fasteners and associated fittings, to be sure of returning everything to its correct place on installation. In some cases the aid of an assistant will be required when removing panels, to help avoid the risk of damage to paintwork. Once the evident fasteners have been removed, try to withdraw the panel as described but DO NOT FORCE IT – if it will not release, check that all fasteners have been removed and try again. Where a panel engages another by means of tabs, be careful not to break the tab or its mating slot or to damage the paintwork. Remember that a few moments of patience at this stage will save you a lot of money in replacing broken fairing panels!

4 When installing a body panel, first study it closely, noting any fasteners and associated fittings removed with it, to be sure of returning

everything to its correct place. Check that all fasteners are in good condition, including all trim clips and rubber mounts; any of these that are faulty must be replaced with new ones before the panel is reassembled. Check also that all mounting brackets are straight, and repair or renew them if necessary before attempting to install the panel. Where assistance was required to remove a panel, make sure your assistant is on hand to install it.

5 Tighten the fasteners securely, but be careful not to overtighten any of them or the panel may break (not always immediately) due to the uneven stress.

Trim clips

6 Three types of plastic trim clip are used, so carefully note which fits where when removing the fairing panels.

7 The first type has a centre pin which you

1.7 Centre pin type trim clip

To remove the trim clip, push its centre pin (A) inwards and withdraw the clip from the panel (B)

To install the trim clip, depress the pawls and push the centre pin outwards so that the clip can be inserted in the panel (C), then press the centre pin in level with the head of the clip to lock it in place (D).

push into the body of the clip to allow the clip to be drawn out of the panel **(see illustration)**. To install the clip, first expand the pawls of the clip body and push the centre pin back out. Now fit the clip body into its hole, then push the centre pin in so that it is flush with the clip head. The clip should now be locked in place.
8 The second type of trim clip has a Phillips screw head. To release them unscrew the centre of the clip, then pull the body of the clip out of the panel. When installing them, unscrew the centre of the clip and insert it in the panel then push the centre fully into the body. As they are made of plastic, the threads easily become worn in which case the centres may not unscrew. If this happens, lever the centre out of the body using a small screwdriver and replace the trim clip with a new one.

2 Seats

1 To remove the rider's seat, pull up each rear corner of the seat to access the bolts that retain it, then unscrew the bolts and remove the seat, noting how the tab at the front locates under the tank bracket **(see illustrations)**.
2 To remove the passenger seat, insert the ignition key into the seat lock located on the left-hand side of the bike, and turn it anti-clockwise **(see illustration)**. Lift up the front of the seat and draw it forwards, noting how the tabs at the back and sides locate. Installation is the reverse of removal. Push down on the front of the passenger seat to engage the latch.

3 Fairing and body panels

Upper seat cowling – 2006 and 2007 models

1 Remove the seats (see Section 2).
2 Release and remove the four trim clips under the rider's seat **(see illustration)**.

2.1a Lift the rear corners of the seat and unscrew the bolts . . .

2.1b . . . then lift the seat towards the rear and off

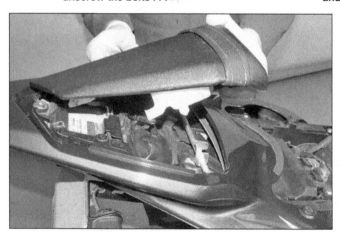

2.2 Unlock the pillion seat and lift it forwards and off

3.2 Release the four trim clips under the rider's seat . . .

3.3a . . . depress the pins and release the three clips under the pillion seat . . .

3.3b . . . and unscrew the bolt at the rear . . .

Collect the damper washers for the trim clips from the sub-frame.

3 Depress the pins and remove the two trim clips under the passenger seat and unscrew the screw at the back **(see illustrations)**. Collect the damper washers for the trim clips from the sub-frame or the back of the cowling.

4 Depress the pins and remove the two clips which hold the front of the upper cowling to the lower cowling **(see illustration)**. Unscrew

and remove the four screws and their washers **(see illustration)**.

5 Carefully lift the front of the cowling and the draw it rearwards and off the bike **(see illustration)**.

6 Installation is the reverse of removal.

Upper seat cowling – 2008-on models

7 Remove the seats (see Section 2).

8 Depress the pins and remove the six trim

clips under the passenger's seat and unscrew the screw at the back **(see illustrations)**. Collect the damper washers for the trim clips from the sub-frame or the back of the cowling.

9 Release the pin at the front of the upper rear cowling from the front rear cowling **(see illustration)**. Raise the front of the cowling to free the tabs and draw it off the bike **(see illustration)**.

10 Remove the four screws under the rider's

3.4a Depress the pins and release the clips holding the upper cowling to the lower one . . .

3.4b . . . and unscrew the four bolts

3.5 Raise the front of the cowling and draw it off to the rear

3.8 Depress the pins and release the six clips (A) and unscrew the bolt (B)

3.9a Lift the pin to free it . . .

3.9b . . . then raise the front of the cowling to clear the tabs (arrowed) and draw it off to the rear

3.10a Remove the two screws from each underside . . .

3.10b . . . the trim clip from each front edge . . .

3.10c . . . and the four trim clips (arrowed) from the top

3.11 Removing the upper seat cowling front section

3.14a Unscrew the bolts and remove the passenger footrest brackets

seat that secure the front upper cowling (see illustration). Depress the pins and remove the two trim clips securing the front upper cowling to the front lower cowling (see illustration). Remove the four trim clips from the top edge of the cowling, noting that they are of the Phillips head type (see Section 1) (see illustration).

11 Draw the cowling forwards and off the bike (see illustration).

12 Installation is the reverse of removal.

Lower seat cowling – 2006 and 2007 models

13 Remove the upper seat cowling (see Steps 1 to 5)

14 Unscrew the bolts and remove the pillion footrests or blanking plates (see illustration). Release the outer of the passenger seat release cable from its bracket on the catch and free the inner cable from the operating arm (see illustration).

15 Disconnect the wiring connectors for the left and right turn signals and licence plate light, then unplug the connector for the rear light and release it from the clip (see illustrations). Release and remove the two trim clips securing the lower cowling to the underside of the sub-frame (see illustration).

16 Counterhold the nuts and unscrew the four bolts securing the licence plate holder and remove it and the lower cowling, feeding the wiring through the sub-frame (see

3.14b Free the seat release cable

3.15a Unplug the wiring connectors for the licence plate light, turn signals . . .

3.15b . . . and the tail light

3.15c Free the wiring from the clip . . .

3.15d . . . then depress the pins and remove the clips

3.16a Counterhold the bolts and unscrew them . . .

3.16b . . . then remove the cowling and licence plate holder

3.20a Unscrew the bolts securing the cowl to the bracket (A) and then the bolts securing the bracket (B)

illustrations). Separate the cowling from the licence plate holder. *Note: Almost inevitably the standard licence plate holder will have been replaced with an aftermarket 'tail tidy' as in the illustrations but the method of removal is the same.*

17 If required the rear light can be removed by releasing the two trim clips that secure it, raising the front end and drawing it forward and the seat catch lock can be removed by sliding the clip off the lock body releasing it and the cable stay bracket.

18 Installation is the reverse of removal

Lower seat cowling – 2008-on models

19 Remove the upper seat cowling (see Steps 7 to 11). Remove the fuel tank (see Chapter 4). Remove the battery (see Chapter 8). Remove the toolkit.

20 Unscrew and remove the four bolts securing the lower cowling to the mounting bracket, and then unscrew the four bolts securing the mounting bracket to the sub-frame and remove it **(see illustrations)**.

21 Remove the R-clip and the nylon washer that secure the shaft of the seat catch **(see illustrations)**. Unscrew the bolts securing the catch to the left-hand side of the sub-frame noting the nylon bearing block **(see illustrations)**. Disconnect the cable and remove the catch. Disconnect the wiring connectors for the left and right turn signals, licence plate light, and the rear light **(see illustrations)**.

3.20b Remove the bracket

3.21a Remove the R-clip and its nylon washer . . .

3.21b . . . unscrew the bolts securing the left-hand side of the catch . . .

3.21c Note the nylon bearing block

3.21d Uncouple the tail light . . .

3.21e . . . turn signal wiring . . .

3.21f . . . and licence plate light connectors

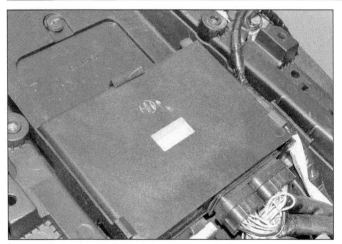

3.22a Ease back the clips securing the ECU . . .

3.22b . . . and uncouple the connectors before removing it

3.23 Release and remove the clips (arrowed) securing the battery tray

22 Disconnect the wiring connectors for the ECU and unclip remove the ECU **(see illustrations)**.

23 Release and remove the three clips securing the battery tray **(see illustration)**. If fitted, remove the pillion footrests or blanking plates. Carefully lift the rear of the battery to reveal the licence plate holder bolts.

24 Release and remove the two trim clips securing the front of the cowling to the bottom of the sub-frame **(see illustration)**. Counterhold the nuts and unscrew the four bolts securing the licence plate holder to the sub-frame **(see illustration)**. Remove the cowling and the licence plate holder **(see illustration)**. *Note: Almost inevitably the standard licence*

plate holder will have been replaced with an aftermarket 'tail tidy' as in the illustrations, but the method of removal is the same.

25 If required the lower cowling can be separated by removing the clips securing the two sections together, and the rear light can be removed by removing the trim clips securing it and sliding it forwards.

26 Installation is the reverse of removal

Fairing side panels – 2006 and 2007 models

27 Unscrew the screws securing the cockpit trim panels **(see illustrations)**. Carefully release the pin fixing from its retainer **(see illustration)**.

3.24a Release and remove the two trim clips (arrowed) . . .

3.24b . . . raise the rear of the battery tray and unscrew the bolts . . .

3.24c . . . then remove the cowling

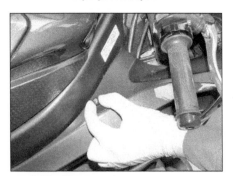

3.27a Unscrew the two screws . . .

3.27b . . . retaining the cockpit trim panel . . .

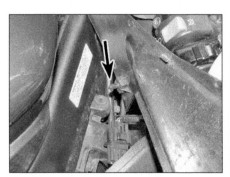

3.27c . . . and carefully release the pin (arrowed)

3.28a Depress the pin and release the clip

3.28b Unscrew the two bolts at the front . . .

28 Depress the pin and remove the trim clip securing the top side fairing panel to the lower side fairing panel **(see illustration)**. Unscrew and remove the four screws securing the top side fairing panel **(see illustrations)**. Slide the panel forwards to disengage the tabs and remove it **(see illustration)**. *Note: If the bike is fitted with 'crash buttons' as in the illustration it* *may be necessary to remove the left-hand side one to allow the panel to slide forwards and free the tabs due to the panel having been notched to clear the crash button (see illustration).*

3.28c . . . the one at the rear . . .

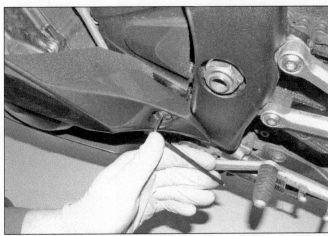

3.28d . . . and lower edge of the side fairing

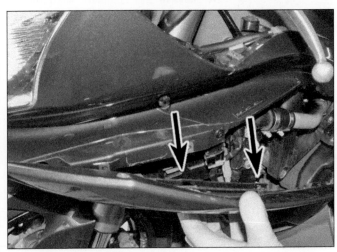

3.28e Slide the panel forward to free the tabs (arrowed)

3.28f If crash buttons are fitted remove them first if the panel has been notched (arrowed) around the button

3.29a Depress the pin and release the clip at the front . . .

3.29b . . . and rear of the top side fairing

3.29c Undo the screws at the front . . .

3.29d . . . and the rear . . .

3.29e . . . of the panel . . .

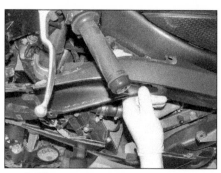

3.29f . . . and draw it off to the rear

29 Depress the pins and remove the trim clips securing the lower side fairing panel to the fairing and the air duct **(see illustrations)**.

Unscrew and remove the screw securing the upper fairing side panel to the fairing **(see illustration)**. Unscrew and remove

the two screws securing the panel to the frame, slide the panel to the rear to free it from the front fairing and remove it **(see illustration)**.

30 Disconnect the wiring loom connector for the turn signals **(see illustration)**. Depress the pin and remove the trim clips securing the bottom fairing panels to the fairing, noting there are two on the right hand side, and three on the left hand side **(see illustration)**. Unscrew and remove the screw securing the bottom fairing panels to the fairing **(see illustration)**.

31 Release the fasteners securing the bottom fairing panels to the radiator **(see illustration)**.

32 Unscrew and remove the screws securing the two bottom fairing panels to each other

3.30a Disconnect the turn signal wiring connectors

3.30b Depress the pin and release the trim clips securing the lower fairing to the fairing . . .

3.30c . . . noting that there are three on the left-hand side

3.30d Undo the screws securing the lower fairing to the fairing

3.31 Unscrew and release the fasteners securing the lower fairing to the radiator

3.32a Unscrew the bolts securing the panels to each other at the front . . .

3.32b . . . and at the rear

3.32c Unscrew the bolts securing the panels to the sump . . .

3.32d . . . and the one securing the left-hand panel to the exhaust

3.32e Remove the panel

3.34a Depress the pin . . .

(see illustrations). Unscrew and remove the screw securing the bottom fairing panel to the bracket on the sump and for the left-hand panel the one securing it to the exhaust (see illustration). Remove the panel complete with the turn signal and air duct (see illustration).
33 Installation is the reverse of removal.

Fairing side panels – 2008-on models

Note: The cockpit trim panels (Step 39) can be removed on their own if required.
34 Depress the pins and remove the six trim clips securing the fairing inner panel to the lower fairing side panels and the fairing (see illustrations). Remove the fairing inner panel (see illustration).
35 Release the fasteners securing the lower fairing side panels to the radiator (see

illustration). Depress the pin and remove the trim clips securing the upper fairing side panels to the air ducts (see illustration).

Depress the pin and remove the trim clip securing the lower fairing side panel to the upper fairing side panel (see illustration).

3.34b . . . and remove the trim clips . . .

3.34c . . . to release the fairing inner panel

3.35a Release the fasteners securing the lower fairing to the radiator . . .

3.35b . . . and depress the pins and release the clips securing the upper side panel to the air duct . . .

3.35c . . . and securing the lower side panel to the upper side panel

3.36a Unscrew the bolts securing the lower fairing side panel to the upper fairing side panel . . .

3.36b . . . and the bolts securing the lower fairing side panels to each other at the rear . . .

3.36c . . . and at the front

36 Unscrew and remove the screws securing the lower fairing side panels to the upper fairing side panels (see illustration). Unscrew and remove the screws securing the lower fairing side panels to each other (see illustrations).

37 Unscrew and remove the screw securing the right-hand lower fairing side panel to the mounting bracket near the brake pedal (see illustration) or alternatively remove the screw securing the bracket to the frame. Unscrew and remove the screw securing the right-hand lower fairing side panel to the bracket on the oil

sump (see illustration). Unscrew and remove the three screws securing the left-hand fairing side panel to the frame, oil sump, and exhaust (see illustration).

38 Ease the front of the lower fairing side panel away from the front fairing (see illustration) and slide the lower fairing side panel forwards to disengage the tabs joining it to the front fairing (see illustration). Ease the panel away and disconnect the turn signal wiring loom connector (see illustration). Remove the panel along with the turn signal and air duct.

3.37a Unscrew the bolt securing the right-hand fairing panel to the bracket by the brake pedal . . .

3.37b . . . and the bolt securing it to the bracket on the oil sump

3.37c Unscrew the three bolts (arrowed) securing the left-hand fairing side panel

3.38a Ease the front of the panel out and slide it forwards . . .

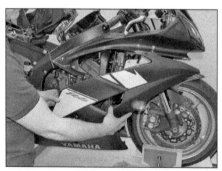

3.38b . . . to release the tabs and free the panel . . .

3.38c . . . then disconnect the turn signal wiring connector and remove the panel

3.39a Undo the screws (arrowed) to free the cockpit panel

3.39b Wiring clamp projection on inside of top fairing side panel

3.40 Remove the trim clip (A) and screws (B)

39 Remove the screws securing the cockpit trim panel **(see illustration)** and remove the panel. Open the wiring clamp on the inside of the top fairing side panel by pressing on the clamp projection and separate the wiring from the panel **(see illustration)**.
40 Release the trim clip from the front underside of the top fairing side panel, then remove the screws securing the panel to the front fairing and frame **(see illustration)**.
41 Slide the panel to the rear to free the tab and remove it **(see illustration)**.
42 Installation is the reverse of removal.

Windshield – 2006 and 2007 models

43 Remove the mirrors (see Section 4). Undo the two screws on each side noting the washers and draw the windshield out **(see illustration)**. Note that the screws thread into rubber-bodied wellnuts set in the windshield.

44 Installation is the reverse of removal. Do not overtighten the screws.

Windshield – 2008-on models

45 Remove the mirrors (see Section 4).Undo the two screws on each side, noting the washers, and draw the windshield out **(see illustration)**. Note that the screws thread into rubber-bodied wellnuts set in the fairing **(see illustration)**.
46 Installation is the reverse of removal. Do not overtighten the screws.

Fairing – 2006 and 2007 models

47 Remove the fairing side panels (Steps 27 to 30)
48 Remove the mirrors (see Section 4) and the windshield (Step 43)
49 Disconnect the two wiring loom connectors between the headlight/instruments

wiring loom and the main wiring loom **(see illustration)**. Free the headlight loom from the cable-ties. Disconnect the wiring loom connectors from the instrument cluster, the intake air temperature sensor and the sidelight.
50 Unscrew the four mounting bolts and remove the fairing **(see illustration 3.56)**.
51 If required, remove the headlight (see Chapter 8)
52 Installation is the reverse of removal.

Fairing – 2008-on models

53 Remove the fairing side panels (Steps 34 to 41)
54 Remove the mirrors (see Section 4) and the windshield (Step 45). Release the fasteners securing the fairing to the fairing stay **(see illustration)**.
55 Disconnect the headlight and sidelight

3.41 Slide the panel to the rear to free the tab (arrowed)

3.43 Windshield location with fairing – 2006/7 models

3.45a Undo the screws and remove the windshield (2008-on models) . . .

3.45b . . . collecting the rubber wellnuts that secure the windshield

3.49 Uncouple the two wiring connectors for the headlamp loom

3.54 Release the trim clip securing the fairing to the mirror stay

3.55a Disconnect the two headlamp wiring connectors . . .

3.55b . . . and the sidelight wiring connector

3.55c Slide the headlight relays from their mounting tabs

wiring loom connectors **(see illustrations)**. Slide the headlamp relays off their mounting tabs **(see illustration)**.
56 Unscrew the four mounting bolts and remove the fairing **(see illustration)**.
57 If required remove the headlight (see Chapter 8)
58 Installation is the reverse of removal

4 Mirrors

1 Unscrew the two nuts securing each mirror and remove the mirror **(see illustration)**. Note the rubber pad with collars for the mirror bolts **(see illustration)**.

2 Installation is the reverse of removal.

5 Front mudguard

1 Unscrew the screws securing the mudguard to the fork noting that there is a nut on the inside of the rear screw **(see illustrations)**.
2 Draw the mudguard forward from between the forks and remove it from the motorcycle **(see illustration)**.
3 Note the collars and bushes in the mudguard mounting holes and remove them if they are loose; replace them with new ones if they are worn or perished.
4 Installation is the reverse of removal.

3.56 Fairing is retained by two bolts on each side

4.1a Unscrew the nuts and remove the mirror . . .

4.1b . . . noting the rubber pad and its collars

5.1a Undo the screws . . .

5.1b . . . noting the rear one has a nut

5.2 Draw the mudguard off to the front

Chapter 8
Electrical system

Contents

Degrees of difficulty

| Easy, suitable for novice with little experience | | Fairly easy, suitable for beginner with some experience | | Fairly difficult, suitable for competent DIY mechanic | | Difficult, suitable for experienced DIY mechanic | | Very difficult, suitable for expert DIY or professional | |

Specifications

Battery

Capacity	12V, 8.6Ah
Type	Yuasa YTZ10S
Charge condition	
Fully charged	12.8V
Half-charged	12.4V
Discharged	12V or less
Charging time	Until fully charged (12.8V) (see Section 4)
Current leakage	1mA (max)

Oil level sensor

Resistance	
Upright	114 to 126 ohms @ 20°C
Upside down	484 to 536 ohms @ 20°C

Starter motor

Brush length	
Standard	10.0 mm
Service limit (min)	3.5 mm
Commutator diameter	
Standard	28 mm
Service limit (min)	27 mm
Mica undercut	0.7 mm

Starter relay

Coil resistance . . . .   4.18 to 4.62 ohms

Charging system

Alternator nominal output. . . . .   14V, 420W @ 5000 rpm
Alternator stator coil resistance . . . .   0.12 to 0.18 ohms @ 20°C
Regulated voltage output (no load) . . . .   14.1 to 14.9V @ 5000 rpm

Fuses

Europe models
  Main 50A
  Fuel injection system 15A
  Fans . . . .   15A x 2
  Signal (turn signals, brake light, horn) 10A
  Ignition 15A
  Tail light. 7.5A
  Headlights 15A
  Back-up (odometer, clock, immobiliser). 7.5A
  Throttle servo (YCC-T) 7.5A
US and Canada models
  Main 50A
  Fuel injection system 15A
  Fans . . . .   15A x 2
  Signal (turn signals, brake light, horn) 10A
  Ignition 15A
  Headlights 15A
  Back-up (odometer, clock). 7.5A
  Throttle servo (YCC-T) 7.5A

Bulbs

Headlight . . . .   55W halogen x 2
Sidelight . . . .   5W (2006 and 2007 models), LED (2008-on models)
Brake/tail light . . . .   LED
Turn signal lights
  UK models . . . .   21W x 4
  US models . . . .   21/5W x 2 (front with running light), 21W x 2 (rear)
Instrument illumination and warning . . . .   LED
Licence plate illumination. 5W

Torque wrench settings

Alternator stator screws. . . . .   10 Nm
Alternator stator wiring clamp bolt. . . . .   10 Nm
Ignition switch bolts . . . .   26 Nm
Neutral switch. . . . .   20 Nm
Oil level sensor bolts . . . .   10 Nm
Starter motor bolts . . . .   10 Nm
Starter motor terminal locknut . . . .   7 Nm

1 General information

All models have a 12 volt electrical system charged by a three-phase alternator with a separate regulator/rectifier.

The regulator maintains the charging system output within the specified range to prevent overcharging, and the rectifier converts the ac (alternating current) output of the alternator to dc (direct current) to power the lights and other components and to charge the battery. The alternator is driven off the left-hand end of the crankshaft, and the starter clutch is on the back of the alternator.

The starting system includes the starter motor, the battery, the starter relay and the starter circuit relay and the various wires and switches. If the engine kill switch is in the RUN position and the ignition switch is ON, the starter circuit relay allows the starter motor to operate only with the transmission in neutral (neutral switch on) or, with the transmission is in gear, the clutch lever pulled into the handlebar and the sidestand up. The starter motor is mounted on the top of the crankcase, behind the cylinders.

Note: *Keep in mind that electrical parts, once purchased, cannot be returned. To avoid unnecessary expense, make very sure the faulty component has been positively identified before buying a replacement part.*

2 Electrical system fault finding

1 A typical electrical circuit consists of an electrical component, the switches, relays, etc, related to that component and the wiring and connectors that link the component to the battery and the frame.
2 Before tackling any troublesome electrical circuit, first study the wiring diagram thoroughly to get a complete picture of what makes up that individual circuit. Trouble spots, for instance, can often be narrowed down by noting if other components related to that circuit are operating properly or

2.4a A digital multimeter can be used for all electrical tests

2.4b A battery-powered continuity tester

2.4c A simple test light is useful for voltage tests

not. If several components or circuits fail at one time, chances are the fault lies either in the fuse or in a common earth (ground) connection, as several circuits are often routed through the same fuse and earth (ground) connections.

3 Electrical problems often stem from simple causes, such as loose or corroded connections or a blown fuse. Prior to any electrical fault finding, always visually check the condition of the fuse, wires and connections in the problem circuit. Intermittent failures can be especially frustrating, since you can't always duplicate the failure when it's convenient to test. In such situations, a good practice is to clean all connections in the affected circuit, whether or not they appear to be good – where possible use a dedicated electrical cleaning spray along with sandpaper, wire wool or other abrasive material to remove corrosion, and a dedicated electrical protection spray to prevent further problems. All of the connections and wires should also be wiggled to check for looseness which can cause intermittent failure.

4 If you don't have a multimeter it is highly advisable to obtain one – they are not expensive and will enable a full range of electrical tests to be made **(see illustration)**. Go for a modern digital one with LCD display as they are easier to use. A continuity tester and/or test light are useful for certain electrical checks as an alternative, though are limited in their usefulness compared to a multimeter **(see illustrations)**.

Continuity checks

5 The term continuity describes the uninterrupted flow of electricity through an electrical circuit. Continuity can be checked with a multimeter set either to its continuity function (a beep is emitted when continuity is found), or to the resistance (ohms / Ω) function, or with a dedicated continuity tester. Both instruments are powered by an internal battery, therefore the checks are made with the ignition OFF. As a safety precaution, always disconnect the battery negative (-) lead before making continuity checks, particularly if ignition switch checks are being made.

6 If using a multimeter, select the continuity

function if it has one, or the resistance (ohms) function. Touch the meter probes together and check that a beep is emitted or the meter reads zero, which indicates continuity. If there is no continuity there will be no beep or the meter will show infinite resistance. After using the meter, always switch it OFF to conserve its battery.

7 A continuity tester can be used in the same way – its light should come on or it should beep to indicate continuity in the switch ON position, but should be off or silent in the OFF position.

8 Note that the polarity of the test probes doesn't matter for continuity checks, although care should be taken to follow specific test procedures if a diode or solid-state component is being checked.

Switch continuity checks

9 If a switch is at fault, trace its wiring to the wiring connectors. Separate the connectors and inspect them for security and condition. A build-up of dirt or corrosion here will most likely be the cause of the problem – clean up and apply a water dispersant such as WD40, or alternatively use a dedicated contact cleaner and protection spray.

10 If using a multimeter, select the continuity function if it has one, or the resistance (ohms) function, and connect its probes to the terminals in the connector **(see illustration)**. Simple ON/OFF type switches, such as brake light switches, only have two wires whereas combination switches, like the handlebar switches, have many wires. Study the wiring

diagram to ensure that you are connecting to the correct pair of wires. Continuity should be indicated with the switch ON and no continuity with it OFF.

Wiring continuity checks

11 Many electrical faults are caused by damaged wiring, often due to incorrect routing or chaffing on frame components. Loose, wet or corroded wire connectors can also be the cause of electrical problems.

12 A continuity check can be made on a single length of wire by disconnecting it at each end and connecting the meter or continuity tester probes to each end of the wire **(see illustration)**. Continuity (low or no resistance – 0 ohms) should be indicated if the wire is good. If no continuity (high resistance) is shown, suspect a broken wire.

13 To check for continuity to earth in any earth wire connect one probe of your meter or tester to the earth wire terminal in the connector and the other to the frame, engine, or battery earth (-) terminal. Continuity (low or no resistance – 0 ohms) should be indicated if the wire is good. If no continuity (high resistance) is shown, suspect a broken wire or corroded or loose earth point (see below).

Voltage checks

14 A voltage check can determine whether power is reaching a component. Use a multimeter set to the dc voltage scale, or a test light. The test light is the cheaper component, but the meter has the advantage of being able to give a voltage reading.

2.10 Continuity should be indicated across switch terminals when lever is operated

2.12 Wiring continuity check. Connect the meter probes across each end of the same wire

15 Connect the meter or test light in parallel, i.e. across the load **(see illustration)**.
16 First identify the relevant wiring circuit by referring to the wiring diagram at the end of this manual. If other electrical components share the same power supply (i.e. are fed from the same fuse), take note whether they are working correctly – this is useful information in deciding where to start checking the circuit.
17 If using a meter, check first that the meter leads are plugged into the correct terminals on the meter (red to positive (+), black to negative (-). Set the meter to the dc volts function, where necessary at a range suitable for the battery voltage – 0 to 20 vdc. Connect the meter red probe (+) to the power supply wire and the black probe to a good metal earth (ground) on the bike's frame or directly to the battery negative terminal. Battery voltage should be shown on the meter with the ignition switch, and if necessary any other relevant switch, ON.
18 If using a test light, connect its positive (+) probe to the power supply terminal and its negative (-) probe to a good earth (ground) on the bike's frame. With the switch, and if necessary any other relevant switch, ON, the test light should illuminate.
19 If no voltage is indicated, work back towards the fuse continuing to check for voltage. When you reach a point where there is voltage, you know the problem lies between that point and your last check point.

Earth (ground) checks

20 Earth connections are made either directly to the engine or frame via the mounting of the component, or by a separate wire into the earth circuit of the wiring harness. Alternatively a short earth wire is sometimes run from the component directly to the bike's frame.
21 Corrosion is a common cause of a poor earth connection, as is a loose earth terminal fastener.
22 If total or multiple component failure is experienced, check the security of the main earth lead from the negative (-) terminal of the battery, the earth lead bolted to the engine, and the main earth point(s) on the frame. If corroded, dismantle the connection and clean all surfaces back to bare metal. Remake the connection and prevent further corrosion from

2.15 Voltage check. Connect the meter positive probe to the component and the negative probe to earth

forming by smearing battery terminal grease over the connection.
23 To check the earth of a component, use an insulated jumper wire to temporarily bypass its earth connection **(see illustration)** – connect one end of the jumper wire to the earth terminal or metal body of the component and the other end to the bike's frame. If the circuit works with the jumper wire installed, the earth circuit is faulty.
24 To check an earth wire first check for corroded or loose connections, then check the wiring for continuity (Step 13) between each connector in the circuit in turn, and then to its earth point, to locate the break.

3 Battery

Caution: Be extremely careful when handling or working around the battery. The electrolyte is very caustic and an explosive gas (hydrogen) is given off when the battery is charging.

Removal and installation

1 Remove the fuel tank (see Chapter 4). Unscrew the four bolts securing the tank bracket and remove it **(see illustration)**.
2 Unscrew the negative (–) terminal bolt first and disconnect the lead from the battery **(see illustration)**. Lift up the insulating cover to access the positive (+) terminal, then unscrew the bolt and disconnect the lead. Release the

2.23 A selection of insulated jumper wires

battery strap and remove the battery from the bike **(see illustration)**.
3 On installation, ensure the battery terminals and lead ends are clean (see Step 6), then reconnect the leads, connecting the positive (+) terminal first.
4 Fit the tank bracket, then install the tank (see Chapter 4).

> **HAYNES HINT** *Battery corrosion can be kept to a minimum by applying a layer of petroleum jelly to the terminals after the leads have been connected.*

Inspection and maintenance

5 The battery is of the maintenance-free (sealed) gel type, therefore requiring no specific maintenance. Do not attempt to open the battery as resulting damage will mean it will be unfit for further use. However, the following checks should still be regularly performed.
6 Check the battery terminals and leads for tightness and corrosion. If corrosion is evident, unscrew the terminal bolts and disconnect the leads from the battery, disconnecting the negative (–) terminal first. Clean the terminals and lead ends with a wire brush or penknife and steel wool. Reconnect the leads, connecting the negative (–) terminal last, and apply a thin coat of petroleum jelly (Vaseline) or battery grease to the connections to slow further corrosion. DO NOT use a mineral-based grease.
7 The battery case should be kept clean to prevent current leakage, which can discharge

3.1 Unscrew the bolts on each side and remove the bracket

3.2a Disconnect the negative lead first, then disconnect the positive lead

3.2b Release the battery strap and remove the battery

H45526

3.10 Measure the voltage and assess the condition of the battery using the chart

H45525

4.2 Measure the voltage to determine the required charging time

4.4 If the charger doesn't have an ammeter built in, connect one in series as shown. DO NOT connect the ammeter between the battery terminals or it will be ruined

the battery over a period of time (especially when it sits unused). Remove the battery from the motorcycle and wash the outside of the case with a solution of baking soda and water. Rinse the battery thoroughly, then dry it.

8 Look for cracks in the case and replace the battery with a new one if any are found.

9 If the motorcycle sits unused for long periods of time, disconnect the leads from the battery terminals, negative (–) terminal first. Refer to Section 4 and charge the battery once every month to six weeks or connect a trickle-charger which will maintain battery charge on the machine.

10 The condition of the battery can be assessed by measuring the voltage present at the battery terminals, and comparing the figure against the chart **(see illustration and 4.2)**. Connect the voltmeter positive (+) probe to the battery positive (+) terminal, and the negative (–) probe to the battery negative (–) terminal. When fully charged, there should be 12.8 volts (or more) present. If the voltage falls below 12.0 volts the battery must be removed, disconnecting the negative (–) terminal first, and recharged as described in Section 4.

Note that there are many bike-specific chargers available from good suppliers that are designed for the maintenance and recovery of motorcycle batteries, in particular catering for the requirements of heavily discharged MF batteries. They are not expensive, and are a worthwhile investment, especially if the bike is not used over winter.

4 Battery charging

Caution: Be extremely careful when handling or working around the battery. The electrolyte is very caustic and an explosive gas (hydrogen) is given off when the battery is charging.

1 Ensure the charger is suitable for charging a 12V battery.

2 Remove the battery from the motorcycle (see Section 3). If not already done, refer to Section 3, Step 10, and check the open circuit voltage of the battery. Refer to the chart **(see illustration)** and read off the charging time required according to the voltage reading taken.

3 Connect the charger to the battery BEFORE switching the charger ON. Make sure that the positive (+) lead on the charger is connected to the positive (+) terminal on the battery, and the negative (–) lead is connected to the negative (–) terminal. The battery should be charged for the specified time (reference the table), or until the voltage across the terminals reaches 12.8V (allow the battery to stabilise for 30 minutes after charging, before taking a voltage reading). Exceeding this charging time can cause the battery to overheat, buckling the plates and rendering it useless.

4 Charge the battery at the rate marked on its casing, i.e. 0.8A for 5 to 10 hours. Few owners will have access to an expensive current controlled charger, so if a normal domestic

charger is used check that after a possible initial peak, the charge rate falls to a safe level **(see illustration)**. If the battery becomes hot during charging **STOP**. Further charging will cause damage. **Note:** *In emergencies the battery can be charged at a higher rate of around 3.0 amps for a period of 1 hour. However, this is not recommended and the low amp charge is by far the safer method of charging the battery.*

5 If the recharged battery discharges rapidly when left disconnected it is likely that an internal short caused by physical damage or sulphation has occurred. A new battery will be required. A sound battery will tend to lose its charge at about 1% per day.

6 Install the battery (see Section 3).

7 If the motorcycle sits unused for long periods of time, charge the battery once every month to six weeks and leave it disconnected. Alternatively purchase a trickle charger which allows the battery to remain connected.

5 Fuses

1 The electrical system is protected by fuses of different ratings. The fuel injection system fuse and its spare are integral with the starter relay, which is located under the rider's seat **(see illustration)**. The main fuse is in a separate holder which is also under the rider's seat **(see illustration)**. The fuse for the YCC-T,

5.1a Fuel injection system fuse (A) and its spare (B)

5.1b The main fuse is in a separate holder

5.1c The fuses for the odometer and immobiliser back up (A), YCC-T (B), and a spare (C) are under the seat

5.1d All other fuses are in a fusebox behind the left-hand fairing panel (arrowed)

the fuse for the memory for the odometer, clock, and on Europe models the immobiliser, and a spare are also located under the seat **(see illustration)**. All other fuses and spare fuses, are housed in the fusebox, which is located behind the left-hand fairing side panel **(see illustration)**.

2 To access the fusebox fuses remove the left-hand fairing cockpit trim panel (see Chapter 7) and unclip the fusebox lid **(see illustration)**. To access the fuel injection system fuse remove the rider's seat and unclip the fuse cover **(see illustration 5.1a)**. To access the main fuse, remove the rider's seat, then release the fuse holder from its mount **(see illustration 5.1b)**.

3 The fuses can be removed and checked visually. If you can't pull the fuse out with your fingertips, use a suitable pair of pliers. A blown fuse is easily identified by a break in the element **(see illustration)**, or the fuse can be tested for continuity using an ohmmeter or continuity tester – if there is no continuity, it has blown. Each fuse is clearly marked with its rating and must only be replaced by a fuse of the same rating. Spare fuses are provided in the fusebox and the starter relay, but note there is no spare main fuse. If a spare fuse is used, always replace it with a new one so that a spare of each rating is carried on the bike at all times.

5.2 Unclip the lid to access the fusebox fuses

⚠ *Warning: Never put in a fuse of a higher rating or bridge the terminals with any other substitute, however temporary it may be. Serious damage may be done to the circuit, or a fire may start.*

4 If a fuse blows, be sure to check the wiring circuit very carefully for evidence of a short-circuit. Look for bare wires and chafed, melted or burned insulation. If the fuse is renewed before the cause is located, the new fuse will blow immediately.

5 Occasionally a fuse will blow or cause an open-circuit for no obvious reason. Corrosion of the fuse ends and fusebox terminals may occur and cause poor fuse contact. If this happens, remove the corrosion with a penknife or steel wool, then spray the fuse end and terminals with electrical contact cleaner.

6 Lighting system check

Note: *If the ignition is switched ON for any checks, remember to switch it OFF again before proceeding further or removing any electrical component from the system.*

1 The battery provides power for operation of the headlight, tail light, brake light, turn signals and instrument cluster lights. If none of the

5.3 A blown fuse can be identified by a break in its element

lights operate, check battery condition before proceeding. Low battery voltage indicates either a faulty battery or a defective charging system. Refer to Section 3 for battery checks and Section 30 for charging system tests. Also, check the condition of the fuses (see Section 5). When checking for a blown filament in a bulb, it is advisable to back up a visual check with a continuity test of the filament as it is not always apparent that a bulb has blown. When testing for continuity, remember that on tail light and turn signal bulbs it is often the metal body of the bulb that is the ground or earth.

Headlight and relays

2 If one of the bulbs in the headlight fails to work, check the bulb first (see Section 7). If all bulbs fail to work check the headlight fuse (Section 5), and then the ON/OFF relay (Step 6). If the HI beam bulbs fail to work check the dimmer relay (Step 7).

3 Next disconnect the relevant headlight wiring (Section 7, Step 2), and check for battery voltage on the supply side of the wiring connector with a test light or multimeter – connect the negative probe of the multimeter to the black wire (earth) and the positive probe to the black/yellow wire for the high beam bulb connectors or the black/green wire for the low beam bulb connectors, with the ignition switch ON. Don't forget to select either high or low beam as appropriate at the handlebar switch while conducting this test. If no voltage is indicated at the terminal, check the wiring between the headlight connector, relay, dimmer switch and the ignition switch, referring to *Wiring Diagrams* at the end of the chapter, then check the switches themselves.

4 If voltage is indicated, check for continuity between the black wire connector terminal and earth (ground). If there is no continuity, check the earth (ground) circuit for an open or poor connection.

5 To check the headlight relays (one is the main ON/OFF relay, the other is the dimmer relay), first remove the cockpit trim panels (see Chapter 7) – the relays are mounted one either side of the

6.5 Headlight relays are located on each side of the fairing

Red/Yellow

Black/Green

Red/Yellow

Yellow/Black

H48581

6.6 Connect the meter positive to A, meter negative to B, then battery positive to C and battery negative to D

headlight unit **(see illustration)**. Remove the relevant relay and use a continuity tester (or a multimeter set to the resistance range) and a 12V battery with insulated jumper wires according to the relevant procedure below.

6 Test the ON/OFF relay by connecting the multimeter probes between the red/yellow and black/green wire terminals on the relay; there should be no continuity. Leaving the meter in place, use the jumper wires to connect the battery positive (+) terminal to the red/yellow wire terminal and the battery negative (–) terminal to the yellow/black wire terminal; use the correct red/yellow wire in each case **(see illustration)**. The relay should now close and continuity (0 ohms) should be shown on the meter.

7 Test the dimmer relay by connecting the meter probes between the black/green and black/yellow wire terminals on the relay; there should be no continuity. Leaving the meter in place, use the jumper wires to connect the battery positive (+) terminal to the yellow wire terminal and the battery negative (-) terminal to the black wire terminal. The relay should now close and continuity (0 ohms) should be shown on the meter.

Tail light

8 The tail light consists of a number of LEDs in a sealed unit. When a single LED fails it cannot be replaced with a new one, however the failure of one LED will not affect the function of the others. If enough LEDs have failed so as to impair the safe operation of the motorcycle, replace the tail light unit with a new one (Section 10).

9 If the tail light fails to work completely, first check the fuse, then the wiring connector **(see illustration 10.2)**. Next check for battery voltage at the blue/red wire terminal on the supply side of the tail light wiring connector, with the ignition switch ON.

10 If no voltage is indicated, check the wiring between the tail light, fusebox and the ignition switch, then check the switch itself.

11 If voltage is indicated, check for continuity between the black wire terminal and earth (ground). If there is no continuity, check the earth (ground) circuit for a broken or poor connection.

Sidelight (Europe only)

12 If the sidelights fail to work with the ignition switch either in the ON position or in the P position check the fuse, then check the bulb and the bulb terminals and wiring connector for 2006 and 2007 models; 2008-on models have an LED sidelight and just require the connector to be checked. Next check for battery voltage at the blue/red wire terminal on the supply side of the sidelight wiring connector, with the ignition switch first in the ON position, then in the P position.

13 If no voltage is indicated in either position, check the wiring between the sidelight, fusebox and the ignition switch, then check the switch (Section 19).

14 If voltage is indicated, check for continuity between the wiring connector terminals on the light side of the wiring connector and the corresponding terminals in the bulbholder if fitted; no continuity indicates a break in the circuit. If continuity is present, check for continuity between the black wire terminal and earth (ground). If there is no continuity, check the earth (ground) circuit for a broken or poor connection.

15 If the sidelight bulb works with the ignition switch in one position (ON or P) but not the other then the switch is faulty.

Brake light

16 The brake light consists of a number of LEDs in a sealed unit. When a single LED fails it cannot be replaced with a new one, however the failure of one LED will not affect the function of the others. If enough LEDs have failed so as to impair the safe operation of the motorcycle, replace the tail light unit with a new one (Section 10).

17 If the brake light fails to work completely, first check the fuse, then the wiring connector **(see illustration 10.2)**. Next check for battery voltage at the yellow wire terminal on the supply side of the tail light wiring connector, with the ignition switch ON and the brake lever or pedal applied.

18 If no voltage is indicated, check the brake light switches (see Section 14), then the wiring between the tail light and the switches.

19 If voltage is indicated, check for continuity between the black wire terminal and earth (ground). If there is no continuity, check the earth (ground) circuit for a broken or poor connection.

Licence plate light

20 If the light fails to work, first check the bulb and the bulb terminals (Section 9), then the fuse (Section 5), then the wiring connectors **(see illustration)** – remove the seat cowling to access them (see Chapter 7). Next check for battery voltage at the blue/red wire terminal on the supply side of the wiring connector, with the ignition switch ON.

21 If no voltage is indicated, check the wiring between the tail light, fusebox and the ignition switch, then check the switch itself.

22 If voltage is indicated, check for continuity between the black wire terminal and earth (ground). If there is no continuity, check the earth (ground) circuit for a broken or poor connection.

Turn signal lights

23 If one light fails to work, check the bulb and the bulb terminals (see Section 12), then the wiring connector. If none of the turn signals work, first check the battery, main fuse and circuit fuse.

24 If the fuse is good, check the turn signal relay (see Section 11).

Instrument cluster lights

25 See Section 17.

6.20 Licence plate light wiring connectors

7.2a Remove the cover . . .

7.2b . . . and disconnect the wiring connector

7.2c Release the clip . . .

7 Headlight bulbs and sidelight bulbs

Note: *The headlight bulbs are of the quartz-halogen type. Do not touch the bulb glass as skin acids will shorten the bulb's service life. If the bulb is accidentally touched, it should be wiped carefully when cold with a rag soaked in methylated spirit and dried before fitting.*

Headlight

1 Remove the relevant cockpit trim panel (see Chapter 7).
2 To remove a headlight bulb remove the cover by turning it anti-clockwise, then disconnect the wiring connector from the back of the headlight bulb **(see illustrations)**.

Release the bulb retaining clip, noting how it fits, then remove the bulb from the back of the reflector **(see illustrations)**.
3 Fit the new bulb, bearing in mind the information in the **Note** above. Make sure the tabs on the bulb flange are aligned with the slots in the back of the reflector, and secure the bulb in position with the retaining clip.
4 Connect the wiring connector then fit the cover, turning it clockwise to lock it in place.
5 Check the operation of the headlight.

Sidelight – 2006 and 2007 models

6 Pry out the rubber plug, and loosen the screw securing the lens **(see illustrations)**. Remove the lens **(see illustration)**.
7 Carefully pull the bulb out of the holder **(see illustration)**.
8 Fit the new bulb and check the operation of the light, then fit the lens,

HAYNES HiNT *Always use a paper towel or dry cloth when handling new bulbs to prevent injury if the bulb should break, and to increase bulb life.*

9 Replace the screw and tighten it. Refit the rubber plug

Sidelight LED unit – 2008-on models

10 Remove the fairing (see Chapter 7).
11 Remove the headlights from the fairing (see Chapter 7).
12 Unscrew the screws securing the sidelight and remove it **(see illustration)**.
13 Fit a new LED light, replace the screws and tighten them.
14 Reassembly is the reverse of removal.

7.2d . . . and remove the bulb

7.6a Prise out the rubber plug . . .

7.6b . . . then undo the screw . . .

7.6c . . . and carefully prise the lens free

7.7 Carefully pull the bulb from its holder

7.12 Unscrew the screws and remove the light unit

8.3 Undo the screws (arrowed) and remove the light unit

8.6 Horizontal alignment adjuster (A), and vertical alignment adjuster (B)

8 Headlight units and headlight aim

Removal and installation

1 Remove the fairing (see Chapter 7).
2 Remove the headlight bulbs from headlight unit (see Section 7). Unclip the relays from the headlight unit (see illustration 6.5).
3 Remove the screws securing the headlight unit and lift it out of the fairing (see illustration).
4 Installation is the reverse of removal. Make sure all the wiring is correctly connected and secured. Check the operation of the headlights and sidelights. Check the headlight aim.

Headlight aim

Note: *An improperly adjusted headlight may cause problems for oncoming traffic or provide poor, unsafe illumination of the road ahead. Before adjusting the headlight aim, be sure to consult with local traffic laws and regulations – for UK models refer to MOT Test Checks in the Reference section.*

5 The headlight beams can be adjusted both horizontally and vertically. Before making any adjustment, check that the tyre pressures are correct and the suspension is adjusted as required. Make any adjustments to the headlight aim with the machine on level ground, with the fuel tank half full and with

an assistant sitting on the seat. If the bike is usually ridden with a passenger on the back, have a second assistant to do this.
6 Horizontal adjustment is made by turning the adjuster screw on the top/outer of the relevant beam unit (see illustration). For the left-hand headlight turn the adjuster anti-clockwise to move the beam to the right and clockwise to move the beam to the left. For the right-hand headlight this is reversed.
7 Vertical adjustment is made by turning the adjuster screw on the lower/inner of the relevant beam unit (see illustration 8.6). Turn it anti-clockwise to move the beam up, and clockwise to move the beam down.

9 Brake/tail light LEDs and licence plate bulb

Brake/tail light LEDs

1 If one or more of the LEDs within the brake or tail light unit has failed, replace the entire tail light assembly with a new one – individual LEDs are not available (see Section 10).

Licence plate light bulb

Note: *It is a good idea to use a paper towel or dry cloth when handling a new bulb to prevent injury if it breaks, and to increase bulb life.*
2 Undo the screws securing the licence plate light lens and remove it (see illustration).

3 Release the bulbholder. Carefully pull the bulb out of its socket and replace it with a new one.
4 Fit the bulbholder and check the light works, then fit the lens – do not overtighten the screws as the lens or threads could be damaged.

10 Tail light unit

1 Remove the seat cowling (see Chapter 7).
2 Disconnect the tail light wiring connector and feed the wiring back to the light, noting its routing (see illustration).
3 Release the trim clips securing the light unit and remove it (see illustration). Refer to Chapter 7, Section 1 for details on how to release the trim clips, if required.
4 Installation is the reverse of removal. Check the operation of the tail light and the brake light, then replace the seat cowling.

11 Turn signal circuit check

1 Most turn signal problems are the result of a burned-out bulb or corroded socket. This is especially true when the turn signals function properly in one direction, but fail to

9.2 Two screws retain the licence plate light lens

10.2 Disconnect the wiring connector (arrowed)

10.3 Release the trim clips (arrowed) and remove the tail light

11.2 Turn signal relay (arrowed)

12.1 Undo the screw and remove the lens

12.2 Release the bulb and replace it with a new one

flash in the other direction. Check the bulbs and the sockets (see Section 12) and the wiring connectors. Also, check the fuse (see Section 5) and the switch (see Section 19).

2 If the bulbs, sockets, connectors, fuses, switch and battery are good, remove the rider's seat (see Chapter 7) and check the turn signal relay as follows **(see illustration)**.

3 Disconnect the relay connector and check for voltage at the brown wire terminal in the connector with the ignition ON. If no voltage is indicated, refer to the appropriate wiring diagram at the end of this Chapter and check the wiring between the relay, signal fuse and the ignition switch for continuity.

4 If voltage is indicated, reconnect the relay connector and check for voltage at the brown/white wire terminal in the connector with the ignition ON, and with the signal switch turned to either LEFT or RIGHT.

5 If no voltage is indicated, replace the relay with a new one.

6 If voltage is indicated, check the wiring between the relay, turn signal switch and turn signal lights for continuity.

12 Turn signal bulbs

1 Remove the screw securing the turn signal lens and remove the lens, noting how it fits **(see illustration)**.

2 Push the bulb into the holder and twist it anti-clockwise to remove it **(see illustration)**. Check the socket terminals for corrosion and clean them, if necessary. Line up the pins of

the new bulb with the slots in the socket, then push the bulb in and turn it clockwise until it locks into place. **Note:** *On US models fitted with front running lights, the dual filament bulbs have offset pins and can only be fitted one way in their holders.*

3 Fit the lens onto the holder, making sure the foam cushion is in place and the tab locates correctly **(see illustration)**. Do not overtighten the screw as the lens or threads could be damaged.

13 Turn signal assemblies

Front

1 Remove the fairing side panel from the side concerned, then remove the inner panel from the side panel (see Chapter 7).

2 Unclip the turn signal mounting plate and draw it off the wiring **(see illustration 13.6)**. Push the turn signal stem through the panel, noting how it fits and remove the turn signal. Take care not to snag the wiring as you pull it through the panel.

3 Installation is the reverse of removal. Make sure the wiring is correctly routed and securely connected. Check the operation of the turn signals.

Rear

4 Remove the seat cowling (see Chapter 7).

5 Trace the wiring back from the turn signal and disconnect it at the connectors **(see illustration)**. Feed it through to the turn signal, noting its routing.

6 Unclip the turn signal mounting plate and draw

12.3 Make sure the lens locates correctly

it off the wiring **(see illustration)**. Push the turn signal stem through the mudguard, noting how it fits and remove the turn signal. Take care not to snag the wiring as you pull it through the panel.

7 Installation is the reverse of removal. Make sure the wiring is correctly routed and securely connected. Check the operation of the turn signals.

14 Brake light switches

Circuit check

1 Before checking the switches, check the brake light circuit (see Section 6).

2 The front brake light switch is mounted on the underside of the brake master cylinder. Disconnect the wiring connectors from the switch **(see illustration)**. Using a continuity

13.5 Disconnect the relevant wiring connector

13.6 Release the mounting plate and push the stem through

14.2 Front brake switch wiring connectors (arrowed)

14.3 Rear brake switch wiring connector

14.9 Unhook the spring (A) and undo the screw (B) to remove the switch

tester, connect its probes to the terminals of the switch. With the brake lever at rest, there should be no continuity. With the brake lever applied, there should be continuity. If the switch does not behave as described, replace it with a new one.

3 The rear brake light switch is mounted on the inside of the rider's right-hand footrest bracket, above the brake pedal. Raise and support the fuel tank (see Chapter 4) to access its 2-pin brown wiring connector and disconnect it (see illustration). Using a continuity tester, connect the probes to the two terminals on the switch side of the wiring connector. With the brake pedal at rest, there should be no continuity. With the brake pedal applied, there should be continuity. If the switch does not behave as described, replace it with a new one.

4 If the switches are good, connect the wiring and check for voltage at the brown wire terminal on the supply side of the connector with the ignition switch ON. If no voltage is indicated, check the wiring between the switch, signal fuse and the ignition switch (see *Wiring Diagrams* at the end of this Chapter).

Switch removal and installation

Front brake light switch

5 The switch is mounted on the underside of the brake master cylinder. Disconnect the wiring connectors from the switch (see illustration 14.2).

6 Undo the single screw securing the switch to the bottom of the master cylinder and remove the switch (see illustration 5.6 in Chapter 6).

7 Installation is the reverse of removal. The switch is not adjustable.

Rear brake light switch

8 The switch is mounted on the inside of the rider's right-hand footrest bracket. Raise and support the fuel tank (see Chapter 4) to access the 2-pin wiring connector, then trace the wiring from the switch and disconnect it (see illustration 14.3). Feed it through to the switch, noting its routing, and cut any cable-ties.

9 Detach the lower end of the switch spring from the pin on the back of the brake pedal (see illustration). Undo the screw securing the switch bracket to the footrest bracket and remove the switch assembly.

10 Thread the switch out of its adjuster nut in the bracket, then press the nut ears in and draw it out of the bracket – note the bush and spacer in the switch bracket and remove them if they are loose.

11 Installation is the reverse of removal, noting the following:

● Replace the switch bracket bush with a new one if it is worn or perished.
● Ensure the end of the switch spring is correctly located on the brake pedal pin (see illustration 14.9).
● Secure the wiring to the footrest bracket with a new cable-tie.
● Adjust the switch as necessary (see Chapter 1, Section 12).

15 Instrument cluster removal and installation

1 Remove the fairing (see Chapter 7).
2 Undo the screws securing the instrument cluster to the fairing stay (see illustration). Pull the cluster off, noting how the three pins on the back locate in three bushes. Pull back the rubber boot and disconnect the wiring connector (see illustration).
3 Installation is the reverse of removal. If the bushes in the stay are worn or perished replace them with new ones.

16 Instrument check and replacement

Check

1 If all instrument and display functions fail at the same time, check the circuit fuse and the wiring and connectors, referring to the *Wiring Diagrams* at the end of the Chapter.

Tachometer

2 No test details are available for the tachometer. If it fails a new instrument cluster must be fitted.

Oil level display

3 The oil level display is controlled by the oil level sensor – refer to Section 26 for test details.

15.2a Undo the screws and remove the instrument cluster . . .

15.2b . . . pull back the rubber boot and disconnect the wiring connector

16.6 Disconnect the speed sensor wiring connector (arrowed)

16.8 Undo the screw and remove the sensor

Coolant temperature display

4 The coolant temperature display is controlled by the coolant temperature sensor – refer to Chapter 3 for test details.

Speedometer

5 The speedometer is controlled by the speed sensor, which is mounted in the back of the crankcase. To test the output from the sensor, place the motorcycle on an auxiliary stand so the rear wheel is off the ground. Make sure the transmission is in neutral.

6 Perform the diagnostic routine for the speed sensor (see Chapter 4) If the results aren't as expected, and if the wiring between the speed sensor and the connector is good (see illustration), replace the speed sensor with a new one (Steps 8 and 9).

7 If the diagnostic reading is correct, refer to Wiring Diagrams at the end of this Chapter and check the wiring and connectors between the sensor, ECU and the instrument cluster for continuity. If no fault can be found, the instrument cluster is faulty and must be replaced with a new one.

8 To fit a new sensor, raise or remove the fuel tank (see Chapter 4). Trace the wiring from the sensor and disconnect it at the wiring connector (see illustration 16.6). Feed it down to the sensor, noting its routing through the

cable-tie. Unscrew the bolt and withdraw the sensor from the crankcase (see illustration). Check the condition of the O-ring and replace it with a new one if it is damaged.

9 Smear the sensor O-ring with grease, then fit the sensor into the crankcase and tighten the bolt, not forgetting to secure the wiring clamp with it (see illustration). Connect the sensor wiring connector, then install the fuel tank (see Chapter 4).

Replacement

10 No parts are available from Yamaha to repair the instruments, so a new unit must be purchased. It may be worth checking with a specialist automotive electronic repairer to see if a failed unit can be repaired.

17 Instrument and warning lights

1 The warning and indicator functions (neutral, high beam, turn signals, fuel level, oil level and coolant temperature) are all illuminated by LEDs on the instrument cluster circuit board.

2 The fuel level, oil level and coolant temperature indicator lights should come on for a few seconds when the ignition is switched

ON as a check of the LEDs, and then go off. If the lights do not go off, first check the fuel and oil levels, and if the engine has been running the temperature readout on the LCD display, and if all is good then check the LED circuit (see Step 4). If the lights do not come on, test the LEDs as described below.

3 To test whether an LED has failed, remove the windshield (see Chapter 7), then pull back the rubber boot and disconnect the instrument cluster wiring connector. If required for better access remove the instrument cluster (see Section 15). Using a fully charged 12V battery and two suitable jumper wires, refer to Wiring Diagrams at the end of this Chapter and connect the positive (+) battery wire to the relevant terminal on the instrument cluster connector pin. The negative (-) battery wire should be connected to the black/white wire pin in the connector for all LEDs except the neutral light where testing is not possible.

4 If the LED comes on, the fault lies elsewhere in the electrical circuit for the LED in question. Check the fuse and wiring, and the operation of the component linked to the LED.

5 If the LED has failed a new instrument must be installed (see Section 16).

18 Ignition switch

⚠ Warning: To prevent the risk of short circuits, disconnect the battery negative (–) lead before making any ignition switch checks.

Check

1 Remove the left-hand cockpit trim panel from the fairing (see Chapter 7). Trace the ignition switch wiring back from the switch and disconnect it at the white connectors (see illustration). Make the checks on the switch side of the connector.

2 Using a multimeter or a continuity tester, check the continuity of the connector terminal

16.9 Smear the O-ring (arrowed) with grease

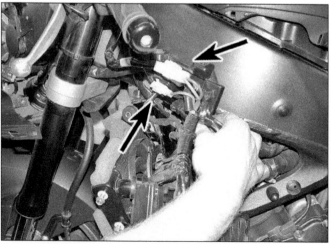

18.1 Ignition switch wiring connectors (arrowed)

18.4 Remove the cover and uncouple the wiring connector

18.6 Immobiliser screws (A) and cable-tie (B)

pairs (see *Wiring Diagrams* at the end of this Chapter). Continuity should exist between the terminals connected by a solid line on the diagram when the switch key is turned to the indicated position.

3 If the switch fails any of the tests, replace it with a new one.

Removal

4 Disconnect the battery negative (–) lead (Section 3). Remove the left-hand cockpit trim panel from the fairing (see Chapter 7). Trace the ignition switch wiring back from the switch and disconnect it at the connectors **(see illustration 18.1)**. Where an immobiliser is fitted, raise the fuel tank, remove the air filter housing and the AIS cover (see Chapter 4), the immobiliser wiring connector is under the cover on the reverse of the AIS cover **(see illustration)**. Remove the cover and disconnect the wiring connector, noting the correct routing. Release the wiring from any cable-ties and feed it back to the switch noting the correct routing.

5 Remove the top yoke (see Chapter 5, Section 9).

6 Where an immobiliser is fitted, undo the screws and detach the receiver **(see illustration)**.

7 Two shear-head security bolts mount the switch to the underside of the top yoke **(see illustration)**. The heads of the bolts must be

tapped around using a suitable punch or drift, or drilled off, before the switch can be removed. To do this, mount the yoke in a vice equipped with soft jaws to avoid damaging the yoke.

8 Remove the bolts and discard them as new ones must be used on reassembly, then withdraw the switch from the top yoke.

Installation

9 Installation is the reverse of removal, noting the following:
● Ensure the switch is installed in the yoke the correct way round before tightening the shear-head bolts.
● Obtain the correct type shear-head bolts from a Yamaha dealer – do not use another type of bolt. Tighten the bolts until their heads shear off.
● Ensure the wiring is securely connected and correctly routed.
● Ensure all top yoke and handlebar nuts and bolts are tightened to the torque settings specified in Chapter 5.

19 Handlebar switch check

1 Generally speaking, the handlebar switch units are reliable and trouble-free. Most

problems, when they do occur, are caused by dirty or corroded contacts, but wear and breakage of internal parts is a possibility that should not be overlooked. If breakage does occur, the entire switch unit and related wiring harness will have to be replaced with a new one, as individual parts are not available.

2 The switches can be checked for continuity using an multimeter or a continuity tester.

3 Remove the fairing cockpit trim panel for the side being checked to access the switch wiring connectors (see Chapter 7). Trace the wiring harness of the switch in question back to its connector (blue for the right-hand switches and off-white for the left-hand) and disconnect it/them **(see illustrations)** noting that they have an integral clip to secure them to the bracket.

4 Check for continuity between the terminals of the switch harness with the switch in the various positions (i.e. switch OFF – no continuity, switch ON – continuity) – see *Wiring Diagrams* at the end of this Chapter.

5 If the continuity check indicates a problem exists, refer to Section 20, displace the switch from the handlebar and spray the switch contacts with electrical contact cleaner. If they are accessible, scrape the contacts clean with a penknife or steel wool. If switch components are damaged or broken, it should be obvious when the switch is disassembled.

18.7 Remove the shear-head bolts (arrowed) as described

19.3a Handlebar switch wiring connector (arrowed) – right-hand side

19.3b Handlebar switch wiring connector (arrowed) – left-hand side

20 Handlebar switch removal and installation

Removal

1 If the switch unit is to be removed from the motorcycle, rather than just displaced from the handlebar, remove the cockpit trim panel for the side being checked to access the switch wiring connectors (see Chapter 7). Trace the wiring harness of the switch in question back to its connector (blue for the right-hand switches and off-white for the left-hand) and disconnect it/them (see illustrations 19.3a or b). Feed the wiring back to the switch, freeing it from any clips and ties and noting its correct routing.

2 Disconnect the wiring connectors from the brake light switch (if removing the right-hand switch unit) or the clutch switch (if removing the left-hand switch unit) (see illustration 14.2 or 23.2).

3 Undo the switch unit screws and free the unit from the handlebar by separating the halves (see illustrations).

Installation

4 Installation is the reverse of removal. Make sure the locating pin in the switch unit locates in the hole in the handlebar. Make sure the wiring is securely connected and correctly routed.

21 Neutral switch

Check

1 Before checking the electrical circuit, check the instrument cluster (backup) fuse (see Section 5).

2 The switch is located on the rear of the crankcase (see illustration). Make sure the transmission is in neutral. If necessary remove the EXUP servo (see Chapter 4) and disconnect the wiring connector from the switch.

3 With the connector disconnected and the

20.3a Right-hand switch housing screws (arrowed)

ignition switched ON, the neutral light should be out. If not, the wire between the connector and instrument cluster must be earthed (grounded) at some point.

4 Check for continuity between the terminal on the switch and the crankcase – with the transmission in neutral, there should be continuity; with the transmission in gear, there should be no continuity. If there is continuity when in gear or no continuity when in neutral, remove the switch (see below), and check that the contact plunger is not damaged or seized in the switch body (see illustration).

5 If the switch is good, check the wire between the connector, relay assembly and the instrument cluster for continuity. Refer to Section 24 for details of checking the diodes in the relay assembly. If there is continuity then check for battery voltage at the neutral switch connector.

6 If no voltage is present check for voltage at the brown wire terminal on the wiring loom side of the instrument cluster connector with the ignition ON – remove the windshield to access the connector (see Chapter 7), then pull back the rubber boot and disconnect it. If no voltage is indicated, first check the ignition fuse, then refer to the wiring diagram at the end of this Chapter and check for continuity between the connector and the fuse terminal.

7 If voltage is indicated check the starter circuit cut-off relay (Section 24) and other components in the starter circuit as described in the relevant Sections of this Chapter. If all components are good, check the wiring between the various components (see Wiring

20.3b Left-hand switch housing screws (arrowed)

Diagrams at the end of this Chapter). If that is good the instrument cluster could be faulty (see Section 16).

Removal and installation

8 The switch is located on the top of the crankcase. Remove the EXUP servo (see Chapter 4). Pull the wire connector off the switch terminal (see illustration 21.2). Unscrew the switch and withdraw it from the casing. Discard the sealing washer as a new one must be used on reassembly.

9 Install the switch using a new sealing washer and tighten it to the torque setting specified at the beginning of this Chapter.

10 Connect the wire to the switch terminal and check the operation of the neutral light.

22 Sidestand switch

Check

1 The sidestand switch is mounted on the back of the sidestand bracket. The switch is part of the safety circuit which prevents or stops the engine running if the transmission is in gear whilst the sidestand is down, and prevents the engine from starting if the transmission is in gear unless the sidestand is up and the clutch lever is pulled in. Before checking the electrical circuit, check the main and ignition fuses (see Section 5).

2 To access the wiring connector, raise or remove the fuel tank (see Chapter 4). Trace

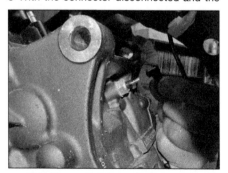

21.2 The switch is on the rear of the crankcase

21.4 Make sure the plunger is not seized or damaged

22.2 Disconnect the sidestand switch wiring connector

22.7a Counter-hold the switch mounting bolts (arrowed) . . .

22.7b . . . and unscrew the nuts (arrowed)

the wiring from the switch and disconnect it at the 2-pin connector **(see illustration)**.

3 Check the operation of the switch using a multimeter or continuity tester. Connect the meter probes to the terminals on the switch side of the wire connector. With the sidestand up there should be continuity (zero resistance) between the terminals, and with the stand down there should be no continuity (infinite resistance).

4 If the switch does not perform as expected, check the plunger is not seized in the switch body. If the plunger is fine replace the switch with a new one.

5 If the switch is good, check for battery voltage at the blue/black wire terminal on the loom side of the connector, and check for continuity to earth in the black wire. Next check the starter circuit cut-off relay (Section 24) and other components in the starter circuit as described in the relevant Sections of this Chapter. If all components are good, check the wiring between the various components (see *Wiring Diagrams* at the end of this Chapter).

Renewal

6 The sidestand switch is mounted on the back of the sidestand bracket. Raise or remove the fuel tank (see Chapter 4), then trace the wiring from the switch and disconnect it at the connector **(see illustration 22.2)**. Release the wiring from any cable-ties and feed it back to the switch, noting its routing.

23.2 Disconnect the clutch switch wiring connectors

7 Remove the lower fairing (see Chapter 7). Remove the plastic cover from the inside of the frame **(see illustration 4.4 in Chapter 5)**. Counter-hold the bolts, unscrew the nuts and remove the switch **(see illustrations)**.

8 Install the new switch, not forgetting the wiring clamp, and tighten the bolts/nuts. Ensure the switch plunger engages correctly with the contact plate on the sidestand.

9 Make sure the wiring is correctly routed up to the connector and retained by all the necessary clips and ties. Reconnect the wiring connector and check the operation of the switch.

23 Clutch switch

Check

1 The clutch switch is mounted on the underside of the clutch lever bracket. The switch is part of the safety circuit which prevents or stops the engine running if the transmission is in gear whilst the sidestand is down, and prevents the engine from starting if the transmission is up and the clutch lever is pulled in. The switch is not adjustable.

2 To check the switch, disconnect the wiring

24.3 Displace the relay assembly and disconnect the connector

connectors **(see illustration)**. Connect the probes of a multimeter or a continuity tester to the two switch terminals. There should be continuity (zero resistance) with the clutch lever pulled in, and no continuity (infinite resistance) with the clutch lever out.

3 If the switch is good, check the starter circuit cut-off relay (Section 24) and other components in the starter circuit as described in the relevant Sections of this Chapter. If all components are good, check the wiring between the various components (see *Wiring Diagrams* at the end of this Chapter).

Renewal

4 The clutch switch is mounted on the underside of the clutch lever bracket.

5 Disconnect the wiring connectors **(see illustration 23.2)**, then undo the screw and remove the switch.

6 Installation is the reverse of removal.

24 Relay assembly

Starter circuit cut-off relay and diodes

1 The starter circuit cut-off relay and its associated diodes are contained within the relay assembly. They are part of the safety circuit which prevents or stops the engine running if the transmission is in gear whilst the sidestand is down, and prevents the engine from starting if the transmission is in gear unless the sidestand is up and the clutch lever is pulled in.

2 The relay assembly is mounted under the rider's seat, Remove the seat for access (see Chapter 7).

3 Disconnect the battery negative (–) lead, then displace the relay and disconnect the wiring connector **(see illustration)**. Move the relay assembly to the bench for testing. Refer to the wiring diagram for your model (see end of Chapter) and the following procedures:

4 To check the operation of the relay, first

24.4 Starter circuit cut-off relay test connections

1	Red/black	3	Blue/white
2	Black/yellow	4	Blue/white (2)

24.6 Diode test connections

1	Light blue	4	Light blue/white
2	Black/yellow	5	Blue/black
3	Blue/yellow (2)		

connect a multimeter set to the ohms x 1 scale, or a continuity tester, between the two blue/white wire terminals (Nos. 3 and 4) of the relay as indicated **(see illustration)**. There should be no continuity.

5 Leave the multimeter or continuity tester connected to the relay. Now, using a fully charged 12V battery and two suitable jumper wires, connect the battery positive (+) terminal to the relay's red/black wire terminal (No. 1) and the battery negative (–) terminal to the relay's black/yellow wire terminal (No. 2). With voltage applied, the test equipment should show continuity. If it doesn't, replace the relay assembly with a new one.

6 The diodes contained within the relay assembly can be checked by performing a continuity test – diodes should show continuity in one direction and no continuity when the meter or tester probes are reversed. Connect the multimeter (set to the ohms or diode test function) or continuity tester across the wire terminals for the diode being tested **(see illustration)** and perform the following tests. If any diode shows the same condition in both directions it is faulty, and the relay assembly must be replaced with a new one.

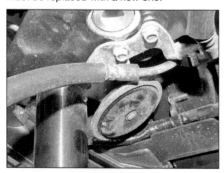

25.2 Horn location

Positive probe (+)	Negative probe (-)	Result
1 Light blue	2 Black/yellow	Continuity
2 Black/yellow	1 Light blue	No continuity
1 Light blue	3 Blue/yellow	Continuity
3 Blue/yellow	1 Light blue	No continuity
1 Light blue	4 Light blue/white	Continuity
4 Light blue/white	1 Light blue	No continuity
5 Blue/black	3 Blue/yellow	Continuity
3 Blue/yellow	5 Blue/black	No continuity

7 If the cut-out relay and diodes are good, but the starting system fault still exists, check all other components in the starting circuit (i.e. the neutral switch, sidestand switch, clutch switch, starter switch and starter relay) as described in the relevant Sections of this Chapter. If all components are good, check the wiring between the various components (see *Wiring Diagrams* at the end of this Chapter).

8 Installation is the reverse of removal.

Fuel pump relay

9 Refer to Chapter 4, Section 8.

25 Horn

Check

1 If the horn doesn't work, first check the circuit fuse (see Section 5) and the battery (see Section 3).

2 The horn is mounted on the bottom yoke

(see illustration). Remove the left-hand fairing side panel for best access to it (see Chapter 7).

3 Pull the wiring connectors off the horn terminals. Using two jumper wires, apply battery voltage directly to the terminals on the horn. If the horn sounds, check the switch (see Section 19) and the wiring between the switch and the horn (see *Wiring Diagrams* at the end of this Chapter).

4 If the horn doesn't sound, replace it with a new one.

Removal and installation

5 Remove the left-hand fairing side panel (see Chapter 7) for best access to the horn.

6 Pull the wiring connectors off the horn terminals. Unscrew the bolt securing the horn and remove it from the bike.

7 Install the horn and tighten the bolt. Connect the wiring connectors and check the operation of the horn, then install the fairing panel.

26 Oil level sensor

Check

1 The oil level warning light will come on for a few seconds when the ignition is switched ON as a check of the warning light LED. It should then go out and the motorcycle can be started. If the warning light remains on and/ or the oil level symbol in the digital display remains illuminated, check the oil level as described in *Pre-ride checks*. If the oil level is correct, check the sensor as described below. Equally if the warning light comes on (and/or flashes) whilst the motorcycle is being ridden, stop the engine allow it to cool and check the oil level immediately.

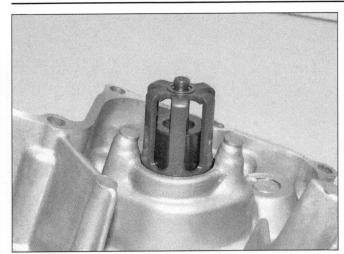

26.3a Sensor float (arrowed) with sensor in upright position

26.3b Sensor float raised

2 If the warning light does not come on when the ignition is switched ON, check the LED as described in Section 17. If there is a fault in the wiring circuit it will be detected by a self diagnosis function and the warning light will flash ten times, then go out for 2.5 seconds, and this will be repeated until the fault is fixed.

3 To check the sensor, remove it from the sump (see Steps 4 to 6). Make sure the sensor float is not stuck and moves freely between its top and bottom positions (see illustrations). Connect one probe of a multimeter set to the ohms x 100 scale to the sensor wire and the other probe to the base of the sensor. With the sensor upright (i.e. in its normal installed position with the wiring at the bottom), the resistance should be as specified at the beginning of the Chapter. Raise the sensor float to the top or turn the sensor upside down and check the resistance – it should be as specified. If either condition does not occur, replace the sensor with a new one.

 HAYNES HiNT *On all models the warning light may flicker during sudden acceleration or deceleration or when riding up or down hill. Note that this is a characteristic of the system and provided the oil level is correct, does not indicate a fault.*

Removal

4 Drain the engine oil (see Chapter 1).

5 Raise or remove the fuel tank (see Chapter 4), then trace the wire back from the sensor and disconnect it at the connector (see illustration). Release the wire from any cable-ties and the clamp secured by one sump bolt (see illustration 26.6), and feed it back to the sensor noting the correct routing.

6 Unscrew the two bolts securing the sensor to the bottom of the sump and withdraw it from the sump, being prepared to catch any residual oil (see illustration).

Installation

7 Fit a new O-ring to the sensor, smearing it with lithium-based grease, then fit the sensor into the sump. Tighten its bolts to the torque setting specified at the beginning of this Chapter.

8 Feed the wiring to the connector (see illustration 26.5) and secure it with new cable-ties. Don't forget to install the clamp and sump bolt (see illustration 26.6).

9 Fill the engine with the specified amount of oil (see Chapter 1) and check the operation of the sensor. Install the fuel tank.

27 Starter relay

Check

1 If the starter circuit is faulty, first check the main fuse and ignition fuse (see Section 5).

26.5 Disconnect the oil level sensor wiring connector

26.6 Unscrew the bolt (A) to free the wiring from the clamp, then unscrew the bolts (B) and withdraw the sensor

27.2a Starter relay (arrowed)

27.2b Remove the cover and disconnect the starter lead

27.9 Disconnect the wiring connector

2 Remove the rider's seat (see Chapter 7). The starter relay is located behind the battery **(see illustration)**. Lift the terminal cover **(see illustration)** and unscrew the bolt securing the starter motor lead to its terminal (marked M); position the lead away from the relay terminal With the ignition switch ON, the engine kill switch in the RUN position, and the transmission in neutral, press the starter switch. The relay should be heard to click.

3 If the relay doesn't click, switch the ignition OFF, remove the relay (see Steps 8 and 9) and test it as follows.

4 Connect a multimeter set to the ohms x 1 scale, or a continuity tester, between the relay's starter motor (black) and battery (red) lead terminals. There should be no continuity.

5 Leave the multimeter or continuity tester connected to the relay. Now, using a fully-charged 12V battery and two suitable jumper wires, connect the battery positive (+) terminal to the relay's red/white wire terminal, and the battery negative (–) terminal to the relay's blue/white wire terminal. With voltage applied, the relay should be heard to click and the test equipment should show continuity. Disconnect the battery and test meter.

6 If the relay does not click when battery voltage is applied and indicates no continuity (infinite resistance) across its terminals, it is faulty and must be replaced with a new one. The relay coil resistance can be checked by connecting a multimeter set to the ohms x 1 range across the red/white and blue/white terminals of the relay wire connector; the value should be as specified at the beginning of this Chapter.

7 If the relay is good, check for battery voltage at the red/white wire terminal on the loom side of the relay wiring connector when the starter button is pressed with the ignition switched ON. If voltage is present, check the other components in the starter circuit as described in the relevant Sections of this Chapter. If no voltage is present, check the wiring between the various components (see *Wiring Diagrams* at the end of this Chapter).

Removal and installation

8 Remove the rider's seat (see Chapter 7). The starter relay is located behind the battery **(see illustration 27.2a)**. Disconnect the battery negative (–) lead before removing the relay.

9 Disconnect the relay wiring connector **(see illustration)**. Unscrew the two bolts securing the starter motor and battery leads (marked M and B respectively) to the relay and detach the leads **(see illustration 27.2b)**. Remove the relay with its rubber sleeve from its mounting lug on the frame.

10 Installation is the reverse of removal. The black starter motor lead connects to the M terminal, and the red battery lead to the B terminal **(see illustration 27.2b)**. Make sure the terminal bolts are tightened securely. Connect the negative (–) lead last when reconnecting the battery.

28.1 Lift the rubber heat shield

28.2 Pull back the terminal cover then unscrew the nut, and detach the lead

28 Starter motor removal and installation

Removal

1 Disconnect the battery negative (–) lead (see Section 3). Remove the throttle bodies (see Chapter 4). The starter motor is mounted on the crankcase, behind the cylinder block. Remove the rubber heat shield to uncover it **(see illustration)**.

2 Peel back the terminal boot, then unscrew the nut and washers (take note of their locations) securing the lead to the starter motor terminal **(see illustration)**.

3 Unscrew the two mounting bolts, then draw the starter motor out of the crankcase and remove it **(see illustrations)**.

4 Remove the O-ring on the end of the starter motor and discard it, as a new one must be used **(see illustration 28.5)**.

28.3a Unscrew the two bolts (arrowed) . . .

28.3b . . . and remove the starter motor

28.5 Fit a new O-ring and lubricate it

29.2 Note the alignment marks (arrowed) then unscrew the two bolts, noting the O-rings

29.3 Remove the front cover

Installation

5 Fit a new O-ring onto the end of the starter motor, making sure it is seated in its groove, and smear it with grease **(see illustration)**.
6 Manoeuvre the motor into position and slide it into the crankcase **(see illustration 28.3b)**. Ensure that the starter motor teeth mesh correctly with those of the starter idler gear. Install the mounting bolts and tighten them to the torque setting specified at the beginning of this Chapter **(see illustration 28.3a)**.
7 Connect the lead to the starter motor terminal and secure it with the nut and washers **(see illustration 28.2)**. Make sure the boot is correctly seated over the terminal.
8 Fit the rubber heat shield and install the throttle bodies (see Chapter 4). Connect the battery negative (–) lead.

29 Starter motor overhaul

Disassembly

1 Remove the starter motor (see Section 28).
2 Note the alignment marks between the main housing and the front and rear covers, or make your own if they are unclear. Unscrew and remove the two long bolts **(see illustration)**.
3 Remove the front cover from the motor **(see illustration)**.
4 Remove the tabbed washer from inside the cover and slide the washers off the front end of the armature **(see illustrations)**.
5 Holding the main housing, draw the armature out, noting that the attraction of the magnets will have to be overcome **(see illustration)**. Slide the washers off the rear end of the armature.
6 Remove the rear cover and brushplate assembly **(see illustration)**. Remove the sealing rings from the housing and discard them as new ones must be fitted on reassembly **(see illustration 29.18a)**.

Inspection

7 Check the general condition of all the starter motor components. The parts that are most likely to require attention are the brushes.

29.4a Remove the tabbed washer . . .

29.4b . . . and the plain washers

29.5 Draw the armature out

29.6 Remove the rear cover and brushplate assembly

Undo the locknut on the cable terminal, remove it and the washers, noting their order, and withdraw the brushplate assembly. Slide the brushes out of their holders, then measure the length of each brush **(see illustration)**. Compare the results to the standard and minimum brush lengths listed in this Chapter's Specifications to assess the degree of wear. If any of the brushes are worn beyond the service limit, fit a new brushplate **(see illustration)**.
8 Inspect the commutator bars on the

29.7a Measure the length of each brush

29.7b Fit the brushplate

29.9 Continuity should exist between the commutator bars

29.10 There should be no continuity between the bars and the armature shaft

29.11 Mica (1) must be the specified depth below the commutator bars (2)

armature for scoring, scratches and discoloration. The commutator can be cleaned and polished with steel wool or crocus cloth, but do not use sandpaper or emery paper. After cleaning, wipe away any residue with a cloth soaked in electrical system cleaner or denatured alcohol.

9 Using a multimeter or a continuity tester, check for continuity between the commutator bars (see illustration). Continuity should exist (Yamaha specify 0.0012 to 0.0022 ohms at 20°C) between each bar and all of the others.

10 Check for continuity between the commutator bars and the armature shaft (see illustration). There should be no continuity (infinite resistance – Yamaha specify a resistance of over 1 M-ohm); if the checks indicate otherwise, the armature is defective.

11 Check the depth of the insulating mica undercut between the commutator bars (see illustration) – if it is less than the amount specified at the beginning of this Chapter, scrape the mica away using a

suitably shaped hacksaw blade until it is correct.

12 Measure the diameter of the commutator and replace the starter motor with a new one if it has worn below the minimum diameter specified (see illustration).

13 Check the starter shaft teeth for wear, cracks and chips and replace the starter motor with a new one if necessary.

14 Inspect the end covers for signs of cracks. Check the oil seal and needle bearing in the front cover and the bush in the rear cover for wear and damage (see illustrations). Inspect the magnets in the main housing and the housing itself for cracks.

15 Make sure the terminal is secure in the rear cover.

Reassembly

16 Ensure the brush spring ends press on the brushes themselves and refit the brushplate into the end cover (see illustration 29.7b) ensuring that the insulating washers are fitted in the correct position (see illustration). Tighten the locknut to the torque specified in the beginning of this Chapter.

17 Lubricate the shaft end with a smear of

29.12 Measure the diameter of the commutator

29.14a Check the oil seal and bearing (arrowed) in the front cover . . .

29.14b . . . and the bush (arrowed) in the rear cover

29.16 Refit the washers and the nut and then tighten it to the specified torque

29.17a Lubricate the rear end of the armature and refit the washers . . .

29.17b . . . push the brushes back with the end of the armature . . .

grease and re-fit the washers (see illustration), then insert the shaft into the rear cover, tilting it to locate the two brushes against the bars, then pushing the brushes back to align the shaft with its bush (see illustrations). Check that each brush is securely pressed against the commutator.

18 Fit new O-rings onto the main housing (see illustration). Fit the housing over the armature and onto the rear cover, aligning the marks (see illustration) – hold the armature to prevent it being drawn out of the rear cover by the attraction of the magnets, and make sure

you do not get your fingers caught between the housing and the rear cover as the housing is drawn into place (see illustration).
19 Slide the washers onto the front end of the armature shaft and lubricate the shaft with a smear of grease (see illustration 29.4b).

29.17c . . . then align it with the bush and insert it into the cover

29.18a Fit new O-rings onto the main housing

29.18b Carefully fit the housing over the armature . . .

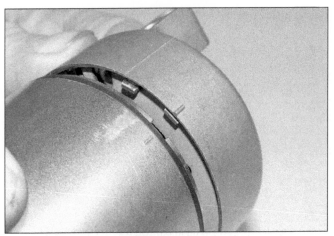

29.18c . . . making sure the marks are aligned

Apply a smear of grease to the inside of the front cover oil seal. Fit the tabbed washer into the cover, making sure the tabs locate correctly **(see illustrations 29.4a)**. Fit the cover onto the main housing, aligning the marks **(see illustration 29.3)**.

20 Check that the marks on the rear cover, main housing and front cover are correctly aligned, then install the bolts with their washers and tighten them **(see illustration 29.2)**.

21 Install the starter motor (see Section 28).

30 Charging system testing

1 If the performance of the charging system is suspect, the system as a whole should be checked first, followed by testing of the individual components. **Note:** *Before beginning the checks, make sure the battery is fully charged and that all system connections are clean and tight.*

2 Checking the output of the charging system and the performance of the various components within the charging system requires the use of a multimeter (with voltage, current and resistance checking facilities).

30.5 Checking the charging system leakage rate – connect the meter as shown

If a multimeter is not available, the job of checking the charging system should be left to a Yamaha dealer or automotive electrician.

3 When making the checks, follow the procedures carefully to prevent incorrect connections or short circuits, as irreparable damage to electrical system components may result if short circuits occur.

Leakage test

Caution: Always connect an ammeter in series, never in parallel with the battery, otherwise it will be damaged. Do not turn the ignition ON or operate the starter motor when the ammeter is connected – a sudden surge in current will blow the meter's fuse.

4 Turn the ignition switch OFF. Remove the rider's seat (see Chapter 7) and disconnect the lead from the battery negative (–) terminal (see Section 3).

5 Set the multimeter to the Amps function and connect its negative (–) probe to the battery negative (–) terminal, and positive (+) probe to the disconnected negative (–) lead **(see illustration)**. Always set the meter to a high amps range initially and then bring it down to the mA (milli Amps) range; if there is a high current flow in the circuit it may blow the meter's fuse.

6 No current flow should be indicated. If current leakage is indicated (generally greater than 1mA, but may be more if an alarm is fitted), there is a short circuit in the wiring. Using the wiring diagrams at the end of this Chapter, systematically disconnect individual electrical components, checking the meter each time until the source is identified.

7 If no leakage is indicated, disconnect the meter and connect the negative (–) lead to the battery, tightening it securely.

Output test

8 Start the engine and warm it up to normal operating temperature. Remove the rider's seat (see Chapter 7).

9 To check the regulated voltage output, allow the engine to idle and connect a multimeter set to the 0 to 20 volts DC scale (voltmeter) across the terminals of the battery, positive (+) lead to battery positive (+) terminal, negative (–) lead to battery negative (–) terminal **(see illustration)**. Slowly increase the engine speed to 5000 rpm and note the reading obtained.

10 The regulated voltage should be as specified at the beginning of the Chapter. If the voltage is outside these limits, check the alternator, then the regulator/rectifier (see Sections 31 and 32).

11 Stop the engine and disconnect the test meter.

31 Alternator rotor and stator

Check

1 Remove the left-hand fairing side panel (see Chapter 7).

2 Locate the alternator wiring connector behind the coolant pipe and uncouple it **(see illustration)**.

3 Using a multimeter set to the ohms x 1 (ohmmeter) scale, measure the resistance between the centre wire terminal and each of the other two on the loom side of the connector, then between the outer two terminals, taking a total of three readings, then check for continuity between each terminal and earth (ground). If the alternator stator coil windings are in good condition the resistance readings should be within the range shown in the Specifications at the beginning of this Chapter and there should be no continuity (infinite resistance) between the terminals and earth (ground). If not, check the fault is not due to damaged wiring between the connector and alternator coils. If the wiring is good, the alternator stator coil assembly is at fault and should be replaced with a new one.

30.9 Charging system regulated voltage check

31.2 Locate the wiring connector (arrowed) and uncouple it

31.5a Unscrew the wiring clamp bolt (A) and the stator screws (B) . . .

31.5b . . . noting the grommet (arrowed) and how it locates

Removal

4 Refer to Chapter 2, Section 14 for removal of the alternator stator and rotor, and to separate the rotor from the starter clutch.
5 To remove the stator, undo the bolt securing the wiring clamp and the three screws securing the stator to the inside of the cover, then remove the assembly, noting how it locates on the cover and how the wiring grommet locates in the edge of the cover (see illustrations).

Installation

6 Fit the stator, aligning the wiring grommet with the recess in the cover, and making sure it locates correctly (see illustration 31.5b). Apply a suitable non-permanent thread locking compound to the stator screw threads, then install the screws and tighten them to the torque setting specified at the beginning of this Chapter.
7 Apply sealant to the wiring grommet, then press it into the recess in the cover (see illustration 31.5a). Apply a non-permanent thread locking compound to the wiring clamp bolt threads, then fit the clamp and tighten the bolt to the specified torque setting.
8 Refer to Chapter 2, Section 14 for installation of the alternator stator and rotor.

32 Regulator/rectifier

Check

1 Yamaha provide no test specifications for the regulator/rectifier other than the charging system output test (see Section 30). If the regulator/rectifier is suspected of being faulty, first check all other components and the wiring and connectors in the charging circuit, referring to the relevant Sections in this Chapter and to the wiring diagrams which follow.
2 If all other components and the wiring are good, remove the unit (see below) and take it to a Yamaha dealer for testing. Alternatively, substitute the suspect unit with a known good one and see if the fault is cured.

 HAYNES HiNT *Clues to a faulty regulator are constantly blowing bulbs, with brightness varying considerably with engine speed, and battery overheating.*

32.4 Unscrew the bolts and remove the bracket

Removal and installation

3 Remove the left-hand fairing side panels (see Chapter 7) to access the regulator/rectifier mounting bracket .
4 Unscrew the bolts securing the regulator/rectifier bracket and remove it (see illustration). Detach the bracket if required. Note the washers.
5 Install the new unit and tighten its bolts, not forgetting the washers. Connect the wiring connectors. Install the fairing panels (see Chapter 7).

Instruments

1 Illumination
2 Illumination
3 High beam warning light
4 LH turn signal warning light
5 RH turn signal warning light
6 Neutral warning light
7 Multifunction display
8 Fuel level warning light
9 Oil level warning light
10 Shift timing warning light
11 Engine trouble warning light
12 Coolant temperature warning light
13 Immobiliser warning light
14 Tachometer

Engine stop switch
Starter switch
Ignition switch
Fuel pump and level sensor
Relay assembly
A Starter cut-off relay
B Fuel pump relay

Front brake light switch
Rear brake light switch

Air temperature sensor

Front right turn signal
Headlight (Hi)
Headlight (Lo)
Front sidelight
Front left turn signal
Headlight relay (on/off)
Headlight relay (dimmer)
Engine cooling fan relay
RH engine cooling fan
LH engine cooling fan

Horn switch
Horn
Passing switch
Dimmer switch
Turn signal switch
Hazard switch
Clutch switch
Turn signal relay
Alarm connector
Oil level switch
Neutral switch
Sidestand switch
Immobiliser control unit

H47549

YZF-R6 2006 and 2007 Europe

ECU

Throttle body position sensor

Throttle cable position sensor

Tip-over sensor

Speed sensor

Throttle servo motor

Oxygen sensor

EXUP servo motor

Crank position sensor

Coolant temperature sensor

Ignition coils and spark plugs

Air induction system cut-off valve

Cylinder identification sensor

Secondary fuel injectors

Primary fuel injectors

Intake air pressure sensor

Atmospheric pressure sensor

Rear right turn signal

Brake and tail LED

Licence plate light

Rear left turn signal

Main fuse

Starter relay and fuel injection fuse

A 7.5A Backup (odometer, clock and immobiliser) fuse
B 7.5A YCC-T throttle servo fuse

1 15A Left radiator fan motor
2 15A Right radiator fan motor
3 10A Signaling system
4 15A Ignition fuse
5 7.5A Taillight fuse
6 15A Headlight

Fuse box

Alternator

Regulator rectifier

Starter motor

Battery

H47550

YZF-R6 2006 and 2007 Europe

Instruments

1 Illumination
2 Illumination
3 High beam warning light
4 LH turn signal warning light
5 RH turn signal warning light
6 Neutral warning light
7 Multifunction display

8 Fuel level warning light
9 Oil level warning light
10 Shift timing warning light
11 Engine trouble warning light
12 Coolant temperature warning light
13 Immobiliser warning light
14 Tachometer

Engine stop switch

Starter switch

Ignition switch

Fuel pump and level sensor

Relay assembly
A Starter cut-off relay
B Fuel pump relay

Front brake light switch

Rear brake light switch

Air temperature sensor

Front right turn signal

Headlight (Hi)

Headlight (Lo)

Front sidelight LED

Front left turn signal

Headlight relay (on/off)

Headlight relay (dimmer)

Engine cooling fan relay

RH engine cooling fan

LH engine cooling fan

Horn switch

Horn

Passing switch

Clutch switch

Dimmer switch

Turn signal switch

Hazard switch

Turn signal relay

Alarm connector

Oil level switch

Neutral switch

Sidestand switch

Immobiliser control unit

H47551

YZF-R6 2008-on Europe

ECU

YCC-I
Intake funnel
servo motor

Throttle body
position
sensor

Throttle cable
position
sensor

Tip-over
sensor

Speed
sensor

Throttle
servo
motor

Oxygen
sensor

EXUP servo
motor

Crank
position
sensor

Coolant
temperature
sensor

Ignition coils
and spark plugs

Air
induction
system
cut-off valve

Cylinder
identification
sensor

Secondary
fuel injectors

Primary
fuel injectors

Intake air
pressure
sensor

Atmospheric
pressure
sensor

Rear right
turn signal

Brake and
tail LED

Licence
plate light

Rear left
turn signal

50A
Main fuse

Starter relay and
fuel injection fuse

15A

A   7.5A   Backup (odometer, clock
            and immobiliser) fuse
B   7.5A   YCC-T throttle servo fuse

1   15A   Left radiator fan motor
2   15A   Right radiator fan motor
3   10A   Signaling system
4   15A   Ignition fuse
5   7.5A Taillight fuse
6   15A   Headlight

Fuse box 2

Alternator

Regulator
rectifier

Starter
motor

Battery

H47552

YZF-R6 2008-on Europe

Instruments
1 Illumination
2 Illumination
3 High beam warning light
4 LH turn signal warning light
5 RH turn signal warning light
6 Neutral warning light
7 Multifunction display

8 Fuel level warning light
9 Oil level warning light
10 Shift timing warning light
11 Engine trouble warning light
12 Coolant temperature warning light
13 Tachometer

Engine stop switch
Starter switch
Ignition switch
Fuel pump and level sensor

Front brake light switch
Rear brake light switch

Relay assembly
A Starter cut-off relay
B Fuel pump relay

ON
OFF

Air temperature sensor

Front right turn signal/position light

Headlight (Hi)

Headlight (Lo)

Front left turn signal/position light

Headlight relay (on/off)

Headlight relay (dimmer)

Engine cooling fan relay

RH engine cooling fan

LH engine cooling fan

Horn switch

Horn

Clutch switch

Dimmer switch
HI
LO

Turn signal switch
L
N
R

Hazard switch
OFF
ON

Turn signal relay

Oil level switch

Neutral switch

Sidestand switch

H47553

YZF-R6 2008-on US

ECU

YCC-I
Intake funnel
servo motor

Throttle body
position
sensor

Throttle cable
position
sensor

Tip-over
sensor

Speed
sensor

Throttle
servo
motor

Oxygen
sensor

EXUP servo
motor

Crank
position
sensor

Coolant
temperature
sensor

Ignition coils
and spark plugs

Air
induction
system
cut-off valve

Cylinder
identification
sensor

Secondary
fuel injectors

Primary
fuel injectors

Intake air
pressure
sensor

Atmospheric
pressure
sensor

Rear right
turn signal

Brake and
tail LED

Licence
plate light

Rear left
turn signal

Main fuse

Starter relay and
fuel injection fuse

A 7.5A Backup (odometer and
          clock) fuse
B 7.5A YCC-T throttle servo fuse

1 15A Left radiator fan motor
2 15A Right radiator fan motor
3 10A Signaling system
4 15A Ignition fuse
5 15A Headlight

Fuse box 2

Alternator

Regulator
rectifier

Starter
motor

Battery

H47554

YZF-R6 2008-on US

Reference

Buying tools

A toolkit is a fundamental requirement for servicing and repairing a motorcycle. Although there will be an initial expense in building up enough tools for servicing, this will soon be offset by the savings made by doing the job yourself. As experience and confidence grow, additional tools can be added to enable the repair and overhaul of the motorcycle. Many of the specialist tools are expensive and not often used so it may be preferable to hire them, or for a group of friends or motorcycle club to join in the purchase.

As a rule, it is better to buy more expensive, good quality tools. Cheaper tools are likely to wear out faster and need to be renewed more often, nullifying the original saving.

> ⚠ **Warning: To avoid the risk of a poor quality tool breaking in use, causing injury or damage to the component being worked on, always aim to purchase tools which meet the relevant national safety standards.**

The following lists of tools do not represent the manufacturer's service tools, but serve as a guide to help the owner decide which tools are needed for this level of work. In addition, items such as an electric drill, hacksaw, files, soldering iron and a workbench equipped with a vice, may be needed. Although not classed as tools, a selection of bolts, screws, nuts, washers and pieces of tubing always come in useful.

For more information about tools, refer to the Haynes *Motorcycle Workshop Practice Techbook* (Bk. No. 3470).

Manufacturer's service tools

Inevitably certain tasks require the use of a service tool. Where possible an alternative tool or method of approach is recommended, but sometimes there is no option if personal injury or damage to the component is to be avoided. Where required, service tools are referred to in the relevant procedure.

Service tools can usually only be purchased from a motorcycle dealer and are identified by a part number. Some of the commonly-used tools, such as rotor pullers, are available in aftermarket form from mail-order motorcycle tool and accessory suppliers.

Maintenance and minor repair tools

1 Set of flat-bladed screwdrivers
2 Set of Phillips head screwdrivers
3 Combination open-end and ring spanners
4 Socket set (3/8 inch or 1/2 inch drive)
5 Set of Allen keys or bits

6 Set of Torx keys or bits
7 Pliers, cutters and self-locking grips (Mole grips)
8 Adjustable spanners
9 C-spanners
10 Tread depth gauge and tyre pressure gauge

11 Cable oiler clamp
12 Feeler gauges
13 Spark plug gap measuring tool
14 Spark plug spanner or deep plug sockets
15 Wire brush and emery paper

16 Calibrated syringe, measuring vessel and funnel
17 Oil filter adapters
18 Oil drainer can or tray
19 Pump type oil can
20 Grease gun

21 Straight-edge and steel rule
22 Continuity tester
23 Battery charger
24 Hydrometer (for battery specific gravity check)
25 Anti-freeze tester (for liquid-cooled engines)

Repair and overhaul tools

1 *Torque wrench (small and mid-ranges)*
2 *Conventional, plastic or soft-faced hammers*
3 *Impact driver set*
4 *Vernier gauge*
5 *Circlip pliers (internal and external, or combination)*
6 *Set of cold chisels and punches*
7 *Selection of pullers*
8 *Breaker bars*
9 *Chain breaking/riveting tool set*
10 *Wire stripper and crimper tool*
11 *Multimeter (measures amps, volts and ohms)*
12 *Stroboscope (for dynamic timing checks)*
13 *Hose clamp (wingnut type shown)*
14 *Clutch holding tool*
15 *One-man brake/clutch bleeder kit*

Specialist tools

1 *Micrometers (external type)*
2 *Telescoping gauges*
3 *Dial gauge*
4 *Cylinder compression gauge*
5 *Vacuum gauges (left) or manometer (right)*
6 *Oil pressure gauge*
7 *Plastigauge kit*
8 *Valve spring compressor (4-stroke engines)*
9 *Piston pin drawbolt tool*
10 *Piston ring removal and installation tool*
11 *Piston ring clamp*
12 *Cylinder bore hone (stone type shown)*
13 *Stud extractor*
14 *Screw extractor set*
15 *Bearing driver set*

1 Workshop equipment and facilities

The workbench

● Work is made much easier by raising the bike up on a ramp - components are much more accessible if raised to waist level. The hydraulic or pneumatic types seen in the dealer's workshop are a sound investment if you undertake a lot of repairs or overhauls **(see illustration 1.1)**.

1.1 Hydraulic motorcycle ramp

● If raised off ground level, the bike must be supported on the ramp to avoid it falling. Most ramps incorporate a front wheel locating clamp which can be adjusted to suit different diameter wheels. When tightening the clamp, take care not to mark the wheel rim or damage the tyre - use wood blocks on each side to prevent this.
● Secure the bike to the ramp using tie-downs **(see illustration 1.2)**. If the bike has only a sidestand, and hence leans at a dangerous angle when raised, support the bike on an auxiliary stand.

1.2 Tie-downs are used around the passenger footrests to secure the bike

● Auxiliary (paddock) stands are widely available from mail order companies or motorcycle dealers and attach either to the wheel axle or swingarm pivot **(see illustration 1.3)**. If the motorcycle has a centrestand, you can support it under the crankcase to prevent it toppling whilst either wheel is removed **(see illustration 1.4)**.

1.3 This auxiliary stand attaches to the swingarm pivot

1.4 Always use a block of wood between the engine and jack head when supporting the engine in this way

Fumes and fire

● Refer to the Safety first! page at the beginning of the manual for full details. Make sure your workshop is equipped with a fire extinguisher suitable for fuel-related fires (Class B fire - flammable liquids) - it is not sufficient to have a water-filled extinguisher.
● Always ensure adequate ventilation is available. Unless an exhaust gas extraction system is available for use, ensure that the engine is run outside of the workshop.
● If working on the fuel system, make sure the workshop is ventilated to avoid a build-up of fumes. This applies equally to fume build-up when charging a battery. Do not smoke or allow anyone else to smoke in the workshop.

Fluids

● If you need to drain fuel from the tank, store it in an approved container marked as suitable for the storage of petrol (gasoline) **(see illustration 1.5)**. Do not store fuel in glass jars or bottles.

1.5 Use an approved can only for storing petrol (gasoline)

● Use proprietary engine degreasers or solvents which have a high flash-point, such as paraffin (kerosene), for cleaning off oil, grease and dirt - never use petrol (gasoline) for cleaning. Wear rubber gloves when handling solvent and engine degreaser. The fumes from certain solvents can be dangerous - always work in a well-ventilated area.

Dust, eye and hand protection

● Protect your lungs from inhalation of dust particles by wearing a filtering mask over the nose and mouth. Many frictional materials still contain asbestos which is dangerous to your health. Protect your eyes from spouts of liquid and sprung components by wearing a pair of protective goggles **(see illustration 1.6)**.

1.6 A fire extinguisher, goggles, mask and protective gloves should be at hand in the workshop

● Protect your hands from contact with solvents, fuel and oils by wearing rubber gloves. Alternatively apply a barrier cream to your hands before starting work. If handling hot components or fluids, wear suitable gloves to protect your hands from scalding and burns.

What to do with old fluids

● Old cleaning solvent, fuel, coolant and oils should not be poured down domestic drains or onto the ground. Package the fluid up in old oil containers, label it accordingly, and take it to a garage or disposal facility. Contact your local authority for location of such sites or ring the oil care hotline.

Note: It is antisocial and illegal to dump oil down the drain. To find the location of your local oil recycling bank in the UK, call 08708 506 506 or visit www.oilbankline.org.uk

In the USA, note that any oil supplier must accept used oil for recycling.

2 Fasteners - screws, bolts and nuts

Fastener types and applications

Bolts and screws

● Fastener head types are either of hexagonal, Torx or splined design, with internal and external versions of each type **(see illustrations 2.1 and 2.2)**; splined head fasteners are not in common use on motorcycles. The conventional slotted or Phillips head design is used for certain screws. Bolt or screw length is always measured from the underside of the head to the end of the item **(see illustration 2.11)**.

2.1 Internal hexagon/Allen (A), Torx (B) and splined (C) fasteners, with corresponding bits

2.2 External Torx (A), splined (B) and hexagon (C) fasteners, with corresponding sockets

● Certain fasteners on the motorcycle have a tensile marking on their heads, the higher the marking the stronger the fastener. High tensile fasteners generally carry a 10 or higher marking. Never replace a high tensile fastener with one of a lower tensile strength.

Washers (see illustration 2.3)

● Plain washers are used between a fastener head and a component to prevent damage to the component or to spread the load when torque is applied. Plain washers can also be used as spacers or shims in certain assemblies. Copper or aluminium plain washers are often used as sealing washers on drain plugs.

2.3 Plain washer (A), penny washer (B), spring washer (C) and serrated washer (D)

● The split-ring spring washer works by applying axial tension between the fastener head and component. If flattened, it is fatigued and must be renewed. If a plain (flat) washer is used on the fastener, position the spring washer between the fastener and the plain washer.

● Serrated star type washers dig into the fastener and component faces, preventing loosening. They are often used on electrical earth (ground) connections to the frame.

● Cone type washers (sometimes called Belleville) are conical and when tightened apply axial tension between the fastener head and component. They must be installed with the dished side against the component and often carry an OUTSIDE marking on their outer face. If flattened, they are fatigued and must be renewed.

● Tab washers are used to lock plain nuts or bolts on a shaft. A portion of the tab washer is bent up hard against one flat of the nut or bolt to prevent it loosening. Due to the tab washer being deformed in use, a new tab washer should be used every time it is disturbed.

● Wave washers are used to take up endfloat on a shaft. They provide light springing and prevent excessive side-to-side play of a component. Can be found on rocker arm shafts.

Nuts and split pins

● Conventional plain nuts are usually six-sided **(see illustration 2.4)**. They are sized by thread diameter and pitch. High tensile nuts carry a number on one end to denote their tensile strength.

2.4 Plain nut (A), shouldered locknut (B), nylon insert nut (C) and castellated nut (D)

● Self-locking nuts either have a nylon insert, or two spring metal tabs, or a shoulder which is staked into a groove in the shaft - their advantage over conventional plain nuts is a resistance to loosening due to vibration. The nylon insert type can be used a number of times, but must be renewed when the friction of the nylon insert is reduced, ie when the nut spins freely on the shaft. The spring tab type can be reused unless the tabs are damaged. The shouldered type must be renewed every time it is disturbed.

● Split pins (cotter pins) are used to lock a castellated nut to a shaft or to prevent slackening of a plain nut. Common applications are wheel axles and brake torque arms. Because the split pin arms are deformed to lock around the nut a new split pin must always be used on installation - always fit the correct size split pin which will fit snugly in the shaft hole. Make sure the split pin arms are correctly located around the nut **(see illustrations 2.5 and 2.6)**.

2.5 Bend split pin (cotter pin) arms as shown (arrows) to secure a castellated nut

2.6 Bend split pin (cotter pin) arms as shown to secure a plain nut

Caution: If the castellated nut slots do not align with the shaft hole after tightening to the torque setting, tighten the nut until the next slot aligns with the hole - never slacken the nut to align its slot.

● R-pins (shaped like the letter R), or slip pins as they are sometimes called, are sprung and can be reused if they are otherwise in good condition. Always install R-pins with their closed end facing forwards **(see illustration 2.7)**.

2.7 Correct fitting of R-pin. Arrow indicates forward direction

Circlips (see illustration 2.8)

● Circlips (sometimes called snap-rings) are used to retain components on a shaft or in a housing and have corresponding external or internal ears to permit removal. Parallel-sided (machined) circlips can be installed either way round in their groove, whereas stamped circlips (which have a chamfered edge on one face) must be installed with the chamfer facing away from the direction of thrust load (**see illustration 2.9**).

2.8 External stamped circlip (A), internal stamped circlip (B), machined circlip (C) and wire circlip (D)

● Always use circlip pliers to remove and install circlips; expand or compress them just enough to remove them. After installation, rotate the circlip in its groove to ensure it is securely seated. If installing a circlip on a splined shaft, always align its opening with a shaft channel to ensure the circlip ends are well supported and unlikely to catch (**see illustration 2.10**).

THRUST LOAD

THRUST WASHER

SHARP EDGE

CHAMFERED EDGE

0650H

2.9 Correct fitting of a stamped circlip

2.10 Align circlip opening with shaft channel

● Circlips can wear due to the thrust of components and become loose in their grooves, with the subsequent danger of becoming dislodged in operation. For this reason, renewal is advised every time a circlip is disturbed.

● Wire circlips are commonly used as piston pin retaining clips. If a removal tang is provided, long-nosed pliers can be used to dislodge them, otherwise careful use of a small flat-bladed screwdriver is necessary. Wire circlips should be renewed every time they are disturbed.

Thread diameter and pitch

● Diameter of a male thread (screw, bolt or stud) is the outside diameter of the threaded portion (**see illustration 2.11**). Most motorcycle manufacturers use the ISO (International Standards Organisation) metric system expressed in millimetres, eg M6 refers to a 6 mm diameter thread. Sizing is the same for nuts, except that the thread diameter is measured across the valleys of the nut.

● Pitch is the distance between the peaks of the thread (**see illustration 2.11**). It is expressed in millimetres, thus a common bolt size may be expressed as 6.0 x 1.0 mm (6 mm thread diameter and 1 mm pitch). Generally pitch increases in proportion to thread diameter, although there are always exceptions.

● Thread diameter and pitch are related for conventional fastener applications and the accompanying table can be used as a guide. Additionally, the AF (Across Flats), spanner or socket size dimension of the bolt or nut (**see illustration 2.11**) is linked to thread and pitch specification. Thread pitch can be measured with a thread gauge (**see illustration 2.12**).

AF

L

D

P

2.11 Fastener length (L), thread diameter (D), thread pitch (P) and head size (AF)

2.12 Using a thread gauge to measure pitch

AF size	Thread diameter x pitch (mm)
8 mm	M5 x 0.8
8 mm	M6 x 1.0
10 mm	M6 x 1.0
12 mm	M8 x 1.25
14 mm	M10 x 1.25
17 mm	M12 x 1.25

● The threads of most fasteners are of the right-hand type, ie they are turned clockwise to tighten and anti-clockwise to loosen. The reverse situation applies to left-hand thread fasteners, which are turned anti-clockwise to tighten and clockwise to loosen. Left-hand threads are used where rotation of a component might loosen a conventional right-hand thread fastener.

Seized fasteners

● Corrosion of external fasteners due to water or reaction between two dissimilar metals can occur over a period of time. It will build up sooner in wet conditions or in countries where salt is used on the roads during the winter. If a fastener is severely corroded it is likely that normal methods of removal will fail and result in its head being ruined. When you attempt removal, the fastener thread should be heard to crack free and unscrew easily - if it doesn't, stop there before damaging something.

● A smart tap on the head of the fastener will often succeed in breaking free corrosion which has occurred in the threads (**see illustration 2.13**).

● An aerosol penetrating fluid (such as WD-40) applied the night beforehand may work its way down into the thread and ease removal. Depending on the location, you may be able to make up a Plasticine well around the fastener head and fill it with penetrating fluid.

2.13 A sharp tap on the head of a fastener will often break free a corroded thread

● If you are working on an engine internal component, corrosion will most likely not be a problem due to the well lubricated environment. However, components can be very tight and an impact driver is a useful tool in freeing them **(see illustration 2.14)**.

2.14 Using an impact driver to free a fastener

● Where corrosion has occurred between dissimilar metals (eg steel and aluminium alloy), the application of heat to the fastener head will create a disproportionate expansion rate between the two metals and break the seizure caused by the corrosion. Whether heat can be applied depends on the location of the fastener - any surrounding components likely to be damaged must first be removed **(see illustration 2.15)**. Heat can be applied using a paint stripper heat gun or clothes iron, or by immersing the component in boiling water - wear protective gloves to prevent scalding or burns to the hands.

2.15 Using heat to free a seized fastener

● As a last resort, it is possible to use a hammer and cold chisel to work the fastener head unscrewed **(see illustration 2.16)**. This will damage the fastener, but more importantly extreme care must be taken not to damage the surrounding component.

Caution: Remember that the component being secured is generally of more value than the bolt, nut or screw - when the fastener is freed, do not unscrew it with force, instead work the fastener back and forth when resistance is felt to prevent thread damage.

2.16 Using a hammer and chisel to free a seized fastener

Broken fasteners and damaged heads

● If the shank of a broken bolt or screw is accessible you can grip it with self-locking grips. The knurled wheel type stud extractor tool or self-gripping stud puller tool is particularly useful for removing the long studs which screw into the cylinder mouth surface of the crankcase or bolts and screws from which the head has broken off **(see illustration 2.17)**. Studs can also be removed by locking two nuts together on the threaded end of the stud and using a spanner on the lower nut **(see illustration 2.18)**.

2.17 Using a stud extractor tool to remove a broken crankcase stud

2.18 Two nuts can be locked together to unscrew a stud from a component

● A bolt or screw which has broken off below or level with the casing must be extracted using a screw extractor set. Centre punch the fastener to centralise the drill bit, then drill a hole in the fastener **(see illustration 2.19)**. Select a drill bit which is approximately half to three-quarters the diameter of the fastener

2.19 When using a screw extractor, first drill a hole in the fastener . . .

and drill to a depth which will accommodate the extractor. Use the largest size extractor possible, but avoid leaving too small a wall thickness otherwise the extractor will merely force the fastener walls outwards wedging it in the casing thread.

● If a spiral type extractor is used, thread it anti-clockwise into the fastener. As it is screwed in, it will grip the fastener and unscrew it from the casing **(see illustration 2.20)**.

2.20 . . . then thread the extractor anti-clockwise into the fastener

● If a taper type extractor is used, tap it into the fastener so that it is firmly wedged in place. Unscrew the extractor (anti-clockwise) to draw the fastener out.

Warning: Stud extractors are very hard and may break off in the fastener if care is not taken - ask an engineer about spark erosion if this happens.

● Alternatively, the broken bolt/screw can be drilled out and the hole retapped for an oversize bolt/screw or a diamond-section thread insert. It is essential that the drilling is carried out squarely and to the correct depth, otherwise the casing may be ruined - if in doubt, entrust the work to an engineer.

● Bolts and nuts with rounded corners cause the correct size spanner or socket to slip when force is applied. Of the types of spanner/socket available always use a six-point type rather than an eight or twelve-point type - better grip

2.21 Comparison of surface drive ring spanner (left) with 12-point type (right)

is obtained. Surface drive spanners grip the middle of the hex flats, rather than the corners, and are thus good in cases of damaged heads **(see illustration 2.21)**.

● Slotted-head or Phillips-head screws are often damaged by the use of the wrong size screwdriver. Allen-head and Torx-head screws are much less likely to sustain damage. If enough of the screw head is exposed you can use a hacksaw to cut a slot in its head and then use a conventional flat-bladed screwdriver to remove it. Alternatively use a hammer and cold chisel to tap the head of the fastener around to slacken it. Always replace damaged fasteners with new ones, preferably Torx or Allen-head type.

HAYNES HiNT

A dab of valve grinding compound between the screw head and screwdriver tip will often give a good grip.

Thread repair

● Threads (particularly those in aluminium alloy components) can be damaged by overtightening, being assembled with dirt in the threads, or from a component working loose and vibrating. Eventually the thread will fail completely, and it will be impossible to tighten the fastener.

● If a thread is damaged or clogged with old locking compound it can be renovated with a thread repair tool (thread chaser) **(see illustrations 2.22 and 2.23)**; special thread

2.22 A thread repair tool being used to correct an internal thread

2.23 A thread repair tool being used to correct an external thread

chasers are available for spark plug hole threads. The tool will not cut a new thread, but clean and true the original thread. Make sure that you use the correct diameter and pitch tool. Similarly, external threads can be cleaned up with a die or a thread restorer file **(see illustration 2.24)**.

2.24 Using a thread restorer file

● It is possible to drill out the old thread and retap the component to the next thread size. This will work where there is enough surrounding material and a new bolt or screw can be obtained. Sometimes, however, this is not possible - such as where the bolt/screw passes through another component which must also be suitably modified, also in cases where a spark plug or oil drain plug cannot be obtained in a larger diameter thread size.

● The diamond-section thread insert (often known by its popular trade name of Heli-Coil) is a simple and effective method of renewing the thread and retaining the original size. A kit can be purchased which contains the tap, insert and installing tool **(see illustration 2.25)**. Drill out the damaged thread as size drill specified **(see illustration 2.26)**. Carefully retap the thread **(see illustration 2.27)**. Install the

2.25 Obtain a thread insert kit to suit the thread diameter and pitch required

2.26 To install a thread insert, first drill out the original thread . . .

2.27 . . . tap a new thread . . .

2.28 . . . fit insert on the installing tool . . .

2.29 . . . and thread into the component . . .

2.30 . . . break off the tang when complete

insert on the installing tool and thread it slowly into place using a light downward pressure **(see illustrations 2.28 and 2.29)**. When positioned between a 1/4 and 1/2 turn below the surface withdraw the installing tool and use the break-off tool to press down on the tang, breaking it off **(see illustration 2.30)**.

● There are epoxy thread repair kits on the market which can rebuild stripped internal threads, although this repair should not be used on high load-bearing components.

Thread locking and sealing compounds

● Locking compounds are used in locations where the fastener is prone to loosening due to vibration or on important safety-related items which might cause loss of control of the motorcycle if they fail. It is also used where important fasteners cannot be secured by other means such as lockwashers or split pins.

● Before applying locking compound, make sure that the threads (internal and external) are clean and dry with all old compound removed. Select a compound to suit the component being secured - a non-permanent general locking and sealing type is suitable for most applications, but a high strength type is needed for permanent fixing of studs in castings. Apply a drop or two of the compound to the first few threads of the fastener, then thread it into place and tighten to the specified torque. Do not apply excessive thread locking compound otherwise the thread may be damaged on subsequent removal.

● Certain fasteners are impregnated with a dry film type coating of locking compound on their threads. Always renew this type of fastener if disturbed.

● Anti-seize compounds, such as copper-based greases, can be applied to protect threads from seizure due to extreme heat and corrosion. A common instance is spark plug threads and exhaust system fasteners.

3   Measuring tools and gauges

Feeler gauges

● Feeler gauges (or blades) are used for measuring small gaps and clearances (see illustration 3.1). They can also be used to measure endfloat (sideplay) of a component on a shaft where access is not possible with a dial gauge.

● Feeler gauge sets should be treated with care and not bent or damaged. They are etched with their size on one face. Keep them clean and very lightly oiled to prevent corrosion build-up.

3.1 Feeler gauges are used for measuring small gaps and clearances - thickness is marked on one face of gauge

● When measuring a clearance, select a gauge which is a light sliding fit between the two components. You may need to use two gauges together to measure the clearance accurately.

Micrometers

● A micrometer is a precision tool capable of measuring to 0.01 or 0.001 of a millimetre. It should always be stored in its case and not in the general toolbox. It must be kept clean and never dropped, otherwise its frame or measuring anvils could be distorted resulting in inaccurate readings.

● External micrometers are used for measuring outside diameters of components and have many more applications than internal micrometers. Micrometers are available in different size ranges, eg 0 to 25 mm, 25 to 50 mm, and upwards in 25 mm steps; some large micrometers have interchangeable anvils to allow a range of measurements to be taken. Generally the largest precision measurement you are likely to take on a motorcycle is the piston diameter.

● Internal micrometers (or bore micrometers) are used for measuring inside diameters, such as valve guides and cylinder bores. Telescoping gauges and small hole gauges are used in conjunction with an external micrometer, whereas the more expensive internal micrometers have their own measuring device.

External micrometer

Note: *The conventional analogue type instrument is described. Although much easier to read, digital micrometers are considerably more expensive.*

● Always check the calibration of the micrometer before use. With the anvils closed (0 to 25 mm type) or set over a test gauge

3.2 Check micrometer calibration before use

(for the larger types) the scale should read zero **(see illustration 3.2)**; make sure that the anvils (and test piece) are clean first. Any discrepancy can be adjusted by referring to the instructions supplied with the tool. Remember that the micrometer is a precision measuring tool - don't force the anvils closed, use the ratchet (4) on the end of the micrometer to close it. In this way, a measured force is always applied.

● To use, first make sure that the item being measured is clean. Place the anvil of the micrometer (1) against the item and use the thimble (2) to bring the spindle (3) lightly into contact with the other side of the item **(see illustration 3.3)**. Don't tighten the thimble down because this will damage the micrometer - instead use the ratchet (4) on the end of the micrometer. The ratchet mechanism applies a measured force preventing damage to the instrument.

● The micrometer is read by referring to the linear scale on the sleeve and the annular scale on the thimble. Read off the sleeve first to obtain the base measurement, then add the fine measurement from the thimble to obtain the overall reading. The linear scale on the sleeve represents the measuring range of the micrometer (eg 0 to 25 mm). The annular scale

3.3 Micrometer component parts

1	Anvil	3	Spindle	5	Frame
2	Thimble	4	Ratchet	6	Locking lever

on the thimble will be in graduations of 0.01 mm (or as marked on the frame) - one full revolution of the thimble will move 0.5 mm on the linear scale. Take the reading where the datum line on the sleeve intersects the thimble's scale. Always position the eye directly above the scale otherwise an inaccurate reading will result.

In the example shown the item measures 2.95 mm **(see illustration 3.4)**:

Linear scale	2.00 mm
Linear scale	0.50 mm
Annular scale	0.45 mm
Total figure	2.95 mm

3.4 Micrometer reading of 2.95 mm

3.5 Micrometer reading of 46.99 mm on linear and annular scales . . .

3.6 . . . and 0.004 mm on vernier scale

3.7 Expand the telescoping gauge in the bore, lock its position . . .

3.8 . . . then measure the gauge with a micrometer

3.9 Expand the small hole gauge in the bore, lock its position . . .

3.10 . . . then measure the gauge with a micrometer

Most micrometers have a locking lever (6) on the frame to hold the setting in place, allowing the item to be removed from the micrometer.
● Some micrometers have a vernier scale on their sleeve, providing an even finer measurement to be taken, in 0.001 increments of a millimetre. Take the sleeve and thimble measurement as described above, then check which graduation on the vernier scale aligns with that of the annular scale on the thimble **Note:** *The eye must be perpendicular to the scale when taking the vernier reading - if necessary rotate the body of the micrometer to ensure this.* Multiply the vernier scale figure by 0.001 and add it to the base and fine measurement figures.

In the example shown the item measures 46.994 mm **(see illustrations 3.5 and 3.6)**:

Linear scale (base)	46.000 mm
Linear scale (base)	00.500 mm
Annular scale (fine)	00.490 mm
Vernier scale	00.004 mm
Total figure	46.994 mm

Internal micrometer

● Internal micrometers are available for measuring bore diameters, but are expensive and unlikely to be available for home use. It is suggested that a set of telescoping gauges and small hole gauges, both of which must be used with an external micrometer, will suffice for taking internal measurements on a motorcycle.
● Telescoping gauges can be used to measure internal diameters of components. Select a gauge with the correct size range, make sure its ends are clean and insert it into the bore. Expand the gauge, then lock its position and withdraw it from the bore **(see illustration 3.7)**. Measure across the gauge ends with a micrometer **(see illustration 3.8)**.
● Very small diameter bores (such as valve guides) are measured with a small hole gauge. Once adjusted to a slip-fit inside the component, its position is locked and the gauge withdrawn for measurement with a micrometer **(see illustrations 3.9 and 3.10)**.

Vernier caliper

Note: *The conventional linear and dial gauge type instruments are described. Digital types are easier to read, but are far more expensive.*
● The vernier caliper does not provide the precision of a micrometer, but is versatile in being able to measure internal and external diameters. Some types also incorporate a depth gauge. It is ideal for measuring clutch plate friction material and spring free lengths.
● To use the conventional linear scale vernier, slacken off the vernier clamp screws (1) and set its jaws over (2), or inside (3), the item to be measured **(see illustration 3.11)**. Slide the jaw into contact, using the thumb-wheel (4) for fine movement of the sliding scale (5) then tighten the clamp screws (1). Read off the main scale (6) where the zero on the sliding scale (5) intersects it, taking the whole number to the left of the zero; this provides the base measurement. View along the sliding scale and select the division which

lines up exactly with any of the divisions on the main scale, noting that the divisions usually represents 0.02 of a millimetre. Add this fine measurement to the base measurement to obtain the total reading.

3.11 Vernier component parts (linear gauge)

1	Clamp screws	3	Internal jaws	5	Sliding scale	7	Depth gauge
2	External jaws	4	Thumbwheel	6	Main scale		

In the example shown the item measures 55.92 mm **(see illustration 3.12)**:

Base measurement	55.00 mm
Fine measurement	00.92 mm
Total figure	**55.92 mm**

3.12 Vernier gauge reading of 55.92 mm

3.13 Vernier component parts (dial gauge)

1	Clamp screw	5	Main scale
2	External jaws	6	Sliding scale
3	Internal jaws	7	Dial gauge
4	Thumbwheel		

● Some vernier calipers are equipped with a dial gauge for fine measurement. Before use, check that the jaws are clean, then close them fully and check that the dial gauge reads zero. If necessary adjust the gauge ring accordingly. Slacken the vernier clamp screw (1) and set its jaws over (2), or inside (3), the item to be measured **(see illustration 3.13)**. Slide the jaws into contact, using the thumbwheel (4) for fine movement. Read off the main scale (5) where the edge of the sliding scale (6) intersects it, taking the whole number to the left of the zero; this provides the base measurement. Read off the needle position on the dial gauge (7) scale to provide the fine measurement; each division represents 0.05 of a millimetre. Add this fine measurement to the base measurement to obtain the total reading.

In the example shown the item measures 55.95 mm **(see illustration 3.14)**:

Base measurement	55.00 mm
Fine measurement	00.95 mm
Total figure	**55.95 mm**

3.14 Vernier gauge reading of 55.95 mm

Plastigauge

● Plastigauge is a plastic material which can be compressed between two surfaces to measure the oil clearance between them. The width of the compressed Plastigauge is measured against a calibrated scale to determine the clearance.

● Common uses of Plastigauge are for measuring the clearance between crankshaft journal and main bearing inserts, between crankshaft journal and big-end bearing inserts, and between camshaft and bearing surfaces. The following example describes big-end oil clearance measurement.

● Handle the Plastigauge material carefully to prevent distortion. Using a sharp knife, cut a length which corresponds with the width of the bearing being measured and place it carefully across the journal so that it is parallel with the shaft **(see illustration 3.15)**. Carefully install both bearing shells and the connecting rod. Without rotating the rod on the journal tighten its bolts or nuts (as applicable) to the specified torque. The connecting rod and bearings are then disassembled and the crushed Plastigauge examined.

3.15 Plastigauge placed across shaft journal

● Using the scale provided in the Plastigauge kit, measure the width of the material to determine the oil clearance **(see illustration 3.16)**. Always remove all traces of Plastigauge after use using your fingernails.

Caution: Arriving at the correct clearance demands that the assembly is torqued correctly, according to the settings and sequence (where applicable) provided by the motorcycle manufacturer.

3.16 Measuring the width of the crushed Plastigauge

Dial gauge or DTI (Dial Test Indicator)

● A dial gauge can be used to accurately measure small amounts of movement. Typical uses are measuring shaft runout or shaft endfloat (sideplay) and setting piston position for ignition timing on two-strokes. A dial gauge set usually comes with a range of different probes and adapters and mounting equipment.

● The gauge needle must point to zero when at rest. Rotate the ring around its periphery to zero the gauge.

● Check that the gauge is capable of reading the extent of movement in the work. Most gauges have a small dial set in the face which records whole millimetres of movement as well as the fine scale around the face periphery which is calibrated in 0.01 mm divisions. Read off the small dial first to obtain the base measurement, then add the measurement from the fine scale to obtain the total reading.

In the example shown the gauge reads 1.48 mm (see illustration 3.17):

Base measurement	1.00 mm
Fine measurement	0.48 mm
Total figure	1.48 mm

3.17 Dial gauge reading of 1.48 mm

● If measuring shaft runout, the shaft must be supported in vee-blocks and the gauge mounted on a stand perpendicular to the shaft. Rest the tip of the gauge against the centre of the shaft and rotate the shaft slowly whilst watching the gauge reading (see illustration 3.18). Take several measurements along the length of the shaft and record the

3.18 Using a dial gauge to measure shaft runout

maximum gauge reading as the amount of runout in the shaft. Note: The reading obtained will be total runout at that point - some manufacturers specify that the runout figure is halved to compare with their specified runout limit.

● Endfloat (sideplay) measurement requires that the gauge is mounted securely to the surrounding component with its probe touching the end of the shaft. Using hand pressure, push and pull on the shaft noting the maximum endfloat recorded on the gauge (see illustration 3.19).

3.19 Using a dial gauge to measure shaft endfloat

● A dial gauge with suitable adapters can be used to determine piston position BTDC on two-stroke engines for the purposes of ignition timing. The gauge, adapter and suitable length probe are installed in the place of the spark plug and the gauge zeroed at TDC. If the piston position is specified as 1.14 mm BTDC, rotate the engine back to 2.00 mm BTDC, then slowly forwards to 1.14 mm BTDC.

Cylinder compression gauges

● A compression gauge is used for measuring cylinder compression. Either the rubber-cone type or the threaded adapter type can be used. The latter is preferred to ensure a perfect seal against the cylinder head. A 0 to 300 psi (0 to 20 Bar) type gauge (for petrol/gasoline engines) will be suitable for motorcycles.

● The spark plug is removed and the gauge either held hard against the cylinder head (cone type) or the gauge adapter screwed into the cylinder head (threaded type) (see illustration 3.20). Cylinder compression is measured with the engine turning over, but not running. The

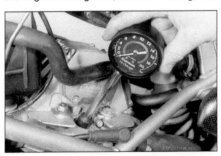

3.20 Using a rubber-cone type cylinder compression gauge

gauge will hold the reading until manually released.

Oil pressure gauge

● An oil pressure gauge is used for measuring engine oil pressure. Most gauges come with a set of adapters to fit the thread of the take-off point (see illustration 3.21). If the take-off point specified by the motorcycle manufacturer is an external oil pipe union, make sure that the specified replacement union is used to prevent oil starvation.

3.21 Oil pressure gauge and take-off point adapter (arrow)

● Oil pressure is measured with the engine running (at a specific rpm) and often the manufacturer will specify pressure limits for a cold and hot engine.

Straight-edge and surface plate

● If checking the gasket face of a component for warpage, place a steel rule or precision straight-edge across the gasket face and measure any gap between the straight-edge and component with feeler gauges (see illustration 3.22). Check diagonally across the component and between mounting holes (see illustration 3.23).

3.22 Use a straight-edge and feeler gauges to check for warpage

3.23 Check for warpage in these directions

● Checking individual components for warpage, such as clutch plain (metal) plates, requires a perfectly flat plate or piece or plate glass and feeler gauges.

4 Torque and leverage

What is torque?

● Torque describes the twisting force about a shaft. The amount of torque applied is determined by the distance from the centre of the shaft to the end of the lever and the amount of force being applied to the end of the lever; distance multiplied by force equals torque.

● The manufacturer applies a measured torque to a bolt or nut to ensure that it will not slacken in use and to hold two components securely together without movement in the joint. The actual torque setting depends on the thread size, bolt or nut material and the composition of the components being held.

● Too little torque may cause the fastener to loosen due to vibration, whereas too much torque will distort the joint faces of the component or cause the fastener to shear off. Always stick to the specified torque setting.

Using a torque wrench

● Check the calibration of the torque wrench and make sure it has a suitable range for the job. Torque wrenches are available in Nm (Newton-metres), kgf m (kilograms-force metre), lbf ft (pounds-feet), lbf in (inch-pounds). Do not confuse lbf ft with lbf in.

● Adjust the tool to the desired torque on the scale **(see illustration 4.1)**. If your torque wrench is not calibrated in the units specified, carefully convert the figure (see Conversion Factors). A manufacturer sometimes gives a torque setting as a range (8 to 10 Nm) rather than a single figure - in this case set the tool midway between the two settings. The same torque may be expressed as 9 Nm ± 1 Nm. Some torque wrenches have a method of locking the setting so that it isn't inadvertently altered during use.

4.1 Set the torque wrench index mark to the setting required, in this case 12 Nm

● Install the bolts/nuts in their correct location and secure them lightly. Their threads must be clean and free of any old locking compound. Unless specified the threads and flange should be dry - oiled threads are necessary in certain circumstances and the manufacturer will take this into account in the specified torque figure. Similarly, the manufacturer may also specify the application of thread-locking compound.

● Tighten the fasteners in the specified sequence until the torque wrench clicks, indicating that the torque setting has been reached. Apply the torque again to double-check the setting. Where different thread diameter fasteners secure the component, as a rule tighten the larger diameter ones first.

● When the torque wrench has been finished with, release the lock (where applicable) and fully back off its setting to zero - do not leave the torque wrench tensioned. Also, do not use a torque wrench for slackening a fastener.

Angle-tightening

● Manufacturers often specify a figure in degrees for final tightening of a fastener. This usually follows tightening to a specific torque setting.

● A degree disc can be set and attached to the socket **(see illustration 4.2)** or a protractor can be used to mark the angle of movement on the bolt/nut head and the surrounding casting **(see illustration 4.3)**.

4.2 Angle tightening can be accomplished with a torque-angle gauge . . .

4.3 . . . or by marking the angle on the surrounding component

Loosening sequences

● Where more than one bolt/nut secures a component, loosen each fastener evenly a little at a time. In this way, not all the stress of the joint is held by one fastener and the components are not likely to distort.

● If a tightening sequence is provided, work in the REVERSE of this, but if not, work from the outside in, in a criss-cross sequence **(see illustration 4.4)**.

4.4 When slackening, work from the outside inwards

Tightening sequences

● If a component is held by more than one fastener it is important that the retaining bolts/nuts are tightened evenly to prevent uneven stress build-up and distortion of sealing faces. This is especially important on high-compression joints such as the cylinder head.

● A sequence is usually provided by the manufacturer, either in a diagram or actually marked in the casting. If not, always start in the centre and work outwards in a criss-cross pattern **(see illustration 4.5)**. Start off by securing all bolts/nuts finger-tight, then set the torque wrench and tighten each fastener by a small amount in sequence until the final torque is reached. By following this practice,

4.5 When tightening, work from the inside outwards

REF•14 **Tools and Workshop Tips**

the joint will be held evenly and will not be distorted. Important joints, such as the cylinder head and big-end fasteners often have two- or three-stage torque settings.

Applying leverage

● Use tools at the correct angle. Position a socket wrench or spanner on the bolt/nut so that you pull it towards you when loosening. If this can't be done, push the spanner without curling your fingers around it **(see illustration 4.6)** - the spanner may slip or the fastener loosen suddenly, resulting in your fingers being crushed against a component.

4.6 If you can't pull on the spanner to loosen a fastener, push with your hand open

● Additional leverage is gained by extending the length of the lever. The best way to do this is to use a breaker bar instead of the regular length tool, or to slip a length of tubing over the end of the spanner or socket wrench.
● If additional leverage will not work, the fastener head is either damaged or firmly corroded in place (see Fasteners).

5 Bearings

Bearing removal and installation

Drivers and sockets

● Before removing a bearing, always inspect the casing to see which way it must be driven out - some casings will have retaining plates or a cast step. Also check for any identifying markings on the bearing and if installed to a certain depth, measure this at this stage. Some roller bearings are sealed on one side - take note of the original fitted position.
● Bearings can be driven out of a casing using a bearing driver tool (with the correct size head) or a socket of the correct diameter. Select the driver head or socket so that it contacts the outer race of the bearing, not the balls/rollers or inner race. Always support the casing around the bearing housing with wood blocks, otherwise there is a risk of fracture. The bearing is driven out with a few blows on the driver or socket from a heavy mallet. Unless access is severely restricted (as with wheel bearings), a pin-punch is not recommended unless it is moved around the bearing to keep it square in its housing.

● The same equipment can be used to install bearings. Make sure the bearing housing is supported on wood blocks and line up the bearing in its housing. Fit the bearing as noted on removal - generally they are installed with their marked side facing outwards. Tap the bearing squarely into its housing using a driver or socket which bears only on the bearing's outer race - contact with the bearing balls/rollers or inner race will destroy it **(see illustrations 5.1 and 5.2)**.
● Check that the bearing inner race and balls/rollers rotate freely.

5.1 Using a bearing driver against the bearing's outer race

5.2 Using a large socket against the bearing's outer race

Pullers and slide-hammers

● Where a bearing is pressed on a shaft a puller will be required to extract it **(see illustration 5.3)**. Make sure that the puller clamp or legs fit securely behind the bearing and are unlikely to slip out. If pulling a bearing

5.3 This bearing puller clamps behind the bearing and pressure is applied to the shaft end to draw the bearing off

off a gear shaft for example, you may have to locate the puller behind a gear pinion if there is no access to the race and draw the gear pinion off the shaft as well **(see illustration 5.4)**.

> *Caution: Ensure that the puller's centre bolt locates securely against the end of the shaft and will not slip when pressure is applied. Also ensure that puller does not damage the shaft end.*

5.4 Where no access is available to the rear of the bearing, it is sometimes possible to draw off the adjacent component

● Operate the puller so that its centre bolt exerts pressure on the shaft end and draws the bearing off the shaft.
● When installing the bearing on the shaft, tap only on the bearing's inner race - contact with the balls/rollers or outer race with destroy the bearing. Use a socket or length of tubing as a drift which fits over the shaft end **(see illustration 5.5)**.

5.5 When installing a bearing on a shaft use a piece of tubing which bears only on the bearing's inner race

● Where a bearing locates in a blind hole in a casing, it cannot be driven or pulled out as described above. A slide-hammer with knife-edged bearing puller attachment will be required. The puller attachment passes through the bearing and when tightened expands to fit firmly behind the bearing **(see illustration 5.6)**. By operating the slide-hammer part of the tool the bearing is jarred out of its housing **(see illustration 5.7)**.
● It is possible, if the bearing is of reasonable weight, for it to drop out of its housing if the casing is heated as described opposite.

5.6 Expand the bearing puller so that it locks behind the bearing . . .

5.7 . . . attach the slide hammer to the bearing puller

If this method is attempted, first prepare a work surface which will enable the casing to be tapped face down to help dislodge the bearing - a wood surface is ideal since it will not damage the casing's gasket surface. Wearing protective gloves, tap the heated casing several times against the work surface to dislodge the bearing under its own weight **(see illustration 5.8)**.

5.8 Tapping a casing face down on wood blocks can often dislodge a bearing

● Bearings can be installed in blind holes using the driver or socket method described above.

Drawbolts

● Where a bearing or bush is set in the eye of a component, such as a suspension linkage arm or connecting rod small-end, removal by drift may damage the component. Furthermore, a rubber bushing in a shock absorber eye cannot successfully be driven out of position. If access is available to a engineering press, the task is straightforward. If not, a drawbolt can be fabricated to extract the bearing or bush.

5.9 Drawbolt component parts assembled on a suspension arm

1 *Bolt or length of threaded bar*
2 *Nuts*
3 *Washer (external diameter greater than tubing internal diameter)*
4 *Tubing (internal diameter sufficient to accommodate bearing)*
5 *Suspension arm with bearing*
6 *Tubing (external diameter slightly smaller than bearing)*
7 *Washer (external diameter slightly smaller than bearing)*

5.10 Drawing the bearing out of the suspension arm

● To extract the bearing/bush you will need a long bolt with nut (or piece of threaded bar with two nuts), a piece of tubing which has an internal diameter larger than the bearing/bush, another piece of tubing which has an external diameter slightly smaller than the bearing/bush, and a selection of washers **(see illustrations 5.9 and 5.10)**. Note that the pieces of tubing must be of the same length, or longer, than the bearing/bush.

● The same kit (without the pieces of tubing) can be used to draw the new bearing/bush back into place **(see illustration 5.11)**.

5.11 Installing a new bearing (1) in the suspension arm

Temperature change

● If the bearing's outer race is a tight fit in the casing, the aluminium casing can be heated to release its grip on the bearing. Aluminium will expand at a greater rate than the steel bearing outer race. There are several ways to do this, but avoid any localised extreme heat (such as a blow torch) - aluminium alloy has a low melting point.

● Approved methods of heating a casing are using a domestic oven (heated to 100°C) or immersing the casing in boiling water **(see illustration 5.12)**. Low temperature range localised heat sources such as a paint stripper heat gun or clothes iron can also be used **(see illustration 5.13)**. Alternatively, soak a rag in boiling water, wring it out and wrap it around the bearing housing.

> ⚠ **Warning: All of these methods require care in use to prevent scalding and burns to the hands. Wear protective gloves when handling hot components.**

5.12 A casing can be immersed in a sink of boiling water to aid bearing removal

5.13 Using a localised heat source to aid bearing removal

● If heating the whole casing note that plastic components, such as the neutral switch, may suffer - remove them beforehand.

● After heating, remove the bearing as described above. You may find that the expansion is sufficient for the bearing to fall out of the casing under its own weight or with a light tap on the driver or socket.

● If necessary, the casing can be heated to aid bearing installation, and this is sometimes the recommended procedure if the motorcycle manufacturer has designed the housing and bearing fit with this intention.

● Installation of bearings can be eased by placing them in a freezer the night before installation. The steel bearing will contract slightly, allowing easy insertion in its housing. This is often useful when installing steering head outer races in the frame.

Bearing types and markings

● Plain shell bearings, ball bearings, needle roller bearings and tapered roller bearings will all be found on motorcycles **(see illustrations 5.14 and 5.15)**. The ball and roller types are usually caged between an inner and outer race, but uncaged variations may be found.

5.14 Shell bearings are either plain or grooved. They are usually identified by colour code (arrow)

5.15 Tapered roller bearing (A), needle roller bearing (B) and ball journal bearing (C)

● Shell bearings (often called inserts) are usually found at the crankshaft main and connecting rod big-end where they are good at coping with high loads. They are made of a phosphor-bronze material and are impregnated with self-lubricating properties.
● Ball bearings and needle roller bearings consist of a steel inner and outer race with the balls or rollers between the races. They require constant lubrication by oil or grease and are good at coping with axial loads. Taper roller bearings consist of rollers set in a tapered cage set on the inner race; the outer race is separate. They are good at coping with axial loads and prevent movement along the shaft - a typical application is in the steering head.
● Bearing manufacturers produce bearings to ISO size standards and stamp one face of the bearing to indicate its internal and external diameter, load capacity and type **(see illustration 5.16)**.
● Metal bushes are usually of phosphor-bronze material. Rubber bushes are used in suspension mounting eyes. Fibre bushes have also been used in suspension pivots.

5.16 Typical bearing marking

Bearing fault finding

● If a bearing outer race has spun in its housing, the housing material will be damaged. You can use a bearing locking compound to bond the outer race in place if damage is not too severe.
● Shell bearings will fail due to damage of their working surface, as a result of lack of lubrication, corrosion or abrasive particles in the oil **(see illustration 5.17)**. Small particles of dirt in the oil may embed in the bearing material whereas larger particles will score the bearing and shaft journal. If a number of short journeys are made, insufficient heat will be generated to drive off condensation which has built up on the bearings.

5.17 Typical bearing failures

● Ball and roller bearings will fail due to lack of lubrication or damage to the balls or rollers. Tapered-roller bearings can be damaged by overloading them. Unless the bearing is sealed on both sides, wash it in paraffin (kerosene) to remove all old grease then allow it to dry. Make a visual inspection looking to dented balls or rollers, damaged cages and worn or pitted races **(see illustration 5.18)**.
● A ball bearing can be checked for wear by listening to it when spun. Apply a film of light oil to the bearing and hold it close to the ear - hold the outer race with one hand and spin the

5.18 Example of ball journal bearing with damaged balls and cages

5.19 Hold outer race and listen to inner race when spun

inner race with the other hand **(see illustration 5.19)**. The bearing should be almost silent when spun; if it grates or rattles it is worn.

6 Oil seals

Oil seal removal and installation

● Oil seals should be renewed every time a component is dismantled. This is because the seal lips will become set to the sealing surface and will not necessarily reseal.
● Oil seals can be prised out of position using a large flat-bladed screwdriver **(see illustration 6.1)**. In the case of crankcase seals, check first that the seal is not lipped on the inside, preventing its removal with the crankcases joined.

6.1 Prise out oil seals with a large flat-bladed screwdriver

● New seals are usually installed with their marked face (containing the seal reference code) outwards and the spring side towards the fluid being retained. In certain cases, such as a two-stroke engine crankshaft seal, a double lipped seal may be used due to there being fluid or gas on each side of the joint.

● Use a bearing driver or socket which bears only on the outer hard edge of the seal to install it in the casing - tapping on the inner edge will damage the sealing lip.

Oil seal types and markings

● Oil seals are usually of the single-lipped type. Double-lipped seals are found where a liquid or gas is on both sides of the joint.
● Oil seals can harden and lose their sealing ability if the motorcycle has been in storage for a long period - renewal is the only solution.
● Oil seal manufacturers also conform to the ISO markings for seal size - these are moulded into the outer face of the seal (see illustration 6.2).

6.2 These oil seal markings indicate inside diameter, outside diameter and seal thickness

7 Gaskets and sealants

Types of gasket and sealant

● Gaskets are used to seal the mating surfaces between components and keep lubricants, fluids, vacuum or pressure contained within the assembly. Aluminium gaskets are sometimes found at the cylinder joints, but most gaskets are paper-based. If the mating surfaces of the components being joined are undamaged the gasket can be installed dry, although a dab of sealant or grease will be useful to hold it in place during assembly.
● RTV (Room Temperature Vulcanising) silicone rubber sealants cure when exposed to moisture in the atmosphere. These sealants are good at filling pits or irregular gasket faces, but will tend to be forced out of the joint under very high torque. They can be used to replace a paper gasket, but first make sure that the width of the paper gasket is not essential to the shimming of internal components. RTV sealants should not be used on components containing petrol (gasoline).
● Non-hardening, semi-hardening and hard setting liquid gasket compounds can be used with a gasket or between a metal-to-metal joint. Select the sealant to suit the application: universal non-hardening sealant can be used on virtually all joints; semi-hardening on joint faces which are rough or damaged; hard setting sealant on joints which require a permanent bond and are subjected to high temperature and pressure. **Note:** Check first if the paper gasket has a bead of sealant

impregnated in its surface before applying additional sealant.
● When choosing a sealant, make sure it is suitable for the application, particularly if being applied in a high-temperature area or in the vicinity of fuel. Certain manufacturers produce sealants in either clear, silver or black colours to match the finish of the engine. This has a particular application on motorcycles where much of the engine is exposed.
● Do not over-apply sealant. That which is squeezed out on the outside of the joint can be wiped off, whereas an excess of sealant on the inside can break off and clog oilways.

Breaking a sealed joint

● Age, heat, pressure and the use of hard setting sealant can cause two components to stick together so tightly that they are difficult to separate using finger pressure alone. Do not resort to using levers unless there is a pry point provided for this purpose (see illustration 7.1) or else the gasket surfaces will be damaged.
● Use a soft-faced hammer (see illustration 7.2) or a wood block and conventional hammer to strike the component near the mating surface. Avoid hammering against cast extremities since they may break off. If this method fails, try using a wood wedge between the two components.

Caution: If the joint will not separate, double-check that you have removed all the fasteners.

7.1 If a pry point is provided, apply gently pressure with a flat-bladed screwdriver

7.2 Tap around the joint with a soft-faced mallet if necessary - don't strike cooling fins

Removal of old gasket and sealant

● Paper gaskets will most likely come away complete, leaving only a few traces stuck

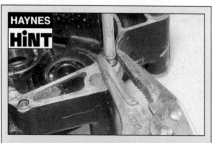

Most components have one or two hollow locating dowels between the two gasket faces. If a dowel cannot be removed, do not resort to gripping it with pliers - it will almost certainly be distorted. Install a close-fitting socket or Phillips screwdriver into the dowel and then grip the outer edge of the dowel to free it.

on the sealing faces of the components. It is imperative that all traces are removed to ensure correct sealing of the new gasket.
● Very carefully scrape all traces of gasket away making sure that the sealing surfaces are not gouged or scored by the scraper (see illustrations 7.3, 7.4 and 7.5). Stubborn deposits can be removed by spraying with an aerosol gasket remover. Final preparation of

7.3 Paper gaskets can be scraped off with a gasket scraper tool . . .

7.4 . . . a knife blade . . .

7.5 . . . or a household scraper

7.6 Fine abrasive paper is wrapped around a flat file to clean up the gasket face

7.7 A kitchen scourer can be used on stubborn deposits

the gasket surface can be made with very fine abrasive paper or a plastic kitchen scourer (**see illustrations 7.6 and 7.7**).

● Old sealant can be scraped or peeled off components, depending on the type originally used. Note that gasket removal compounds are available to avoid scraping the components clean; make sure the gasket remover suits the type of sealant used.

8 Chains

Breaking and joining final drive chains

● Drive chains for all but small bikes are continuous and do not have a clip-type connecting link. The chain must be broken using a chain breaker tool and the new chain securely riveted together using a new soft rivet-type link. Never use a clip-type connecting link instead of a rivet-type link, except in an emergency. Various chain breaking and riveting tools are available, either as separate tools or combined as illustrated in the accompanying photographs - read the instructions supplied with the tool carefully.

> ⚠ **Warning: The need to rivet the new link pins correctly cannot be overstressed - loss of control of the motorcycle is very likely to result if the chain breaks in use.**

● Rotate the chain and look for the soft link. The soft link pins look like they have been

8.1 Tighten the chain breaker to push the pin out of the link . . .

8.2 . . . withdraw the pin, remove the tool . . .

8.3 . . . and separate the chain link

deeply centre-punched instead of peened over like all the other pins (**see illustration 8.9**) and its sideplate may be a different colour. Position the soft link midway between the sprockets and assemble the chain breaker tool over one of the soft link pins (**see illustration 8.1**). Operate the tool to push the pin out through the chain (**see illustration 8.2**). On an O-ring chain, remove the O-rings (**see illustration 8.3**). Carry out the same procedure on the other soft link pin.

> **Caution: Certain soft link pins (particularly on the larger chains) may require their ends to be filed or ground off before they can be pressed out using the tool.**

● Check that you have the correct size and strength (standard or heavy duty) new soft link - do not reuse the old link. Look for the size marking on the chain sideplates (**see illustration 8.10**).

● Position the chain ends so that they are engaged over the rear sprocket. On an O-ring

8.4 Insert the new soft link, with O-rings, through the chain ends . . .

8.5 . . . install the O-rings over the pin ends . . .

8.6 . . . followed by the sideplate

chain, install a new O-ring over each pin of the link and insert the link through the two chain ends (**see illustration 8.4**). Install a new O-ring over the end of each pin, followed by the sideplate (with the chain manufacturer's marking facing outwards) (**see illustrations 8.5 and 8.6**). On an unsealed chain, insert the link through the two chain ends, then install the sideplate with the chain manufacturer's marking facing outwards.

● Note that it may not be possible to install the sideplate using finger pressure alone. If using a joining tool, assemble it so that the plates of the tool clamp the link and press the sideplate over the pins (**see illustration 8.7**). Otherwise, use two small sockets placed over

8.7 Push the sideplate into position using a clamp

8.8 Assemble the chain riveting tool over one pin at a time and tighten it fully

8.9 Pin end correctly riveted (A), pin end unriveted (B)

the rivet ends and two pieces of the wood between a G-clamp. Operate the clamp to press the sideplate over the pins.

● Assemble the joining tool over one pin (following the maker's instructions) and tighten the tool down to spread the pin end securely **(see illustrations 8.8 and 8.9)**. Do the same on the other pin.

> ⚠️ **Warning: Check that the pin ends are secure and that there is no danger of the sideplate coming loose. If the pin ends are cracked the soft link must be renewed.**

Final drive chain sizing

● Chains are sized using a three digit number, followed by a suffix to denote the chain type **(see illustration 8.10)**. Chain type is either standard or heavy duty (thicker sideplates), and also unsealed or O-ring/X-ring type.

● The first digit of the number relates to the pitch of the chain, ie the distance from the centre of one pin to the centre of the next pin **(see illustration 8.11)**. Pitch is expressed in eighths of an inch, as follows:

8.10 Typical chain size and type marking

8.11 Chain dimensions

Sizes commencing with a 4 (eg 428) have a pitch of 1/2 inch (12.7 mm)
Sizes commencing with a 5 (eg 520) have a pitch of 5/8 inch (15.9 mm)
Sizes commencing with a 6 (eg 630) have a pitch of 3/4 inch (19.1 mm)

● The second and third digits of the chain size relate to the width of the rollers, again in imperial units, eg the 525 shown has 5/16 inch (7.94 mm) rollers **(see illustration 8.11)**.

9 Hoses

Clamping to prevent flow

● Small-bore flexible hoses can be clamped to prevent fluid flow whilst a component is worked on. Whichever method is used, ensure that the hose material is not permanently distorted or damaged by the clamp.

a) A brake hose clamp available from auto accessory shops **(see illustration 9.1)**.
b) A wingnut type hose clamp **(see illustration 9.2)**.

9.1 Hoses can be clamped with an automotive brake hose clamp . . .

9.2 . . . a wingnut type hose clamp . . .

c) Two sockets placed each side of the hose and held with straight-jawed self-locking grips **(see illustration 9.3)**.
d) Thick card each side of the hose held between straight-jawed self-locking grips **(see illustration 9.4)**.

9.3 . . . two sockets and a pair of self-locking grips . . .

9.4 . . . or thick card and self-locking grips

Freeing and fitting hoses

● Always make sure the hose clamp is moved well clear of the hose end. Grip the hose with your hand and rotate it whilst pulling it off the union. If the hose has hardened due to age and will not move, slit it with a sharp knife and peel its ends off the union **(see illustration 9.5)**.

● Resist the temptation to use grease or soap on the unions to aid installation; although it helps the hose slip over the union it will equally aid the escape of fluid from the joint. It is preferable to soften the hose ends in hot water and wet the inside surface of the hose with water or a fluid which will evaporate.

9.5 Cutting a coolant hose free with a sharp knife

Introduction

In less time than it takes to read this introduction, a thief could steal your motorcycle. Returning only to find your bike has gone is one of the worst feelings in the world. Even if the motorcycle is insured against theft, once you've got over the initial shock, you will have the inconvenience of dealing with the police and your insurance company.

The motorcycle is an easy target for the professional thief and the joyrider alike and the official figures on motorcycle theft make for depressing reading; on average a motor-cycle is stolen every 16 minutes in the UK!

Motorcycle thefts fall into two categories, those stolen 'to order' and those taken by opportunists. The thief stealing to order will be on the look out for a specific make and model and will go to extraordinary lengths to obtain that motorcycle. The opportunist thief on the other hand will look for easy targets which can be stolen with the minimum of effort and risk.

Whilst it is never going to be possible to make your machine 100% secure, it is estimated that around half of all stolen motorcycles are taken by opportunist thieves. Remember that the opportunist thief is always on the look out for the easy option: if there are two similar motorcycles parked side-by-side, they will target the one with the lowest level of security. By taking a few precautions, you can reduce the chances of your motorcycle being stolen.

Security equipment

There are many specialised motorcycle security devices available and the following text summarises their applications and their good and bad points.

Once you have decided on the type of security equipment which best suits your needs, we recommended that you read one of the many equipment tests regularly carried out by the motorcycle press. These tests compare the products from all the major manufacturers and give impartial ratings on their effectiveness, value-for-money and ease of use.

No one item of security equipment can provide complete protection. It is highly recommended that two or more of the items described below are combined to increase the security of your motorcycle (a lock and chain plus an alarm system is just about ideal). The more security measures fitted to the bike, the less likely it is to be stolen.

Lock and chain

Pros: *Very flexible to use; can be used to secure the motorcycle to almost any immovable object. On some locks and chains, the lock can be used on its own as a disc lock (see below).*

Cons: *Can be very heavy and awkward to carry on the motorcycle, although some types will be supplied with a carry bag which can be strapped to the pillion seat.*

● Heavy-duty chains and locks are an excellent security measure **(see illustration 1).** Whenever the motorcycle is parked, use the lock and chain to secure the machine to a solid, immovable object such as a post or railings. This will prevent the machine from being ridden away or being lifted into the back of a van.

● When fitting the chain, always ensure the chain is routed around the motorcycle frame or swingarm **(see illustrations 2 and 3)**. Never merely pass the chain around one of the wheel rims; a thief may unbolt the wheel and lift the rest of the machine into a van, leaving you with just the wheel! Try to avoid having excess chain free, thus making it difficult to use cutting tools, and keep the chain and lock off the ground to prevent thieves attacking it with a cold chisel. Position the lock so that its lock barrel is facing downwards; this will make it harder for the thief to attack the lock mechanism.

Ensure the lock and chain you buy is of good quality and long enough to shackle your bike to a solid object

Pass the chain through the bike's frame, rather than just through a wheel . . .

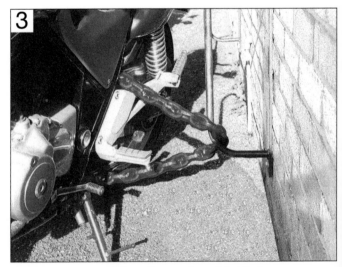

. . . and loop it around a solid object

U-locks

Pros: *Highly effective deterrent which can be used to secure the bike to a post or railings. Most U-locks come with a carrier which allows the lock to be easily carried on the bike.*

Cons: *Not as flexible to use as a lock and chain.*

● These are solid locks which are similar in use to a lock and chain. U-locks are lighter than a lock and chain but not so flexible to use. The length and shape of the lock shackle limit the objects to which the bike can be secured **(see illustration 4)**.

Disc locks

Pros: *Small, light and very easy to carry; most can be stored underneath the seat.*

Cons: *Does not prevent the motorcycle being lifted into a van. Can be very embarrassing if*

U-locks can be used to secure the bike to a solid object – ensure you purchase one which is long enough

you forget to remove the lock before attempting to ride off!

● Disc locks are designed to be attached to the front brake disc. The lock passes through one of the holes in the disc and prevents the wheel rotating by jamming against the fork/ brake caliper **(see illustration 5)**. Some are equipped with an alarm siren which sounds if the disc lock is moved; this not only acts as a theft deterrent but also as a handy reminder if you try to move the bike with the lock still fitted.

● Combining the disc lock with a length of cable which can be looped around a post or railings provides an additional measure of security **(see illustration 6)**.

Alarms and immobilisers

Pros: *Once installed it is completely hassle-free to use. If the system is 'Thatcham' or 'Sold Secure-approved', insurance companies may give you a discount.*

Cons: *Can be expensive to buy and complex to install. No system will prevent the motorcycle from being lifted into a van and taken away.*

● Electronic alarms and immobilisers are available to suit a variety of budgets. There are three different types of system available: pure alarms, pure immobilisers, and the more expensive systems which are combined alarm/immobilisers **(see illustration 7)**.
● An alarm system is designed to emit an audible warning if the motorcycle is being tampered with.
● An immobiliser prevents the motorcycle being started and ridden away by disabling its electrical systems.
● When purchasing an alarm/immobiliser system, check the cost of installing the system unless you are able to do it yourself. If the motorcycle is not used regularly, another consideration is the current drain of the system. All alarm/immobiliser systems are powered by the motorcycle's battery; purchasing a system with a very low current drain could prevent the battery losing its charge whilst the motorcycle is not being used.

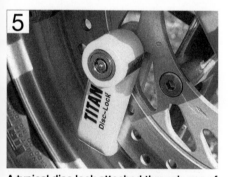

A typical disc lock attached through one of the holes in the disc

A disc lock combined with a security cable provides additional protection

A typical alarm/immobiliser system

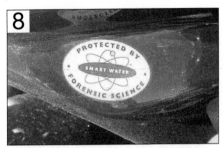

Indelible markings can be applied to most areas of the bike – always apply the manufacturer's sticker to warn off thieves

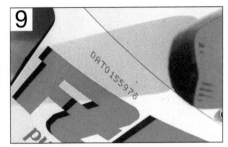

Chemically-etched code numbers can be applied to main body panels . . .

. . . again, always ensure that the kit manufacturer's sticker is applied in a prominent position

Security marking kits

Pros: *Very cheap and effective deterrent. Many insurance companies will give you a discount on your insurance premium if a recognised security marking kit is used on your motorcycle.*

Cons: *Does not prevent the motorcycle being stolen by joyriders.*

● There are many different types of security marking kits available. The idea is to mark as many parts of the motorcycle as possible with a unique security number **(see illustrations 8, 9 and 10)**. A form will be included with the kit to register your personal details and those of the motorcycle with the kit manufacturer. This register is made available to the police to help them trace the rightful owner of any motorcycle or components which they recover should all other forms of identification have been removed. Always apply the warning stickers provided with the kit to deter thieves.

Ground anchors, wheel clamps and security posts

Pros: *An excellent form of security which will deter all but the most determined of thieves.*

Cons: *Awkward to install and can be expensive.*

● Whilst the motorcycle is at home, it is a good idea to attach it securely to the floor or a solid wall, even if it is kept in a securely locked garage. Various types of ground anchors, security posts and wheel clamps are available for this purpose **(see illustration 11)**. These security devices are either bolted to a solid concrete or brick structure or can be cemented into the ground.

Permanent ground anchors provide an excellent level of security when the bike is at home

Security at home

A high percentage of motorcycle thefts are from the owner's home. Here are some things to consider whenever your motorcycle is at home:

● Where possible, always keep the motorcycle in a securely locked garage. Never rely solely on the standard lock on the garage door, these are usual hopelessly inadequate. Fit an additional locking mechanism to the door and consider having the garage alarmed. A security light, activated by a movement sensor, is also a good investment.

● Always secure the motorcycle to the ground or a wall, even if it is inside a securely locked garage.
● Do not regularly leave the motorcycle outside your home, try to keep it out of sight wherever possible. If a garage is not available, fit a motorcycle cover over the bike to disguise its true identity.
● It is not uncommon for thieves to follow a motorcyclist home to find out where the bike is kept. They will then return at a later date. Be aware of this whenever you are returning

home on your motorcycle. If you suspect you are being followed, do not return home, instead ride to a garage or shop and stop as a precaution.
● When selling a motorcycle, do not provide your home address or the location where the bike is normally kept. Arrange to meet the buyer at a location away from your home. Thieves have been known to pose as potential buyers to find out where motorcycles are kept and then return later to steal them.

Security away from the home

As well as fitting security equipment to your motorcycle here are a few general rules to follow whenever you park your motorcycle.
● Park in a busy, public place.
● Use car parks which incorporate security features, such as CCTV.

● At night, park in a well-lit area, preferably directly underneath a street light.
● Engage the steering lock.
● Secure the motorcycle to a solid, immovable object such as a post or railings with an additional lock. If this is not possible,

secure the bike to a friend's motorcycle. Some public parking places provide security loops for motorcycles.
● Never leave your helmet or luggage attached to the motorcycle. Take them with you at all times.

Lubricants and fluids

A wide range of lubricants, fluids and cleaning agents is available for motor-cycles. This is a guide as to what is available, its applications and properties.

Four-stroke engine oil

● Engine oil is without doubt the most important component of any four-stroke engine. Modern motorcycle engines place a lot of demands on their oil and choosing the right type is essential. Using an unsuitable oil will lead to an increased rate of engine wear and could result in serious engine damage. Before purchasing oil, always check the recommended oil specification given by the manufacturer. The manufacturer will state a recommended 'type or classification' and also a specific 'viscosity' range for engine oil.

● The oil 'type or classification' is identified by its API (American Petroleum Institute) rating. The API rating will be in the form of two letters, e.g. SG. The S identifies the oil as being suitable for use in a petrol (gasoline) engine (S stands for spark ignition) and the second letter, ranging from A to J, identifies the oil's performance rating. The later this letter, the higher the specification of the oil; for example API SG oil exceeds the requirements of API SF oil. **Note:** *On some oils there may also be a second rating consisting of another two letters, the first letter being C, e.g. API SF/CD. This rating indicates the oil is also suitable for use in a diesel engines (the C stands for compression ignition) and is thus of no relevance for motorcycle use.*

● The 'viscosity' of the oil is identified by its SAE (Society of Automotive Engineers) rating. All modern engines require multigrade oils and the SAE rating will consist of two numbers, the

first followed by a W, e.g. 10W/40. The first number indicates the viscosity rating of the oil at low temperatures (W stands for winter – tested at –20ºC) and the second number represents the viscosity of the oil at high temperatures (tested at 100ºC). The lower the number, the thinner the oil. For example an oil with an SAE 10W/40 rating will give better cold starting and running than an SAE 15W/40 oil.

● As well as ensuring the 'type' and 'viscosity' of the oil match the recommendations, another consideration to make when buying engine oil is whether to purchase a standard mineral-based oil, a semi-synthetic oil (also known as a synthetic blend or synthetic-based oil) or a fully-synthetic oil. Although all oils will have a similar rating and viscosity, their cost will vary considerably; mineral-based oils are the cheapest, the fully-synthetic oils the most expensive with the semi-synthetic oils falling somewhere in-between. This decision is very much up to the owner, but it should be noted that modern synthetic oils have far better lubricating and cleaning qualities than traditional mineral-based oils and tend to retain these properties for far longer. Bearing in mind the operating conditions inside a modern, high-revving motorcycle engine it is highly recommended that a fully synthetic oil is used. The extra expense at each service could save you money in the long term by preventing premature engine wear.

● As a final note always ensure that the oil is specifically designed for use in motorcycle engines. Engine oils designed primarily for use in car engines sometimes contain additives or friction modifiers which could cause clutch slip on a motorcycle fitted with a wet-clutch.

Two-stroke engine oil

● Modern two-stroke engines, with their high power outputs, place high demands on their oil. If engine seizure is to be avoided it is essential that a high-quality oil is used. Two-stroke oils differ hugely from four-stroke oils. The oil lubricates only the crankshaft and piston(s) (the transmission has its own lubricating oil) and is used on a total-loss basis where it is burnt completely during the combustion process.

● The Japanese have recently introduced a classification system for two-stroke oils, the JASO rating. This rating is in the form of two letters, either FA, FB or FC – FA is the lowest classification and FC the highest. Ensure the oil being used meets or exceeds the recommended rating specified by the manufacturer.

● As well as ensuring the oil rating matches the recommendation, another consideration to make when buying engine oil is whether to purchase a standard mineral-based oil, a semi-synthetic oil (also known as a synthetic blend or synthetic-based oil) or a fully-synthetic oil. The cost of each type of oil varies considerably; mineral-based oils are the cheapest, the fully-synthetic oils the most expensive with the semi-synthetic oils falling somewhere in-between. This decision is very much up to the owner, but it should be noted that modern synthetic oils have far better lubricating properties and burn cleaner than traditional mineral-based oils. It is therefore recommended that a fully synthetic oil is used. The extra expense could save you money in the long term by preventing premature engine wear, engine performance will be improved, carbon deposits and exhaust smoke will be reduced.

● Always ensure that the oil is specifically designed for use in an injector system. Many high quality two-stroke oils are designed for competition use and need to be pre-mixed with fuel. These oils are of a much higher viscosity and are not designed to flow through the injector pumps used on road-going two-stroke motorcycles.

Transmission (gear) oil

● On a two-stroke engine, the transmission and clutch are lubricated by their own separate oil bath which must be changed in accordance with the Maintenance Schedule.
● Although the engine and transmission units of most four-strokes use a common lubrication supply, there are some exceptions where the engine and gearbox have separate oil reservoirs and a dry clutch is used.
● Motorcycle manufacturers will either recommend a monograde transmission oil or a four-stroke multigrade engine oil to lubricate the transmission.
● Transmission oils, or gear oils as they are often called, are designed specifically for use in transmission systems. The viscosity of these oils is represented by an SAE number, but the scale of measurement applied is different to that used to grade engine oils. As a rough guide a SAE90 gear oil will be of the same viscosity as an SAE50 engine oil.

Shaft drive oil

● On models equipped with shaft final drive, the shaft drive gears are will have their own oil supply. The manufacturer will state a recommended 'type or classification' and also a specific 'viscosity' range in the same manner as for four-stroke engine oil.
● Gear oil classification is given by the number which follows the API GL (GL standing for gear lubricant) rating, the higher the number, the higher the specification of the oil, e.g. API GL5 oil is a higher specification than API GL4 oil. Ensure the oil meets or

exceeds the classification specified and is of the correct viscosity. The viscosity of gear oils is also represented by an SAE number but the scale of measurement used is different to that used to grade engine oils. As a rough guide an SAE90 gear oil will be of the same viscosity as an SAE50 engine oil.
● If the use of an EP (Extreme Pressure) gear oil is specified, ensure the oil purchased is suitable.

Fork oil and suspension fluid

● Conventional telescopic front forks are hydraulic and require fork oil to work. To ensure the forks function correctly, the fork oil must be changed in accordance with the Maintenance Schedule.
● Fork oil is available in a variety of viscosities, identified by their SAE rating; fork oil ratings vary from light (SAE 5) to heavy (SAE 30). When purchasing fork oil, ensure the viscosity rating matches that specified by the manufacturer.
● Some lubricant manufacturers also produce a range of high-quality suspension fluids which are very similar to fork oil but are designed mainly for competition use. These fluids may have a different viscosity rating system which is not to be confused with the SAE rating of normal fork oil. Refer to the manufacturer's instructions if in any doubt.

Brake and clutch fluid

● All disc brake systems and some clutch systems are hydraulically operated. To ensure correct operation, the hydraulic fluid must be changed in accordance with the Maintenance Schedule.
● Brake and clutch fluid is classified by its DOT rating with most motorcycle manufacturers specifying DOT 3 or 4 fluid. Both fluid types are glycol-based and can be mixed together without adverse effect; DOT 4 fluid exceeds the requirements of DOT 3

fluid. Although it is safe to use DOT 4 fluid in a system designed for use with DOT 3 fluid, never use DOT 3 fluid in a system which specifies the use of DOT 4 as this will adversely affect the system's performance. The type required for the system will be marked on the fluid reservoir cap.
● Some manufacturers also produce a DOT 5 hydraulic fluid. DOT 5 hydraulic fluid is silicone-based and is not compatible with the glycol-based DOT 3 and 4 fluids. Never mix DOT 5 fluid with DOT 3 or 4 fluid as this will seriously affect the performance of the hydraulic system.

Coolant/antifreeze

● When purchasing coolant/antifreeze, always ensure it is suitable for use in an aluminium engine and contains corrosion inhibitors to prevent possible blockages of the internal coolant passages of the system. As a general rule, most coolants are designed to be used neat and should not be diluted whereas antifreeze can be mixed with distilled water to provide a coolant solution of the required strength. Refer to the manufacturer's instructions on the bottle.
● Ensure the coolant is changed in accordance with the Maintenance Schedule.

Chain lube

● Chain lube is an aerosol-type spray lubricant specifically designed for use on motorcycle final drive chains. Chain lube has two functions, to minimise friction between the final drive chain and sprockets and to prevent corrosion of the chain. Regular use of a good-quality chain lube will extend the life of the drive chain and sprockets and thus maximise the power being transmitted from the transmission to the rear wheel.
● When using chain lube, always allow some time for the solvents in the lube to evaporate before riding the motorcycle. This will minimise the amount of lube which will

'fling' off from the chain when the motorcycle is used. If the motorcycle is equipped with an 'O-ring' chain, ensure the chain lube is labelled as being suitable for use on 'O-ring' chains.

Degreasers and solvents

● There are many different types of solvents and degreasers available to remove the grime and grease which accumulate around the motorcycle during normal use. Degreasers and solvents are usually available as an aerosol-type spray or as a liquid which you apply with a brush. Always closely follow the manufacturer's instructions and wear eye protection during use. Be aware that many solvents are flammable and may give off noxious fumes; take adequate precautions when using them (see *Safety First!*).
● For general cleaning, use one of the many solvents or degreasers available from most motorcycle accessory shops. These solvents are usually applied then left for a certain time before being washed off with water.

Brake cleaner is a solvent specifically designed to remove all traces of oil, grease and dust from braking system components. Brake cleaner is designed to evaporate quickly and leaves behind no residue.

Carburettor cleaner is an aerosol-type solvent specifically designed to clear carburettor blockages and break down the hard deposits and gum often found inside carburettors during overhaul.

Contact cleaner is an aerosol-type solvent designed for cleaning electrical components. The cleaner will remove all traces of oil and dirt from components such as switch contacts or fouled spark plugs and then dry, leaving behind no residue.

Gasket remover is an aerosol-type solvent designed for removing stubborn gaskets from engine components during overhaul. Gasket remover will minimise the amount of scraping required to remove the gasket and therefore reduce the risk of damage to the mating surface.

Spray lubricants

● Aerosol-based spray lubricants are widely available and are excellent for lubricating lever pivots and exposed cables and switches. Try to use a lubricant which is of the dry-film type as the fluid evaporates, leaving behind a dry-film of lubricant. Lubricants which leave behind an oily residue will attract dust and dirt which will increase the rate of wear of the cable/lever.

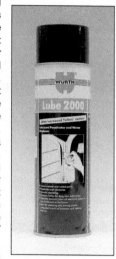

● Most lubricants also act as a moisture dispersant and a penetrating fluid. This means they can also be used to 'dry out' electrical components such as wiring connectors or switches as well as helping to free seized fasteners.

Greases

● Grease is used to lubricate many of the pivot-points. A good-quality multi-purpose grease is suitable for most applications but some manufacturers will specify the use of specialist greases for use on components such as swingarm and suspension linkage bushes. These specialist greases can be purchased from most motorcycle (or car) accessory shops; commonly specified types include molybdenum disulphide grease, lithium-based grease, graphite-based grease, silicone-based grease and high-temperature copper-based grease.

Gasket sealing compounds

● Gasket sealing compounds can be used in conjunction with gaskets, to improve their sealing capabilities, or on their own to seal metal-to-metal joints. Depending on their type, sealing compounds either set hard or stay relatively soft and pliable.

● When purchasing a gasket sealing compound, ensure that it is designed specifically for use on an internal combustion engine. General multi-purpose sealants available from DIY stores may appear visibly similar but they are not designed to withstand the extreme heat or contact with fuel and oil encountered when used on an engine (see 'Tools and Workshop Tips' for further information).

Thread locking compound

● Thread locking compounds are used to secure certain threaded fasteners in position to prevent them from loosening due to vibration. Thread locking compounds can be purchased from most motorcycle (and car) accessory shops. Ensure the threads of the both components are completely clean and dry before sparingly applying the locking compound (see 'Tools and Workshop Tips' for further information).

Fuel additives

● Fuel additives which protect and clean the fuel system components are widely available. These additives are designed to remove all traces of deposits that build up on the carburettors/injectors and prevent wear, helping the fuel system to operate more efficiently. If a fuel additive is being used, check that it is suitable for use with your motorcycle, especially if your motorcycle is equipped with a catalytic converter.

● Octane boosters are also available. These additives are designed to improve the performance of highly-tuned engines being run on normal pump-fuel and are of no real use on standard motorcycles.

Conversion factors

Length (distance)

Inches (in)	x 25.4	= Millimetres (mm)	x 0.0394	= Inches (in)
Feet (ft)	x 0.305	= Metres (m)	x 3.281	= Feet (ft)
Miles	x 1.609	= Kilometres (km)	x 0.621	= Miles

Volume (capacity)

Cubic inches (cu in; in³)	x 16.387	= Cubic centimetres (cc; cm³)	x 0.061	= Cubic inches (cu in; in³)
Imperial pints (Imp pt)	x 0.568	= Litres (l)	x 1.76	= Imperial pints (Imp pt)
Imperial quarts (Imp qt)	x 1.137	= Litres (l)	x 0.88	= Imperial quarts (Imp qt)
Imperial quarts (Imp qt)	x 1.201	= US quarts (US qt)	x 0.833	= Imperial quarts (Imp qt)
US quarts (US qt)	x 0.946	= Litres (l)	x 1.057	= US quarts (US qt)
Imperial gallons (Imp gal)	x 4.546	= Litres (l)	x 0.22	= Imperial gallons (Imp gal)
Imperial gallons (Imp gal)	x 1.201	= US gallons (US gal)	x 0.833	= Imperial gallons (Imp gal)
US gallons (US gal)	x 3.785	= Litres (l)	x 0.264	= US gallons (US gal)

Mass (weight)

Ounces (oz)	x 28.35	= Grams (g)	x 0.035	= Ounces (oz)
Pounds (lb)	x 0.454	= Kilograms (kg)	x 2.205	= Pounds (lb)

Force

Ounces-force (ozf; oz)	x 0.278	= Newtons (N)	x 3.6	= Ounces-force (ozf; oz)
Pounds-force (lbf; lb)	x 4.448	= Newtons (N)	x 0.225	= Pounds-force (lbf; lb)
Newtons (N)	x 0.1	= Kilograms-force (kgf; kg)	x 9.81	= Newtons (N)

Pressure

Pounds-force per square inch (psi; lbf/in²; lb/in²)	x 0.070	= Kilograms-force per square centimetre (kgf/cm²; kg/cm²)	x 14.223	= Pounds-force per square inch (psi; lbf/in²; lb/in²)
Pounds-force per square inch (psi; lbf/in²; lb/in²)	x 0.068	= Atmospheres (atm)	x 14.696	= Pounds-force per square inch (psi; lbf/in²; lb/in²)
Pounds-force per square inch (psi; lbf/in²; lb/in²)	x 0.069	= Bars	x 14.5	= Pounds-force per square inch (psi; lbf/in²; lb/in²)
Pounds-force per square inch (psi; lbf/in²; lb/in²)	x 6.895	= Kilopascals (kPa)	x 0.145	= Pounds-force per square inch (psi; lbf/in²; lb/in²)
Kilopascals (kPa)	x 0.01	= Kilograms-force per square centimetre (kgf/cm²; kg/cm²)	x 98.1	= Kilopascals (kPa)
Millibar (mbar)	x 100	= Pascals (Pa)	x 0.01	= Millibar (mbar)
Millibar (mbar)	x 0.0145	= Pounds-force per square inch (psi; lbf/in²; lb/in²)	x 68.947	= Millibar (mbar)
Millibar (mbar)	x 0.75	= Millimetres of mercury (mmHg)	x 1.333	= Millibar (mbar)
Millibar (mbar)	x 0.401	= Inches of water (inH₂O)	x 2.491	= Millibar (mbar)
Millimetres of mercury (mmHg)	x 0.535	= Inches of water (inH₂O)	x 1.868	= Millimetres of mercury (mmHg)
Inches of water (inH₂O)	x 0.036	= Pounds-force per square inch (psi; lbf/in²; lb/in²)	x 27.68	= Inches of water (inH₂O)

Torque (moment of force)

Pounds-force inches (lbf in; lb in)	x 1.152	= Kilograms-force centimetre (kgf cm; kg cm)	x 0.868	= Pounds-force inches (lbf in; lb in)
Pounds-force inches (lbf in; lb in)	x 0.113	= Newton metres (Nm)	x 8.85	= Pounds-force inches (lbf in; lb in)
Pounds-force inches (lbf in; lb in)	x 0.083	= Pounds-force feet (lbf ft; lb ft)	x 12	= Pounds-force inches (lbf in; lb in)
Pounds-force feet (lbf ft; lb ft)	x 0.138	= Kilograms-force metres (kgf m; kg m)	x 7.233	= Pounds-force feet (lbf ft; lb ft)
Pounds-force feet (lbf ft; lb ft)	x 1.356	= Newton metres (Nm)	x 0.738	= Pounds-force feet (lbf ft; lb ft)
Newton metres (Nm)	x 0.102	= Kilograms-force metres (kgf m; kg m)	x 9.804	= Newton metres (Nm)

Power

Horsepower (hp)	x 745.7	= Watts (W)	x 0.0013	= Horsepower (hp)

Velocity (speed)

Miles per hour (miles/hr; mph)	x 1.609	= Kilometres per hour (km/hr; kph)	x 0.621	= Miles per hour (miles/hr; mph)

Fuel consumption*

Miles per gallon, Imperial (mpg)	x 0.354	= Kilometres per litre (km/l)	x 2.825	= Miles per gallon, Imperial (mpg)
Miles per gallon, US (mpg)	x 0.425	= Kilometres per litre (km/l)	x 2.352	= Miles per gallon, US (mpg)

Temperature

Degrees Fahrenheit = (°C x 1.8) + 32

Degrees Celsius (Degrees Centigrade; °C) = (°F - 32) x 0.56

It is common practice to convert from miles per gallon (mpg) to litres/100 kilometres (l/100km), where mpg x l/100 km = 282

About the MOT Test

In the UK, all vehicles more than three years old are subject to an annual test to ensure that they meet minimum safety requirements. A current test certificate must be issued before a machine can be used on public roads, and is required before a road fund licence can be issued. Riding without a current test certificate will also invalidate your insurance.

For most owners, the MOT test is an annual cause for anxiety, and this is largely due to owners not being sure what needs to be checked prior to submitting the motorcycle for testing. The simple answer is that a fully roadworthy motorcycle will have no difficulty in passing the test.

This is a guide to getting your motorcycle through the MOT test. Obviously it will not be possible to examine the motorcycle to the same standard as the professional MOT tester, particularly in view of the equipment required for some of the checks. However, working through the following procedures will enable you to identify any problem areas before submitting the motorcycle for the test.

It has only been possible to summarise the test requirements here, based on the regulations in force at the time of printing. Test standards are becoming increasingly stringent, although there are some exemptions for older vehicles. More information about the MOT test can be

obtained from the TSO publications, *How Safe is your Motorcycle* and *The MOT Inspection Manual for Motorcycle Testing*.

Many of the checks require that one of the wheels is raised off the ground. If the motorcycle doesn't have a centre stand, note that an auxiliary stand will be required. Additionally, the help of an assistant may prove useful.

Certain exceptions apply to machines under 50 cc, machines without a lighting system, and Classic bikes - if in doubt about any of the requirements listed below seek confirmation from an MOT tester prior to submitting the motorcycle for the test.

Check that the frame number is clearly visible.

Electrical System

Lights, turn signals, horn and reflector

● With the ignition on, check the operation of the following electrical components. **Note:** *The electrical components on certain small-capacity machines are powered by the generator, requiring that the engine is run for this check.*

a) *Headlight and tail light. Check that both illuminate in the low and high beam switch positions.*
b) *Position lights. Check that the front position (or sidelight) and tail light illuminate in this switch position.*
c) *Turn signals. Check that all flash at the correct rate, and that the warning light(s) function correctly. Check that the turn signal switch works correctly.*
d) *Hazard warning system (where fitted). Check that all four turn signals flash in this switch position.*
e) *Brake stop light. Check that the light comes on when the front and rear brakes are independently applied. Models first used on or after 1st April 1986 must have a brake light switch on each brake.*
f) *Horn. Check that the sound is continuous and of reasonable volume.*

● Check that there is a red reflector on the rear of the machine, either mounted separately or as part of the tail light lens.
● Check the condition of the headlight, tail light and turn signal lenses.

Headlight beam height

● The MOT tester will perform a headlight beam height check using specialised beam setting equipment **(see illustration 1)**. This equipment will not be available to the home mechanic, but if you suspect that the headlight is incorrectly set or may have been maladjusted in the past, you can perform a rough test as follows.
● Position the bike in a straight line facing a brick wall. The bike must be off its stand, upright and with a rider seated. Measure the height from the ground to the centre of the headlight and mark a horizontal line on the wall at this height. Position the motorcycle 3.8 metres from the wall and draw a vertical

Headlight beam height checking equipment

line up the wall central to the centreline of the motorcycle. Switch to dipped beam and check that the beam pattern falls slightly lower than the horizontal line and to the left of the vertical line **(see illustration 2)**.

Home workshop beam alignment check

Exhaust System and Final Drive

Exhaust

● Check that the exhaust mountings are secure and that the system does not foul any of the rear suspension components.
● Start the motorcycle. When the revs are increased, check that the exhaust is neither holed nor leaking from any of its joints. On a linked system, check that the collector box is not leaking due to corrosion.

● Note that the exhaust decibel level ("loudness" of the exhaust) is assessed at the discretion of the tester. If the motorcycle was first used on or after 1st January 1985 the silencer must carry the BSAU 193 stamp, or a marking relating to its make and model, or be of OE (original equipment) manufacture. If the silencer is marked NOT FOR ROAD USE, RACING USE ONLY or similar, it will fail the MOT.

Final drive

● On chain or belt drive machines, check that the chain/belt is in good condition and does not have excessive slack. Also check that the sprocket is securely mounted on the rear wheel hub. Check that the chain/belt guard is in place.
● On shaft drive bikes, check for oil leaking from the drive unit and fouling the rear tyre.

Steering and Suspension

Steering

● With the front wheel raised off the ground, rotate the steering from lock to lock. The handlebar or switches must not contact the fuel tank or be close enough to trap the rider's hand. Problems can be caused by damaged lock stops on the lower yoke and frame, or by the fitting of non-standard handlebars.
● When performing the lock to lock check, also ensure that the steering moves freely without drag or notchiness. Steering movement can be impaired by poorly routed cables, or by overtight head bearings or worn bvearings. The tester will perform a check of the steering head bearing lower race by mounting the front wheel on a surface plate, then performing a lock to lock check with the weight of the machine on the lower bearing (see illustration 3).
● Grasp the fork sliders (lower legs) and attempt to push and pull on the forks

Front wheel mounted on a surface plate for steering head bearing lower race check

(see illustration 4). Any play in the steering head bearings will be felt. Note that in extreme cases, wear of the front fork bushes can be misinterpreted for head bearing play.
● Check that the handlebars are securely mounted.
● Check that the handlebar grip rubbers are secure. They should by bonded to the bar left end and to the throttle cable pulley on the right end.

Front suspension

● With the motorcycle off the stand, hold the front brake on and pump the front forks up and down (see illustration 5). Check that they are adequately damped.

Checking the steering head bearings for freeplay

Hold the front brake on and pump the front forks up and down to check operation

Inspect the area around the fork dust seal for oil leakage (arrow)

Bounce the rear of the motorcycle to check rear suspension operation

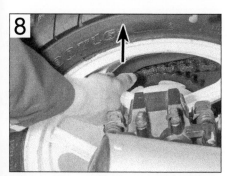

Checking for rear suspension linkage play

● Inspect the area above and around the front fork oil seals **(see illustration 6)**. There should be no sign of oil on the fork tube (stanchion) nor leaking down the slider (lower leg). On models so equipped, check that there is no oil leaking from the anti-dive units.

● On models with swingarm front suspension, check that there is no freeplay in the linkage when moved from side to side.

Rear suspension

● With the motorcycle off the stand and an assistant supporting the motorcycle by its handlebars, bounce the rear suspension **(see illustration 7)**. Check that the suspension components do not foul on any of the cycle parts and check that the shock absorber(s) provide adequate damping.

● Visually inspect the shock absorber(s) and check that there is no sign of oil leakage from its damper. This is somewhat restricted on certain single shock models due to the location of the shock absorber.

● With the rear wheel raised off the ground, grasp the wheel at the highest point and attempt to pull it up **(see illustration 8)**. Any play in the swingarm pivot or suspension linkage bearings will be felt as movement. **Note:** *Do not confuse play with actual suspension movement.* Failure to lubricate suspension linkage bearings can lead to bearing failure **(see illustration 9)**.

● With the rear wheel raised off the ground, grasp the swingarm ends and attempt to move the swingarm from side to side and forwards and backwards - any play indicates wear of the swingarm pivot bearings **(see illustration 10)**.

Worn suspension linkage pivots (arrows) are usually the cause of play in the rear suspension

Grasp the swingarm at the ends to check for play in its pivot bearings

Brake pad wear can usually be viewed without removing the caliper. Most pads have wear indicator grooves (arrowed) and some also have indicator tangs or cut-outs.

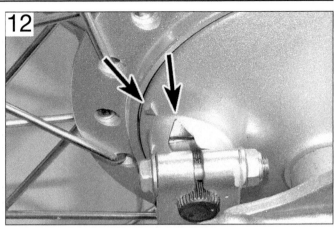

On drum brakes, check the angle of the operating lever with the brake fully applied. Most drum brakes have a wear indicator pointer or scale.

Brakes, Wheels and Tyres

Brakes

● With the wheel raised off the ground, apply the brake then free it off, and check that the wheel is about to revolve freely without brake drag.

● On disc brakes, examine the disc itself. Check that it is securely mounted and not cracked.

● On disc brakes, view the pad material through the caliper mouth and check that the pads are not worn down beyond the limit **(see illustration 11)**.

● On drum brakes, check that when the brake is applied the angle between the operating lever and cable or rod is not too great **(see illustration 12)**. Check also that the operating lever doesn't foul any other components.

● On disc brakes, examine the flexible hoses from top to bottom. Have an assistant hold the brake on so that the fluid in the hose is under pressure, and check that there is no sign of fluid leakage, bulges or cracking. If there are any metal brake pipes or unions, check that these are free from corrosion and damage. Where a brake-linked anti-dive system is fitted, check the hoses to the anti-dive in a similar manner.

● Check that the rear brake torque arm is secure and that its fasteners are secured by self-locking nuts or castellated nuts with split-pins or R-pins **(see illustration 13)**.

● On models with ABS, check that the self-check warning light in the instrument panel works.

● The MOT tester will perform a test of the motorcycle's braking efficiency based on a calculation of rider and motorcycle weight. Although this cannot be carried out at home, you can at least ensure that the braking systems are properly maintained. For hydraulic disc brakes, check the fluid level, lever/pedal feel (bleed of air if its spongy) and pad material. For drum brakes, check adjustment, cable or rod operation and shoe lining thickness.

Wheels and tyres

● Check the wheel condition. Cast wheels should be free from cracks and if of the built-up design, all fasteners should be secure. Spoked wheels should be checked for broken, corroded, loose or bent spokes.

● With the wheel raised off the ground, spin the wheel and visually check that the tyre and wheel run true. Check that the tyre does not foul the suspension or mudguards.

● With the wheel raised off the ground, grasp the wheel and attempt to move it about the axle (spindle) **(see illustration 14)**. Any play felt here indicates wheel bearing failure.

Brake torque arm must be properly secured at both ends

Check for wheel bearing play by trying to move the wheel about the axle (spindle)

Checking the tyre tread depth

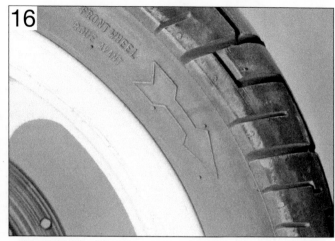

Tyre direction of rotation arrow can be found on tyre sidewall

Castellated type wheel axle (spindle) nut must be secured by a split pin or R-pin

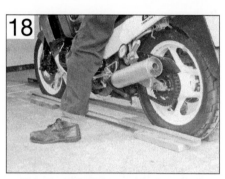

Two straightedges are used to check wheel alignment

● Check the tyre tread depth, tread condition and sidewall condition **(see illustration 15)**.
● Check the tyre type. Front and rear tyre types must be compatible and be suitable for road use. Tyres marked NOT FOR ROAD USE, COMPETITION USE ONLY or similar, will fail the MOT.

● If the tyre sidewall carries a direction of rotation arrow, this must be pointing in the direction of normal wheel rotation **(see illustration 16)**.
● Check that the wheel axle (spindle) nuts (where applicable) are properly secured. A self-locking nut or castellated nut with a split-pin or R-pin can be used **(see illustration 17)**.
● Wheel alignment is checked with the motorcycle off the stand and a rider seated. With the front wheel pointing straight ahead, two perfectly straight lengths of metal or wood and placed against the sidewalls of both tyres **(see illustration 18)**. The gap each side of the front tyre must be equidistant on both sides. Incorrect wheel alignment may be due to a cocked rear wheel (often as the result of poor chain adjustment) or in extreme cases, a bent frame.

General checks and condition

● Check the security of all major fasteners, bodypanels, seat, fairings (where fitted) and mudguards.

● Check that the rider and pillion footrests, handlebar levers and brake pedal are securely mounted.

● Check for corrosion on the frame or any load-bearing components. If severe, this may affect the structure, particularly under stress.

Sidecars

A motorcycle fitted with a sidecar requires additional checks relating to the stability of the machine and security of attachment and swivel joints, plus specific wheel alignment (toe-in) requirements. Additionally, tyre and lighting requirements differ from conventional motorcycle use. Owners are advised to check MOT test requirements with an official test centre.

Preparing for storage

Before you start

If repairs or an overhaul is needed, see that this is carried out now rather than left until you want to ride the bike again.

Give the bike a good wash and scrub all dirt from its underside. Make sure the bike dries completely before preparing for storage.

Engine

● Remove the spark plug(s) and lubricate the cylinder bores with approximately a teaspoon of motor oil using a spout-type oil can **(see illustration 1)**. Reinstall the spark plug(s). Crank the engine over a couple of times to coat the piston rings and bores with oil. If the bike has a kickstart, use this to turn the engine over. If not, flick the kill switch to the OFF position and crank the engine over on the starter **(see illustration 2)**. If the nature on the ignition system prevents the starter operating with the kill switch in the OFF position, remove the spark plugs and fit them back in their caps; ensure that the plugs are earthed (grounded) against the cylinder head when the starter is operated **(see illustration 3)**.

> ⚠️ **Warning: It is important that the plugs are earthed (grounded) away from the spark plug holes otherwise there is a risk of atomised fuel from the cylinders igniting.**

> **HAYNES HINT** *On a single cylinder four-stroke engine, you can seal the combustion chamber completely by positioning the piston at TDC on the compression stroke.*

● Drain the carburettor(s) otherwise there is a risk of jets becoming blocked by gum deposits from the fuel **(see illustration 4)**.

● If the bike is going into long-term storage, consider adding a fuel stabiliser to the fuel in the tank. If the tank is drained completely, corrosion of its internal surfaces may occur if left unprotected for a long period. The tank can be treated with a rust preventative especially for this purpose. Alternatively, remove the tank and pour half a litre of motor oil into it, install the filler cap and shake the tank to coat its internals with oil before draining off the excess. The same effect can also be achieved by spraying WD40 or a similar water-dispersant around the inside of the tank via its flexible nozzle.

● Make sure the cooling system contains the correct mix of antifreeze. Antifreeze also contains important corrosion inhibitors.

● The air intakes and exhaust can be sealed off by covering or plugging the openings. Ensure that you do not seal in any condensation; run the engine until it is hot,

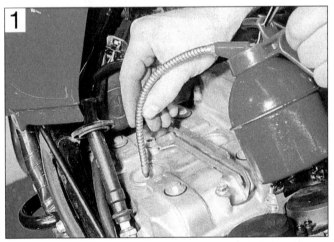

Squirt a drop of motor oil into each cylinder

Flick the kill switch to OFF . . .

. . . and ensure that the metal bodies of the plugs (arrows) are earthed against the cylinder head

Connect a hose to the carburettor float chamber drain stub (arrow) and unscrew the drain screw

Exhausts can be sealed off with a plastic bag

Disconnect the negative lead (A) first, followed by the positive lead (B)

Use a suitable battery charger - this kit also assess battery condition

then switch off and allow to cool. Tape a piece of thick plastic over the silencer end(s) **(see illustration 5)**. Note that some advocate pouring a tablespoon of motor oil into the silencer(s) before sealing them off.

Battery

● Remove it from the bike - in extreme cases of cold the battery may freeze and crack its case **(see illustration 6)**.

● Check the electrolyte level and top up if necessary (conventional refillable batteries). Clean the terminals.
● Store the battery off the motorcycle and away from any sources of fire. Position a wooden block under the battery if it is to sit on the ground.
● Give the battery a trickle charge for a few hours every month **(see illustration 7)**.

Tyres

● Place the bike on its centrestand or an auxiliary stand which will support the motorcycle in an upright position. Position wood blocks under the tyres to keep them off the ground and to provide insulation from damp. If the bike is being put into long-term storage, ideally both tyres should be off the ground; not only will this protect the tyres, but will also ensure that no load is placed on the steering head or wheel bearings.
● Deflate each tyre by 5 to 10 psi, no more or the beads may unseat from the rim, making subsequent inflation difficult on tubeless tyres.

Pivots and controls

● Lubricate all lever, pedal, stand and footrest

pivot points. If grease nipples are fitted to the rear suspension components, apply lubricant to the pivots.
● Lubricate all control cables.

Cycle components

● Apply a wax protectant to all painted and plastic components. Wipe off any excess, but don't polish to a shine. Where fitted, clean the screen with soap and water.
● Coat metal parts with Vaseline (petroleum jelly). When applying this to the fork tubes, do not compress the forks otherwise the seals will rot from contact with the Vaseline.
● Apply a vinyl cleaner to the seat.

Storage conditions

● Aim to store the bike in a shed or garage which does not leak and is free from damp.
● Drape an old blanket or bedspread over the bike to protect it from dust and direct contact with sunlight (which will fade paint). This also hides the bike from prying eyes. Beware of tight-fitting plastic covers which may allow condensation to form and settle on the bike.

Getting back on the road

Engine and transmission

● Change the oil and replace the oil filter. If this was done prior to storage, check that the oil hasn't emulsified - a thick whitish substance which occurs through condensation.
● Remove the spark plugs. Using a spout-type oil can, squirt a few drops of oil into the cylinder(s). This will provide initial lubrication as the piston rings and bores comes back into contact. Service the spark plugs, or fit new ones, and install them in the engine.

● Check that the clutch isn't stuck on. The plates can stick together if left standing for some time, preventing clutch operation. Engage a gear and try rocking the bike back and forth with the clutch lever held against the handlebar. If this doesn't work on cable-operated clutches, hold the clutch lever back against the handlebar with a strong elastic band or cable tie for a couple of hours **(see illustration 8)**.
● If the air intakes or silencer end(s) were blocked off, remove the bung or cover used.
● If the fuel tank was coated with a rust

Hold clutch lever back against the handlebar with elastic bands or a cable tie preventative, oil or a stabiliser added to the fuel, drain and flush the tank and dispose of the fuel sensibly. If no action was taken with the fuel tank prior to storage, it is advised that the old fuel is disposed of since it will go off over a period of time. Refill the fuel tank with fresh fuel.

Frame and running gear

● Oil all pivot points and cables.
● Check the tyre pressures. They will definitely need inflating if pressures were reduced for storage.
● Lubricate the final drive chain (where applicable).
● Remove any protective coating applied to the fork tubes (stanchions) since this may well destroy the fork seals. If the fork tubes weren't protected and have picked up rust spots, remove them with very fine abrasive paper and refinish with metal polish.
● Check that both brakes operate correctly. Apply each brake hard and check that it's not possible to move the motorcycle forwards, then check that the brake frees off again once released. Brake caliper pistons can stick due to corrosion around the piston head, or on the sliding caliper types, due to corrosion of the slider pins. If the brake doesn't free after repeated operation, take the caliper off for examination. Similarly drum brakes can stick

due to a seized operating cam, cable or rod linkage.
● If the motorcycle has been in long-term storage, renew the brake fluid and clutch fluid (where applicable).
● Depending on where the bike has been stored, the wiring, cables and hoses may have been nibbled by rodents. Make a visual check and investigate disturbed wiring loom tape.

Battery

● If the battery has been previously removal and given top up charges it can simply be reconnected. Remember to connect the positive cable first and the negative cable last.
● On conventional refillable batteries, if the battery has not received any attention, remove it from the motorcycle and check its electrolyte level. Top up if necessary then charge the battery. If the battery fails to hold a charge and a visual checks show heavy white sulphation of the plates, the battery is probably defective and must be renewed. This is particularly likely if the battery is old. Confirm battery condition with a specific gravity check.
● On sealed (MF) batteries, if the battery has not received any attention, remove it from the motorcycle and charge it according to the information on the battery case - if the battery fails to hold a charge it must be renewed.

Starting procedure

● If a kickstart is fitted, turn the engine over a couple of times with the ignition OFF to distribute oil around the engine. If no kickstart is fitted, flick the engine kill switch OFF and the ignition ON and crank the engine over a couple of times to work oil around the upper cylinder components. If the nature of the ignition system is such that the starter won't work with the kill switch OFF, remove the spark plugs, fit them back into their caps and earth (ground) their bodies on the cylinder head. Reinstall the spark plugs afterwards.
● Switch the kill switch to RUN, operate the choke and start the engine. If the engine won't start don't continue cranking the engine - not only will this flatten the battery, but the starter motor will overheat. Switch the ignition off and try again later. If the engine refuses to start, go through the fault finding procedures in this manual. **Note:** *If the bike has been in storage for a long time, old fuel or a carburettor blockage may be the problem. Gum deposits in carburettors can block jets - if a carburettor cleaner doesn't prove successful the carburettors must be dismantled for cleaning.*
● Once the engine has started, check that the lights, turn signals and horn work properly.
● Treat the bike gently for the first ride and check all fluid levels on completion. Settle the bike back into the maintenance schedule.

This Section provides an easy reference-guide to the more common faults that are likely to afflict your machine. Obviously, the opportunities are almost limitless for faults to occur as a result of obscure failures, and to try and cover all eventualities would require a book. Indeed, a number have been written on the subject.

Successful troubleshooting is not a mysterious 'black art' but the application of a bit of knowledge combined with a systematic and logical approach to the problem. Approach any troubleshooting by first accurately identifying the symptom and then checking through the list of possible causes, starting with the simplest or most obvious and progressing in stages to the most complex.

Take nothing for granted, but above all apply liberal quantities of common sense.

The main symptom of a fault is given in the text as a major heading below which are listed the various systems or areas which may contain the fault. Details of each possible cause for a fault and the remedial action to be taken are given, in brief, in the paragraphs below each heading. Further information should be sought in the relevant Chapter.

1 Engine doesn't start or is difficult to start

- [ ] Starter motor doesn't rotate
- [ ] Starter motor rotates but engine does not turn over
- [ ] Starter works but engine won't turn over (seized)
- [ ] No fuel flow
- [ ] Engine flooded
- [ ] No spark or weak spark
- [ ] Compression low
- [ ] Stalls after starting
- [ ] Rough idle

2 Poor running at low speed

- [ ] Spark weak
- [ ] Fuel/air mixture incorrect
- [ ] Compression low
- [ ] Poor acceleration

3 Poor running or no power at high speed

- [ ] Firing incorrect
- [ ] Fuel/air mixture incorrect
- [ ] Compression low
- [ ] Knocking or pinking
- [ ] Miscellaneous causes

4 Overheating

- [ ] Engine overheats
- [ ] Firing incorrect
- [ ] Fuel/air mixture incorrect
- [ ] Compression too high
- [ ] Engine load excessive
- [ ] Lubrication inadequate
- [ ] Miscellaneous causes

5 Clutch problems

- [ ] Clutch slipping
- [ ] Clutch not disengaging completely

6 Gearchanging problems

- [ ] Doesn't go into gear, or lever doesn't return
- [ ] Jumps out of gear
- [ ] Overselects

7 Abnormal engine noise

- [ ] Knocking or pinking
- [ ] Piston slap or rattling
- [ ] Valve noise
- [ ] Other noise

8 Abnormal driveline noise

- [ ] Clutch noise
- [ ] Transmission noise
- [ ] Final drive noise

9 Abnormal frame and suspension noise

- [ ] Front end noise
- [ ] Shock absorber noise
- [ ] Brake noise

10 Oil level warning light comes on

- [ ] Engine lubrication system
- [ ] Electrical system

11 Excessive exhaust smoke

- [ ] White smoke
- [ ] Black smoke
- [ ] Brown smoke

12 Poor handling or stability

- [ ] Handlebar hard to turn
- [ ] Handlebar shakes or vibrates excessively
- [ ] Handlebar pulls to one side
- [ ] Poor shock absorbing qualities

13 Braking problems

- [ ] Brakes are spongy, don't hold
- [ ] Brake lever or pedal pulsates
- [ ] Brakes drag

14 Electrical problems

- [ ] Battery dead or weak
- [ ] Battery overcharged

1 Engine doesn't start or is difficult to start

Starter motor doesn't rotate

☐ Engine kill switch OFF.
☐ Main fuse blown (Chapter 8).
☐ Battery voltage low. Check and recharge battery (Chapter 8).
☐ Starter motor defective. Make sure the wiring to the starter is secure. Make sure the starter relay clicks when the start button is pushed. If the relay clicks, then the fault is in the wiring or motor (see Chapter 8).
☐ Starter switch not contacting. The contacts could be wet, corroded or dirty. Disassemble and clean the switch (Chapter 8).
☐ Wiring open or shorted. Check all wiring connections and harnesses to make sure that they are dry, tight and not corroded. Also check for broken or frayed wires that can cause a short to ground (earth) (see Wiring diagrams, Chapter 8).
☐ Ignition switch defective. Check the switch and replace with a new one if it is defective (see Chapter 8).
☐ Engine kill switch defective. Check for wet, dirty or corroded contacts. Clean or replace the switch with a new one as necessary (see Chapter 8).
☐ Faulty neutral switch, sidestand switch or clutch switch. Check the wiring to each switch and the switch itself (see Chapter 8).
☐ Faulty starter circuit cut-off relay or diodes (Chapter 8).
☐ Fuel injection system shutdown due to system fault (Chapter 4).

Starter motor rotates but engine does not turn over

☐ Starter clutch defective. Inspect and repair or replace with a new one (see Chapter 2).
☐ Damaged idler or starter gears. Inspect and replace the damaged parts (see Chapter 2).

Starter works but engine won't turn over (seized)

☐ Seized engine caused by one or more internally damaged components. Failure due to wear, abuse or lack of lubrication. Damage can include seized valves, followers, camshafts, pistons, crankshaft, connecting rod bearings, or transmission gears or bearings. Refer to Chapter 2 for engine disassembly.

No fuel flow

☐ No fuel in tank.
☐ Fuel tank breather hose obstructed.
☐ Faulty fuel pump relay. Check the relay (see Chapter 4).
☐ Fuel pump faulty or its filter is blocked (see Chapter 4).
☐ Fuel hose clogged. Remove the fuel hose and carefully blow through it.

☐ Fuel rail or injectors clogged. For all of the injectors to be clogged, either a very bad batch of fuel with an unusual additive has been used, or some other foreign material has entered the tank. In some cases, if a machine has been unused for several months, the fuel turns to a varnish-like liquid which can cause an injector needle to stick to its seat. Drain the tank and clean the fuel system (Chapter 4).

Engine flooded

☐ Injector needle valve worn or stuck open. A piece of dirt, rust or other debris can cause the needle to seat improperly, causing excess fuel to be admitted to the throttle body. In this case, the injector should be cleaned and the needle and seat inspected (see Chapter 4). If the needle and seat are worn, then the leaking will persist and the parts should be replaced with new ones.
☐ Starting technique incorrect. Under normal circumstances (i.e. if all the components of the fuel injection system are good) the machine should start with the throttle closed.

No spark or weak spark

☐ Ignition switch OFF.
☐ Engine kill switch turned to the OFF position.
☐ Ignition or kill switch shorted. This is usually caused by water, corrosion, damage or excessive wear. The switches can be disassembled and cleaned with electrical contact cleaner. If cleaning does not help, replace the switches (see Chapter 8).
☐ Battery voltage low. Check and recharge the battery as necessary (Chapter 8).
☐ Ignition coil not making good contact. Make sure that the coils fit snugly over the plug ends.
☐ Spark plugs dirty, defective or worn out. Locate reason for fouled plugs using spark plug condition chart on the inside back cover and follow the plug maintenance procedures (see Chapter 1).
☐ Incorrect spark plugs. Wrong type or heat range. Check and install correct plugs (see Chapter 1).
☐ Ignition coil defective. Test and renew if necessary (Chapter 4).
☐ Fuel injection system shutdown due to system fault (Chapter 4).
☐ Cylinder identification sensor defective (see Chapter 4).
☐ Crankshaft position sensor defective (see Chapter 4).
☐ Engine control unit (ECU) defective (see Chapter 4).
☐ Wiring shorted or broken between:
   a) Ignition switch and engine kill switch (or blown fuse)
   b) ECU and engine kill switch
   c) ECU and ignition coils
   d) ECU and crankshaft position sensor
☐ Make sure that all wiring connections are clean, dry and tight. Look for chafed and broken wires (see Chapters 4 and 8).

1 Engine doesn't start or is difficult to start (continued)

Compression low

- ☐ Spark plugs loose. Remove the plugs and inspect their threads. Reinstall and tighten securely (see Chapter 1).
- ☐ Cylinder head not sufficiently tightened down. If a cylinder head is suspected of being loose, then there's a chance that the gasket or head is damaged if the problem has persisted for any length of time. The head nuts should be tightened to the proper torque and in the correct sequence (Chapter 2).
- ☐ Improper valve clearance. This means that the valve is not closing completely and compression pressure is leaking past the valve. Check and adjust the valve clearances (Chapter 1).
- ☐ Cylinder and/or piston worn. Excessive wear will cause compression pressure to leak past the rings. This is usually accompanied by worn rings as well. A top-end overhaul is necessary (Chapter 2).
- ☐ Piston rings worn, weak, broken, or sticking. Broken or sticking piston rings usually indicate a lubrication or fuelling problem that causes excess carbon deposits to form on the pistons and rings. Top-end overhaul is necessary (Chapter 2).
- ☐ Piston ring-to-groove clearance excessive. This is caused by excessive wear of the piston ring lands. Piston renewal is necessary (Chapter 2).
- ☐ Cylinder head gasket damaged. If a head is allowed to become loose, or if excessive carbon build-up on the piston crown and combustion chamber causes extremely high compression, the head gasket may leak. Retorquing the head is not always sufficient to restore the seal, so a new gasket is necessary (Chapter 2).
- ☐ Cylinder head warped. This is caused by overheating or improperly tightened head nuts. Machine shop resurfacing or head renewal is necessary (Chapter 2).
- ☐ Valve spring broken or weak. Caused by component failure or wear; the springs must be renewed (Chapter 2).
- ☐ Valve not seating properly. This is caused by a bent valve (from over-revving or improper valve adjustment), burned valve or seat (incorrect air/fuel mixture) or an accumulation of carbon deposits on the seat. The valves must be cleaned and/or renewed and the seats serviced (Chapter 2).

Stalls after starting

- ☐ Incorrect valve clearances (see Chapter 1).
- ☐ Air filter dirty or incorrectly fitted (see Chapter 1).
- ☐ Ignition malfunction (see Chapter 4).
- ☐ Fuel injection system malfunction (see Chapter 4).
- ☐ Fuel contaminated. The fuel can be contaminated with either dirt or water, or can change chemically if the machine has been unused for several months. Drain the tank and fuel system (Chapter 4).
- ☐ Intake air leak. Check for loose throttle body-to-intake manifold connections, loose or damaged AIS vacuum hose or throttle body vacuum hoses (Chapter 4).

Rough idle

- ☐ Incorrect valve clearances (see Chapter 1).
- ☐ Air filter dirty or incorrectly fitted (see Chapter 1).
- ☐ Ignition fault (see Chapter 4).
- ☐ Throttle body air screws not synchronised. Adjust them as described in Chapter 1.
- ☐ Fuel injection system malfunction (see Chapter 4).
- ☐ Fuel contaminated. The fuel can be contaminated with either dirt or water, or can change chemically if the machine has been unused for several months. Drain the tank and the fuel system (Chapter 4).
- ☐ Intake air leak. Check for loose throttle body-to-intake manifold connections, loose or damaged AIS vacuum hose or throttle body vacuum hoses (Chapter 4).
- ☐ Air filter clogged. Clean the air filter element or replace it with a new one (Chapter 1).

2 Poor running at low speeds

Spark weak

- ☐ Battery voltage low. Check and recharge battery (see Chapter 8).
- ☐ Ignition coils not making good contact. Make sure that the coils fit snugly over the plug ends.
- ☐ Spark plugs dirty, defective or worn out. Locate reason for fouled plugs using spark plug condition chart on the inside back cover and follow the plug maintenance procedures (see Chapter 1).
- ☐ Incorrect spark plugs. Wrong type or heat range. Check and install correct plugs (see Chapter 1).
- ☐ Ignition coil defective. Test and renew if necessary (see Chapter 4).

Fuel/air mixture incorrect

- ☐ Fuel tank breather hose obstructed.
- ☐ Fuel pump faulty, or its filter is blocked (see Chapter 4).
- ☐ Fuel hose clogged. Remove the fuel hose and carefully blow through it.
- ☐ Fuel rail or injector clogged. For all of the injectors to be clogged, either a very bad batch of fuel with an unusual additive has been used, or some other foreign material has entered the tank. Check the fuel pump filter. In some cases, if a machine has been unused for several months, the fuel turns to a varnish-like liquid which can cause an injector needle to stick to its seat. Drain the tank and fuel system (Chapter 4).
- ☐ Intake air leak. Check for loose throttle body-to-intake manifold connections, loose or damaged AIS vacuum hose or throttle body vacuum hoses (Chapter 4).
- ☐ Air filter clogged. Clean the air filter element or replace it with a new one (Chapter 1).

Compression low

Check by performing a compression test (see Chapter 2).
- ☐ Spark plugs loose. Remove the plugs and inspect their threads. Reinstall and tighten securely (see Chapter 1).
- ☐ Cylinder head not sufficiently tightened down. If a cylinder head is suspected of being loose, then there's a chance that the gasket or head is damaged if the problem has persisted for any length of time. The head nuts should be tightened to the proper torque and in the correct sequence (Chapter 2).
- ☐ Improper valve clearance. This means that the valve is not closing completely and compression pressure is leaking past the valve. Check and adjust the valve clearances (Chapter 1).
- ☐ Cylinder and/or piston worn. Excessive wear will cause compression pressure to leak past the rings. This is usually accompanied by worn rings as well. A top-end overhaul is necessary (Chapter 2).
- ☐ Piston rings worn, weak, broken, or sticking. Broken or sticking piston rings usually indicate a lubrication or fuelling problem that causes excess carbon deposits to form on the pistons and rings. Top-end overhaul is necessary (Chapter 2).
- ☐ Piston ring-to-groove clearance excessive. This is caused by excessive wear of the piston ring lands. Piston renewal is necessary (Chapter 2).
- ☐ Cylinder head gasket damaged. If the head is allowed to become loose, or if excessive carbon build-up on the piston crown and combustion chamber causes extremely high compression, the head gasket may leak. Retorquing the head is not always sufficient to restore the seal, so a new gasket is necessary (Chapter 2).
- ☐ Cylinder head warped. This is caused by overheating or improperly tightened head nuts. Machine shop resurfacing or head renewal is necessary (Chapter 2).
- ☐ Valve spring broken or weak. Caused by component failure or wear; the springs must be renewed (Chapter 2).
- ☐ Valve not seating properly. This is caused by a bent valve (from over-revving or improper valve adjustment), burned valve or seat (improper fuelling) or an accumulation of carbon deposits on the seat (from fuelling or lubrication problems). The valves must be cleaned and/or renewed and the seats serviced (Chapter 2).

Poor acceleration

- ☐ Timing not advancing. The crankshaft position sensor or the engine control unit (ECU) may be defective (see Chapter 4). If so, they must be renewed.
- ☐ Engine oil viscosity too high. Using a heavier oil than that recommended in Chapter 1 can damage the oil pump or lubrication system and cause drag on the engine.
- ☐ Brakes dragging. Usually caused by debris which has entered the brake caliper piston seals, or from a warped disc or bent axle (see Chapter 6).

3 Poor running or no power at high speed

Firing incorrect

- [ ] Ignition coils not making good contact. Make sure that the coils fit snugly over the plug ends and that the wiring is secure.
- [ ] Spark plugs dirty, defective or worn out. Locate reason for fouled plugs using spark plug condition chart on the inside back cover and follow the plug maintenance procedures (see Chapter 1).
- [ ] Incorrect spark plugs. Wrong type or heat range. Check and install correct plugs (see Chapter 1).
- [ ] Ignition coil defective. Test and renew if necessary (see Chapter 4).
- [ ] Faulty ECU (engine control unit) (see Chapter 4).

Fuel/air mixture incorrect

- [ ] Fuel tank breather hose obstructed.
- [ ] Fuel pump faulty, or its filter is blocked (see Chapter 4).
- [ ] Fuel hose clogged. Remove the fuel hose and carefully blow through it.
- [ ] Fuel rail or injector clogged. For all of the injectors to be clogged, either a very bad batch of fuel with an unusual additive has been used, or some other foreign material has entered the tank. Check the pump filter. In some cases, if a machine has been unused for several months, the fuel turns to a varnish-like liquid which can cause an injector needle to stick to its seat. Drain the tank and fuel system (Chapter 4).
- [ ] Intake air leak. Check for loose throttle body-to-intake manifold connections, loose or damaged AIS vacuum hose or throttle body vacuum hoses (Chapter 4).
- [ ] Air filter clogged. Clean the air filter element or replace it with a new one (Chapter 1).

Compression low

Check by performing a compression test (see Chapter 2).

- [ ] Spark plugs loose. Remove the plugs and inspect their threads. Reinstall and tighten securely (see Chapter 1).
- [ ] Cylinder head not sufficiently tightened down. If a cylinder head is suspected of being loose, then there's a chance that the gasket or head is damaged if the problem has persisted for any length of time. The head nuts should be tightened to the proper torque and in the correct sequence (Chapter 2).
- [ ] Improper valve clearance. This means that the valve is not closing completely and compression pressure is leaking past the valve. Check and adjust the valve clearances (Chapter 1).
- [ ] Cylinder and/or piston worn. Excessive wear will cause compression pressure to leak past the rings. This is usually accompanied by worn rings as well. A top-end overhaul is necessary (Chapter 2).
- [ ] Piston rings worn, weak, broken or sticking. Broken or sticking piston rings usually indicate a lubrication or fuelling problem that causes excess carbon deposits to form on the pistons and rings. Top-end overhaul is necessary (Chapter 2).
- [ ] Piston ring-to-groove clearance excessive. This is caused by excessive wear of the piston ring lands. Piston renewal is necessary (Chapter 2).
- [ ] Cylinder head gasket damaged. If a head is allowed to become loose, or if excessive carbon build-up on the piston crown and combustion chamber causes extremely high compression, the head gasket may leak. Retorquing the head is not always sufficient to restore the seal, so a new gasket is necessary (Chapter 2).
- [ ] Cylinder head warped. This is caused by overheating or improperly tightened head nuts. Machine shop resurfacing or head renewal is necessary (Chapter 2).
- [ ] Valve spring broken or weak. Caused by component failure or wear; the springs must be replaced with new ones (Chapter 2).
- [ ] Valve not seating properly. This is caused by a bent valve (from over-revving or improper valve adjustment), burned valve or seat (improper fuelling) or an accumulation of carbon deposits on the seat (from fuelling or lubrication problems). The valves must be cleaned and/or renewed and the seats serviced (Chapter 2).

Knocking or pinking

- [ ] Carbon build-up in combustion chamber. Use of a fuel additive that will dissolve the adhesive bonding the carbon particles to the piston crown and chamber is the easiest way to remove the build-up. Otherwise, the cylinder head will have to be removed and decarbonised (Chapter 2).
- [ ] Incorrect or poor quality fuel. Old or improper grades of fuel can cause detonation. This causes the piston to rattle, thus the knocking or pinking sound. Drain old fuel and always use the recommended fuel grade.
- [ ] Spark plug heat range incorrect. Uncontrolled detonation indicates the plug heat range is too hot. The plug in effect becomes a glow plug, raising cylinder temperatures. Install the proper heat range plug (Chapter 1).
- [ ] Improper air/fuel mixture. This will cause the cylinders to run hot, which leads to detonation. A blockage in the fuel system or an air leak can cause this imbalance (see Chapter 4).

Miscellaneous causes

- [ ] YCC-T or YCC-I fault (see Chapter 4).
- [ ] Clutch slipping due loose or worn clutch components (see Chapter 2).
- [ ] Timing not advancing. The crankshaft position sensor (CKP) or the engine control unit (ECU) may be defective (see Chapter 4). If so, they must be replaced with new ones.
- [ ] Engine oil viscosity too high. Using a heavier oil than the one recommended in Chapter 1 can damage the oil pump or lubrication system and cause drag on the engine.
- [ ] Brakes dragging. Usually caused by debris which has entered the brake caliper piston seals, or from a warped disc or bent axle (see Chapter 6).

4 Overheating

Engine overheats

- ☐ Coolant level low. Check and add coolant (see *Pre-ride checks*).
- ☐ Leak in cooling system. Check cooling system hoses and radiator for leaks and other damage. Repair or renew parts as necessary (see Chapter 3).
- ☐ Faulty thermostat. Check and renew as described in Chapter 3.
- ☐ Faulty radiator cap. Remove the cap and have it pressure tested.
- ☐ Coolant passages clogged. Drain, flush and refill with fresh coolant (Chapter 1).
- ☐ Water pump defective. Remove the pump and check the components (see Chapter 3).
- ☐ Clogged or damaged radiator fins (see Chapter 3).
- ☐ Faulty cooling fan, fan relay or coolant temperature sensor (see Chapters 3 and 4).

Firing incorrect

- ☐ Wrongly connected ignition coil wiring.
- ☐ Spark plugs dirty, defective or worn out. Locate reason for fouled plugs using spark plug condition chart on the inside back cover and follow the plug maintenance procedures (see Chapter 1).
- ☐ Incorrect spark plugs. Wrong type or heat range. Check and install correct plugs (see Chapter 1).
- ☐ Ignition coil defective. Test and replace with a new one if necessary (see Chapter 4).
- ☐ Faulty ECU (engine control unit) (see Chapter 4).

Fuel/air mixture incorrect

- ☐ Fuel tank breather hose obstructed.
- ☐ Fuel pump faulty, or its filter is blocked (see Chapter 4).
- ☐ Fuel hose clogged. Remove the fuel hose and carefully blow through it.
- ☐ Fuel rail or injector clogged. For all of the injectors to be clogged, either a very bad batch of fuel with an unusual additive has been used, or some other foreign material has entered the tank. Check the pump filter. In some cases, if a machine has been unused for several months, the fuel turns to a varnish-like liquid which can cause an injector needle to stick to its seat. Drain the tank and fuel system (Chapter 4).
- ☐ Intake air leak. Check for loose throttle body-to-intake manifold connections, loose or damaged AIS vacuum hose or throttle body vacuum hoses (Chapter 4).
- ☐ Air filter clogged. Clean the air filter element or replace it with a new one (Chapter 1).

Compression too high

Check by performing a compression test (see Chapter 2).

- ☐ Carbon build-up in combustion chamber. Use of a fuel additive that will dissolve the adhesive bonding the carbon particles to the piston crown and chamber is the easiest way to remove the build-up. Otherwise, the cylinder head will have to be removed and decarbonised (Chapter 2).
- ☐ Improperly machined head surface or installation of incorrect gasket during engine assembly.

Engine load excessive

- ☐ Clutch slipping due loose or worn clutch components (see Chapter 2).
- ☐ Engine oil level too high. Too much oil will cause pressurisation of the crankcase and inefficient engine operation. Check Specifications and drain to proper level (Chapter 1 and *Pre-ride checks*).
- ☐ Engine oil viscosity too high. Using a heavier oil than the one recommended in Chapter 1 can damage the oil pump or lubrication system as well as cause drag on the engine.
- ☐ Brakes dragging. Usually caused by debris which has entered the brake caliper piston seals, or from a warped disc or bent axle (see Chapter 6).

Lubrication inadequate

- ☐ Engine oil level too low. Friction caused by intermittent lack of lubrication or from oil that is overworked can cause overheating. The oil provides a definite cooling function in the engine. Check the oil level (see *Pre-ride checks*).
- ☐ Low engine oil pressure. Check the pressure (see Chapter 2).
- ☐ Blocked oil filter or oil cooler (see Chapter 2).

Miscellaneous causes

- ☐ Modification to exhaust system. Most aftermarket exhaust systems cause the engine to run leaner, which make them run hotter. When installing an accessory exhaust system, always check with the manufacturer/supplier as to whether the fuel system requires adjustment.

5 Clutch problems

Clutch slipping

- [ ] Incorrectly assembled clutch (see Chapter 2).
- [ ] Insufficient clutch cable freeplay. Check and adjust (see Chapter 1).
- [ ] Clutch plates worn or warped. Overhaul the clutch assembly (see Chapter 2).
- [ ] Clutch springs broken or weak. Old or heat-damaged (from slipping clutch) springs should be renewed (Chapter 2).
- [ ] Faulty clutch release mechanism – wear between gear teeth on release shaft and pullrod. Replace any defective parts with new ones (see Chapter 2).
- [ ] Clutch centre or housing unevenly worn. This causes improper engagement of the plates. Replace the damaged or worn parts (see Chapter 2).
- [ ] Incorrect oil used in engine. Oils designed for car engines often contain friction modifiers which if used in an engine with a wet clutch can promote clutch slip. Always use an oil designed for motorcycle engines (see Pre-ride checks).

Clutch not disengaging completely

- [ ] Excessive clutch cable freeplay. Check and adjust (see Chapter 1).
- [ ] Clutch plates warped or damaged. This will cause clutch drag, which in turn will cause the machine to creep. Overhaul the clutch assembly (see Chapter 2).
- [ ] Clutch springs fatigued or broken. Check and renew the springs (see Chapter 2).
- [ ] Incorrect alignment of the clutch plates, hub and/or pressure plate (see Chapter 2).
- [ ] Engine oil deteriorated. Old, thin oil will not provide proper lubrication for the plates, causing the clutch to drag. Renew the oil and filter (see Chapter 1).
- [ ] Engine oil viscosity too high. Using a heavier oil than recommended in Chapter 1 can cause the plates to stick together. Change to the correct weight oil.
- [ ] Clutch housing bearing seized on the transmission input shaft. Lack of lubrication, severe wear or damage can cause the bearing to seize. Overhaul of the clutch, and perhaps transmission, may be necessary to repair the damage (see Chapter 2).
- [ ] Faulty clutch release mechanism. Renew any defective parts (see Chapter 2).
- [ ] Loose clutch centre nut. Causes housing and centre misalignment putting a drag on the engine. Engagement adjustment continually varies. Overhaul the clutch assembly (see Chapter 2).

6 Gearchanging problems

Doesn't go into gear or lever doesn't return

- [ ] Clutch not disengaging (see above).
- [ ] Gearchange mechanism stopper arm spring weak or broken, or arm roller broken or worn. Replace the spring or arm with a new one (see Chapter 2).
- [ ] Selector fork(s) bent, worn or seized. Overhaul the transmission (see Chapter 2).
- [ ] Gear(s) stuck on shaft. Most often caused by a lack of lubrication or excessive wear in transmission bearings and bushes. Overhaul the transmission shafts (see Chapter 2).
- [ ] Selector drum binding. Caused by lubrication failure or excessive wear. Replace the drum and/or its bearing with a new one (see Chapter 2).
- [ ] Gearchange mechanism return spring weak or broken (see Chapter 2).
- [ ] Gearchange linkage arm broken. Splines stripped out of arm or shaft, caused by a loose linkage arm pinch bolt or from dropping the machine (see Chapter 2).

Jumps out of gear

- [ ] Selector fork(s) worn (see Chapter 2).
- [ ] Selector fork groove(s) in selector drum worn (see Chapter 2).
- [ ] Gear pinion dogs or dog slots worn or damaged. The gear pinions should be inspected and renewed. No attempt should be made to repair the worn parts.

Overselects

- [ ] Gearchange mechanism stopper arm spring weak or broken, or arm roller broken or worn. Renew the spring or arm (see Chapter 2).
- [ ] Gearchange mechanism return spring weak or broken (see Chapter 2).

7 Abnormal engine noise

Knocking or pinking

☐ Carbon build-up in combustion chamber. Use of a fuel additive that will dissolve the adhesive bonding the carbon particles to the piston crown and chamber is the easiest way to remove the build-up. Otherwise, the cylinder head will have to be removed and decarbonised (Chapter 2).

☐ Incorrect or poor quality fuel. Old or improper grades of fuel can cause detonation. This causes the pistons to rattle, thus the knocking or pinking sound. Drain old fuel and always use the recommended fuel grade.

☐ Spark plug heat range incorrect. Uncontrolled detonation indicates the plug heat range is too hot. The plug in effect becomes a glow plug, raising cylinder temperatures. Install the proper heat range plug (Chapter 1).

☐ Improper air/fuel mixture. This will cause the cylinders to run hot, which leads to detonation. A blockage in the fuel system or an air leak can cause this imbalance (see Chapter 4).

Piston slap or rattling

☐ Cylinder-to-piston clearance excessive. Cylinder and/or piston worn, usually accompanied by worn rings as well. A top-end overhaul is necessary (see Chapter 2).

☐ Piston ring(s) worn, broken or sticking. Overhaul the top-end (see Chapter 2).

☐ Piston pin, piston pin bore or connecting rod small-end worn from high mileage or seized due to lack of lubrication (see Chapter 2).

☐ Piston seizure damage. Usually from lack of lubrication or overheating. Replace the pistons and cylinder block/crankcases, as necessary (see Chapter 2).

☐ Connecting rod big-end clearance excessive. Caused by excessive wear or lack of lubrication. Replace worn parts.

☐ Connecting rod bent. Caused by over-revving, trying to start a badly flooded engine or from ingesting a foreign object into the combustion chamber. Replace the damaged parts (Chapter 2).

Valve noise

☐ Incorrect valve clearances – check and adjust (see Chapter 1).

☐ Valve spring broken or weak. Check and replace weak valve springs with new ones (see Chapter 2).

☐ Camshaft or camshaft journals in the cylinder head worn or damaged. Lubrication failure at high rpm is usually the cause of damage due to insufficient oil or failure to change the oil at the recommended intervals. Since there are no replaceable bearings in the head, the head itself will have to be replaced with a new one (see Chapter 2).

Other noise

☐ Cylinder head gasket leaking. Check around the joint for blowing with the engine running.

☐ Exhaust pipe leaking at cylinder head connection. Caused by incorrect fit of pipe(s), loose exhaust flange or damaged gasket. All exhaust system fasteners should be tightened evenly and carefully to avoid leaks (see Chapter 4).

☐ Crankshaft runout excessive. Caused by a bent crankshaft (from over-revving) or damage from an upper cylinder component failure. Can also be attributed to dropping the machine on either of the crankshaft ends.

☐ Engine mounting bolts loose – ensure all the bolts are tightened to the specified torque settings (see Chapter 2).

☐ Crankshaft main bearings worn (see Chapter 2).

☐ Cam chain rattle, due to worn chain or defective tensioner. Also worn chain tensioner/guide blades (see Chapter 2).

8 Abnormal driveline noise

Clutch noise

☐ Clutch housing/friction plate clearance excessive (Chapter 2).

☐ Wear between the inner pressure plate splines and input shaft splines (Chapter 2).

☐ Component matchmarks not correctly aligned following clutch reassembly (Chapter 2).

☐ Loose clutch nut (Chapter 2).

☐ Worn release bearing in outer pressure plate (Chapter 2).

Transmission noise

☐ Bearings worn. Also includes the possibility that the shafts are worn. Overhaul the transmission (Chapter 2).

☐ Gears worn or chipped (Chapter 2).

☐ Metal chips jammed in gear teeth. Probably pieces from a broken clutch, gear or selector mechanism that were picked up by the gears. This will cause early bearing failure (Chapter 2).

☐ Engine oil level too low. Causes a howl from transmission. Also affects engine power and clutch operation. Top up oil (Pre-ride checks).

Final drive noise

☐ Chain not adjusted properly (Chapter 1).

☐ Front or rear sprocket loose. Tighten fasteners (Chapter 6).

☐ Sprockets and/or chain worn. Fit new sprockets and chain (Chapter 6).

☐ Rear sprocket warped. Fit a new sprocket (Chapter 6).

☐ Rubber dampers in rear wheel worn (Chapter 6).

☐ Rear sprocket carrier bearing worn (Chapter 6).

9 Abnormal frame and suspension noise

Front end noise

☐ Low fluid level or improper viscosity oil in forks. This can sound like spurting and is usually accompanied by irregular fork action (Chapter 5).

☐ Spring weak or broken. Makes a clicking or scraping sound. Fork oil, when drained, will have a lot of metal particles in it (Chapter 5).

☐ Steering head bearings loose or damaged. Clicks when braking. Check and adjust or replace with new ones as necessary (Chapters 1 and 5).

☐ Fork yoke clamp bolts loose – ensure all the bolts are tightened to the specified torque (Chapter 6).

☐ Forks bent. Good possibility if machine has been dropped. Replace the inner and outer fork tubes with new ones as required (Chapter 5).

☐ Front axle or axle pinch bolts loose. Tighten them to the specified torque (Chapter 6).

☐ Loose or worn wheel bearings. Check and replace with new ones as needed (Chapters 1 and 6).

Shock absorber noise

☐ Fluid level incorrect. Indicates a leak caused by defective seal. Shock will be covered with oil. Replace shock with a new one or seek advice on repair from a suspension specialist (Chapter 5).

☐ Defective shock absorber with internal damage. This is in the body of the shock and can't be remedied. The shock must be replaced with a new one or rebuilt (Chapter 5).

☐ Bent or damaged shock body. Replace the shock with a new one (Chapter 5).

☐ Loose or worn suspension linkage components. Check and replace with new ones as necessary (Chapter 5).

Brake noise

☐ Squeal caused by pad shim not installed or positioned correctly (where fitted) (Chapter 6).

☐ Squeal caused by dust on brake pads. Usually found in combination with glazed pads. Clean using brake cleaning solvent (Chapter 6).

☐ Pads glazed. Caused by excessive heat from prolonged hard use or from contamination. DO NOT use sandpaper, emery cloth, carborundum cloth or any other abrasive to roughen the pad surfaces as abrasives will stay in the pad material and damage the disc. A very fine flat file can be used, but new pads is the best remedy (Chapter 6).

☐ Contamination of brake pads. Oil or brake fluid can cause the brake pads to chatter or squeal. Fit new pads. Identify the cause of the contamination, especially check the caliper piston seals for leaking fluid. Clean the disc thoroughly with brake system cleaner (Chapter 6).

☐ Disc warped. Can cause a chattering, clicking or intermittent squeal. Usually accompanied by a pulsating lever and uneven braking. Replace the disc with new one (Chapter 6).

☐ Loose or worn wheel bearings. Check and replace with new ones as needed (Chapters 1 and 6).

10 Oil level warning light comes on

Engine lubrication system

☐ Engine oil level low. Inspect for leak or other problem causing low oil level and add recommended oil (see *Pre-ride checks*).

☐ Engine oil pump defective, blocked oil strainer gauze or failed pressure relief valve. Carry out an oil pressure check (Chapter 2).

☐ Engine oil viscosity too low. Very old, thin oil or an improper weight of oil used in the engine. Change to correct oil (Chapter 1).

☐ Camshaft or crankshaft journals worn. Excessive wear causing drop in oil pressure. Abnormal wear could be caused by oil starvation at high rpm from low oil level or improper weight or type of oil (Chapter 1).

Electrical system

☐ Oil level sensor defective. Check the switch according to the procedure in Chapter 8. Replace it with a new one it if it is defective.

☐ Oil level warning LED or symbol defective. Check for pinched, shorted, disconnected or damaged wiring (Chapter 8).

11 Excessive exhaust smoke

White smoke

- [ ] Piston rings worn or broken, causing oil from the crankcase to be pulled past the piston into the combustion chamber. Replace the rings with new ones (Chapter 2).
- [ ] Cylinders worn or scored. Caused by overheating or oil starvation. Install new cylinder block/crankcases (Chapter 2).
- [ ] Valve stem oil seal damaged or worn. Replace the oil seals with new ones (Chapter 2).
- [ ] Valve guide worn. Perform a complete valve job (Chapter 2).
- [ ] Engine oil level too high, which causes the oil to be forced past the rings. Drain oil to the proper level (see Chapter 1 and *Pre-ride checks*).
- [ ] Head gasket broken between oil return and cylinder. Causes oil to be pulled into the combustion chamber. Replace the head gasket with a new one and check the head for warpage (Chapter 2).
- [ ] Abnormal crankcase pressurisation which forces oil past the rings, usually caused by a clogged breather.

Black smoke

- [ ] Air filter clogged. Clean the air filter element or replace it with a new one (Chapter 1).
- [ ] Fuel injection system malfunction (Chapter 4).

Brown smoke

- [ ] Air filter poorly sealed or not installed (Chapter 1).
- [ ] Fuel injection system malfunction (Chapter 4).

12 Poor handling or stability

Handlebars hard to turn

- [ ] Steering head bearing adjuster nut too tight. Check adjustment as described in Chapter 1.
- [ ] Bearings damaged. Roughness can be felt as the bars are turned from side-to-side. Replace the bearings with new ones (Chapter 5).
- [ ] Races dented or worn. Denting results from wear in only one position (e.g., straight ahead), from a collision or hitting a pothole or from dropping the machine. Replace the bearings with new ones (Chapter 5).
- [ ] Steering stem lubrication inadequate. Causes are grease getting hard from age or being washed out by high pressure car washes. Disassemble steering head and repack bearings (Chapter 5).
- [ ] Steering stem bent. Caused by a collision, hitting a pothole or by dropping the machine. Replace damaged part. Don't try to straighten the steering stem (Chapter 5).
- [ ] Front tyre air pressure too low (*Pre-ride checks*).

Handlebar shakes or vibrates excessively

- [ ] Tyres worn or out of balance (Chapter 6).
- [ ] Swingarm bearings worn. Replace the bearings with new ones (Chapter 5).
- [ ] Wheel rim(s) warped or damaged. Inspect wheels for runout (Chapter 6).
- [ ] Wheel bearings worn. Worn front or rear wheel bearings can cause poor tracking. Worn front bearings will cause wobble (Chapters 1 and 6).
- [ ] Fork yoke clamp bolts or handlebar clamp bolts loose. Tighten them to the specified torque (Chapter 5).
- [ ] Engine mounting bolts loose. Will cause excessive vibration with increased engine rpm – ensure all the bolts are tightened to the specified torque settings (see Chapter 2).

Machine pulls to one side

- [ ] Frame bent. Definitely suspect this if the machine has been dropped. May be accompanied by cracking near the steering head, swingarm mountings or engine mountings. Replace the frame with a new one (Chapter 5).
- [ ] Wheels out of alignment. Caused by failure to observe wheel alignment marks when adjusting drive chain, improper location of axle spacers or from bent steering stem or frame (Chapters 1, 5 and 6).
- [ ] Forks bent. Disassemble the forks and replace the damaged parts (Chapter 5).
- [ ] Swingarm bent or twisted. Replace the arm with a new one (Chapter 5).
- [ ] Fork oil level uneven. Check and add or drain as necessary (Chapter 5).
- [ ] Fork adjustment uneven. The adjustment settings should be the same on both forks (Chapter 5).

Poor shock absorbing qualities

- [ ] Too hard:
  - a) Suspension settings incorrect (Chapter 5).
  - b) Fork oil level excessive (Chapter 5).
  - c) Fork oil viscosity too high. Use a lighter oil (see the Specifications in Chapter 5).
  - d) Fork tube bent. Causes a harsh, sticking feeling (Chapter 5).
  - e) Fork internal damage (Chapter 5).
  - f) Shock shaft or body bent or damaged (Chapter 5).
  - g) Shock internal damage.
  - h) Tyre pressure too high (Pre-ride checks).
- [ ] Too soft:
  - a) Suspension settings incorrect (Chapter 5).
  - b) Fork oil level too low (Chapter 5).
  - c) Fork oil viscosity too light (Chapter 5).
  - d) Fork springs weak or broken (Chapter 5).
  - e) Fork or shock oil leaking (Chapter 5).
  - f) Shock internal damage (Chapter 5).

13 Braking problems

Brakes are spongy, don't hold

☐ Low brake fluid level (see *Pre-ride checks*).
☐ Air in hydraulic system. Caused by inattention to master cylinder fluid level or by leakage. Locate problem and bleed brakes (Chapter 6).
☐ Pad or disc worn (Chapters 1 and 6).
☐ Contaminated pads. Caused by contamination with oil, grease, brake fluid, etc. Fit new pads. Identify the cause of the contamination, especially check the caliper piston seals for leaking fluid. Clean disc thoroughly with brake system cleaner (Chapter 6).
☐ Brake fluid deteriorated. Fluid is old or contaminated. Drain system, replenish with new fluid and bleed the system (Chapter 6).
☐ Master cylinder internal seals worn or damaged causing fluid to bypass (Chapter 6).
☐ Master cylinder bore scratched by foreign material or broken spring. Fit a new master cylinder (Chapter 6).
☐ Disc warped. Replace disc with new one (Chapter 6).

Brake lever or pedal pulsates

☐ Disc warped. Replace disc with new one (Chapter 6).
☐ Axle bent. Replace axle with new one (Chapter 6).
☐ Brake caliper bolts loose – tighten the bolts to the specified torque (Chapter 6).
☐ Wheel warped or otherwise damaged (Chapter 6).
☐ Wheel bearings damaged or worn (Chapters 1 and 6).

Brakes drag

☐ Master cylinder piston seized. Caused by wear or damage to piston or cylinder bore (Chapter 6).
☐ Lever balky or stuck. Check pivot and lubricate (Chapter 6).
☐ Brake caliper piston seized in bore. Caused by corrosion or ingestion of dirt past deteriorated seal (Chapter 6).
☐ Caliper sticking on slider pins due to corrosion (rear caliper). Clean and lubricate pins and check dust boots (Chapter 6).
☐ Brake pad damaged. Pad material separated from backing plate. Usually caused by faulty manufacturing process or from contact with chemicals. Fit new pads (Chapter 6).
☐ Pads improperly installed (Chapter 6).
☐ Brake caliper incorrectly installed (Chapter 6).

14 Electrical problems

Battery dead or weak

☐ Battery faulty. Caused by sulphated plates which are shorted through sedimentation. Confirm by terminal voltage check (Chapter 8).
☐ Broken battery terminal making only occasional contact.
☐ Battery leads making poor contact (Chapter 8).
☐ Load excessive. Caused by addition of high wattage lights or other electrical accessories.
☐ Ignition switch defective. Switch either earths (grounds) internally or fails to shut off system. Renew the switch (Chapter 8).
☐ Regulator/rectifier defective (Chapter 8).
☐ Alternator stator coil open or shorted (Chapter 8).
☐ Charging system fault. Check for excessive current leakage (Chapter 8).
☐ Wiring faulty. Wiring earthed (grounded) or connections loose in ignition, charging or lighting circuits (Chapter 8).

Battery overcharged

☐ Regulator/rectifier defective. Overcharging is noticed when battery gets excessively warm (Chapter 8).
☐ Battery faulty. Confirm with battery terminal voltage check (Chapter 8).
☐ Battery amperage too low, wrong type or size of battery. Install manufacturer's specified amp-hour battery to handle charging load (Chapter 8)

A

ABS (Anti-lock braking system) A system, usually electronically controlled, that senses incipient wheel lockup during braking and relieves hydraulic pressure at wheel which is about to skid.

Aftermarket Components suitable for the motorcycle, but not produced by the motorcycle manufacturer.

Allen key A hexagonal wrench which fits into a recessed hexagonal hole.

Alternating current (ac) Current produced by an alternator. Requires converting to direct current by a rectifier for charging purposes.

Alternator Converts mechanical energy from the engine into electrical energy to charge the battery and power the electrical system.

Ampere (amp) A unit of measurement for the flow of electrical current. Current = Volts ÷ Ohms.

Ampere-hour (Ah) Measure of battery capacity.

Angle-tightening A torque expressed in degrees. Often follows a conventional tightening torque for cylinder head or main bearing fasteners **(see illustration)**.

Angle-tightening con-rod bolts

Antifreeze A substance (usually ethylene glycol) mixed with water, and added to the cooling system, to prevent freezing of the coolant in winter. Antifreeze also contains chemicals to inhibit corrosion and the formation of rust and other deposits that would tend to clog the radiator and coolant passages and reduce cooling efficiency.

Anti-dive System attached to the fork lower leg (slider) to prevent fork dive when braking hard.

Anti-seize compound A coating that reduces the risk of seizing on fasteners that are subjected to high temperatures, such as exhaust clamp bolts and nuts.

API American Petroleum Institute. A quality standard for 4-stroke motor oils.

Asbestos A natural fibrous mineral with great heat resistance, commonly used in the composition of brake friction materials. Asbestos is a health hazard and the dust created by brake systems should never be inhaled or ingested.

ATF Automatic Transmission Fluid. Often used in front forks.

ATU Automatic Timing Unit. Mechanical device for advancing the ignition timing on early engines.

ATV All Terrain Vehicle. Often called a Quad.

Axial play Side-to-side movement.

Axle A shaft on which a wheel revolves. Also known as a spindle.

B

Backlash The amount of movement between meshed components when one component is held still. Usually applies to gear teeth.

Ball bearing A bearing consisting of a hardened inner and outer race with hardened steel balls between the two races.

Bearings Used between two working surfaces to prevent wear of the components and a build-up of heat. Four types of bearing are commonly used on motorcycles: plain shell bearings, ball bearings, tapered roller bearings and needle roller bearings.

Bevel gears Used to turn the drive through 90°. Typical applications are shaft final drive and camshaft drive **(see illustration)**.

Bevel gears are used to turn the drive through 90°

BHP Brake Horsepower. The British measurement for engine power output. Power output is now usually expressed in kilowatts (kW).

Bias-belted tyre Similar construction to radial tyre, but with outer belt running at an angle to the wheel rim.

Big-end bearing The bearing in the end of the connecting rod that's attached to the crankshaft.

Bleeding The process of removing air from an hydraulic system via a bleed nipple or bleed screw.

Bottom-end A description of an engine's crankcase components and all components contained there-in.

BTDC Before Top Dead Centre in terms of piston position. Ignition timing is often expressed in terms of degrees or millimetres BTDC.

Bush A cylindrical metal or rubber component used between two moving parts.

Burr Rough edge left on a component after machining or as a result of excessive wear.

C

Cam chain The chain which takes drive from the crankshaft to the camshaft(s).

Canister The main component in an evaporative emission control system (California market only); contains activated charcoal granules to trap vapours from the fuel system rather than allowing them to vent to the atmosphere.

Castellated Resembling the parapets along the top of a castle wall. For example, a castellated wheel axle or spindle nut.

Catalytic converter A device in the exhaust system of some machines which converts certain pollutants in the exhaust gases into less harmful substances.

Charging system Description of the components which charge the battery, ie the alternator, rectifer and regulator.

Circlip A ring-shaped clip used to prevent endwise movement of cylindrical parts and shafts. An internal circlip is installed in a groove in a housing; an external circlip fits into a groove on the outside of a cylindrical piece such as a shaft. Also known as a snap-ring.

Clearance The amount of space between two parts. For example, between a piston and a cylinder, between a bearing and a journal, etc.

Coil spring A spiral of elastic steel found in various sizes throughout a vehicle, for example as a springing medium in the suspension and in the valve train.

Compression Reduction in volume, and increase in pressure and temperature, of a gas, caused by squeezing it into a smaller space.

Compression damping Controls the speed the suspension compresses when hitting a bump.

Compression ratio The relationship between cylinder volume when the piston is at top dead centre and cylinder volume when the piston is at bottom dead centre.

Continuity The uninterrupted path in the flow of electricity. Little or no measurable resistance.

Continuity tester Self-powered bleeper or test light which indicates continuity.

Cp Candlepower. Bulb rating commonly found on US motorcycles.

Crossply tyre Tyre plies arranged in a criss-cross pattern. Usually four or six plies used, hence 4PR or 6PR in tyre size codes.

Cush drive Rubber damper segments fitted between the rear wheel and final drive sprocket to absorb transmission shocks **(see illustration)**.

Cush drive rubbers dampen out transmission shocks

D

Decarbonisation The process of removing carbon deposits - typically from the combustion chamber, valves and exhaust port/system.

Degree disc Calibrated disc for measuring piston position. Expressed in degrees.

Detonation Destructive and damaging explosion of fuel/air mixture in combustion chamber instead of controlled burning.

Dial gauge Clock-type gauge with adapters for measuring runout and piston position. Expressed in mm or inches.

Diaphragm The rubber membrane in a master cylinder or carburettor which seals the upper chamber.

Diaphragm spring A single sprung plate often used in clutches.

Direct current (dc) Current produced by a dc generator.

Diode An electrical valve which only allows current to flow in one direction. Commonly used in rectifiers and starter interlock systems.

Disc valve (or rotary valve) A induction system used on some two-stroke engines.

Double-overhead camshaft (DOHC) An engine that uses two overhead camshafts, one for the intake valves and one for the exhaust valves.

Drivebelt A toothed belt used to transmit drive to the rear wheel on some motorcycles. A drivebelt has also been used to drive the camshafts. Drivebelts are usually made of Kevlar.

Driveshaft Any shaft used to transmit motion. Commonly used when referring to the final driveshaft on shaft drive motorcycles.

E

Earth return The return path of an electrical circuit, utilising the motorcycle's frame.

ECU (Electronic Control Unit) A computer which controls (for instance) an ignition system, or an anti-lock braking system.

EGO Exhaust Gas Oxygen sensor. Sometimes called a Lambda sensor.

Electrolyte The fluid in a lead-acid battery.

EMS (Engine Management System) A computer controlled system which manages the fuel injection and the ignition systems in an integrated fashion.

Endfloat The amount of lengthways movement between two parts. As applied to a crankshaft, the distance that the crankshaft can move side-to-side in the crankcase.

Endless chain A chain having no joining link. Common use for cam chains and final drive chains.

EP (Extreme Pressure) Oil type used in locations where high loads are applied, such as between gear teeth.

Evaporative emission control system Describes a charcoal filled canister which stores fuel vapours from the tank rather than allowing them to vent to the atmosphere. Usually only fitted to California models and referred to as an EVAP system.

Expansion chamber Section of two-stroke engine exhaust system so designed to improve engine efficiency and boost power.

F

Feeler blade or gauge A thin strip or blade of hardened steel, ground to an exact thickness, used to check or measure clearances between parts.

Final drive Description of the drive from the transmission to the rear wheel. Usually by chain or shaft, but sometimes by belt.

Firing order The order in which the engine cylinders fire, or deliver their power strokes, beginning with the number one cylinder.

Flooding Term used to describe a high fuel level in the carburettor float chambers, leading to fuel overflow. Also refers to excess fuel in the combustion chamber due to incorrect starting technique.

Free length The no-load state of a component when measured. Clutch, valve and fork spring lengths are measured at rest, without any preload.

Freeplay The amount of travel before any action takes place. The looseness in a linkage, or an assembly of parts, between the initial application of force and actual movement. For example, the distance the rear brake pedal moves before the rear brake is actuated.

Fuel injection The fuel/air mixture is metered electronically and directed into the engine intake ports (indirect injection) or into the cylinders (direct injection). Sensors supply information on engine speed and conditions.

Fuel/air mixture The charge of fuel and air going into the engine. See Stoichiometric ratio.

Fuse An electrical device which protects a circuit against accidental overload. The typical fuse contains a soft piece of metal which is calibrated to melt at a predetermined current flow (expressed as amps) and break the circuit.

G

Gap The distance the spark must travel in jumping from the centre electrode to the side electrode in a spark plug. Also refers to the distance between the ignition rotor and the pickup coil in an electronic ignition system.

Gasket Any thin, soft material - usually cork, cardboard, asbestos or soft metal - installed between two metal surfaces to ensure a good seal. For instance, the cylinder head gasket seals the joint between the block and the cylinder head.

Gauge An instrument panel display used to monitor engine conditions. A gauge with a movable pointer on a dial or a fixed scale is an analogue gauge. A gauge with a numerical readout is called a digital gauge.

Gear ratios The drive ratio of a pair of gears in a gearbox, calculated on their number of teeth.

Glaze-busting see **Honing**

Grinding Process for renovating the valve face and valve seat contact area in the cylinder head.

Gudgeon pin The shaft which connects the connecting rod small-end with the piston. Often called a piston pin or wrist pin.

H

Helical gears Gear teeth are slightly curved and produce less gear noise that straight-cut gears. Often used for primary drives.

Helicoil A thread insert repair system. Commonly used as a repair for stripped spark plug threads **(see illustration)**.

Installing a Helicoil thread insert

Honing A process used to break down the glaze on a cylinder bore (also called glaze-busting). Can also be carried out to roughen a rebored cylinder to aid ring bedding-in.

HT (High Tension) Description of the electrical circuit from the secondary winding of the ignition coil to the spark plug.

Hydraulic A liquid filled system used to transmit pressure from one component to another. Common uses on motorcycles are brakes and clutches.

Hydrometer An instrument for measuring the specific gravity of a lead-acid battery.

Hygroscopic Water absorbing. In motorcycle applications, braking efficiency will be reduced if DOT 3 or 4 hydraulic fluid absorbs water from the air - care must be taken to keep new brake fluid in tightly sealed containers.

I

lbf ft Pounds-force feet. An imperial unit of torque. Sometimes written as ft-lbs.

lbf in Pound-force inch. An imperial unit of torque, applied to components where a very low torque is required. Sometimes written as in-lbs.

IC Abbreviation for Integrated Circuit.

Ignition advance Means of increasing the timing of the spark at higher engine speeds. Done by mechanical means (ATU) on early engines or electronically by the ignition control unit on later engines.

Ignition timing The moment at which the spark plug fires, expressed in the number of crankshaft degrees before the piston reaches the top of its stroke, or in the number of millimetres before the piston reaches the top of its stroke.

Infinity (∞) Description of an open-circuit electrical state, where no continuity exists.

Inverted forks (upside down forks) The sliders or lower legs are held in the yokes and the fork tubes or stanchions are connected to the wheel axle (spindle). Less unsprung weight and stiffer construction than conventional forks.

J

JASO Quality standard for 2-stroke oils.

Joule The unit of electrical energy.

Journal The bearing surface of a shaft.

K

Kickstart Mechanical means of turning the engine over for starting purposes. Only usually fitted to mopeds, small capacity motorcycles and off-road motorcycles.

Kill switch Handebar-mounted switch for emergency ignition cut-out. Cuts the ignition circuit on all models, and additionally prevent starter motor operation on others.

km Symbol for kilometre.

kmh Abbreviation for kilometres per hour.

L

Lambda (λ) sensor A sensor fitted in the exhaust system to measure the exhaust gas oxygen content (excess air factor).

Lapping see Grinding.
LCD Abbreviation for Liquid Crystal Display.
LED Abbreviation for Light Emitting Diode.
Liner A steel cylinder liner inserted in a aluminium alloy cylinder block.
Locknut A nut used to lock an adjustment nut, or other threaded component, in place.
Lockstops The lugs on the lower triple clamp (yoke) which abut those on the frame, preventing handlebar-to-fuel tank contact.
Lockwasher A form of washer designed to prevent an attaching nut from working loose.
LT Low Tension Description of the electrical circuit from the power supply to the primary winding of the ignition coil.

M

Main bearings The bearings between the crankshaft and crankcase.
Maintenance-free (MF) battery A sealed battery which cannot be topped up.
Manometer Mercury-filled calibrated tubes used to measure intake tract vacuum. Used to synchronise carburettors on multi-cylinder engines.
Micrometer A precision measuring instrument that measures component outside diameters **(see illustration)**.

Tappet shims are measured with a micrometer

MON (Motor Octane Number) A measure of a fuel's resistance to knock.
Monograde oil An oil with a single viscosity, eg SAE80W.
Monoshock A single suspension unit linking the swingarm or suspension linkage to the frame.
mph Abbreviation for miles per hour.
Multigrade oil Having a wide viscosity range (eg 10W40). The W stands for Winter, thus the viscosity ranges from SAE10 when cold to SAE40 when hot.
Multimeter An electrical test instrument with the capability to measure voltage, current and resistance. Some meters also incorporate a continuity tester and buzzer.

N

Needle roller bearing Inner race of caged needle rollers and hardened outer race. Examples of uncaged needle rollers can be found on some engines. Commonly used in rear suspension applications and in two-stroke engines.
Nm Newton metres.
NOx Oxides of Nitrogen. A common toxic pollutant emitted by petrol engines at higher temperatures.

O

Octane The measure of a fuel's resistance to knock.
OE (Original Equipment) Relates to components fitted to a motorcycle as standard or replacement parts supplied by the motorcycle manufacturer.
Ohm The unit of electrical resistance. Ohms = Volts ÷ Current.
Ohmmeter An instrument for measuring electrical resistance.
Oil cooler System for diverting engine oil outside of the engine to a radiator for cooling purposes.
Oil injection A system of two-stroke engine lubrication where oil is pump-fed to the engine in accordance with throttle position.
Open-circuit An electrical condition where there is a break in the flow of electricity - no continuity (high resistance).
O-ring A type of sealing ring made of a special rubber-like material; in use, the O-ring is compressed into a groove to provide the sealing action.
Oversize (OS) Term used for piston and ring size options fitted to a rebored cylinder.
Overhead cam (sohc) engine An engine with single camshaft located on top of the cylinder head.
Overhead valve (ohv) engine An engine with the valves located in the cylinder head, but with the camshaft located in the engine block or crankcase.
Oxygen sensor A device installed in the exhaust system which senses the oxygen content in the exhaust and converts this information into an electric current. Also called a Lambda sensor.

P

Plastigauge A thin strip of plastic thread, available in different sizes, used for measuring clearances. For example, a strip of Plastigauge is laid across a bearing journal. The parts are assembled and dismantled; the width of the crushed strip indicates the clearance between journal and bearing.
Polarity Either negative or positive earth (ground), determined by which battery lead is connected to the frame (earth return). Modern motorcycles are usually negative earth.
Pre-ignition A situation where the fuel/air mixture ignites before the spark plug fires. Often due to a hot spot in the combustion chamber caused by carbon build-up. Engine has a tendency to 'run-on'.
Pre-load (suspension) The amount a spring is compressed when in the unloaded state. Preload can be applied by gas, spacer or mechanical adjuster.
Premix The method of engine lubrication on older two-stroke engines. Engine oil is mixed with the petrol in the fuel tank in a specific ratio. The fuel/oil mix is sometimes referred to as "petroil".
Primary drive Description of the drive from the crankshaft to the clutch. Usually by gear or chain.
PS Pfedestärke - a German interpretation of BHP.
PSI Pounds-force per square inch. Imperial measurement of tyre pressure and cylinder pressure measurement.
PTFE Polytetrafluroethylene. A low friction substance.
Pulse secondary air injection system A process of promoting the burning of excess fuel present in the exhaust gases by routing fresh air into the exhaust ports.

Q

Quartz halogen bulb Tungsten filament surrounded by a halogen gas. Typically used for the headlight **(see illustration)**.

Quartz halogen headlight bulb construction

R

Rack-and-pinion A pinion gear on the end of a shaft that mates with a rack (think of a geared wheel opened up and laid flat). Sometimes used in clutch operating systems.
Radial play Up and down movement about a shaft.
Radial ply tyres Tyre plies run across the tyre (from bead to bead) and around the circumference of the tyre. Less resistant to tread distortion than other tyre types.
Radiator A liquid-to-air heat transfer device designed to reduce the temperature of the coolant in a liquid cooled engine.
Rake A feature of steering geometry - the angle of the steering head in relation to the vertical **(see illustration)**.

Steering geometry

Rebore Providing a new working surface to the cylinder bore by boring out the old surface. Necessitates the use of oversize piston and rings.

Rebound damping A means of controlling the oscillation of a suspension unit spring after it has been compressed. Resists the spring's natural tendency to bounce back after being compressed.

Rectifier Device for converting the ac output of an alternator into dc for battery charging.

Reed valve An induction system commonly used on two-stroke engines.

Regulator Device for maintaining the charging voltage from the generator or alternator within a specified range.

Relay A electrical device used to switch heavy current on and off by using a low current auxiliary circuit.

Resistance Measured in ohms. An electrical component's ability to pass electrical current.

RON (Research Octane Number) A measure of a fuel's resistance to knock.

rpm revolutions per minute.

Runout The amount of wobble (in-and-out movement) of a wheel or shaft as it's rotated. The amount a shaft rotates 'out-of-true'. The out-of-round condition of a rotating part.

S

SAE (Society of Automotive Engineers) A standard for the viscosity of a fluid.

Sealant A liquid or paste used to prevent leakage at a joint. Sometimes used in conjunction with a gasket.

Service limit Term for the point where a component is no longer useable and must be renewed.

Shaft drive A method of transmitting drive from the transmission to the rear wheel.

Shell bearings Plain bearings consisting of two shell halves. Most often used as big-end and main bearings in a four-stroke engine. Often called bearing inserts.

Shim Thin spacer, commonly used to adjust the clearance or relative positions between two parts. For example, shims inserted into or under tappets or followers to control valve clearances. Clearance is adjusted by changing the thickness of the shim.

Short-circuit An electrical condition where current shorts to earth (ground) bypassing the circuit components.

Skimming Process to correct warpage or repair a damaged surface, eg on brake discs or drums.

Slide-hammer A special puller that screws into or hooks onto a component such as a shaft or bearing; a heavy sliding handle on the shaft bottoms against the end of the shaft to knock the component free.

Small-end bearing The bearing in the upper end of the connecting rod at its joint with the gudgeon pin.

Spalling Damage to camshaft lobes or bearing journals shown as pitting of the working surface.

Specific gravity (SG) The state of charge of the electrolyte in a lead-acid battery. A measure of the electrolyte's density compared with water.

Straight-cut gears Common type gear used on gearbox shafts and for oil pump and water pump drives.

Stanchion The inner sliding part of the front forks, held by the yokes. Often called a fork tube.

Stoichiometric ratio The optimum chemical air/fuel ratio for a petrol engine, said to be 14.7 parts of air to 1 part of fuel.

Sulphuric acid The liquid (electrolyte) used in a lead-acid battery. Poisonous and extremely corrosive.

Surface grinding (lapping) Process to correct a warped gasket face, commonly used on cylinder heads.

T

Tapered-roller bearing Tapered inner race of caged needle rollers and separate tapered outer race. Examples of taper roller bearings can be found on steering heads.

Tappet A cylindrical component which transmits motion from the cam to the valve stem, either directly or via a pushrod and rocker arm. Also called a cam follower.

TCS Traction Control System. An electronically-controlled system which senses wheel spin and reduces engine speed accordingly.

TDC Top Dead Centre denotes that the piston is at its highest point in the cylinder.

Thread-locking compound Solution applied to fastener threads to prevent slackening. Select type to suit application.

Thrust washer A washer positioned between two moving components on a shaft. For example, between gear pinions on gearshaft.

Timing chain See **Cam Chain**.

Timing light Stroboscopic lamp for carrying out ignition timing checks with the engine running.

Top-end A description of an engine's cylinder block, head and valve gear components.

Torque Turning or twisting force about a shaft.

Torque setting A prescribed tightness specified by the motorcycle manufacturer to ensure that the bolt or nut is secured correctly. Undertightening can result in the bolt or nut coming loose or a surface not being sealed. Overtightening can result in stripped threads, distortion or damage to the component being retained.

Torx key A six-point wrench.

Tracer A stripe of a second colour applied to a wire insulator to distinguish that wire from another one with the same colour insulator. For example, Br/W is often used to denote a brown insulator with a white tracer.

Trail A feature of steering geometry. Distance from the steering head axis to the tyre's central contact point.

Triple clamps The cast components which extend from the steering head and support the fork stanchions or tubes. Often called fork yokes.

Turbocharger A centrifugal device, driven by exhaust gases, that pressurises the intake air. Normally used to increase the power output from a given engine displacement.

TWI Abbreviation for Tyre Wear Indicator. Indicates the location of the tread depth indicator bars on tyres.

U

Universal joint or U-joint (UJ) A double-pivoted connection for transmitting power from a driving to a driven shaft through an angle. Typically found in shaft drive assemblies.

Unsprung weight Anything not supported by the bike's suspension (ie the wheel, tyres, brakes, final drive and bottom (moving) part of the suspension).

V

Vacuum gauges Clock-type gauges for measuring intake tract vacuum. Used for carburettor synchronisation on multi-cylinder engines.

Valve A device through which the flow of liquid, gas or vacuum may be stopped, started or regulated by a moveable part that opens, shuts or partially obstructs one or more ports or passageways. The intake and exhaust valves in the cylinder head are of the poppet type.

Valve clearance The clearance between the valve tip (the end of the valve stem) and the rocker arm or tappet/follower. The valve clearance is measured when the valve is closed. The correct clearance is important - if too small the valve won't close fully and will burn out, whereas if too large noisy operation will result.

Valve lift The amount a valve is lifted off its seat by the camshaft lobe.

Valve timing The exact setting for the opening and closing of the valves in relation to piston position.

Vernier caliper A precision measuring instrument that measures inside and outside dimensions. Not quite as accurate as a micrometer, but more convenient.

Wet liner arrangement

VIN Vehicle Identification Number. Term for the bike's engine and frame numbers.

Viscosity The thickness of a liquid or its resistance to flow.

Volt A unit for expressing electrical "pressure" in a circuit. Volts = current x ohms.

W

Water pump A mechanically-driven device for moving coolant around the engine.

Watt A unit for expressing electrical power. Watts = volts x current.

Wear limit see **Service limit**

Wet liner A liquid-cooled engine design where the pistons run in liners which are directly surrounded by coolant **(see illustration)**.

Wheelbase Distance from the centre of the front wheel to the centre of the rear wheel.

Wiring harness or loom Describes the electrical wires running the length of the motorcycle and enclosed in tape or plastic sheathing. Wiring coming off the main harness is usually referred to as a sub harness.

Woodruff key A key of semi-circular or square section used to locate a gear to a shaft. Often used to locate the alternator rotor on the crankshaft.

Wrist pin Another name for gudgeon or piston pin.

Note: *References throughout this index are in the form - "Chapter number" • "Page number"*

EF•54 Notes